DATE DUE

~~AP 27 97~~			
~~MY 28 97~~			
~~OC 24 00~~			
~~NO 15 00~~			
~~AE 6 07~~			

DEMCO 38-296

BEARING WITNESS

12

Henry L. Feingold

BEARING WITNESS

How America and Its Jews
Responded to the Holocaust

Syracuse University Press

Copyright © 1995 by Syracuse University Press
Syracuse, New York 13244-5160

All Rights Reserved

First Edition 1995
95 96 97 98 99 01 02   6 5 4 3 2 1

The paper used in this publication meets the minimum requirements of American
National Standard for Information Sciences—Permanence of Paper for Printed Library
Materials, ANSI Z39.48-1984. ∞™

Library of Congress Cataloging-in-Publication Data
Feingold, Henry L., 1931–
    Bearing witness : How America and Its Jews Responded to the Holocaust
Henry L. Feingold
        p. cm.
    Includes bibliographical references and index.
    ISBN 0-8156-2669-X (cloth : alk. paper). — ISBN 0-8156-2670-3
(pbk. : alk. paper)
        1. Holocaust, Jewish (1939–1945)—Historiography. 2. Holocaust,
Jewish (1939–1945)—Foreign public opinion, American. 3. Public
opinion—United States. 4. United States—Foreign
relations—1933–1945. 5. Jews—United States—Politics and
government. 6. United States—Ethnic relations. I. Title.
D804.3.F45 1995
940.53'18—dc20   95-15862

Manufactured in the United States of America

*This book is dedicated to the memory of
the Regenbogens and Singers and all the other Jewish families
who found no haven in a hostile world.*

HENRY L. FEINGOLD, a professor of history at Baruch College and the Graduate Center of the City University of New York, specializes in American Jewish history, history of the Holocaust, and American diplomatic history. He is the author of several books, including *Zion in America: The American Jewish Experience from Colonial Times to the Present* and is general editor of the highly acclaimed five-volume series, *The Jewish People in America*.

Contents

PART THREE
American Jewry and the Holocaust

BEARING WITNESS

Introduction

THIS BOOK deals mostly with the witness role of the American government and American Jewry. Witnesses here are those governments, international agencies, and individual leaders who shared the historical stage during the years of the Holocaust. I assume, perhaps, foolishly, that before National Socialism strove for total separation, European Jewry had largely become part of what Helen Fein identified as a "universe of obligation," the sense of concern we naturally feel when we see the travail of our fellow man.[1] But that concern, in which the obligation of bearing witness is rooted, was little in evidence during the years of the Holocaust. Examined here are the implications of that absence.

The title, *Bearing Witness*, also refers to my personal witness to the Holocaust. My family arrived on American shores on the eve of the Holocaust. By the time I has reached my early adolescence, I was aware that this event had shaken me to my innermost core. Yet, I remember nothing that might have traumatized me. Of course, there was endless worried talk about visas and affidavits, and I remember the trip to the American consulate in Stuttgart. But for me, a boy of eight, these were adventures. I recall only joy of being on a big oceanliner, which we boarded in Antwerp. If there were worried looks on the faces of the refugee passengers, they did not impress themselves on me. Nor was I shattered by the straitened circumstances of my family. It was only years later when personal letters and Red Cross cables arrived informing of the fate of relatives, when photos and stories began to appear in the press, that I realized how lucky my family had been. I became an obsessive reader of everything that related to the destruction of the Jews of Europe. I realize

1

now, in thinking how easily it could have happened to me and mine, that I was experiencing a kind of vicarious terror. I think that I began to research and write about the Holocaust in an effort to exorcise it from my imagination. My research interest went on to examine the condition of American Jewry during the interwar period. But I soon discovered that it was more a continuity than a change of interest. I now wanted to discover why other families failed to find a haven in America. I learned that America did not want the refugees and that American Jewry lacked the cohesiveness and influence to help.

That reluctance and lack of influence were the subject of my first book, *The Politics of Rescue: The Roosevelt Administration and the Holocaust, 1938–1945*[2] I concluded *Politics* by wondering if nation-states were in fact capable of making human responses to catastrophes like the Holocaust, especially during times of economic depression and war. The American government, like all sovereign agencies, finally had to come down on the side of *raison d'état*. My sense that a retroactive indictment of the Roosevelt administration and American Jewry, both of which could be written with ease, lacked historicity and was born out by subsequent events. Despite its utter gruesomeness, the destruction of European Jewry during World War II did not bring a halt to the penchant for genocidal mass murder. It seems that some governments, in their insecurity, were actually far more prone to commit mass murder than to prevent it. That fact is born out by lesser-scale, post-Holocaust genocides in places like Cambodia, Nigeria, Rwanda, and Bosnia.

Still within that nation-state framework, we can assume that democratic governments are less likely to do such violence and that they will take their responsibility as witnesses more seriously. Democracies are, after all, subject to pressure from social agencies like churches, which exert pressure on society to make it everything that they believe it should be. In the America of the thirties, that sensitizing role fell primarily, although not exclusively, on its Jewry, which had a tie of kinship and a liberal humanitarian motivation to act as an advocate to prevent European Jewry from perishing. As it turned out, despite comparatively good resources that included political experience in projecting pressure on government, good congressional representation, and a supposed influential position in the Roosevelt administration, American Jewry was not effective in its advocacy during the war years. What went wrong? Anti-Semitic rhetoric endlessly pictured Jewry as a highly organized conspiracy. Yet, American Jewry was so disunited during the crisis that its organizational life in which the various social, ideological, and religious components of the community were represented, was characterized by an absence of communication and a lack of elementary civility. Because secularization, the passport for entering modernity, is above all a process of individuation and detribalization, some loss of cohesiveness in postemancipation Jewish communities should have been expected. But American Jewry seemed to be more divided against itself than usual, especially in the face of such a crisis. Suspecting that the answer to the puzzle might be found in these historic processes that were weakening the bonds that held Jews together, I turned to examining them.

Surprisingly, no one seemed to notice that my conclusions were quite different from those reached in two books published a year before *Politics*.[3] I was not a disappointed Roosevelt admirer like Arthur Morse, nor did I possess an outraged Christian conscience like David Wyman. I do not blame American Jews for being what they had become in the thirties. I do not wish they were something they could no longer be. In short, I do not argue with history but rather try to explain what happened to the communal bindings under the impact of modernization and acculturation that American Jewry experienced simultaneously. That is the balance I have tried to strike in these essays. It was not easy for me to maintain that balance. I note with chagrin that in the earlier essays contained here, my anger and disappointment sometimes got the better of me. This introduction, which presents the major observations and themes of each essay, is presented to the reader in the spirit of *caveat emptor*. The reader should be informed beforehand about the compass that guides the author.

We begin with the problem of finding an approach to the study of the Holocaust. The reader will note that I am not much concerned with the current debate between "intentionalists," those who are convinced that genocide was intended from the outset, and "functionalists," those who believe that its hallmark was inadvertancy, best understood in the framework of World War II and the events leading to it. These are concerns of historians of the twentieth-century European experience like Arno Mayer, whose quest is causation.[4] I accept a great deal from both positions without discomfort. But my priorities are shaped primarily by what has happened on the

Jewish historical canvas, and my approach to the Holocaust is therefore inevitably Judeo-centric. I believe the historical uniqueness of the Holocaust, its valence, or weight, stems primarily from the people it sought to destroy.

In "The Uniqueness of the Holocaust," I suggest that, rather than the scale of the slaughter or its intentionality, it was the fact that European Jewry was producing a universalizing elite in the sciences, political theory, communications, literature, theater, philosophy, and commerce that was reshaping European life and pushing it beyond the confines of the nation-state that gives the Holocaust its historical weight. It is the destruction of the population base that produced that small universalizing elite that makes the Holocaust a turning point in European history. In the multinational European civilization, its Jewry was no ordinary subculture. It is in that sense that its historic weight is not in the same class as the mass murder of the Armenians or the Romanies. I am of course aware that this is after all how the radical anti-Semitism introduced by National Socialism imagined the Jews to be, but it nevertheless needs to be understood in nondemonic terms. I do not mean by the claim of uniqueness the kind that every group has in its arsenal as part of what makes it separateness necessary and worthwhile. Nor do I imagine a new form of covenantal chosenness. This uniqueness is based on its importance in the historical development of Europe.

Fortunately, the claim of uniqueness does not depend for validation on the analytic or reconstructive talents of a historian whose connection with that destroyed people places his objectivity in question. Rather, it is based on the flow of subsequent history. If, as is claimed, the Holocaust is a major turning point in history, like the discovery of the wheel or the French Revolution, it is bound to produce a historical echo or resonance. We should notice a change in the trajectory of European and Jewish history. For the last mentioned, the sea changes brought by the Holocaust are apparent, not necessarily in the disproportionate number of Jewish scholars that event continues to draw, but in the actual post-Holocaust experience of the Jewish people. The establishment of a Jewish state has totally altered the internal dynamics of Jewish communal life. It has also left in its wake a seemingly intractable conflict between Palestinians and Israelis. But such radical changes in course are barely discernable on the European stage. The Holocaust has entered the consciousness and vocabulary of Western civilization; but its influence on the actual course of events, if it exists at all, remains latent. In the twenty years after "The Uniqueness of the Holocaust" was written, little is discernably different since Europe's Jews were slaughtered. Europe is doing well economically without its Jews, whom it certainly does not miss. Occasionally, one hears that today's Germany is boring. But those who experienced its turbulent prewar life during the Weimar years may find that preferable. Predictably, some German historians, concerned about building a "usable past," have somehow tried to fit "the Final Solution to the Jewish question" into the flow of history by purging it of its horrendous particularity. Europe's passivity regarding "ethnic cleansing" in Bosnia is taken by some to indicate that, though the Holocaust was often in the background of the dialogue on intervention, it had little influence in actually shaping government policy. In fact, it may be the events in Bosnia that offer the first clue to how much the self-confidence of Europe has been shaken by the Holocaust in its closet. The nations of Europe behave as if they were afraid of themselves and tremble at what can be done in the name of nationalism and totalistic ideologies. But generally, it is difficult to avoid the conclusion that, today as during the war years, the majority of Europeans remain unable to fathom what the death factories may signify for their time in history.

If Jews were prominent among Europe's modernizing elites, some believe that they were not prominent enough in resisting those who wanted to destroy them. They supposedly went like "sheep to the slaughter." The question of Jewish resistance and the related problem of complicity by its leadership are the most sensitive in Holocaust historiography. That they touch a nerve is evidenced by the number of books that are published yearly on these questions alone. One of the best of these books was written by Isaiah Trunk in 1972 in response to Hannah Arendt's charge in *Eichmann in Jerusalem* that Jewish leadership was complicitous in implementing the Final Solution.[5] The charge tore at the spirit of a people still mourning its heavy losses. Jews were being told that not only did victims of the Holocaust go "like sheep to the slaughter" but they were also betrayed by their leadership.

Using the data on the German-organized Jewish Councils retrieved by Trunk, I show in "Like Sheep to the Slaughter: The *Judenrat*," that the survival strategies conceived by the Jewish Councils varied from place to place and were based on a realistic perception of their situation. They assumed their tormentors, who were involved in a bitter *Vernichtungskrieg* in the East, would be practical and behave rationally and that Jews would be therefore allowed to survive as long as they made themselves useful to the German war effort. It was the same reasoning used by Oscar Schindler and others to save lives. Despite their life-threatening circumstances, Jews did not abandon hope lightly. They clung to the belief that some could survive. That belief lay behind the councils' "rescue through work" strategy adopted in most ghettos examined by Trunk. What they could not perceive was that, on the Jewish question, the German occupiers were not rational, a fact already in evidence when the Germans rid themselves of the brilliant Jewish scientists who went on to play a crucial role in the Manhattan project to build the first atom bomb. The behavior of the Jewish Councils was in fact composed of an amalgam in which heroism, operational necessity, and rank opportunism lived side by side.

"The Resistance Question," was written when there as a proliferation of books and articles that followed hard upon Arendt's charges. A group of researchers found almost exclusively on finding evidence of physical resistance, as if to redeem the lost honor of the Jewish people. Those, like myself, who never believed there was such a loss, resented this searching through the dead, mostly women and children, for evidence of martial courage. In the sense that they seek the good opinion of mankind, these books and articles concerning Jewish resistance seem to be part of a developing apologetic history. The search for heroes is more concerned with finding a kernel of courage to redeem a fallen image than to understand what it means to live powerlessly in a murderous world.

That anti-Semitism would be found at the center of any historic inquiry concerning the causes of the Holocaust was predictable. But as "Allied Foreign Policy and the Holocaust" shows, it is problematic in any analysis of causes. The noted Zionist historian Ben Halpern observed that anti-Semitism is an "overloaded" term.[6] That idea becomes especially apparent in the study of the Holocaust where the conclusion that we are seeing the culmination of European anti-Semitism is almost irresistible. What else could explain it? But then, one is confronted with the discontinuities between the radical political anti-Semitism of National Socialism that makes the omnipresent normative anti-Semitism seem almost benevolent.

It was that kind of familiar anti-Semitism that was present at the grass roots in the general population of the United States, Britain, and the Soviet Union. In the United States, it reached its apogee in 1944. The nations that were spilling blood and spending treasure to defeat a power that placed anti-Semitism at the center of its cosmology were themselves subject to a more benevolent strain of the dread malady. That paradox cannot be overlooked when we examine the Allied witness role. Churchill, Roosevelt, and Stalin were undoubtedly aware of the danger of allowing German propaganda to depict the war as one to save the Jews. That is one reason that, although Berlin spoke endlessly about the Jews, mention of their fate is rarely found in public statements of the Allies or on the agenda of their wartime conferences. Still, little or no mention of the Jews by the Allies does not necessarily reflect feelings of anti-Semitism among them or indifference to the Jews' plight. Roosevelt's earlier refusal to tamper with the restrictive antirefugee policy could just as easily be blamed on the persistence of the Great Depression. Unemployment rose sharply in 1937. Similarly, the British White Paper of May 1939, which limited Jewish immigration to Palestine, can be viewed as a response to the national interest that placed the need for Arab oil and friendship in the impending war before the Jewish need for haven. And the charge against Soviet authorities that they compelled Jews to live in an information vacuum, depriving them of knowledge of the dire threat they faced should war come, does not stand up very well. The Russian people themselves were kept in a larger information vacuum; and until the victory at Stalingrad in 1943, the special crucible of Russian Jewry was overshadowed by the terrible loss of life endured by the Russian people in a bitter ideological war.

The conclusion that during World War II anti-Semitism was "in the air" on both sides seems unavoidable. But there was also a notable difference. The researcher occasionally encounters random evidence in which a government official vents anti-Semitic feelings; but in the Allied camp, it was far more discernable on the grass-roots level than among the makers of policy. Roosevelt, Churchill, and Stalin could not have been unaware of its prevalence in the populace and the danger it posed should Berlin successfully play the Jewish card. In the final months of the war, anti-Semitism had become the mainstay of Nazi propaganda. But a conscious, clear, and continuous anti-Semitic impact on policy is hard to detect among Allied leaders. More likely to account for Allied indifference, especially during the refugee phase of the Holocaust (1933–1941), is the changed perception of Jewish power. During World War I, that faintly anti-Semitic perception of great Jewish power held by both sides contributed to London's issuance of the Balfour Declaration in 1917, pledging British support of the establishment of a Jewish home in Palestine. During the interwar years, that exaggerated sense of Jewish power was nowhere to be found. What the unchallenged depredations against German and other European Jewries may really have achieved was to reveal how powerless and isolated Jews had become. That lack of power is a requisite precondition of all history's victims.

Part 2, "America and the Holocaust," begins with a discussion of the posture of the Roosevelt administration in relation to the Holocaust. "Roosevelt's New Deal Humanitarianism" is included primarily to furnish the uninformed reader with the basic facts of the case. It also reveals some of the paradoxes and ironies of the refugee rescue issue. Until the final months of 1943, when it suddenly threatened to explode in the press, the rescue question was a comparatively minor blip on the public-awareness monitor. Not anxious to assume an unecessary political risk, Roosevelt usually avoided addressing the issue directly. But administration spokesmen expressed concern when it was considered politically necessary to do so. Roosevelt, for example, several times called for greater care for refugees and eventually invited thirty-two nations to attend an international refugee conference to be convened at Evian, France, in July 1938. The details of the State Department's obstructionist policy, which was finally revealed by the Treasury Department in the early weeks of 1944, led to the establishment of the War Refugee Board (WRB), the high point of Roosevelt's rescue policy. Little came of these gestures, and it is possible that little was intended to come of them. It is for that reason that I call it a policy of "gestures." It refers to the yawning gap that had developed between the administration's benevolent rhetoric and what the bureaucrats were actually doing on their level. This essay sets the stage for our consideration of Roosevelt's search for resettlement havens, a recourse which contemporary researchers rarely consider but which actually became a major part of his administration's rescue effort.

Between 1939 and 1942, the word *resettlement* was for both sides the favored solution for what Berlin called the Jewish problem and what had become for the Allied receiving nations, the refugee problem. In both cases, there was an element of opportunism in hoping to tuck a despised minority away, usually near some arid desert or tropical rain forest. But the National Socialists intended something more drastic in their policy of *Umsiedlung*, the term sometimes applied to the deportation stage that became the code word for the Final Solution. In Berlin, "resettlement" was briefly considered before the war in the East created an opportunity for directed genocide. I say "directed" because it is likely, given what we know of Nazi intent, that the Madagascar and other schemes to deport the Jewish population to Madagascar and other out-of-the-way places would probably have resulted in a slower, more random, but ultimately no less-bloody and destructive policy.

"Could Resettlement Have Saved European Jewry?," examines the prospect of such schemes and finds them wanting. Based on archival sources, various resettlement schemes considered by the Roosevelt administration are examined, as is Roosevelt's penchant for large state-building projects for "political refugees" anywhere except in the United States. In promoting this idea, Roosevelt's keen political instincts are much in evidence. Resettlement not only held out the promise of lessening pressure concerning the refugee crisis at home but also deflected Zionist pressure regarding the British White Paper. The remoteness of realization did not therefore deter Roosevelt from conducting an avid search for likely areas where Europe's Jews might be deposited, at least for the emergency.

Yet clearly demographically and occupationally, European Jewry was hardly suitable human material for pioneering in remote areas. Members of the Zionist movement, which had finally gained dominance in Jewish communities of the Diaspora, viewed the resettlement idea with great suspicion because it threatened the funding of the prestate Jewish community in Palestine (Yishuv), which they considered the most logical and desirable resettlement area. But in 1943, the Bergsonites, and Irgun (militant Zionist Revisionist) group that followed Peter Bergson's (Hillel Kook) view, had become active in the rescue arena in the United States. Realizing that there was little hope of undoing the British White Paper, the Bergsonites pushed to separate the "homeland" goal that had become the centerpiece of the Zionist program, from the rescue goal, which they perceived to be working at cross purposes. But the Zionists, who were the most successful mass resettlers of the twentieth century, remained adamantly opposed. Except for the experiment to send a small number of Jews to the Dominican Republic, most Jews who escaped Europe did so by infiltration into settled communities. Still, the idea of resettlement taunts those who continue to wonder whether it offered a practical way to rescue thousands of Europe's doomed Jews.

The reader comes away form these essays with the sense that the Roosevelt administration was unwilling to confront the problem of rescue directly. It was politically too risky; and given the virulence of domestic anti-Semitism, it posed a threat to the difficult task of mobilizing the American people for a European war they were reluctant to enter. Occasionally, a gesture was made to mollify American Jewry, which had become the Democratic Party's most loyal ethnic constituency. Roosevelt was aware and appreciative of the Jewish voter's strong commitment to the New Deal. But he also knew that there was little danger that Jewish leaders could remove the support of Jewish voters.

Not until the fortunes of war began to favor the Allies in the spring of 1943 did a greater willingness to confront the death camps develop. It is in that context that the establishment of the War Refugee Board in January 1944 is best viewed. It came just in time to deal with the threat facing the Jews of Hungary, the sole surviving sizable European Jewish community, whose number had been swollen by escapees from the charnel house Europe had become. Based on an examination of available archival sources, "The American Effort To Save the Jews of Hungary" presents the background of such actions as the recruitment of Raoul Wallenberg by Iver Olsen, an agent of the WRB, the unresolved bombing question of whether to bomb the camps and the railroads leading to them, and the diplomatic effort to convince the Hungarian Regent regime Miklós Horthy to resist Berlin's entreaties to cooperate in the deportation of its Jews.

The Hungarian episode also illustrates how committed Berlin was to the liquidation of European Jewry. Despite the certain knowledge that the war was lost, the death mills of Auschwitz continued to grind until November 1944. The Final Solution had achieved a momentum of its own. The WRB was too little and came too late to save Hungarian Jewry. It leaves us with a tantalizing picture of what might have been done had the will to save Jewish lives matched Berlin's will to take them.

We next turn to two essays in which I evaluate the Roosevelt administration's response to the Holocaust. Publication of these essays was separated by a period of fourteen years. That juxtaposition gives the reader an opportunity to see the development of my thinking. "PBS's Roosevelt: Deceit and Indifference or Politics and Powerlessness?," develops many of the ideas expressed in "Governmental Response to Human Crisis," but it contextualizes Roosevelt's response by viewing it against the background of domestic politics and the threatening situation abroad.

This essay was written in response to a highly accusatory documentary, "America and the Holocaust," shown on PBS channels in April 1994 and based largely on the work of David Wyman. That documentary shows how the historian's view of the actions of the Roosevelt administration during the Holocaust years is in some measure shaped by his values and assumptions concerning humankind generally. Although I do not take exception to the basic facts presented by Wyman, I show that the failure to contextualize the Roosevelt response can lead to a misreading of history. When viewed in the context of domestic politics and the degraded condition of international relations in the years before and during the war, the characterization of Roosevelt's response to the refugee crisis as one of "deceit and indifference" appears unbalanced. These two essays also demonstrate the difference between history and retroactive investigative journalism, a difference that has become blurred in recent years.

Part 3, "American Jewry and the Holocaust," contains three essays dealing with the American Jewish response to the Holocaust, a touchy subject yet to be fully explored. They will be especially welcome to those who have been regaled with arguments that the indictment of witnessing governments and agencies like the Vatican, which has been a major part of Holocaust historiography, is really part of a Jewish conspiracy to garner the income our caring society reserves for its victims. Recent research concerning the role of the *Yishuv* and my own preliminary research on American Jewry's role during those terrible years should demonstrate that Jewish historians have been no less sparing in their examination of the Jewish witness. These articles discuss American Jewry, warts and all.

"Was There Communal Failure Among American Jews?" sets the stage for responding to that question by providing information of what the actual political, economic, and social condition of American Jewry had become after Word War I. With bloody wars as bookends and impacted by a worldwide depression, the interwar years suffer from a historical overload that makes the search for continuities and discontinuities problematic. One can sense, for example, that the Great Depression nourished the radical stream in Jewish political culture among the young, just as the virulent anti-Semitism of the thirties fueled an abiding insecurity in the older generation. Both situations bear on the Jews' ineffective response to the Holocaust. Rapid acculturation and secularization wore down the communal bonds that held Jews together. Religious authority, once a mainstay of communalism, gave way to voluntarism based on a sense of common ethnic culture viewed largely in secular terms. But secularism and the freedom it carried proved to be too weak to generate the cohesiveness that especially became necessary in the life-and-death crisis soon to be faced by the Jews of Europe.

On the eve of the Holocaust, American Jewry discovered it was no longer, if it ever really had been, a community able to speak to power with one voice. The shared values, language, culture, history, and aspirations were rapidly being reconfigured by the seductive culture of America. The children of the immigrants cherished America's freedom and used it to free themselves from the confining, yet also binding, religious mandates that had once governed their lives and made them identifiably Jewish. During the Holocaust, it was these subtle changes that partly prevented a more effective American Jewish response to the threat faced by their European brethren.

To "speak truth to power" there must exist not only mutually recognized community leaders but also channels of communication. There was no scarcity of such leaders and channels during the Holocaust years; but with the new democratic voluntaristic organizational structure, one could no longer be certain whether followers would follow where leaders led. Democracy, which is the crucial centerpiece of secular modernity, produces autonomous individuated citizens who are free to accept or reject the mandate of the community. For decades, American Jewry had been in the throes of a democratizing impulse. That was what the Congress movement of the first two decades of the century was all about. But democracy also tended to weaken authority; it brought with it fragmentation until one almost wished that there was Marshall law again. Marshall law refers to a period before his death in 1929, when Louis Marshall, president of the American Jewish Committee (AJC), dominated the community leadership and frequently was virtually able to dictate policy.

"Jewish Leadership During the Roosevelt Years" identifies the several channels through which American Jewry spoke to the Roosevelt administration. One should note that they included not only the traditional channel, the *shtadlan* (the influential "court Jew" who, by dint of wealth or stature, has access to power), but those Jews who had gained prominence in several new power centers operating in American society—the law establishment, business and commerce, organized labor, the social work nexus, the university, science and technology centers, and the media. For American Jewry, the social work nexus; the nascent professional political nexus (speech writers, assistants, fund-raisers, pundits, campaign managers); the science establishment (recently enhanced by the presence of many Jewish refugee scientists); and the New York intellectuals (who were at least nominally Jewish); could serve as conduits to the Oval Office.

How did Jews associated with these centers help amplify the Jewish cry for help? The answer is—very little. The problem was twofold. The strata of Jewish leadership were bifurcated between those who were leaders in the Jewish community, like Rabbi Stephen Wise, and those who were close to Roosevelt, the so-called "Jew Deal," composed of Henry Morgenthau Jr., Herbert Lehman, Samuel Rosenman, Felix Frankfurter, and others. The members of the "Jew Deal," through whom Jews could speak to Roosevelt, did not deny their Jewishness; but they no longer viewed themselves as exclusively Jewish. They thought of themselves as prominent Americans who happened incidentally to be Jewish. Except for Morgenthau, Roosevelt's secretary of the treasury who became involved in the establishment of the WRB, they were not anxious to be over-identified with Jewish causes. The simpler days when Theodore Roosevelt spoke to the Jewish community through Jacob Schiff or Oscar Straus, men who felt obliged to lead, were no more.

"Rescue and the Secular Perception" was first delivered at a conference that linked rescue, which seems always to be a need in Jewish history, to the notion of *pidyon shivuim*, the religious injunction regarding community responsibility to ransom prisoners. Modernization not only weakened the ability of Jewish communities to respond to this need, it left no commanding force that might compell Jews to act on behalf of their brethren. Yet, Jewish secular recruits formed a disproportionate percentage of the young men sent to help Loyalist Spain defend itself against the "scourge of fascism," which they viewed as a universal threat. They saw Jews as part of the human family but could not understand that part of that family had become intent on wiping Jews off the face of the earth. Often without their awareness, that sense of belonging to a caring world served as a cover to abandon their Jewishness without feeling the self-abnegating effects of assimilation.

One source of disunity among Jews was the different speeds and terms with which various constituencies in the community responded to modernity. Modernization, of which secularization was a primary part, progressed especially rapidly in the United States. It gradually undermined a strong sense of being, bound together by the same historical experience and destiny that allowed Jews to see themselves as a people rooted in time, represented by history rather than space. Secularism eroded a built-in sense of corporateness, or peoplehood, that was inherent in premodern Jewish communal culture. It changed the character of American Jewry who would soon be called upon to advocate the rescue of their beleaguered European brethren. Growing numbers of American Jews in the prewar years, having forgotten who they were, could no longer fathom why they should be so called. Their ineffective response to the crisis went beyond an inability to sense a specific threat to Jewish enterprise. They had become disarmed in an unfriendly world that paradoxically had no similar problem in identifying them as Jews.

Yet, there is little assurance that, had there been greater unity in American Jewry, history would have taken a different turn. During the thirties and forties, American Jewry was not winning medals for popularity. The negative impact of German propaganda, which spoke of the "Jewish war," would have been enhanced by an open advocacy of rescue of European Jewry. It is unlikely that before the spring of 1943, when an Allied victory was fairly certain, that the Roosevelt administration would have permitted the rescue of Europe's Jews to become part of the nation's war aims. After that period, it still remained difficult to get even an informal recognition that somehow the annihilation of European Jewry was an intrinsic part of what the war was about. For most Americans, World War II had little to do with the dire fate of the Jews. David Wyman may be overestimating the influence of American Jewry and underestimating American anti-Semitism when he insists that sufficient public pressure could have been generated in 1943 to force Roosevelt to take a more active stance. The American public was preoccupied with winning the war as quickly as possible and "bringing the boys home." Nothing that could be construed as interfering with that objective could be allowed to stand, and most steps suggested by rescue advocates were so interpreted.

Based on the version of events propounded by the Bergson group, an indictment of American Jewry for its supposed indifference and lack of courage can easily be drawn up. Several researchers have done so. The reader will find little evidence of that polemic in these essays. Primarily Palestinian Jews, the Bergsonites viewed the organization and the power of American Jewry in terms of the only reality they knew, the *Yishuv*. They had almost no understanding of how American Jewry was organized and held a much-overblown idea of its power and influence. The responsibility assumed by American Jewry, to rescue the Jews of Europe, was, in fact, far beyond its power to fulfill. Not a sovereign nation and therefore bereft of armed might, American Jewry could not remotely

match the power of a modern nation-state utterly intent on genocide. Those friendly Allied governments from whom Jews sought
succor, and through whom they were obliged to act, were opposed
to rescue as a matter of wartime policy. The gap between power and
responsibility was unbridgeable. Failure of American Jewry was thus
preordained.

We soon learn that determining whether there was communal
failure is not a problem that can be easily handled, much less
solved, by historians because what American Jewry did and failed to
do during those bitter years ultimately comes down to a moral judgment. Predictably, for the moral athlete there can be no limit on
what should have been done. But the historian is better equipped to
make a reasonable determination regarding what the possibilities for
certain actions were. Even here, there are often conflicting judgments. There is, for example, little agreement today on the efficacy
of bombing the death chambers and the rail lines to them. Evidence
accumulates that bombing was not the "silver bullet" of rescue that
early researchers thought they had found.[7]

For those who want to judge the witness role of American
Jewry, the most effective research strategy would be to compare
American Jewish action during the Holocaust to the effectiveness of
other American ethnic groups (Cuban, German, Irish, and Greek
Americans) who were similarly faced with an urgent need to influence American foreign policy. We should be aware that none com-
pares in urgency with the situation faced by American Jewry, who
actually witnessed their kith and kin being processed to death by
modern industrial machinery. But to the extent that it can be drawn,
that comparison furnishes the historian with some measure of what
could reasonably have been expected. Such a comparative approach
reveals that the ability of ethnic groups to pull American foreign
policy in the direction of their interest is limited and that, in this
respect, American Jewry did comparatively well in the past.

Finally, researchers tend to read the unity that characterized
postwar American Jewry, exemplified by its role in helping to wring
recognition of Israel in 1948, back into the pre-Holocaust period. The
discussions presented here emphasize the fact that a unified community, bound together by a common history and culture, did not
exist in those years. It first developed in the postwar period, and
one of its principle building blocks was the radical losses suffered by
Jewry during the Holocaust.

Bearing Witness concludes with "Who Shall Bear Guilt for the
Holocaust?", which again reminds the reader how limited is the abil-

ity of government to protect a despised group that is not legally linked to it and is held captive in enemy territory. Governments, we are reminded, are merely human-made institutions, not humans themselves. They can seem to act morally only to the extent that the men and women who control them wish to act morally. That happens rarely in history and did not happen at all during World War II in regard to victims of the Holocaust. There were several instances during these years when the American government might have made such a humane response. The refugee crisis of the thirties is one example; another might have come with an announcement of retributive or retaliatory bombing or the sending of food packages to the camps despite the blockade. Such actions would have encouraged others, including the people in occupied Europe, to help those in desparate need. But in every case, such suggestions were usually rejected as impractical, illegal, or simply undoable. European Jewry was allowed to perish because no place could be found for its rescue among the war priorities of the Allies.

Despite the many convincing explanations for inaction—the need to give priority to winning the war, the absence of direct legal responsibility, the difficulty of getting the story believed—none seems adequate to explain the stark silence while so many millions of lives were systematically taken. "If 6,000,000 cattle had been slaughtered," Congressman Emanuel Celler quotes an old rabbi as saying, "there would have been more interest. A way would have been found."[8] But no way was ever found; and that truth makes a statement about the condition of the world at that time, perhaps in our time, too.

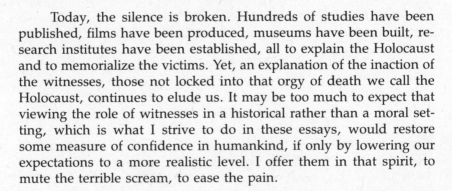

Today, the silence is broken. Hundreds of studies have been published, films have been produced, museums have been built, research institutes have been established, all to explain the Holocaust and to memorialize the victims. Yet, an explanation of the inaction of the witnesses, those not locked into that orgy of death we call the Holocaust, continues to elude us. It may be too much to expect that viewing the role of witnesses in a historical rather than a moral setting, which is what I strive to do in these essays, would restore some measure of confidence in humankind, if only by lowering our expectations to a more realistic level. I offer them in that spirit, to mute the terrible scream, to ease the pain.

PART ONE

Holocaust
The Historical Problem

The Uniqueness of the Holocaust

The tragic paradox of the Jews in modern times has been the fact that their existence and success have been dependent upon the triumph of the idea of oneness as represented by liberal democracy and socialism, while the very phenomenon of Jewry is an unparalleled demonstration of the enormous power of the element of uniqueness. The Jews did not want and could not escape the fact of their uniqueness. The Gentiles would not and could not be made oblivious to it.

—J. L. Talmon,
The Unique and the Universal, 123.

THE CONTINUING DIALOGUE on how best to determine a meaning for the Holocaust has reached a critical juncture. What must be decided is whether the event was historically unique, a *mysterium tremendum*, as Arthur Cohen has called it, or merely one in a series of genocidal acts for which humankind has always had a penchant.[1] For convenience sake, we might view it as a debate between universalizers, anxious to distill lessons regarding the true nature of humankind and society, and particularists, who are wary of comparisons because the meaning of the event lies precisely in its uniqueness.

On its face, it is difficult to take issue with those who view the Holocaust from a universal perspective. The Armenian analogy im-

This essay appeared originally in *Shoal* 2, no. 2 (Spring 1981): 3–11, under the title "Determining the Uniqueness of the Holocaust: The Factor of Historical Valence."

mediately comes to mind. Historians have discovered in that slaughter a direct link to Hitler's plans for the Jews. In musing over the possibility of liquidating Poland's intellectual elite and the Jews, Hitler purportedly observed that there was little talk of the Armenian slaughter. Indeed, when the observation was made in 1939, voices concerning the actions of the Turks had fallen silent. Yet, if the slaughter of the Armenians serves for some as a historic precedent for planned genocide, the silence in evidence in 1939 seems to offer a sharp contrast with the Holocaust. Auschwitz is coming increasingly to occupy a special place in the lexicon of the West, as if to emphasize that what transpired there and in the other death camps of Nazi Europe was not merely another incidence in the long history of human barbarism. The burden of this essay is to seek out these differences.

Why does the argument between the universalists and particularists come to the fore now? Those who keep one eye on the cultural scene cannot help but note that Theodor Adorno's prescription concerning the impossibility of creating poetry after Auschwitz is increasingly disregarded. Writers and playwrights seem to be especially anxious to test their mettle against the intractable event of the Holocaust. Although thus far it has yielded little in the way of transcendent meaning, the creative mind seems naturally prone to seek universal truths, which somehow requires a muting and even denial of the Holocaust's specific Jewish dimension.

Like writers, curriculum developers tend to stress the universal aspects of the Holocaust. The New York City Holocaust curriculum informs teachers that the Holocaust is one of several episodes of genocide throughout history. "Students could study the experience of enslaved Blacks in North and South America, of Native American Indians defeated in wars with the United States, of Christian Armenians exterminated by the government of Turkey." The list is extended to the mass murder of Cambodians and to the "fracticidal conflict in Northern Ireland and Lebanon."[2] In short, all contemporary bloodletting can be classified as genocide, and the Holocaust is subsumed under a generalized scream of ethnic pain. Yet, how can it be otherwise for curriculum designers? In most school districts, Jewish students compose only a small fraction of the student body. A curriculum that focuses on their fate exclusively and does not deal with the persecution of other groups would soon be condemned for disturbing the careful balance of ethnic interest that educators today, especially in larger cities, strive to maintain.

The staunchest proponents of the universalist/comparative approach stem from the world of scholarship, especially the discipline of sociology. In that field, a comparative approach, what Max Weber once called nomotheticism, frequently comes into play. Apparently, similar happenings or processes are grouped together in order to find common patterns or laws that govern their development. In her book *Accounting for Genocide,* for example, Helen Fein begins by comparing the slaughter of European Jewry and the Armenians. Predictably, the comparison yields a number of commonalities that placed both groups outside the "universe of obligation," the ties of mutual obligation and responsibility that define all societies. Once the group is placed outside that universe, the prerequisite for the actual process of mass murder is in place.[3] But again, the discovery that something different happened at Auschwitz is not only not possible using a nomothetic approach, it would also be a disturbing counterweight to the notion that similar historical events have equal historical valence.

The universalizing tendency is enhanced by the fact that the post-Holocaust period did not bring a respite from the gruesome phenomenon of mass murder. Large-scale massacres occurred in Indonesia, Biafra, Burundi, Uganda, and Cambodia. In the seventies, Aleksandr I. Solzhenitsyn's revelations regarding the Soviet Gulag reminded us that the world of the concentration camp was the experience of millions in the Soviet orbit; and while murder through modern mass-production techniques was not the rule in the Gulag, the KGB was no less astute than the SS in the techniques of cheapening life.[4] It appears as if existence in Soviet and Nazi camps shared much in common.

Finally, the discreet properties of the Holocaust were further diffused by a tendency of every aggrieved and vulnerable minority to employ the Holocaust metaphor to signal the danger it felt.[5] The very use of Auschwitz as a measuring rod inadvertently indicated that something radically different has occurred in the death camps. They understood that the Nazis had conceived and implemented an alternate solution to the perennial problem of how men can live together though different. The thrust of liberalism, pluralism, and religious interdenominationalism had been to raise the tolerance threshhold so that one would ultimately be able "to love thy neighbor as thyself." Now, one rediscovered that one could simply eliminate the neighbor and the world would make no protest. That frightening truth emanating from the Holocaust haunts all powerless people. Yet, spokesmen of such groups who wanted to signal the danger they felt tended to be facile about the comparison with the fate of the Jews under Nazi control. Every real or imagined trespass became part of a genocidal conspiracy. It cast doubt on the credibility of the grievance and incidentally on the Holocaust with which it was compared.

It is estimated that at least 5,000,000 Poles, Russians, Gypsies, and other members of Europe's "undesirable" minorities met their death at Nazi hands. The Nazi death machine avidly searched out and slaughtered other groups, too. How then can the particularist, whose position is customarily Judeocentric, maintain that the event is unique? Is that not part of an unseemly Jewish tendency to mourn out loud?[6] For the neo-Nazi propagandists who maintain that the Final Solution never happened at all, one can collect data that are massive and irrefutable.[7] But what response can there be for those who insist that the Jews were not the only or even the principal victims?

This position is elaborated by John Cuddihy, a professor of sociology and author of a provocative work on Jewish culture, *The Ordeal of Civility.* He views the emphasis on the specifically Jewish aspects of the Holocaust and the wide publicity given to the event by the media as a group strategy for garnering ethnic gratification. It is based, he observes, on a "secularized (and sometimes not so secularized) conviction of Jewish chosenness." Its purpose is to give to Jews a "sacred particularity," which according to Robert Merton, is a common drive among status-starved groups for "enthusiastic esteem," or glory.[8] Cuddihy does not go as far as the inversion of victim and victimizer, which might be noted in Soviet charges of racial genocide by Israel. But by insisting that the Holocaust experience was not exclusively a Jewish one, and suspecting a Jewish conspiracy to reap rewards by touting their travail through the media, Cuddihy achieves a similar effect. The Holocaust's unique and specifically Jewish aspect is diminished. It is not sufficient to point out that anti-Gypsyism never became the focal point of an otherwise empty ideology or that Witnesses of Jehovah, Russian war prisoners, homosexuals, and other despised groups who sometimes shared the Jewish fate were not hunted down by a zealous bureaucracy even in the remotest mountains of Bulgaria. It avails little to

point out that the "Jewish question" impinged on everything the
Nazis did, including major decisions of strategy; that it was such an
overwhelming preoccupation that every enemy had somehow to be
converted to being Jewish or that the systematized slaughter of
6,000,000 required elaborate organization, which the Nazi bureaucratic apparatus was more than willing to expend.

Like the universalists, those who argue that what transpired in
the death camps of occupied Europe is a *novum* not comparable to
other bloodlettings in history, do not cut their argument from a single cloth. Some argue that the manner of the slaughter and its sheer
scale differentiate it from other cases of genocide. Those with theological inclinations speak of the radicalness of the evil released by
the Nazis. Death was not merely a by-product of the Nazi system,
the philosopher Emil Fackenheim points out, it was the end product.[9] That observation is borne out by statements made by Nazi
leaders who understood that what they were doing was so horrendous that, once begun, the process could not be stopped. They of
course did not speak of radical evil because, paradoxically enough,
they were still subject to some of the basic thrusts of Western civilization. The Final Solution was in part a massive social-engineering
scheme based on a theory of radical eugenics designed to improve
society. For Nazi ideologues, it was simply a necessary program to
ensure the continued progress of Western civilization on whose behalf they were acting. Yet, in a physical sense, the targeted German
Jews, the first to bear the sting of Nazi racialism, were no longer
observably different. Target-centering them posed a problem for the
Nazi bureaucracy, which conceived of a "pseudo-scientific" set of
racial guidelines later embodied in the Nuremberg laws, so that the
desired objective of making the Reich *Judenrein* could be achieved.
Had the Nazis been willing to be patient, assimilation and natural
attrition would have eliminated German Jewry by the end of the
century.[10]

Not only were the methods used to liquidate the Jews recognizably part of European industrial technology and managerial know-
how, discernible from the way the bureaucracy identified and finally
brought the victims to the death camps, but the objectives of the
Final Solution itself were an intrinsic part of the assumption of progress and development that spurred European civilization forward.

"Progress," that is, a solution to a problem, would be achieved not by building a dam or discovering a vaccine but by mass murder. The assumptions behind the Final Solution and its implementation are reflections of the European industrial system.

It is no accident that the term "Final Solution" was finally chosen to indicate a program of mass murder. It is an operational rather than an ideological term. The Jews were the problem and Auschwitz was the solution. Heinrich Himmler frequently reminded his commanders that the world would someday be thankful for what Germany had the iron will to achieve.[11]

Had the verdict of history been otherwise, the Final Solution might today be viewed in precisely the terms set down by Himmler. Instead, Auschwitz may ultimately come to represent what absolute evil signifies. It is coming to mean absolute terror not only for those who experienced it but for all who live with anxiety and fear. It is, after all, the experience of a Jewish adolescent, Anne Frank, that embodies the classic paranoic nightmare of our time. She was forced to live in a world that wanted her dead for a crime she could not fathom. It gave her no haven. That vision haunts all thinking people and is part of the historical echo left by the Holocaust. The existence of such echoes may in itself be the surest sign that we are dealing with no ordinary event. On the other side, the Nazi-inspired killing machine has become the symbol of demonism. That is the meaning of Nazi paraphernalia—helmets, black leather jackets, and medals—that are worn by motorcycle gangs like the Hell's Angels. Those who want to project evil and danger instinctively seem to know where to find their symbols.

I have noted that the manner of implementing this mass murder serves as a principle dividing line between it and prior acts of genocide. The Final Solution used the industrial processes and the managerial techniques that enabled European civilization to dominate the world. Those mountains of shoes, human hair, eyeglasses, and suitcases were by-products of a modern manufacturing process. They were destined to be reintegrated into the consumer economy. To be sure, there were some notable differences in this manufacturing process. The raw material for these factories was not ore or lumber or mineral substance but human beings; and the end product was not shiny, new industrial goods, but death. In keeping with the most advanced management techniques, an accurate record of production was maintained—so many units produced per day and week—and constant improvement of efficiency was encouraged.

Testifying by affidavit at the Nuremberg trial, Rudolf Hess, the camp commandant of Auschwitz, recalled his achievement in this area. "The Camp Commandant at Treblinka told me that he had liquidated 80,000 in the course of one-half year, he used monoxide gas and I did not think his methods were very efficient. So when I set up the extermination building at Auschwitz, I used Cyclon B. . . . [sic] Another improvement we made over Treblinka was that we built our gas chambers to accommodate 2,000 people at one time, whereas at Treblinka their ten gas chambers only accommodated 200 people each."[12] For Hess, the concentration camp was not "another planet" but rather a mundane extension of normal manufacturing procedures. If the manufacture of death meant that it was a world turned upside down, Hess's testimony gave little evidence of it.

There are then compelling reasons for differentiating the Holocaust from prior acts of mass murder in history, but they merely hint at the larger historical framework that is used here to bring its uniqueness into focus. To do that, we must consider the effect of the event on the subsequent flow of history. Central historical events, such as the French or Russian revolutions, alter the course of history. Did the destruction of European Jewry create such a change? The contention here is that although all the evidence is not yet in, the Holocaust has created such a sharp break. It did so by annihilating a group that somehow was producing a disproportionate share of a special sort of modernizing or universalizing elite that in the realm of ideas, science, and technology, was on the road to creating the basis of a society beyond the lethal nation-state.[13]

There has been endless speculation on the reasons Jewish thinkers were so prominent in conceiving of a universalist vision. Undoubtedly, it is linked to the sense of detachment stemming from the anomalous position of Jews in postemancipation European society. By the end of the nineteenth century, the full promise of emancipation seemed unrealizable. Not only were there powerful elements in the new secular societies unwilling to extend full rights and access to Jews, but Jews also held reservations regarding the total purging of Judaic elements in their social and private lives as required by the transaction. Jews lived in European society but were not precisely of it. Their dual identity often permitted them, on the one hand, to become the most avid generators and carriers of the national cultures where they resided and, on the other, to become predisposed to transnational ideas and activities. While Jewish masses touted the greatness of the national cultures with which they had cast their lot, the writers, critics, and political thinkers stemming from them were the most universal of universalists. It would be this small group whose influence would prove most enduring. They produced, according to George Steiner, a "revolution of spirit so great that our inner lives, and those of western civilization, would scarcely be recognized without them."[14]

The Final Solution not only cut short the lives of many members of this group, it destroyed the cultural matrix from which it stemmed. The impact of that event on Jewish history is already apparent, but the consequences for European civilization can only be speculated about. In the end, it is hardly conceivable that what transpired in the death camps, which were after all conceived by one of Europe's most advanced countries and ignored or abetted by the others, can be divorced from what some today perceive as a loss of élan and self-confidence in European society. The important difference between the Holocaust and other cases of genocide in history is that European Jewry was not a dissident minority in a remote corner of the world but, by virtue of its thinkers, an important component of European civilization, which dominated the pre-Holocaust world. What died in Auschwitz was not merely the corpus of a people but Europe's hope that its social system could endure. From one perspective, one can view the Holocaust as Europe's turning on the group whose thinkers played a key role in paving the way for the entrance of European society into modernity and hereafter confronting the social, economic, and personal problems left in the wake of the transition from traditional to modern society. Who can escape the bitter irony that European Jewry was destroyed by a perverse use of the very industrial process that everywhere is the hallmark of modernity.

Understood correctly, the claim for the Holocaust's uniqueness and particularity rests not on the fact that Jews experienced more pain and greater suffering than others or that the evil they were compelled to confront was crueler. It is based on comparative historical development of modern Europe. Although it is impossible, in the short space of this essay, to relate the many varied components of what major Jewish thinkers submitted to European intellectual thought, much less to determine what was Jewish about those concepts, certain components can be isolated, foremost among them the notion of universalism. Universalism became a constant whether Jewish thinkers spoke of the brotherhood of man, the internationalism of the proletariat, or the universal applicability of the axioms of the new sciences. It was a universalism that did not so much reject national loyalties as it refused to be contained by them. Moreover, it went beyond political ideology whose universalism could be found on the left side of the political spectrum. Sometimes, as in the case of science or the creation of a new universal language like Esperanto, which for a time attracted a disproportionate number of Jews to its banner, it was not political at all.

A disproportionate Jewish presence could also be observed in agencies and professions that were international in character. Jews were attracted early to the international Masonic order. They were among the first to achieve prominence in the field of international law and were staunch supporters of such international agencies as the World Court, the League of Nations, and the United Nations. Their prominence in international peace movements is well known. A disproportionate Jewish presence might also be observed in international commerce. Jews were prominent in the new fields of transportation and communication. The first international news agency was established by a Jew, and generally Jews were well represented in the development of the modern press.[15] They also played a considerable part in financing the earliest railroad lines. In a word, there was an important Jewish presence in almost every activity that tended to bind distant people and cultures together.

That Jews achieved some prominence in organizations that sought to build a web of international comity should not surprise us. The support such organizations received from Jews reflected not only their physical distribution among many nations but also their vulnerability in some of them. Jewish internationalism was a physical as well as an ideological datum. The protection and civil rights of these Jewish communities was a standard item on the agenda of various international conferences in the nineteenth century. The turning of the Jewish communities to international agencies for succor and protection did not begin with the Holocaust. In their quest for diplomatic intercession against anti-Jewish depredations in Switzerland, Morocco, Romania, and Russia, Jewish leaders called into play the principles of the Enlightenment that they tried to establish in international law. They pressed their case at the Congress of Vienna (1815), the Congress of Berlin (1878), the negotiations at Versailles (1919), and at several smaller international conferences held in the nineteenth and twentieth centuries. They may themselves a standing challenge to the humanity and tolerance of the European nation-state system. When the nations proved reluctant to grant such rights, Jews pressed for recognition of their special minority status protected by the international community in the new nations emerging after World War I. Finally, they pressed for recognition of their own state in the Middle East. It is conceivable that had Jews been more successful in wresting protection by the intercession of an international community, this last-mentioned step might never had taken place. But such an international authority proved far too weak to effect basic change. Jewish leaders first imagined it into existence and then asked the nations to be better than they wanted to be. For our purpose, it is important to recall that Jewish internationalism was not merely a form of idealism but also had roots in nineteenth- and early twentieth-century international politics and diplomacy.

Similarly, the burgeoning field of science in the nineteenth and twentieth centuries attracted Jewish thinkers whose conceptualization transcended national boundaries. It was universalism of a different sort, yet it too dealt with universal truths and required international contact to maintain its vitality. It was natural that recently emancipated Jews should be attracted to the sciences because its concepts tended to validate the spirit of the Enlightenment on which the emancipation was based. At the same time, the optimism and confidence that characterized post-Enlightenment European civilization were partly based on the hope that science and technology would ultimately solve the eternal problem of scarcity. Jewish thinkers especially saw in the development of science the possibility of releasing a lucid rationality associated with scientific method that would mute the passions of belief and tribe that heretofore had kept Jews a people apart. The racial underpinnings of the Holocaust have a particular irony because, rather than carrying forward the assumption of intraspecie biological sameness, a pseudo science based on racial genetics, introduced in the late nineteenth century, gained dominance. The value-free truths of science were easy prey to power wielders who could impose on them any coloration they desired. The science that was so attractive to Jewish thinkers could prove lethal when wielded by a bureaucracy imbued with racialist Nazi ideology.

The universalist truths projected outward by its modernizing elite also found ready acceptance within the Jewish constituency. Virtually every ideology embraced by the Jewish masses in the post-Enlightenment period possesses a universalist component. It can be discerned in early Zionist thinkers like Achad Ha'Am (Asher Ginsberg), the Diaspora nationalism of Simon Dubnow, in movements like Bundism, Labor Zionism, and the religious Reform movement that made its debut in Germany in the second decade of the nineteenth century. Finding roots among Jewish masses still steeped in the ancient Jewish tradition was not always easy for the secular universalists. Those like Leon Trotsky, Julius Martov, or Rosa Luxemburg, who had gone completely to the other world, could not speak to Jews who remained linked to, if not precisely the religious tradition, then some notion of Jewish peoplehood. It would be a group of Jewish socialists unable to gain recognition of their special case by the international socialist movement who would address themselves to their Jewish constituency.

But the gulf between the Jewish masses and their universalizing elites remained wide, especially in Germany. Delegates elected to the assembly in Germany by Jewish voters between 1867 and 1877 were overwhelmingly from right-wing and centrist parties. Between 1893 and 1916, a growing gap between elected Jewish officeholders and the Jewish electorate can be discerned: 72 percent of the former were now affiliated with the Socialist Party, but only 19 percent of the Jewish electorate followed these elites, and 61 percent continued their allegiance to the parties of the Right and Center. As late as the election of 1930, the German Jewish voter was markedly more conservative than those Jews who sought and won political office. Sixty-five percent voted for the centrist German Democratic Party, and 30 percent for the Social Democratic Party (SPD).

The remarkable disparity between the general Jewish voting behavior and the political tendencies of Jewish officeholders is partly related to the fact that the latter belonged to the educated Jewish opinion-making elite. They were writers, journalists, and sundry intellectuals prone to seek answers for the Jewish dilemma in secular universalist movements. Of the four hundred Jews active in German politics between 1867 and 1914, a striking 31 percent were employed as editors, writers, journalists, and sundry word wielders for the SPD. It would be these professions from which the Jewish universalizing elite stemmed.

They, of course, shared much in common with non-Jews who were similarly attracted to the universalist ideal. But even within the various branches of the socialist movement where many found their place, the universalism of Jewish thinkers seemed made of sturdier stuff. The more intellectual and theoretical the task within the party, the more Jews it attracted. Jewish socialists were not only more inclined to the theoretical, they were also more concerned with legality and were more international minded. The same pattern held true among Jewish members of the Russian Communist Party. Practically all the Soviet negotiators at the Treaty of Brest Litovsk were of Jewish origin, as were the Soviet representatives at the various socialist international congresses and the Comintern.[16]

The development of the Bund in eastern Europe illustrates the way universalism was turned inward to serve the Jewish constituency. Established in 1897, the Bund was interested primarily in organizing Russian workers, among whom the growing number of Jewish workers would be included. To establish that connection, Jewish religion, nationalism, and all forms of particularism were studiously ignored. Zionist ideology particularly was an anathema because it sought to organize the Jewish masses along national rather than class lines. But the reality of Jewish separateness and the notable absence of socialist fraternalism toward Jews finally caused Bundist leaders to seek out a Jewish constituency. Between 1901 and 1907, the centralist class orientation of the Russian Social Democrats was gradually abandoned in favor of the more flexible position of the Austro-Hungarian Marxists. Conditioned by years of experience organizing in a multinational empire, the Austrian socialists were more sensitive to the problem of national culture. The Bundists were not ready to abandon socialist universalism, they wanted merely to amalgamate it with the reality of a strong spirit of national separatism. "The nation is the peculiar form into which the universal is formed," proclaimed Vladimir Medem, the leading theoretician of the early Bund. After the bloody pogroms of 1905, the Bund abandoned the "neutralist" position and openly affirmed a separate Jewish road to socialism. It began to participate actively in the establishment of Jewish schools, where Yiddish culture and socialism could be taught. It promoted the development of curricula that combined the two and teacher training. That policy was maintained until it was swept away by the Holocaust.

The development of the Bund was specific to eastern Europe, where a self-conscious Jewish community possessing many of the characteristics of nationhood did in fact exist. In western Europe, however, where Jewish ethnicity was weaker, Jewish universalists acted out their roles in the larger non-Jewish arena, where they were indistinguishable from other secular universalists. Even here, there were exceptions like Moses Hess, who in mid-life perceived Jewish nationalism as a necessary prerequisite for Jewish regeneration. But predominantly western Jewish universalists remained under the impression that they were entering upon the larger historical stage, where their influence would be greater.

The development of the Reform movement in Germany and its counterpart in the United States affords evidence that those universalists who chose to act within a Jewish context ultimately had a greater historical impact. The early history of the Reform movement bears noteworthy parallels to the development of the Bund in eastern Europe. Here, too, in the first flush of enthusiasm for the principles of the Enlightenment, the early leaders proposed a universalistic position almost totally emptied of a particularistic Judaic content. They were also confronted by Jewish masses who clung tenaciously to their religious and ethnic loyalties. David Friedlander, a disciple of Moses Mendelsohn, who became a leader of Prussian Jewry in his own right, located the essence of Judaism in the ethical principles of "natural" religion. Predictably, these principles corresponded neatly with those of the Enlightenment, even as they echoed those of the prophets. They, he thought, would become the ideological core of Reform Judaism.

Abraham Geiger approached the tensions between particularism and universalism from another vantage. He was more sensitive to the communal ties that persisted in German Jewry and therefore did not facilely identify the tenets of the Enlightenment with those of Judaism. Like Medem, he began with a total commitment to universalism; but like Friedlander, he ultimately sought to find a rationale for them in the Hebrew prophets. The problem was how to convince the Jewish faithful of the relatedness of the tenets. For Geiger, the answer was to begin with the reality of particularism. "While leaning on particularism," he wrote, "the clergyman must continually lead away from it and toward universalism of the religion of humanity." He counseled spiritual leaders to imbue worshippers with the spirit of *Menshheit*, the common humanity that he saw as the basis of all religion. He was convinced that Judaism always espoused such principles, even during the intensely particularistic biblical period and the Second Commonwealth. Particularism, he thought, was sometimes necessary to weld the monotheistic principle, in which the universalist ethos was embedded, firmly to the Jewish people. It was that linkage between universalism and monotheism that would permit the Jewish people to carry out the "priestly mission of Israel" that was the purpose of the dispersion. That conception, with its powerful universalizing aspect, became the classical Reform position.

There existed in the nineteenth century several patterns of universalism among Jewish thinkers. A secular variety usually led to adherence in the various branches of the socialist movement. It sometimes served as an instrument for those who wanted to project their critique outward to the general society. Their tenuous connection to Judaism was often most clearly reflected in their quarrel with its confining strictures, its tribalism. They were radicals who happened to be Jewish rather than Jewish radicals who sought to express their search for roots and reason through a Jewish instrument. Yet, a third variety of universalist found among Jews were scientists, writers, and those involved in the so-called creative arts. These people generated a universalism of a neutral, nonpolitical kind. It was best articulated by Einstein but can also be noted in the public pronouncements of Freud and Kafka. Their universalism was not linked to any particular ideology but seemed to emerge out of a broad humanitarian impulse or directly out of the discipline they followed. But all varieties of the modernizing elite held in common a compelling need to go beyond their national cultures and the nation-states to which they were confined to seek a larger truth about the general human condition. National cultures were confining, and the nation-state that served as their container warrants for men like George Steiner only "a provisional, constantly reexamined loyalty."[17] Hannah Arendt's response to Gershom Sholem, who questioned her love of Israel after reading *Eichmann in Jerusalem*, followed along similar lines. "You are quite right," she responded, "I am not moved by any love of this sort, and for two reasons: I have never in my life 'loved' any people or collective—neither the German people, nor the French, nor the Americans. . . . Indeed I 'love' only my friends and the only kind of love I know and believe in is the love of persons."[18]

The persistent failure of Jewish intellectuals to find a full nurture within the confines of a single national culture may have stemmed in part from the certain knowledge that they could never be fully immersed in it. They were, to be sure, citizens of the state, members of the *pays légal*, but not members of the organic community, the *pays réel*. As part of the emancipation transaction, they had left the confines of the ghetto and the gates had closed behind them. Only then did they discover that access to the organic community was denied them. Precisely at the juncture when the Weimar Constitution (1919) granted them full rights of citizenship, the German Worker's Party (DAP) began to prattle that Jews were merely guests in Germany. By the time of the 1935 Nuremberg Laws that deprived

Jews of the rights of German citizenship and prohibited marriage between Jews and non-Jews, it was clear that they were not even welcome guests.

Yet, the pariah status placed Jews in a strategic position to make value-free judgments about the workings of a society of which they could never fully be a part. The quest for acceptance was not lightly abandoned. Yitzhak Peretz, who in some respects might be considered the father of Yiddish literature, continued to speak of the necessity of "cross fertilization," which he thought was the only possibility for "human development." "Humanity," he insisted, "must be the synthesis, the sum, the quintessence of all national cultural forms and philosophies." Peretz had developed further than some in acknowledging that there existed a separate Yiddish culture to be melded into "humanity."[19] The noted proponent of Jewish nationalism Simon Dubnow was similarly convinced that Judaism would stand or fall on the ability of mankind to make progress to a more equitable and human social order.[20] Martin Buber saw in that striving for a just universal order the motor force of Jewish creativity. It all emanated from the concept of oneness, of unity. "Striving to evolve unity out of the divisions of the human community, he (the Jew) conceived of the idea of universal justice. Striving to evolve unity out of the division of all human matter, he conceived of the idea of universal love."[21] Here, the quest for universalism is rooted in the religioculture.

Hannah Arendt assigned a more temporal source to her unique version of Jewish universalism. She observed that many Jews solved the problem posed by their otherness by settling for the "radiance of fame" or otherwise becoming parvenus mimicking the ways of established society. There were others who assumed a more human and noble position and idealized their pariah status. For Arendt, the conscious pariah was the real though hidden tradition of the best Jewish thinkers. It allowed them to become rebels struggling with other dispossessed groups to wring justice from a recalcitrant social system.[22] The universalism of these Jewish thinkers emanated not so much from the prophetic tradition and the Enlightenment, whose principles they articulated, but from the immediate and far less glorious condition of powerlessness. The weak, Arendt noted, often cry for justice because they require it to survive.

The existence of related Jewish communities maintaining personal and institutional ties while belonging to separate nation-states made for a shadowy international presence. The connectedness of

Jewish communities emerges most clearly in the defense organizations among nineteenth-century Jewries. The founding of the British Board of Deputies (1860), the Board of Delegates of American Israelites (1859), the Alliance Israelite Universelle (1860), the Hilfsverein (1890), and finally, the American Jewish Committee (1906) not only set the stage for monitoring the Jewish condition in related communities abroad. It also meant an active Jewish participation in foreign affairs based on a Jewish interest and a new type of unofficial presence in the international arena. To defend the Jewish interest by making a case for international protection, there was Jewish representation at every major meeting of the European state system between the Congress of Vienna (1815) and the negotiations ending World War I at Versailles (1919). There were, in addition, Jewish requests for intercession and protection in response to major anti-Semitic incidents throughout the nineteenth century. These defense activities not only bore testimony to the bonds that tied Jews everywhere together, but it seemed almost as if Jewish representatives found themselves forced to conjure up an international order and to remind the world of the need for order where none existed. It is in that context that the staunch support given by Jews to international bodies like the World Court, the League of Nations, and the United Nations is best understood. Jewish support for international agencies, and after World War II for organizations like the World Federalists, represented a pious and ultimately unrealized hope rather than a world conspiracy.

Finally, the rapid urbanization of European Jewry in the second half of the nineteenth century created population aggregates sufficient to generate a cosmopolitan spirit. This cosmopolitanism served as a kind of halfway house in which universalistic ideologies were acceptable, even desirable. Cosmopolitanism did not mean disloyalty to the nation, merely a different conception of the purpose of the national community. "Cosmopolitan feeling is not identical with anti-nationalist or anti-patriotic conviction," writes Eduard Bernstein, the Jewish revisionist Marxist who had come to have a sense that Jews were a "mediating link" between the nations. "It is preferably compatible with the recognition of individual nations as legitimate members of the great organism of civilized humanity, with their own needs and their own interests."[23] The urban center permitted Jews, who were in any case disdained by the folk culture, a special vantage to view the society. "It is in the nature of marginal communities, especially ones living in metropolitan centers, to acquire the refined sensitivity of an exposed nerve and to be the first to detect the trend and shape of things to come" observes J. L. Talmon.[24]

That sensitivity was no more prevalent than among the Jews of Germany, where the process of urbanization moved forward rapidly. By 1910, 54.4 percent of Prussian Jewry resided in cities of 100,000 or more; and by 1925, half of German Jewry lived in the seven major cities of that country in contrast to 13 percent of the general population. In 1933, on the eve of the Holocaust, 70.7 percent of German Jewry, including foreign Jews, lived in cities of 100,000 or more. (The comparable figure for the general population was 30 percent.) The urban setting in which an urbane, cosmopolitan culture could thrive was manifest. One historian who examined that spirit in the Berlin of Weimar, characterized it as "rootless, restless," alienated from soil and tradition, disrespectful of authority, "full of mordant wit and possessing an unerring instinct for quality."[25] It was not precisely the same character observed by Talmon but rather the underside of the cosmopolitan spirit. One might take note of an important distinction between this urban culture and the all-encompassing culture to which anthropologists refer. It was the former against which the Nazi ideologue Hans Rosenberg would reach for his gun and the latter which was idealized in peculiar form by Nazi ideology. What the Nazis despised was the contrived culture—writing, the theater, arts, painting, and dance, journalism and political commentary—by which a people explains itself to itself and others. How could they abide the fact that such a function should be so much in the hands of a minority whom they considered merely guests in Germany?

There exists some danger of making too much of the differentiation caused by living in cities and overestimating the impact of the small number of Jewish thinkers who became opinion leaders. Undoubtedly, most Jews who moved to cities continued to live parochial, circumscribed lives. Yet, one can note early in their hunger for secular education a portent of things to come. For the period of 1859–1860, when Jews were about 1 percent of the population of Prussia, they composed 6.8 percent of all secondary students. By 1906, a remarkable 58.9 percent of the potential Jewish secondary school population were receiving such an education, compared to 7.9 percent of the general population. By 1921, the comparable figures had risen to 60.5 percent and 9.7 percent respectively. The figures for university education, which must be projected backwards from 1886, are even more remarkable. Despite restrictions on Jewish enrollment, they again emerge as enthusiastic consumers of secular education, especially in the fields of medicine, law, philosophy, and fields relating to German culture. In these faculties, Jewish enrollment was five times as high as for the Protestant and Catholic segments of the population. Moreover, despite strong opposition to having Jews hold teaching posts in the university, especially strong before 1847, 9.4 percent of university positions, primarily in the lower ranks, were held by Jews in 1874. By the year 1889–1890, the figure had risen to 12 percent, and twenty years later, to 14 percent. The Jewish rush into the arts and sciences was, according to Einstein, motivated by a "burning enthusiasm" that energized German academic life. Ironically, although the historian Heinrich von Treitschke dreaded the *Mischkultur* that the descendants of the flood of Jewish "trouser peddlers" from the East would create, it was the indigenous Jewish population of Germany that was energetically preparing itself to play a major role as Germany's culture carriers. By 1881, Berlin's Jews were already 7.9 percent of the city's lawyers, 11.7 percent of its doctors, and 8.6 percent of its writers and journalists. The figures would rise to even more astounding proportions in decades to come. Unable to find an anchor in the volk culture of *Deutschtum*, this educated, urban elite would furnish central Europe not only with a good share of the carriers of the "high culture" of music, art, and literature but also a good many of the universalistic thinkers who would ultimately oblige Europe to rethink the nation-state organization of society. For Jews, "town air" was indeed "free air," but the contrived cosmopolitan culture of the city was alien to the countryside. The political Right could point out, without much fear of contradiction, that the culture of Weimar Berlin was more familiar to a resident of London or New York than it was to a Prussian farmer. It was a culture that crossed national lines more readily than it seeped down to the masses. More important, it was a culture, in the words of Hannah Arendt, that permitted "Jewish creative spirits [to] weave the strands of their Jewish genius into the general texture of European life."[26]

We can sometimes measure the importance of an event by its impact on subsequent historical development. The more important the event, the louder the echo in history. How does the Holocaust measure on such a scale? What we need to know to answer that question is what, if anything, changed in Jewish and European civilization as a result of the murder of the Jews.

There probably can be no clear answer to that question because insufficient time has elapsed and because of a malaise within the historical enterprise. Customarily, each generation seeks its own special truths from the record of the past, so that at a given moment we can rarely point to one acceptable truth. In the case of the Holocaust, the situation is made more complex because it is already such a core datum that finding its meaning has a present value not only for Jews but also for Germans, Arabs, Leftists, and Rightists—even those like African Americans who were only remotely related to the event. All groups have learned that capturing the history of the past is, in some measure, to control the present and the future. That is why those who dominate the present seek to place their stamp on the past. History has become a battlefield in which the truth is often the first casualty. Jewish researchers of the Holocaust already stand accused of seeking a "sacred particularity," which they garner by touting Jewish victimization. Given the circumstances surrounding it, we will not soon have a historical verdict regarding its valence. Yet, there are preliminary signs that the Holocaust will ultimately be considered an event of extraordinary importance, perhaps seminal, in Jewish and European history.

Predictably, that a radical alteration of the Jewish historical pattern has occurred is clearer than in the case of European history. Paradoxically, while the Holocaust created a consensus and an irresistable rationale for the creation of a Jewish commonwealth, it destroyed the humanity that might have populated it. The perception that such a nation-state was requisite for Jewish survival was at the opposite pole from the distinctive universalist ethos so characteristic of postemancipation Diaspora Jewry. The establishment of a Jewish state in 1948, after millenia of dispersion, marks a radical alteration in Jewish history whose impact on contemporary events has been profound and sustained. Israel is in fact one of several flash points in the modern world capable of triggering a cataclysmic world conflict. The creation of the state caused the displacement of the Palestinians, who project their grievance upon an aroused Islamic, oil-rich, and yet sorely afflicted world. If such a conflict should occur, it would be the final link in a chain of events that began with the destruction of the Jews of Europe. Unlike the destruction of the Armenians or the Gypsies, the resonance of Auschwitz has a sustained worldwide implication. It remains linked in a chain of causation, rather than standing as an isolated event that occurred on the periphery of the historical canvas.

The Zionist consensus and the establishment of the Jewish state also mark a shattering of the universalist thrust that characterized much of the political culture of pre-Holocaust Jewry. The basic assumption that informs the universalist ideal that there is a caring, concerned world that will intercede with its power to halt the slaughter, proved to be nonexistent. The European Jewish masses who, more than most, dreamed that noble dream were wiped out. There are those who would argue that they were the victims of their own universalistic assumptions. As Auschwitz symbolizes the end of the old universalist Jewish dream, so Entebbe represents the new Jewish particularism. There, a sovereign Jewish state sent its sons, armed with weapons of its own manufacture, to rescue its endangered citizens who had again been selected for "special handling."

Evidence that Auschwitz has changed the character and direction of European history is more difficult to come by. Did the destruction by modern industrial and managerial processes at the very heart of that system of a people who produced the inventors and communicators of that culture in disproportionate numbers make a difference to its historical development? The "modernizing elite," or at least its Jewish portion, is no longer there. Search Europe's laboratories, lecture halls, theaters, political parties; search among its journalists and pundits; its authors—you will find few Jews. Yet, Europe goes on, its streets are bustling, its life is filled with the conveniences of modern civilization. It is as if the Jews were never there.

But in terms of the flow of power, it is no longer the same Europe. Not only has it lost its dominance, but it often seems that it does not possess the confidence and desire to defend itself. Europe is afraid to assume responsibility for its security, noted William Pfaff in an article in *The New Yorker* (September 1980). Because of its "suicidal record," postwar Europe seemed to be afraid of itself. "The second World War and genocide left Europe's survivors reluctant to be alone with one another," observed Pfaff. The malaise just below the surface has been the subject of wonderment for many other observers. There is difficulty in reconciling the two Europes even on the level of the symbolic. The chimneys that proudly symbolize Europe's industrial technology, the very technology that once permitted it to dominate the known world, are also the symbols of its shame. It is the chimneys of the crematoria that inform mankind what the ultimate destiny of that system may be. It is that link to the decline of a once powerful, world-dominating system that marks the Holocaust off from other acts of mass murder in history. The growing interest in what transpired in those camps, in how the system went awry and began to consume itself, is not the product of some promotional hype but a recognition that it contains one of the keys to unraveling the mystery of our time in history.

That is not true of the other genocides in history. Differentiating the destruction of the Jews need not demean the suffering of other victims of state power. Conceivably, the pain and suffering of the Armenians may have been greater. But we are not in a contest to measure pain or degrees of victimization. What is being measured is the importance of the event in history, and there clearly the Holocaust is an entirely different order of event in terms of its historical weight. History is not democratic; it does not assign equal import to like events. To forget that difference, to permit it to be subsumed in facile comparisons with every trespass human flesh has been heir to, is to risk losing the possibility of retrieving some meaning for the event. When that meaning is found, it will be in its specificity rather than in what it shares with other catastrophies.

Why cannot the uniqueness of the Holocaust be stated openly without triggering accusations of ethnocentrism? Even Jews are coming to believe that the current interest in the Holocaust is part of a promotional scheme designed to bring fame and fortune to those who exploit it. There may be some who have misused the event in that way, but most understand that there is little to be gained by the Jewish people from touting the fact that they were the victims rather than the masters of history. The world has far greater respect for the latter. Those who would question that it ever happened, those who facilely invert victims and tormentors, those who innocently deny the specific Jewish dimension of the event, and those who ignorantly place it side by side with other "atrocities," pose a far greater danger than the promoters. It is not merely that some are motivated by a cruel desire to lash out at the center of Jewish sensibility, which is related to the trauma of the death camps. It is that they thwart the possibility of sensing the portent that may lie concealed in this processed death making. What is that warning and portent? It is that the nation-state, the system under which all mankind governs itself, can and does under certain circumstances unleash forces within society, forces that its purpose is ostensibly to control, that can consume civilization in an orgy of death. The people who have reason to know best are the Jews, who were the principal victims of the last episode of madness. Would their silence today be any less a moral failure than the silence of the world political and spiritual leaders when the mills of Auschwitz were grinding?

2

Like Sheep to the Slaughter

The *Judenrat*

> Wherever Jews lived, there were recognized Jewish leaders, and this leadership, almost without exception, cooperated in one way or another, for one reason or another, with the Nazis. The whole truth was that if the Jewish people had really been unorganized and leaderless, there would have been chaos and plenty of misery but the total number of victims would hardly have been between four and a half and six million people.
>
> Hannah Arendt, *Eichmann in Jerusalem,*
> *A Report on the Banality of Evil*, 125.

THREE DECADES HAVE PASSED since Hannah Arendt labeled the actions of Jewish leadership and communal organizations during the Holocaust "the darkest chapter of Jewish history." Appearing first in an unlikely publication, *The New Yorker*, the indictment raised a storm of protest in the Jewish community. Almost to a person, Jewish spokespersons rejected Arendt's contention. A virtual line-by-line refutation of Arendt's narrative was written by a recognized authority on Holocaust matters.[1]

But despite the big guns, perhaps because of them, the specter

Another version of this essay appeared in *The Holocaust as Historical Experience,* ed. Yehuda Bauer and Nathan Rotenstreich (New York: Holmes and Meier, 1981), 223–31, under the title "The *Judenrat* and the Jewish Response."

of millions of Jews, betrayed by their leadership, going passively to their deaths, was not easily laid to rest. Arendt's indictment slashed the fragile Jewish self-image already seriously scathed by the Holocaust. Jews had scarcely tolled their losses when their comprehension of guilt and responsibility was brutally assaulted. One out of three of their brethren had been slaughtered in the catastrophe, but certain historical events had transpired that allowed them to live, if not with ease then with determination, in the temporal world. The state of Israel, which had risen like a phoenix out of the ashes of the catastrophe, seemed to assure Jewish continuance. Moreover, the government of West Germany had acknowledged the guilt of the German people and was bending every effort to make at least a monetary restoration. Jews were being told that it need not have happened the way it did. Things would have been different had they had better leadership, had they shown more courage—in brief, had they been something other than a defenseless minority. The stinging accusation regarding Jewish leadership, especially its Zionist component, had devastating implications because it was that leadership, or its direct heirs that was still making the community's decisions.

There was an element of futility in the debate over Arendt's book. If the renowned political thinker stood accused of creating "historical falsities," her respondents did not know much more about the events, especially about the role of the Jewish Councils, which the Nazis had everywhere created. A key piece of information was missing.

Ten years later, after the fury over those charges had subsided and the Holocaust dialogue had gone on to examine the role of the Holocaust witness, Isaiah Trunk, a research associate for the YIVO Institute for Jewish Research, provided us with a small study of the *Judenräte*, the Jewish Councils of East Europe.[2]

In this welter of data one can find confirmation and negation for every contention made regarding Jewish behavior under stress. We learn that for every seeming act of knavery and cowardice, there was an exception and even singular acts of courage. What transpired among Jews under Nazi hegemony was effected by the time, place, and personality involved and, frequently, by sheer caprice. Given this glimpse into the extraordinary complexity of human behavior under extreme conditions, no man or woman will lightly want to pass judgments or even conceive of rationales regarding the behavior of those who actually endured the ghettos and the camps. The conditions were such that no generalization conceived ex post facto can fully encompass the reality.

It is difficult to define satisfactorily what the Jewish Councils were and whose history, Jewish or German, should rightly lay claim to them. Were they examples of Jewish self-governance following the precedent of the kehilloth of former times, as Trunk maintains, or were they merely Nazi-controlled administrative instruments designed to create the preconditions for the Final Solution? Evidence indicates that they were both. The paradox inherent in the Jewish condition under the Nazi heel was that the same organization could serve for both life and death. It required organization to keep Jews alive during the ghettoization period, and subsequently, it required organization to dispatch them to their death. In practice, both functions existed side by side in the communal organization. Ultimately, the two sides were joined when council leaders sought to make the death of some serve to assure the life of others.

Amidst the appalling conditions of the ghetto—starvation, congestion, epidemics, people suffering from the trauma of separation—all purposefully created by Nazi policy to wear down the Jewish population, there developed a remarkable continuance of Jewish community life. The dependent part of the Jewish population—the orphans, the aged, and the sick—were nurtured. For a time, the traditional service agencies represented by the Jewish Social Welfare (JSS) and the Joint Distribution Committee (JDC) continued to function in the ghetto. The habit of self-help did not die easily. So successful were the efforts of the Jews to ease the painful transition to their new homes and status that the Nazis masters had to revise their plans regarding the destruction process. Hans Frank, governor general of occupied Poland, for example, was sorely disappointed that the expected death of 1,200,000 Jews in the ghettoization process did not materialize.

The ability of Jews to sustain themselves under the most appalling circumstances was evidenced also in the lively cultural, educational, and economic life that characterized the initial phase of ghettoization. In the midst of a nerve-wracking Darwinian struggle for existence, Jews organized schools, vocational retraining, choirs, theaters (one ghetto established a children's puppet theater), lectures, gardening clubs, orchestras, libraries, museums, factories, and even the manufacture of much-needed pharmaceuticals. In some large ghettos, a shadow of gay prewar café life developed.

Jewish genius lay in that impulse toward community. Rein-

forced as it was by the requirements of the religion, living in community was a central part of Jewish life. The community dissolution
that Arendt suggested was never remotely possible. How could
such a people, with such well-defined civic virtues, ever be convinced that government was based on a fundamental misconception
of traditional Jewish behavior, especially during periods of crisis.

The persistence of those civic virtues explains why it was so
difficult for Jews to fathom that their normal attitude toward community and society had to be reversed. What had been their
strength became a lethal weakness. They searched for violinists for
the orchestra and sought teachers for the children rather than machine gunners and sappers. The former talents proliferated in the
Jewish community; the latter were nonexistent. As the screws of the
Final Solution tightened, Jews understood only vaguely that the same
administrative apparatus that had nurtured them could also be used
to organize them for death. Indeed, the aging, the dependent, the
sick, and the starving—those who had first claim on community
concern—would be the first to be sent to die. "We have in the
ghetto many persons sick with tuberculosis," explained Mordecai
Chaim Rumkowski, "king" of the Lodź ghetto, shortly before a resettlement action planned for September 5, 1942. "Deliver to me
those sick ones and it may be possible to save the healthy ones instead." Time transformed the function of the Jewish Councils from
the life-supporting one Jews automatically assigned to them to the
death-dealing one that the Nazi authorities intended. In the end, it
was those who actually had power, the Nazi authorities, who determined the role of the Jewish Councils.

It is only by ignoring the crucial question of power that Trunk
is able to reach his one major conclusion: The Jewish Councils that
were created by the Nazis are examples of Jewish governance rather
than some "unique and queer" episode. They belong to the stream
of Jewish history. In fact, the role they played is reminiscent of the
kahals, those unique agencies by which Jews governed themselves
in sixteenth-, seventeenth-, and eighteenth-century Russia and Pol-
and. In recruiting poor Jewish youth for military service, these kahals (kehilloth in Poland) also consigned Jews to death, at least in a
symbolic sense, because the brutalization and frequent baptism involved in army service was considered to be a form of death by the
community. Jewish leaders withheld the *gute kep*, the smart ones,
who would be an asset to the community. The merchants and the
wealthy were also able to gain exemption. Though the kahals did

not deliver up life itself, the selection among the poor and powerless was not unlike those made by the councils during the Holocaust. It was a matter of degree rather than of kind, Trunk maintains.

But there is a qualitative difference between the kahals and the councils. The latter possessed far greater power over its subjects than the former, and they possessed it precisely because they ruled by proxy. Although in the early stages of ghettoization the councils were able to alleviate the drastic conditions imposed by the Nazi overlords, it ultimately became apparent that, when the critical "re-settlement" period arrived, they were merely instruments of the Nazis. Power, the defining element in any government equation, was not in their hands. The parallel drawn with the role of the ka-hals in czarist Russia is faulty because it does not take into account that the modern techniques of governing that allow the state to absorb virtually all power available in a society were not yet available to czarist regimes. It was available to Stalin, and those Russians who have experienced both regimes know well the difference between modern totalitarian techniques and those bumbling attempts at autocracy employed by the czars.

In assigning Jewish Council leaders a role for which the necessary power did not exist in the captive Jewish community, Trunk appears to fall into the same pit as did Arendt. The Nazis, it should be recalled, turned on the Jews of East Europe with a special vengeance. The situation they created for Jews in the ghettos and camps was probably the closest we have come to the classic totalitarian condition of the complete powerlessness of the governed when confronted by the complete power of their governors. In such circumstances, it seems perverse to talk of Jewish governance, especially when a theoretic framework concerning the role of power in the government equation is omitted. What such talk does, however, is to extend the idea of betrayal and collaboration back into Jewish history and to diminish the horrendous particularity of the Holocaust.

The councils were established by an administrative order of October 12, 1939, that gave the German Security Police complete power to select the members of the councils and to change the composition of the membership when it saw fit. Thereafter, the councils were to be totally controlled by the Security Police. They were in fact conceived to be an administrative arm of the Nazi occupation. The membership chosen by the Nazis did bear some relationship to the prewar leadership of the Jewish community. About 43 percent had been active in prewar community life, according to Trunk. But the majority were chosen with "arbitrary recklessness" by the Nazi task-masters. Frequently, nothing more than a knowledge of German was sufficient to gain a position on the councils. Those so selected were often alien Jews, resettled from some distant points, who had no knowledge of or relationship to the constituency they were supposed to lead.

Within the councils, the reaction to crisis was far from uniform. Some members "assimilated the morals of the oppressors," especially after the first acts of resettlement, when the struggle for survival became even more pronounced. But there were also instances of courage and self-sacrifice. Some council leaders refused to carry out Nazi orders and were either shot by the Nazis or voluntarily joined the "resettlement" transports to the death camps.

Even the assumption that membership in the council offered a better opportunity to survive is questionable. At best, such a position offered a precarious security. Within the first six months of their creation, 18 percent of the original council members no longer held their positions. In addition, 2.9 percent resigned, 1.8 percent were dismissed, and 1.2 percent committed suicide. An estimate based on a special questionnaire used by Trunk reveals that 25.5 percent of the council members lost their lives before "resettlement." Only 12 percent survived the Holocaust. Furthermore, four of the most powerful council leaders, Mordecai Chaim Rumkowski (Lodź), Roman Merin (eastern Upper Silesia), Jacob Gens (Vilna), and Ephraim Barash (Bialystok) were killed by the Nazis. They ruled supremely in the ghettos, but like all Jews, they were powerless in relation to their Nazi tormentors.

Arendt's model of a passive Jewish community led like sheep to the slaughter by a defective Jewish leadership turns out, on closer examination, to be a caricature. In the first place, the population, especially of the larger ghettos, was highly disparate. Only for the Nazis was a Jew simply a Jew. Class, regional, religious, and political differences among Jews were accentuated by the crisis. The ghetto population was often swollen by refugees from Central Europe, whose cultural style and reaction to the crisis varied markedly from their East European brethren. Frequently stemming from the German *Kulturgebiet*, these aliens tended to be highly legalistic and trusting of government and therefore more easily taken in by Nazi fraud and Potemkin village strategems (fake façades to fool inspectors in czarist Russia). They reported willingly to the collection points, nourishing the illusion that they were to be transported back to their former lives and homes. They tended to believe what the "authorities" told them, thinking fate would differentiate them from the Jews of the East. Indigenous Jews had little love to spare for them, convinced, as they were, that their own had been "resettled" to make room for the aliens. There were also baptized Jews in certain ghettos who were Jews only according to Nazi racial laws and neither thought of themselves or were thought by Jews to be affiliated with Judaism. In one sense, these victims were the most tragic of all because they belonged nowhere, having been rejected by the non-Jewish community to which they sought to belong and also by the Jews whom they had rejected.

It was nigh impossible to grasp that the Nazis intended to liquidate *all* Jews. Logic, they thought, was on their side. Hence, they conceived of "rescue through work" and a "rescue through bribery" strategy. They had daily evidence on the grass-roots level that utilitarian and venal considerations motivated even the most fanatical Nazis. If Jews could prove useful to the Nazi war effort and profitable to local Nazi authorities, surely these officials would not choose to kill the goose that laid the golden egg. Most councils implemented these rescue strategies. The councils of Skalat and Bialystok amassed stocks of precious stones, liquor, rare delicacies, and expensive clothes and furniture to bribe local Nazi officials. They linked their plans for survival to the only reality they knew, the reality of petit capitalism. Had there been an element of bookkeeping rationale in Nazi plans for the Jews, the councils might have had some success. But the totally irrational nature of Nazi thinking on the Jewish question made the council's survival strategems a death sentence for their subjects. It was a failure of mind, however, not a murder conspiracy.

The hope that some might be saved proved to be the strongest obstacle to armed resistance. Shaped by a pre-Nazi mentality, council leaders and their ghetto subjects naturally assumed that survival strategies other than resistance would save more lives. Even today, their logic is difficult to refute. The slightest hint of resistance, even the shirking of compulsory labor, produced Draconian reprisals against the innocent ghetto inhabitants. The council leaders opposed resistance not only because of the predictable toll it would take in lives but also because they felt it would interfere with what they thought were "more practical" rescue strategies. Roman Merin fought the underground movement composed of Zionist youth organizations like Hanoar Hazioni, Hashomer Hatzair, Gordonia, and

Poale Zion and ordered the arrest of Zvi Dunski, the young leader of
the resistance movement. Other council leaders hedged on the question of physical resistance. Jacob Gens opposed flight or the storing
of arms in the ghetto but maintained continuous contact with the
underground and paid for it with his life. At one point, he instigated
a revolt to squelch a planned uprising and forced the commander of
the partisan organization, Yitzhak Witenberg, to give himself up.

Yet, other councils, like those of Piotrków Trybunalski and
Minsk did involve themselves in underground resistance. In one
case Beryl Lopatyn, chairman of the council of the Lachwa ghetto,
set fire to the council building, a signal for the mass of ghetto
dwellers to ignite their own dwellings and flee the ghetto for the
surrounding forest. The result of this strategy was disheartening. Of
the ghetto's 2,000 inmates, only 600 escaped, and of those, only 100
to 120 survived the war. Resistance, in the few instances where it
did occur, did not result in saving lives. The Warsaw ghetto uprising
of April 23–30, 1943 (the first example of urban resistance) was intended not so much as a rescue strategy but as a way of redeeming
Jewish honor. It was led by young, highly politicized men and
women who were concerned about such things. Most significantly,
it occurred when much of the dependent civilian population of the
ghetto had already been "resettled."

Still, the question of resistance is raised over and over again,
especially by young people. Why did they go "like sheep to the
slaughter," rather than leaving us with a heroic model with which
we could live? Before he was himself consumed by the flames of the
Holocaust, Emmanuel Ringelblum, chronicler of the Warsaw ghetto,
posed the same agonized question. "One of the problems of great
import," he wrote, "is the passivity of the Jewish masses, dying
without a whimper. Why are they so quiet? Why are the fathers,
mothers and all the children dying without protest?" Was their passivity ordered by an unscrupulous leadership, seeking to save its
own skin, as Arendt suggested?

Only to the extent that it is possible for those who were not
there to place themselves in the shoes of the ghetto dwellers is it
possible to answer such a question. The answer can never be complete because the agony of the ghetto dwellers can only be experienced vicariously. But what do we know? We know with certainty
that they wanted desperately to live. They dared hope that some
might be spared and, failing that, that their lives might be extended
for a few hours or days. *A shu gelebt is oichet gelebt* (to have lived an

hour is also to have lived) became the conventional wisdom. Each day among the living was a separate victory. They did not lightly abandon their notion of a future because to do so would mean to take the first small steps away from life. Real resistance could not develop until that hope was abandoned. It was part of the diabolical cleverness of the Nazi overlords that they developed all kinds of subterfuges to keep a glimmer of hope alive.

What we see is the behavior of a people who at first would not believe what fate had in store for them and used every alternative, including the sacrifice of life, to keep death from their door. Only when every avenue had been exhausted did they withdraw into passivity and prepare themselves for death. That withdrawal was not unlike that of a person with a terminal illness who, at the irreversible stage, withdraws from life.

The simple model of governance behind the Arendt indictment needs a more rigorous examination. We need to know to what extent the policy followed by the Jewish Councils represented a consensus within the Jewish community rather than a decision imposed by an all-powerful, corrupt Jewish leadership. Unfortunately, Trunk offers relatively little data on this crucial question. There are certain clues, however, that point to a much more complex relationship than the one-way authority of governors over governed that Arendt postulated. For example, few of the respondents to Trunk's questionnaire, all of whom are survivors, condemned the policy of the councils outright. (Sixty-two percent evaluated the activities of the members of the councils positively, 16.4 percent held mixed opinions, and only 14 percent were negative.) There is also some question whether in the initial stages of ghettoization the remarkable economic and cultural activity of the ghetto could have been achieved with a recalcitrant citizenry. Jews chose accommodation because they thought it offered a better chance of survival. After the first taste of Nazi occupation policy, when Jews became aware of the dangers of living among hostile people, relatively few chose the option of trying to "pass" on the outside. When Jews moved into the ghetto, they voted with their feet to face the onslaught with other Jews rather than to take their chances individually. Naturally, they were embittered by the injustice of it all and by the rapid decline of their fortunes, but ghetto existence was still preferable to other alternatives that seemed less hopeful.

Once the first small steps toward a policy of accommodation were taken, imperceptibly small new steps were required by the

Nazi authorities—compulsory labor, limited egress from the ghetto, statistical tabulations, and endless lists. Finally required was the surrender of life for "resettlement," which almost everyone soon knew meant death. Why did the council leaders not stop there? The decision was not taken lightly. In some councils, endless hours of debate on the question occurred. But in the end, most councils, viewing themselves as captains on a sinking ship with a limited number of lifeboats, decided to try to influence the selection, rather than to allow the Nazis to do it themselves. In so doing, they eschewed the well-known counsel of Maimonides not to surrender life[3] in favor of the advice of Rabbi Abraham Duber Shapiro, an elder of the Kaunas (Kovno) ghetto who, shortly before a "resettlement" action scheduled for October 25, 1943, advised the council leaders that "if a Jewish community (may God help it) has been condemned to physical destruction, and there are means of rescuing part of it, the leaders of the community should have the courage to assume the responsibility to act and rescue what is possible." Was the councils' choice attributable to an opportunistic shortsighted leadership willing to condemn Jews to death so that they might live, as Arendt implies?

Of course, opportunism was not absent among the functionaries and leaders of the councils. It was even more conspicuous among the ghetto police, many of whom were not above extorting money from those who wanted to avoid "resettlement." Opportunism and corruption arose wherever the Nazis held sway among both Jews and other subject people. But this situation was not the reason for following the path of Rabbi Shapiro rather than Maimonides.

Virtually every decision taken during the Holocaust by those directly or indirectly involved had inherent some element of choice between life and death. Assistant Secretary of War John J. McCloy decided not to bomb the death camps and the railroad lines leading to them, certain children in France were selected to be spirited across the Pyrenees while others were not, certain Jews were given Palestine certificates while others were not, a ransom proposal to save Hungarian Jewry was rejected—all these decisions involved life-and-death choices. As we see the Jews draw closer to the inferno, the existence of these agonizing choices becomes even more apparent. Those who chose to resist in the Lachwa or Warsaw ghetto were as much involved in the death of innocents as were the leaders of the councils because resistance entailed not only retribution but also conflict against a heavily armed and vengeful enemy whose victory was a foregone conclusion.

Once one realizes that *all* Jews were condemned to die, not by cowardly Jewish or even indifferent Allied leaders but by a demented Nazi leadership, then no decision taken during the Holocaust could have avoided the life-and-death choices that had to be made. In that context, the auxiliary decisions by Jewish leaders were intended to save some of the doomed. Rather than leave the selections to blind fate controlled by the Nazis, they tried to influence the Nazis, but usually without much success. The Arendt charge was callous and obscene, but not because it did not fit the facts. In a superficial sense, what she observed is not false, just as it is not false to say that the surgeon who amputates a gangrenous limb cripples his patient. By ripping the actions of Jewish leaders out of the context in which *all* Jews were condemned to death, the victims become their own murderers.

Even when Arendt's charge is considered in its simplest terms, that fewer Jews would have died had there been no Jewish leadership, it does not stand up. The *Einzatsgruppen*, those special SS killer units that operated behind the German lines in Russia, slaughtered 1,500,000 Jews in relatively short order. Yet in these areas, the Jewish leadership and community infrastructure had been eliminated by a jealous Soviet regime for at least one generation. The labor roundups in the ghetto furnish another example. When they were conducted directly by the SS, they were infinitely crueler and more costly in lives, so much so, that Jewish leaders were obliged to organize their own compulsory labor system in order to avoid the gratuitous violence that accompanied SS actions.

Something perverse occurs when victims, and to some extent witnesses, are singled out for a special share of the responsibility as they have been by Hannah Arendt. There is, of course, an element of truth in all such accusations—Jewish leaders were guilty, the pope was guilty, and Roosevelt was guilty. In fact, we are all guilty. That is the most distinctive aspect of the Holocaust, no one who was touched by it can ever again be innocent. It makes everything gruesome. That is certainly true of the perpetrators; but it is also true, in another sense, of the witnesses and the victims. Although in the face of such an enormous catastrophe enough could never have been done, the witnesses are nevertheless held up for not doing enough. The case of the victims is a special one. They are guilty for not having given us evidence of that kernel of courage to redeem the fallen image of humankind. And so we rummage through the evidence and, behold, the witnesses find that the victims were guilty.

We are off the hook. They were responsible for their own fate, and they are not here to deny it. There is only one problem, when all are guilty—none are guilty. In that sense, there is something more that makes Arendt's charge against Jewish leadership and organization perverse—it lacks particularity. In order to make sense of it, she must tell us how Jewish leaders were more guilty than others touched by the Holocaust. A careful reading of Trunk's book tells us that they were not.

Judenrat is a well-organized compilation of data, a good example of what an assiduous researcher can do. There is in the area of Holocaust research a great need to unearth the facts and in that sense this is an important work. To be a work of historical significance, however, the historian must breathe some life into the material. Vision and synthesis must infuse the subject. Trunk chose not to do this. He felt that the nature of the material, the diverse socio-psychological background of the individuals involved did not permit generalization; and except for a brief moment in the last chapter, he is never tempted to break his own rule. The work thus tends to remain a compendium of data about the Jewish Councils. That makes Trunk's work somewhat quixotic, especially in relation to that of Arendt, which undoubtedly motivated its being undertaken. After years of painstaking research and much thinking on the question of Jewish governance during the Holocaust, Trunk makes only several minor judgments regarding the material. Arendt, on the other hand, with almost no basic research to speak of, makes major judgments on that subject. The one ventures too little; the other, too much. The ideal situation would have been to let Arendt loose on Trunk's data.

Once he decided to use what he calls the "inductive" method, Trunk avoided the secondary works available in the field of government and totalitarianism. This decision not only led him into a rather naïve error regarding the problems of power and governance but it also gave his work a *de novo* flavor that is not warranted by the facts. There are many secondary works, such as *The German Dictatorship* by Karl Dietrich Bracher, *Totalitarian Dictatorship and Democracy* by Carl J. Friedrich, and some of the superb works now available on the SS and other administrative agencies involved with the Final Solution, on whose shoulders Trunk might have stood. Stanley Hoffman's concept of *collaboration d'état*[4] though applied mechanically by

Trunk, nevertheless serves as an indication of how these data might have been brought to life.

Paradoxically, Trunk, who dares not assign meaning to his data, goes to the other extreme in the kinds of evidence he brings to bear. A questionnaire, an example of which the reader is never shown, was used to elicit information from selected survivors. There is a danger that such methodology might skew the evidence. Survivors may not necessarily be living evidence that the rescue strategies chosen by the councils worked, but they are bound to view rescue in a certain light. They may be alive today because they were more ruthless or perhaps more fortunate than others. The mere fact of their survival predisposes them to view the possibility of rescue more favorably. Moreover, those who might present countervailing evidence are not alive to make their case. Trunk, it is true, takes great care in how he uses the evidence elicited. But the statistical data produced give *Judenrat* an artificial glow of health because it is of questionable validity. One wonders why Trunk displays such daring with respect to evidence and such timidity in regard to synthesis.

But what Trunk sets out to do, he does well. He comes close to possessing that clear-eyed open view that asks nothing of the victims except that they render their story. That is a refreshing change after the polemics about an opportunistic leadership on the one hand and heroes and martyrs on the other.

3

The Resistance Question

THE FRENCH are not unduly preoccupied with the late development of resistance to the Nazi occupation or the collaborationist role played by the Vichy regime. The Norwegians prefer to forget about the role of their Quislings, and the Russians are amnesiacs when it comes to Vlasov's army. But the Jews, who bore the brunt of Hitler's murderous intent and possessed none of the wherewithal of resistance, agonize endlessly over "the sheep to slaughter" question. The morbid preoccupation with the question of resistance is reflected in the continuing popular and scholarly literature on the Holocaust.

This circumstance is especially true in Israel. The very name of the Israeli agency for Holocaust research, Yad Vashem Martyrs and Heroes Remembrance Authority, suggests the preoccupation. Indeed, the second international conference sponsored by Yad Vashem held in 1971, and the volume of proceedings published subsequently were exclusively devoted to the resistance question. Nor does Yad Vashem attempt to conceal its interest. Its annual publication is entitled *Yad Vashem Studies on the European Jewish Catastrophe and Resistance.*

Resistance or Complicity?

But although Israel has a special interest in the resistance question, publications on that theme are by no means confined to it. In the West, many Jewish communities commemorate the Holocaust

This essay appeared originally in *The Reconstructionist* 44 (May 1978): 7–11, under the title "Some Thoughts on the Resistance Question."

each April on the anniversary of the Warsaw ghetto uprising, which has become its symbol. Dozens of articles and books too numerous to mention here have appeared in America and Europe. Most popular are *They Fought Back* by Yuri Suhl and *Not as a Lamb* by Lucien Steinberg.[1] It is then no accident that the great debate on the Holocaust between the Arendt-Hilberg approach and what might be classified as the Bauer-Suhl approach occurred precisely over the question of resistance and complicity.

What can be the meaning of this overweening interest? A look at some of the problems of the resistance question may reveal aspects of the emotional state of contemporary Jewry. The purpose of these works is frankly to memorialize the resisters and to redeem Jewish honor, which public opinion at large may feel was lost during the Holocaust. The latest of these books, *The Jewish Resistance: The History of the Jewish Partisans in Lithuania and White Russia 1940–1945*[2] by Lester Eckman and Chaim Lazar may serve as a prototype of this apologetic literature. Its basic cast is heroic, and it is replete with many personal tales of courage and incredible endurance. Although it is poorly written and organized, based on only fragmentary derivative research, and lacks any conceptual framework that could place the resistance question in a proper historical framework (thereby enhancing our understanding of what resistance really entailed in the setting of Nazi totalitarianism), the volume does much to cast light on the existence of a Jewish resistance in the forests of the East. That story is also part of the Holocaust and needs to be told.

Partisans in the Forests

Most students of the Holocaust are aware that the uprising in the Warsaw ghetto marks the first example of any resistance in an urban setting, but the story of Jewish partisans in the forests has also emerged. In many ways, it was a far more difficult kind of resistance. Jews were highly urbanized and had little knowledge of the lore of the forests in which they would live. They had to learn from scratch and at terrible cost how to obtain, use, and maintain weapons, which were always in short supply. Few had military training, and almost none could fall back on a tradition of hunting, so popular among the Gentile natives. They faced determined opposition not only from special antipartisan units but also from their fellow partisans, who were often as murderously anti-Semitic as the Nazis themselves.

To wage successful guerilla warfare, logistical support of the native population is imperative. The guerilla, Mao Tse-tung informed us, swims in a sea of peasants. But for the Jewish partisans, it was a hostile sea. The peasants were likely to betray them. The Jews were forced to wage a lonely and uneven battle with little chance of survival. Jewish resistance groups were compelled to make an agonizing choice at the outset. Should they stay in the ghetto with their families and loved ones and fight the Nazi tormentors there or abandon their families to certain death and escape to the forests?

How Much Resistance to Save Jewish Honor?

The dilemma could not be resolved without splitting the resistance. Moreover, fleeing to the forest was not a means of rescue. Those who did so understood that their fate there was even more uncertain. Resistance in a real sense required the abandoning of hope; and yet to be effective, it also required hope that some might live to tell the tale. Some did survive in the partisan family camps concealed deep in the forests. Others miraculously came through numerous desperate battles waged against the Nazis by such Jewish partisan bands as the Belsky brigade.

It is a heroic story; but ultimately, those who seek to find a widespread Jewish resistance must redefine what is meant by resistance under the conditions posed by the Final Solution and confront the question of scale: How much resistance is necessary to redeem Jewish honor? In the East, for example, the number of Jews who fled to the forests is infinitesimal compared to the 1,500,000 Jews slaughtered by the *Einzatsgruppen*, which followed behind the German armies after June 1941. It is a numbers game that cannot be won by those who are concerned with erasing what they believe is a page of shame in Jewish history.

From the outset, the resistance conundrum revolves around the question of honor. That is what the resisters and contemporary memorialists are concerned about. Mordecai Anielewitcz, the leader of the Warsaw uprising, called Jews to battle in its name, and so did the Jewish partisans. "Even if we are too weak to defend our lives," reads an appeal of the Jewish Defense Organization of the Bialystok ghetto, "we are strong enough to defend our Jewish honor and human dignity." But the question of honor was as complex then as it is today because it conflicted with a basic principle of the Jewish tradition that beseeches Jews to "choose life." Those who opposed open resistance did so because of their reluctance to accept the idea that there was no other hope to save Jewish lives.

Life Versus Abstract Notions of Honor

Many Jews, perhaps the majority, found it impossible to abandon hope completely and to accept the idea that all Jews were slated for death. Amidst the abject misery of the ghetto, they retained some optimism about survival. When balanced against the Draconian reprisals that open resistance would bring, they chose survival strategies, which gave priority to saving lives, rather than to abstract notions like Jewish "honor." The Jewish Councils thought first of saving Jewish lives, and their strategies were conceived with the rational mind-set of the petite bourgeoisie from which most stemmed.

As long as Jews were useful to the German war effort, they believed, they would be allowed to live. All that was required, they thought, was to maintain a tenuous hold on life until the tide of the war turned. In the case of Rumkowsky's Lodź ghetto, that calculating ledger-thinking nearly worked. The ghetto was not liquidated until the Russians were near. But ultimately, their Jewish optimism worked against them. They never understood that the Germans were not rational on the "Jewish question" but chose to destroy a people who could have been useful to them. From the memoirs of Albert Speer we know that he was forced to deport highly skilled Jewish workers in the armaments industry in 1942 when there was a crying need for their skills. Precious rolling stock was used to deport Jews rather than to resupply the German army on the eastern front. Everywhere, the Final Solution received priority.

Zionists' Resistance as the Role Model

What happened to Jewish leadership on the resistance question was in most cases more a failure of mind than of nerve. For most Jews in the context of the times, the decision to resist seemed to offer less hope for life than some form of compliance with and even usefulness to the German war machine. What those preoccupied with the resistance question today fail to realize is that *resistance and the question of Jewish honor related to it could only be mobilized when the hope for survival had totally vanished.* Jews, being what they are, abandoned it only reluctantly.

But let us return to the current preoccupation with resistance and Jewish honor. It is preeminently the Zionist movement in Israel that furnishes the motor force for that concern, and it does so for several reasons. In the ghettos, it was the Zionists, especially its left-wing groups like Hashomer Hatzair, Habonim, Youth Dror, and Hechalutz, that furnished the leadership "cadre" and the ideology for the resistance movement. Aside from their natural desire to inform the Jewish world of their role, which, in retrospect, does them great credit, it also has a crucial reinforcement potential for Israel's continued ability to resist Arab aggression. In 1973, Simon Herman spoke of the need to provide the youth of Israel with a fighting model, a heroic myth to strengthen the fighting will and morale of the young who would be called upon to risk their lives in Israel's defense. Certainly, to imbue them with the passivity inherent in the "sheep to the slaughter" myth, would not have boded well for Israel's security.

Search for Heroes

With respect to the preoccupation with Jewish resistance during the Holocaust, one ought to note that it is no accident that highly secularized Jews, often those who have broken most sharply with the Jewish tradition, concern themselves with the question of honor a concept originally related to the martial virtues of Christian feudalism. For religious Jews, a preoccupation that places the image of man in the center of the cosmos must seem unfamiliar indeed, even a species of idolatry. Jews honor God, their parents, and the sanctity of life, not their own image in world public opinion. One suspects that behind much of the preoccupation with resistance is the gnawing fear that Jewish reactions during the bitter years of the Holocaust were less than honorable. That fear makes some search through the corpses of Jewish dead for heroes. They want the victims in their final anguish to yield something more so that the living can better come to terms with the catastrophe. One wants to tell those preoccupied with this unseemly quest that their search has in it the potential for dishonoring the very victims they seek to honor.

4

Allied Foreign Policy
and the Holocaust

IMAGINE THIS. The millennial scourge of anti-Semitism, which heretofore has nested in the cultural and political crevices of Western civilization, is miraculously dissipated so that when the National Socialists come to power in Germany in January 1993, Germans are neutral about Jews, even philosemitic. I call it a miracle because that is what the suspension of such a persistent historical phenomenon comes to. Few readers would give credence to such a happening. Yet, it is necessary to imagine such a miracle in order to conclude, as some do, that anti-Semitism bears little relation to Allied indifference to the fate of the Jews during the fateful years of the Holocaust.[1]

Paradoxically, the reverse assumption, that the Holocaust is the ultimate and logical expression of European anti-Semitism and lies behind the callous indifference of the witnessing nations is equally untenable. In the case of the Nazi Final Solution, we know today that the mass murder of the Jews was not only discontinuous with prior German and Austrian anti-Semitism but actually became public policy without popular consensus. The position of prominent Germans like Karl Goerdeler, the mayor of Leipzig, may have been more representative of German public opinion at large. He wished the Reich to be *Judenrein* but opposed the genocide being committed in the name of the German people. The implementation of the Final

This essay appeared originally in *Jewish-Christian Encounters over the Centuries: Symbiosis, Prejudice, Holocaust, Dialogue,* ed. Marvin Perry and Frederick M. Schweitzer (New York: Peter Lang, 1994), 313–24, under the title "American Foreign Policy and the Holocaust; The Role of Antisemitism."

Solution required some all-powerful enabler who was the führer. There is good reason to believe that the Holocaust would not have happened without the demonic presence of Hitler on the world stage.[2] He acted as the trigger and through a totalitarian dominance, which rendered the German people as subjects rather than as "citoyens," was able to impose his personal pathological hatred of Jews on a people whom history and circumstance had made ready to accept, or at least not resist, what was being done in their name in the East.

But what of the witnessing nations, what of the Allies? Surely their indifference to the saving of life cannot be considered apart from the prevailing anti-Semitism that was especially virulent during these years. London circumvented its own rules of blockade to feed the occupied Greeks throughout the war, but refused even to consider a change in designation to Prisoner of War for the Jews in concentration camps, much less to allow the sending of food packages. That marked a considerable change from World War I, when the Jewish question did earn considerable attention from the Allies. It was, in fact, partly British concern about Jewish influence in Washington that led to the issuance of the Balfour Declaration in 1917. But despite incessant anti-Semitic rhetoric about Jewish power, no such influence was at play during World War II. There had been a pronounced diminution in the effectiveness of Jewish power and influence during the interwar period.[3]

Can one then conclude that Allied indifference to the fate of the Jews was caused by anti-Semitism? In order to respond to that query, the historian needs first to probe certain assumptions regarding the making of public policy: Can we assume that the prevalence of an anti-Semitic mind-set among policymakers and bureaucrats willy-nilly translated itself into policy? Is there a way we can differentiate anti-Semitism from other motivations that influence a particular policy? There is no certain answer to these questions. In the end, we are left with millions of Jewish dead and the destruction of a dynamic Jewish civilization and no reasonable way to determine what role anti-Semitism might have played in the minds of Allied decision makers.

This discussion limits itself to some observations regarding the policies of the United States, Britain, and the Soviet Union during those fateful years. It does not deal with certain major policies, such as appeasement and isolationism, that indirectly impinged on the Jewish fate by allowing National Socialism to secure and extend its power. Such policies were imagined at the time to serve the national interest. There was no consideration of how they affected European Jewry.

In the case of American policy, it is the immigration laws of 1921 and 1924, passed well before the crisis, that offer the most relevant example of the link of anti-Semitism to public policy. The link is indirect before 1933 and direct after that year. The quota system, which favored immigrants whose national origin was northern and western European, depended on the theory of "Nordicism," also known as "Nordic supremacy." In the Germany of National Socialism, it would be known as "Aryanism." The ideological anchorage on which the Final Solution depended found prior expression in American immigration law. That law, which allowed no distinction between refugees in dire need of haven and normal immigrants, would ultimately contribute much to the destruction of European Jewry. That was especially true during the thirties, when a directive of the Hoover administration calling for strict enforcement of the "likely to become a public charge" (LPC) provision of the law, cut off even those who might have found refuge. Only in 1939 were the relevant quotas filled. The linkage seems clear. Jews were extruded from Germany and later exterminated for the same reason that they were unacceptable immigrants to the United States—they had the wrong blood. That connection has a special relevance for our examination. There is little question today that had Germany succeeded in making the Reich *Judenrein* through immigration, the decision for a final, more drastic solution, might never have been made, or at the least, might have been postponed. Karl Schleunes reminds us that the road to Auschwitz was twisted, and that there was nothing preordained about the Holocaust.[4] We cannot assume that Hitler knew in 1939 precisely how he would solve the "Jewish problem." But the failure to find alternate solutions like emigration, as remote as the possibility of implementation was, certainly contributed to the nexus of circumstances in which the decision for mass murder was made. In a sense, the struggle to save European Jewry was lost in the first round, partly as a result of our restrictive racialist immigration law.

But having noted the racialist origins of the law and the drastic impact of its implementation, we are beset by problems concerning the role of anti-Semitism. Serious questions can be raised whether the intent of the original law was specifically to restrict Jews. From the congressional hearings in 1921 and 1924, we learn that the lawmakers were heavily influenced by rumors that Polish Jewry, which had been utterly devastated by the war, stood poised to "flood" America. In 1920, 119,000 had entered the country, so overburdening reception facilities in New York that ships were rerouted to Boston. But notwithstanding the impassioned voices of the Yiddish press, only one case of anti-Semitism by a State Department official was uncovered. It concerned a memorandum that used well-known pejoratives to describe the potential Jewish immigrants and a vastly exaggerated estimate of the number of those who wanted to enter the United States.[5] The memorandum embarrassed Charles E. Hughes, then secretary of state, who was reminded of its questionable legality by Louis Marshall. He issued corrective directives so that it could not recur. But in the text of the immigration law itself, Jews are not mentioned, and of course, there was no Jewish quota. Paradoxically, Italian Americans can make a far better claim than Jews that the laws were aimed at them. Senator "Cotton Ed" Smith, who was one of the sponsors of restrictive legislation, would have exempted the Jews from the quota system, as they were from the Literacy Test Act of 1917. But he was adamant about keeping Italians out. When a Jewish journalist and activist, Gedaliah Bublick, openly accused the committee members of anti-Semitism at the hearings, it was "coolly" denied by the chairman, who insisted that it was all fortuitous. Had the Jews had the foresight to settle in Scotland, they would have been under the more generous English quota.[6]

Anti-Semitic intent is difficult to prove, and it is even more difficult to demonstrate that the law did what it was intended to do. For example, the "national origins" system was designed to restore the ethnic composition of the nation to what it was in 1890. But we know today that it did no such thing. By the twenties, the pioneering types—Scandinavians, Germans, and English stock—so extolled by the "nordomaniacs," preferred to remain at home and enjoy the benefits of the developing welfare state. Their quotas went unfilled, while those for Italy and Poland were oversubscribed. Those who needed to come were unwanted, and those who were wanted would not come. So much for social engineering through public policy.

Finding a direct link between public policy and anti-Semitism becomes even more elusive during the crucial period between 1933 and 1945. The highly restrictive implementation of the law, initiated by Hoover's LPC directive, exacerbated the refugee crisis, which was a harbinger of the Holocaust. But ostensibly, it was issued, not because of a distaste for Jews, but because the depression had created a virtually unanimous consensus that America must concern herself first with her own unemployed. That was also the opinion of most American Jews. Even so, as the crisis grew in intensity, some exceptions to the directive were allowed for prominent refugee scholars and political leaders and culture carriers.

Yet, every son of a Jewish mother knew that to prepare oneself for a career in the foreign service of the State Department was an exercise in futility. The evidence we have in the memoirs of State Department officials substantiates that they did not misperceive.[7] Jews were not wanted. There was also some anti-Semitism among the consuls who, under the law, made the final decision about the issuance of visas. Yet, a suggestion that the anti-Semitism of State Department officials like Wilbur J. Carr, William Phillips, and Breckinridge Long has to be factored in to explain the inhuman implementation of policy in such cases as the *St. Louis* and the *SS Quanza*, two ships blocked from landing refugees by the State Department, was questioned by younger historians. They doubt "that anti-Semitism was the primary instruction behind the State Department's policies affecting Jewish refugees" and see no evidence of it in the grand policy design. State Department officials were more concerned, and legitimately so they insist, with the fear that spies had infiltrated the refugee stream. I am admonished that "the recognition of anti-Semitism must not become a substitute for the intricate and difficult work of analyzing the political and bureaucratic processes of government during the Holocaust and the preceding decade."[8] Nor can we assume that anti-Semitic officials necessarily implement anti-Semitic policies. There were, for example, many such Endec xenophobic types in the Polish Government-in-Exile, yet in 1940 that government entered into negotiations with Jews to find some *modus vivendi* during the crisis. It was the London Poles who requested retributive bombing in December 1942. From a contemporary perspective, the idea of bombing German cities in 1942–1943 in retaliation for what the SS was doing in the East seems far more realizable than the later proposal to bomb the rail lines and the gas chambers, which only became possible in the spring of 1944, when most of the Jews were already in ashes.[9]

If the restrictive immigration laws and their implementation can serve as a prism to view the question of American policy in relation to the Holocaust, then the White Paper of 1939 serves the same purpose for British policy. Is it conceivable that a policy that severely curtailed Jewish immigration and land sales in Palestine, in the teeth of the crisis, was not at least partly motivated by anti-

Semitism? Palestine was such a logical haven for at least a portion of
the refugees that to deny its availability meant that death was almost
certainly the alternative. That much was clear by the early months of
1943. Yet, the first shots fired in World War II were by British soldiers at Jews trying to enter Palestine, and there is the incredibly
heartless case of the *Struma* and the *Patria,* illegal refugee ships that
went down with heavy loss of Jewish life because of the difficulty of
access to Palestine. Yet, historians like Michael Cohen and others,
although not denying that anti-Semitism was rampant in British rul-
ing circles, give far greater emphasis to national interest as the
source of this ruthless policy. There was a conviction that the impending crisis required strong ties to the Arab world, whose oil and loyalty were requisite for British security.[10]

But anti-Semitism there was, and it was sometimes put to perverse use. British and American officials were wont to cite fear of
arousing anti-Semitism as the reason for not offering Jews haven.
Herbert Morrison, the British home secretary, counseled rejection of
a 1940 Vichy offer to release Jewish children because it would "stir
up an unpleasant degree of anti-Semitism (of which there is a fair
amount just below the surface) and that would be bad for the country and the Jewish community."[11] Breckinridge Long, an assistant
secretary of state, used much the same argument to thwart Jewish
pressure for the admission of more refugees to the United States.
When the archbishop of Canterbury warned the House of Lords that
the use of the fear of arousing anti-Semitism as a strategy to avoid
the rescue of threatened lives was cynical and un-Christian, his
voice was not heard. When the same argument was used to thwart
the policy of retributive bombing, suggested by the Polish Government-in-Exile in 1942, the results were lethal for Jews. Retributive
bombing would have required no change in wartime priorities,
which had become the chief stumbling block to rescue. By 1943, German cities were already being savaged from the air, and all that was
required was that the German people be informed through leaflet-
ting and other means that the bombing was retribution for what was
being done in their name in the East. Had it been used, it would
undoubtedly have created a serious morale problem for Berlin, as
had *Kristallnacht,* when Nazis ravaged Jewish shops in Berlin November 9–10, 1938. More important, it would have opened up the
question of the fate of the Jews who had been deported and lifted
the curtain of silence surrounding the Final Solution. Indeed, Goebbels and Himmler fully expected that the Allies would play this card

and had prepared a counter-atrocity campaign. They were convinced that bombing was a Jewish plot.

But the card was never played. It was rejected by middle-echelon officials in the British and American government bureaucracies because they believed that retributive bombing was illegal. They continued to insist upon that although they knew the extermination of the Jews was occurring because they feared that it would turn the war into one to save the Jews, a linkage German propaganda exploited endlessly. As stated by Chief of the Air Staff Sir Charles Portal on January 2, 1943: "[Hitler] has so often stressed that this is a war by the Jews to exterminate Germany that it might as well be, therefore, that a raid, avowedly conducted on account of the Jews, would be an asset to enemy propaganda."[12] Instead, the bombing of Dresden was carried out in February 1945 but was never announced as a response to the Final Solution, which might have given it some justification. Ironically, that failure allows it to be considered a separate and equivalent atrocity in contemporary Germany.

The amalgamation of ideology and policy makes the case of the Soviet Union more difficult to judge. In the anti-Semitic cosmology of National Socialism, Communism and Judaism were inexorably intertwined. It was a linkage reflected in policy and propaganda. Thus, the Commissar Order, the only written evidence of an order for extermination, which was given to German commanders in 1941, ordered the execution of *Politrunkniks* (political officers, which began at the battalion level in the Soviet army) and Jews. The order was carried out by the *Einsatzgruppen*, the SS murder squads that followed behind the invading *Wehrmacht* in June 1941. The mass killing by starvation of thousands of Soviet POWs served as a model for the operation of the death camps. The first inmates of Auschwitz wore the uniforms of these murdered Soviet POWs. Clearly, the Soviets had much more direct evidence of the murderous Nazi intent and were faced with a direct link to the fate of the Jews. It was to be their fate, too. But that did not lay the groundwork for common cause.

About 2,000,000 Jews found a momentary precarious haven in Russia during the war. About 300,000 of these were able to flee eastward from German-occupied Poland, and additional thousands went from the Baltic states and the reoccupied areas of Romania. They were not rescued as part of a Soviet policy toward threatened Jews but instead fled or were evacuated together with the general population. Only in the Crimea were Jews evacuated collectively. Since the twenties, when a trickle of Jewish Communists had been welcomed to join resettlement projects in the Crimea and later in Birobidzhan, Soviet policy rejected Jewish refugees, not for religious reasons, to be sure, but because they often stemmed from the despised bourgeoisie. Afterward, the Soviet Union was invited to join the League of Nations Refugee Commission that strove vainly to bring order into the refugee chaos. A disproportionate number of Jewish artists and intellectuals were victims of the purges during the thirties. Soviet foreign policy remained adamantly opposed to Zionism and its settlements in Palestine. During the interwar period, thousands of Zionists vanished into the Gulag.

But after the German invasion of the Soviet Union in June 1941, as many as 1,500,000 Jews made their way into the interior of the Soviet Union, where together with other fleeing Russians, they sometimes found a precarious safety. The number rescued might have been much higher had the Holocaust not been preceded in the Soviet Union by a Sovietization policy that deprived Jewish communities of their leadership and destroyed all communal and cultural organizations. The *Einsatzgruppen* thus found their Jewish victims to be an unorganized, leaderless mass, amazingly uninformed about what fate had in store for them. For the preceding decade, Jews had lived virtually in an informational vacuum. Some even greeted German troops as saviors.[13] Of those who were evacuated to the interior, thousands were interned in camps, and many died of malnutrition. When the tide of war turned, the Soviets again proved to be indifferent to the fate of Jews in death camps. They also rejected suggestions to bomb the death chambers, although by 1944 they were in a far better position to do so. Dov Levin's conclusion about Soviet policy might just as easily have been written about the United States and Britain. "The humanitarian component and the desire to save Jews were insignificant."[14] The meaning of the destruction of European Jewry, which should have been especially clear to Soviet leaders because their fate was linked to that of the Jews was deliberately underplayed. Even today, Moscow does not acknowledge the anti-Jewish thrust of the Holocaust in its war memorials. As in Poland, the Jewish victims are granted in death what was never given in life. They are considered honored martyrs of the nation.

Yet as in the United States and Britain, there are extenuating circumstances. Treatment of the Russian people by the occupying Germans was harsh. Soviet losses were extremely heavy. It took a long time to recover from the shock of the invasion, and for almost two years it seemed as if the Soviet Union would not survive. Such a government was hardly in a position to concern itself much about the fate of the Jews or to contemplate the meaning of the death camps. They were probably more concerned that they would be compelled to join the assembly line of death. Moreover, having themselves produced a "world of camps" and their own version of mass murder of kulaks and of Polish prisoners at Katyn, they were hardly fitting subjects for moral suasion concerning Jews. When former Soviet officials are broached on the question of their indifference to the fate of their Jewish subjects, they inevitably cite the Constitution of 1936, which outlawed anti-Semitism. But only the timely death of Stalin in 1953 prevented the deportation of Soviet Jewry to the Gulag, where, undoubtedly, an unhappy fate would have awaited them.

What then might one reasonably conclude regarding the relationship between Allied wartime policy and the Holocaust? That the Jews of Europe were ground to dust between the twin millstones of a murderous Nazi intent and a callous Allied indifference seems evident. But whether that indifference to the saving of life was caused by the fact that it was primarily Jewish life is far less apparent. We have research that indicates that the Catholic Church was equally passive regarding the murder of its own adherents, Poles, Gypsies, and even its priests who died in Dachau and Auschwitz. The Vatican's rescue program for Catholic refugees was underfinanced and poorly organized.[15] The same is true of Soviet inaction regarding the liquidation of its soldiers who had been taken prisoner. It may be that we assume that the nation-state has more power to influence events than it possesses in reality and then assign it a responsibility that it cannot fulfill, at least not during wartime, with an enemy state particularly immune to moral suasion.

Clearly, much of Allied indifference to the fate of the Jews during the Holocaust can be rationalized under the general rubric, "reasons of state." Until the spring of 1943, shortly after the battle of Stalingrad, the Allies thought of themselves as likely potential victims of the Nazi juggernaut. But that leaves unexplained the inaction of the period before the war, the refugee phase of the thirties, and the two years following the spring of 1943, when the light of victory could be seen at the end of the tunnel. Something more substantial is required to explain Allied inaction during these periods. Anti-Semitism was prevalent among Allied decision makers, as it was in the general population. But oddly enough, it is difficult to link it to a specific policy step. That is so because anti-Semitism rarely existed in a vacuum. The historian cannot overlook the fact that the depression conditioned the "hard" implementation of the immigration laws and that national security considerations played a major role in Britain's decision to limit Jewish immigration into Palestine at a critical juncture. Consideration of the Jewish plight did not take precedence over consideration of national interests.

In the case of the Jews, it was not so much that they were hated but that they were not important or powerful enough to be of concern. Ironically, the reality was precisely the reverse of what anti-Semitic propaganda imagined the Jews to be. Beyond the exigencies of war, European Jewry was not considered to be within the "universe of obligation" of Western civilization. Jews were not citizens of a state in the western sphere that could make their case. They had become so much excess baggage on a crowded lifeboat, itself in danger of sinking. But even had they been part of that "universe," there is still no guarantee that the outcome might have been otherwise. The Armenians can attest to that. It may be that the very assumption of assigning states a humanitarian mission, which is an integral part of Jewish political culture, is misplaced. Jews, together with other vulnerable peoples, assume automatically that the state ought to seek justice and that there exists a moral spirit in the world that will protect them. The weak always cry for justice and morality, while the powerful call for order. It is in their interest to have such a caring world. But not everyone makes such assumptions. Japanese Americans, who certainly have a more direct claim against the Roosevelt administration, did not file that claim until very recently, and Armenians do not write books about the inaction of the Wilson administration. The questions "Did Roosevelt do enough?" or "Did the churches do enough?," are quintessentially Jewish ones. They are based on the assumption that one ought to care. This principle is the same as that which lies behind overwhelming Jewish support of welfare-state legislation in the domestic arena.

Finally, there seems little doubt that, especially in the case of the implementation of immigration policy during the refugee phase of the crisis, there was an inurement. Much more might have been done during the thirties to grant haven to those in need. That initial failure spilled over into the war. Of course, there were ample reasons for not opening the gates to Jewish refugees. Few Allied leaders were able to imagine that the alternative would be genocide.

But beyond that point there is something that becomes startlingly apparent to the historian. Policymakers in Washington, London, and Moscow thought that is was happening to someone else, a strange people who were not winning medals for popularity in their own countries. They never understood that the chimneys of the crematoria and the chimneys of the factories, which allowed them to enjoy the highest living standard in the world, were part of the same industrial process. Only the death factories built by the SS were producing so many units of death, tolled by managers of the production line, fed by Europe's extensive railroad grid that brought the human raw material to the death machine. They failed to recognize a familiar industrial process. Their civilization had gone awry and was consuming its own children. They were mostly Jews, but they were European, too. The leaders in the Oval Office, Downing Street, and the Kremlin never remotely understood that it was also their world that was burning.

PART TWO

America and the Holocaust

5

Roosevelt's New Deal
Humanitarianism

THE STORY is told of two concentration-camp inmates who by some miracle succeed in escaping, only to be recaptured. They are placed against a wall for summary execution, but before dispatching them, the officer in charge, as is the custom, asks if they have any last requests. In his last agony, one of the men requests a blindfold, whereupon the other nervously whispers to him "Don't make trouble!"

Much of the early discussion of the Holocaust centered on the reaction of the victims: Why did they not resist? Why did they not "make trouble"? We tended to forget that, whether they fought heroically in the Warsaw ghetto or went passively to their fate at Babi Yar, they remained victims. It was almost as if we were seeking a kernel of courage that would prove to us that death could not be produced in factories. European Jewry would be the Luddites of the twentieth century. Meanwhile, this preoccupation with the role of the victims had the unfortunate effect of momentarily obscuring the posture of the third parties—the Vatican, the neutrals, the Roosevelt administration, the International Red Cross, the rescue agencies. Victims remain victims whether they ask for blindfolds or not, but the role of witnesses is not preordained; their ambit of action is far greater because they were not locked into the Final Solution. What did they do? What follows is a brief description of one of the third

This essay appeared originally in *Judaism* 18, no. 3 (Summer 1969): 259–76, under the title "Roosevelt and the Holocaust: New Deal Humanitarianism." Reprinted by permission of the publisher, American Jewish Congress, copyright 1969.

parties—the Roosevelt administration—in relation to the Holocaust and some attempt to make sense of it.

The Historiographical Context

Holocaust observers such as Reitlinger, Hilberg, and, more recently, Gideon Hausner have made short shrift of the rescue story, dismissing it as at best nonexistent and at worst as tending to play an adjunct role to the operations of the Final Solution. The rescue story is, indeed, a tragic one, replete with incredible ineptness and indifference. But to observe that not enough was done is simply to recite a self-evident truth. Enough can never be done where such catastrophes are concerned. Moreover, such recitations, tinged as they are with righteousness, are not concerned with the reason for the failure or even the context in which it occurred. Yet, such failures often have more to tell us than the successes we experience. After one concludes that not enough was done—and such a conclusion is inescapable—the rescue story can serve for more than simply another sermon about man's inhumanity to man.

In addition to offering an opportunity to examine the authenticity of New Deal humanitarianism, there is in the rescue issue a model of special-interest pleading by a hyphenate group that seemed well equipped to exert pressure. Why did the Jews fail while the Irish "twisted the lion's tail" successfully during the last decades of the nineteenth century? Moreover, the rescue issue offers some fascinating insights into Roosevelt's administrative style. It is replete with overlapping agencies in perpetual conflict and with violent personal antagonisms, which can be traced to the president's uncertain mandate. To trace Roosevelt's devious path between those who insisted that refugees presented a threat to American security and those who insisted that the humanitarian roots of the New Deal had to be watered with something more than mere rhetoric presents us with a superb picture of Roosevelt the fox rather than the lion. And for American Jews, what Roosevelt did and did not do during the Holocaust has a special interest. What they really want to know is whether Roosevelt loved them as much as they loved him. One almost hesitates to burst the bubble.

Phase One: The Evian Initiative and Beyond

Roosevelt's interest in rescue began in earnest with the astonishing and unexplained invitation to thirty-two nations to meet at

Evian, France, to bring order into the chaotic refugee situation brought on by Berlin's extrusion policy. The invitation, extended during March 1938, was astonishing because Roosevelt chose to intrude into a situation in which he was virtually powerless to act, bound as he was by a highly restrictive immigration law. The invitation to Evian was in fact so carefully circumscribed that the conference was actually preordained to failure. No nation, cautioned the invitation, would be required to change its immigration regulations. Certainly, the United States would not. Roosevelt had no intention of directly confronting the restrictionist elements in Congress. And so the American delegation went to Evian with no bargaining power at all, and no amount of verbal maneuvering by Myron Taylor, the former head of United States Steel whom Roosevelt selected to lead the delegation, could conceal the impression that the administration would ultimately embarrass itself by sponsoring an exercise in futility.

Long-winded Latin-style oratory was a prominent feature of the deliberations. Virgilio Molina, the Dominican delegate, trusted "that our conference will be like a peaceful, limpid lake, whose health-giving waters assuage the thirst and add to the fertility of the lands that border it."[1] Ironically, the Trujillo regime was the only one to make a substantial resettlement offer, which became the refugee colony in Sosua. But even here, the offer was based more on a peculiar racist breed of thinking rather than a concern with the plight of the hapless Jewish refugees. Little was done to hide the Roosevelt administration's disappointment at the results of the conference. The hope was that Latin America would offer the havens that the United States could not. Had not the great Argentinian educator and statesman Domingo Sarmiento urged his countrymen to emulate the generous immigration policy of the United States? But by 1938, the policy of the United States had changed, and it was this change that the Latin American republics preferred to emulate. The failure to find suitable mass-resettlement havens became the rock on which the first phase of the rescue effort foundered.

Despite the failure at Evian, the administration chose to sustain its initiative. The decision was all the more remarkable because it was apparent that France and England, already burdened with growing numbers of refugees, were in no mood to open further the Pandora's box of resettlement and, for that reason, strongly supported the relatively innocuous League of Nations Refugee Commission, which was distinguished by its inability, as a League agency, even to deal with Berlin on refugee matters. In 1935, American High

Commissioner James G. McDonald, later to be appointed by Roosevelt to head the President's Advisory Commission on Political Refugees (PACPR), had dramatically resigned from the League Commission because of its impotence.

The Intergovernmental Committee on Political Refugees (IGC), which grew out of the Evian conference, was, therefore, a peculiarly American contribution to the solution of the refugee crisis and was pushed with some vigor by the Roosevelt administration. Its primary goal was to come to some agreement with Berlin, so that order might be imposed on the chaotic refugee situation. In 1938, it was believed in Washington, no less than in London, that the men in Berlin were after all, reasonable and could be talked to. The dream of an equitable solution to the refugee problem via negotiations was an integral part of that species of reasoning that led in September to Munich.

Eventually, Berlin did in fact agree to negotiate. From January to March 1939, George Rublee, an old Groton crony of the president's, assisted by the State Department's Robert Pell, partook in long and difficult negotiations first with the Nazi financial wizard Hjalmar Schacht and then with Helmut Wohlthat, an official in the Economic Affairs Ministry. To the dismay of some and the astonishment of others, Rublee actually succeeded in wresting a Statement of Agreement from Berlin. The agreement, an informal arrangement, was far from a humane solution to the German refugee problem and was soon dubbed a "ransom offer" by Dorothy Parker. That label gave to Holocaust history a ghoulish symmetry. It began with an offer to ransom German Jewry and ended with an offer to ransom the Jews of Hungary.

In fact, the Statement of Agreement was more than a simple ransom deal. It bore a startling resemblance to the Ha'avara agreement that the Jewish Agency had with Berlin. It required the forced sale of capital goods, the establishment of a trust fund from confiscated German Jewish capital, and an outside agency representing "international Jewry" that would purchase capital goods from the Reich that could then be used for resettlement purposes by the receiving nation. In turn, for such a forced sale of German goods, which incidentally would go far to shore up the Reich's precarious exchange balance, Berlin would permit an orderly, phased emigration of the Jewish community, protection for the aged and infirm who would be allowed to remain in Germany, and even some guarantees that overt persecution would be eliminated. Success in carrying out the agreement would depend on three factors: continued stability in Germany, the willingness of outside Jews to cooperate, and the availability of resettlement havens. None of these requirements could be fulfilled. Hitler's abrupt dismissal of Schacht in the midst of the negotiations indicated that events in the Reich were already out of control. Nor would the organization of an international Jewish corporation and the location of resettlement havens prove more successful.

We have a fairly good description of the agonizing decision that had to be made by the American, British, and French Jewish communities in Lewis Strauss's *Men and Decisions*. Involved was the question of whether these Jewish communities, not called upon to participate in the negotiations, should now make themselves over to fit the anti-Semitic image of "International Jewry" that Berlin fantasized. An international corporation to act as financial agent would first have to be created, and millions of dollars would have to be raised. Most galling was the suspicion that Washington and London, half sharing the notion that there was such a thing as international Jewish finance, were urging Jewish leaders to cooperate in subsidizing a government that had vowed to destroy Jews. Jewish leaders were wary of establishing a precedent of aiding Berlin to eliminate a particularly splendid community. The problem of the Jews' cooperation in their own destruction came to the fore three years before the decision to liquidate them and was actively abetted by Washington and London. Jews were shocked by the malevolence of the proposal, and they were also aware that in the wings waited Poland and Romania, anxious to "sell" their Jews. Would it not be better to follow the League precedent of protecting unpopular minorities where they lived rather than starting the sticky business of mass resettlement, especially when there was no place to move to? By the time even a nominal compliance with the agreement had been hammered out, the war was upon them. German Jewry was resettled—eastward.

The Security Psychosis and the Visa Debacle

Yet, thousands had been able to leave the Reich and Austria and would continue to be able to do so for some time. It was this stream of refugees that became a primary concern for the administration. Ultimately, the preoccupation with those who in effect were already rescued would become a gambit in foiling the rescue effort. Washington, as late as June 1943, insisted on focusing on these political refugees exclusively as it closed its eyes to the genocide operation. Not until January 1944 did rescue advocates finally succeed in broadening the administration's focus to include those who faced certain death in the camps.

By 1938, some pressure had developed to liberalize the rigid administrative procedures first initiated by Herbert Hoover at the outset of the depression. From time to time, pronunciamentos emanated from the White House declaring a liberalization of the visa procedure. But it soon became apparent that a gulf existed between the aspirations of the White House and what was happening on the operational level. By a fluke in the immigration law, the consuls had the final say on who could get the visas. With the middle-echelon officialdom of the State Department, they shared opposition to a new influx of immigrants and, in some cases, a barely concealed distaste for Jewish refugees. Thus between 1938 and 1941, when the need for visas was crucial and despite professions to the contrary, visas were consistently underissued.

Nevertheless, the private rescue agencies did succeed in communicating to the administration the urgent need to salvage the cultural and scientific elite of Europe. Accordingly, Roosevelt ordered a special visa procedure whereby the various sponsoring groups within the country compiled lists of rescue clients whose names would then be given to the President's Advisory Commission on Political Refugees, which acted as a conduit to the State Department. In theory, such people would then be given priority in visa consideration. In practice, the State Department had begun by 1940 to wage a relentless campaign to restrict such lists. Only now are researchers finally beginning to compile data that will allow some estimate of the extent to which the American cultural and scientific boom of the fifties and sixties was based on the imported refugee intellectual capital of the war years.

Certainly, the persons in the State Department who administered the visa regulations were barely cognizant of such a potential national asset. They were more inclined to view the refugee as an economic burden or a security risk and, therefore, spared no effort to close the doors. The high point of the resistance is well illustrated by the case of the SS Quanza, which arrived in Norfolk in September 1940 with a cargo of refugees who had been refused entrance to Mexico. The Mexican authorities had issued new visas to some passengers that would allow them to enter any haven but Mexico.

When the *Quanza* docked, ostensibly to refuel, a direct confrontation occurred between those who favored leniency for the admission or at least landing, of these refugees and those around Breckinridge Long, a newly appointed assistant secretary and head of the newly created Special Problems Division of the State Department, who were determined to halt the flow of refugees at any cost. It was one thing to urge Havana to accept the refugees of another steamer, the *St. Louis,* and quite another to bring them here. The violent temper tantrum thrown by Long after he learned that, after screening, most refugees had, after all, been found qualified for visas, went far in helping to identify him as the source of much of the resistance to a more humanitarian refugee policy. The *Quanza* victory was a temporary one. By mid-1941, Long was able to write gleefully in his diary that he had been almost completely successful in halting the flow of all refugees.

The instrument employed to bring the flow of refugees to a halt may be labeled the security gambit. It involved a playing on the fear that Berlin had infiltrated the refugee stream with agents. Even Roosevelt contributed to the security panic by referring in a speech to the Trojan horse tactic by which the Nazis had ostensibly gained the upper hand in France. If Berlin had attempted to shore up its exchange balance by attempting to blackmail Jews, could one reasonably expect that they would forego the opportunity that the refugee stream offered to penetrate the security of the United States? A spate of Hollywood spy thrillers generously abetted that kind of thinking in the mind of the American public. As patently ludicrous as such fears were, it was difficult for rescue advocates to counteract them without placing in jeopardy their own credentials as loyal citizens. The Zionist thrust had generated apprehension about dual loyalties in the Jewish community, so that rescue advocates were perhaps too finely attuned to the loyalty question. In any case, the rescue agencies were completely overwhelmed by the security gambit. Even Stephen Wise assented to stricter visa controls in 1941. Men like Breckinridge Long took considerable pride when they looked back at their work. The rescue effort that began with such loud trumpeting seemed to have fizzled by mid-1941.

The Resettlement Dilemma

The absorption of more refugees into the United States became an academic question once it became apparent that Hitler's scheme would ultimately involve all of European Jewry. The nub of the problem was from the beginning concerned with the possibility of finding and developing a suitable resettlement area. Few expected that over 10,000,000 Jews could be infiltrated into existing states. But the Evian conference had already demonstrated that a parallel reluctance existed for offering mass resettlement havens. The administration pressed for such schemes at the Washington conference of the officers of the IGC in October 1939. Roosevelt, playing his favorite role as statesman and amateur geographer, proposed to Paul Van Zeeland, the new head of the Coordinating Foundation, a grandiose plan for resettling millions. This—even as the French and the British were showing distressing signs that they would not be able to withstand the Nazi juggernaut and might soon themselves become candidates for refuge.

Perhaps the most interesting scheme generated by Roosevelt's enthusiasm was the Baruch-Hoover idea of establishing a United States of Africa, where all refugees would be accepted. Undaunted by the warnings of America's leading geographer, Isaiah Bowman, that mass resettlement of a highly urbanized group was chimerical, and forsaking the warnings of Myron Taylor that Jews did not welcome pioneering resettlement schemes, the administration pressed ahead with a plan to make Angola or perhaps Rhodesia into a refugee republic. America's own experience as a successful resettlement operation was too strong to overcome. While Roosevelt was focusing on Africa as the most likely place where new "huddled masses" could be settled, Whitehall was showing increasing interest in British Guiana in the American sphere. Neither side seemed particularly enthusiastic about committing its own sphere to resettlement. Roosevelt's enthusiasm showed a suspicious increase the further such resettlement schemes were away from home. When Harold Ickes pushed for resettlement in Alaska or the Virgin Islands, the idea was rejected by the administration.

The question of whether resettlement of European Jewry would work, an idea that Berlin, had also toyed with between 1939 and 1941, was never put to the test. The Wansee conference held in the suburbs of Berlin in January 1942, came after Hitler had abandoned the idea that a solution by resettlement was possible. The "Statement of Agreement" came to naught, and the question of whether Berlin might have opted in favor of resettlement had such havens been made available remains to plague us today. Nazi preoccupation with a resettlement solution is hinted at by the camouflage terminology under which the final Solution was carried out. How many Jews entered the cattle cars under the impression that they would be resettled somewhere in the East? Paradoxically, Berlin's decision for mass murder solved not only its Jewish problem but also the Allies' refugee problem. Each cattle car that rolled eastward meant that many fewer refugee clients.

The Department of State and American Jewry

The chief architect of the State Department's rescue policy was Breckinridge Long. Little need be said about him except that his diary, housed in the Manuscript Division of the Library of Congress, can be read with great profit by a psychoanalyst. He viewed his fight against the refugees as primarily a battle against Jewish Communist agitators who were trying to ruin his political career. It was Long who directed the antialien battle in Congress through his friends Senators Richard Russell and Robert Reynolds and Congressman Martin Dies. One of Long's favorite tactics was simply to deny that there was a problem which concerned Jews specifically. As late as April 1943 the State Department used the term "political refugee," despite ample evidence that the Nazis talked of nothing but Jews. While Berlin was "converting" all its enemies, including Roosevelt, to the Jewish faith, the State Department was reconverting Jews to a bland category labeled "political refugees." To avoid having to submit to a more active rescue policy, all one had to do was to deny that the Final Solution existed. Like Berlin, the Roosevelt Administration early discovered the effectiveness of a camouflage terminology to disguise its real purpose or lack of it. The now well-known attempt by the State Department to suppress news of the Final Solution that emanated from Gerhart Riegner, agent of the World Jewish Congress in Bern, fits into the same category.

Of course, it was naïve to imagine that news of such a massive operation could be hidden indefinitely and ultimately, the attempt to do so boomeranged on the department. It was Morgenthau's file detailing the State Department's deliberate sabotage that went far in convincing Roosevelt to create a special board in 1944. By the final months of 1942, the lid was off, and news that a mass-murder operation was in progress shocked the Jewish community. The result was a protracted period of agitation by American Jewry, which was designed primarily to redirect the rescue effort into more active channels.

As in the first phase, American Jewry dissipated much of its formidable organizational resources in internal bickering, until it seemed that it was more anxious to tear itself apart than to rescue its coreligionists. This internal organizational deadlock in the American Jewish community had a negative effect on its ability to focus pressure on the administration. One might almost say that the paralytic reaction pattern noted by Hilberg for European Jewry had its American counterpart. Reading the various organizational positions today can be a frightening experience. That a community that desperately needed unity to operate nevertheless remained divided and thus was never able to speak to Roosevelt with one voice is no small tragedy. The issues that divided Jewry seem amazingly irrelevant today. They are too complex to go into here, but one can nevertheless wonder whether the organizations allowed themselves the luxury of fiddling while Jews burned.

Little attempt seemed to have been made to activate the numerous Jews who had won high places in the Roosevelt administration. The silence of the *shtadlanim* is one of the most puzzling aspects of the rescue story. It was not until Henry Morgenthau Jr., secretary of the treasury and Roosevelt's good friend, was drawn into the rescue effort that rescue advocates succeeded in removing it from the State Department, where sabotage and sheer bureaucratic viscosity had brought the effort to a virtual standstill. Sam Rosenman opposed certain resettlement schemes in 1941 because they smacked too much of a re-ghettoization of the Jews. There is almost no information in the archives on the activities of such men as Felix Frankfurter, David Lilienthal, Isador Lubin, Sidney Hillman, Herbert Lehman, and David Niles. Yet, they represented one of the keys to a more successful effort.

The Bermuda Conference

In the early months of 1943, public pressure to rescue Jews reached a crescendo. In New York's Madison Square Garden, a rally was held on March 1 under the motto "Stop Hitler Now." In London, the agitation was, if anything, even stronger because of the role of Whitehall's Palestine policy. It was this pressure that brought Anthony Eden to suggest, while visiting in Washington in March, that a new refugee conference would go far in alleviating London's painful embarrassment. At first, the State Department was reluctant, but as the agitation increased, it saw the wisdom of the Eden gambit. Diplomatic preparations for a new refugee conference to be held in inaccessible Bermuda were begun.

There can be little doubt today that the primary objective of the Bermuda conference, which was held in April, was to deflect the growing agitation over rescue policy. The agenda, carefully prepared by Long, dealt exclusively with the problem of "political refugees." In 1943, that meant rescue of those who were already fortunate enough to be in the refugee stream and had perhaps found a precarious safety in Spain or North Africa. Those in the death camps were simply to be written off. Long, although he denied this at the November congressional hearings, specifically ruled out any attempt to negotiate with Berlin or the satellites through neutral intermediaries. Mostly, Long wanted to refurbish the IGC, an agency that had never really functioned after the outbreak of the war in 1939. Solomon Bloom, the Jewish chairman of the House Foreign Affairs Committee, was shrewdly selected to still the cry of rescue advocates. Later, he was tagged as the administration's *shabbes goy* (a non-Jew retained to perform tasks on the Sabbath forbidden to observant Jews) for allowing himself to be used in a conference that was generally acknowledged to be a callous mockery of the victims rather than an attempt to rescue them. The sheer malevolence in using such a tactic while a mass-murder operation was in progress served to intensify rather than to still the agitation among rescue advocates.

In the Jewish community, a new organization led by Peter Bergson and called the Emergency Committee to Save the Jewish People of Europe began to gain influence on the periphery of Jewish organizational life. It displayed a special flair for publicity and politics that made it the bane of the mainline organizations. Although it contributed to intensifying the organizational strife within American Jewry, it also succeeded in having introduced into Congress two rescue resolutions that sought to remove the rescue operation from the State Department and to create a new agency for that purpose. Hearings on the rescue resolutions were held in November. Breckinridge Long requested to be allowed to testify in executive session. It is difficult to account for the fiasco that followed. Long suffered severely from ulcers and hypertension, and the now-constant pressure on him emanating from "the radical boys" may have caused him to lose his usual aplomb. He presented the committee with a vastly exaggerated figure of the number of refugees admitted and insisted, despite his own well-known strictures, that the IGC had plenary power to negotiate with the enemy through an intermediary. When the testimony became known, rescue advocates became aware that Long himself had given them all the evidence necessary to prove that deliberate procrastination on rescue had been the policy of the State Department. With the help of Congressman Emanuel Cellar and others, Long's role was publicly exposed. It became the lever by which he was finally pried from continuing in his key rescue post.

Changing the Rescue Ground Rules

It was Morgenthau who delivered the *coup de grâce*. He carried a carefully collected file of evidence on the State Department's sabotage, giving special prominence to the deliberate attempt to squelch news of the Final Solution, to Roosevelt. In January 1944, the president startled rescue advocates by announcing the establishment of the War Refugee Board. Headed by John Pehle, an assistant secretary and director of the Foreign Funds Control Division of the Treasury, the new agency was in fact, if not in theory, almost exclusively a Treasury Department operation; and its charter, which gave it special powers, followed generally along the lines recommended by the private rescue agencies.

An energetic rescue operation was initiated employing not only the fragile underground apparatus in occupied Europe but also developing new techniques in psychological warfare that would prove particularly successful in the satellites. The establishment of the WRB was followed in June by a second breakthrough on the heretofore frozen immigration front. The administration adopted a scheme of temporary havens for refugees. The momentum for the idea, which was as old as the rescue effort itself, was furnished by Samuel Grafton, the syndicated columnist for the *New York Post*, who dubbed the idea "free ports." Using the clever analogy of comparing such interned refugees as having the same status as goods awaiting transshipment, the refugees accepted would simply not be registered as immigrants because they would be interned here temporarily until they could be sent back to their country of origin. Paradoxically, the legal precedent was furnished by an action of Breckinridge Long, who in the throes of the security psychosis, had accepted for internment thousands of unfriendly aliens from Latin America outside the quota system. The adoption of free ports, while it circumvented the immigration law only symbolically, marks the high-water mark of the American rescue effort.

When the victory did come, it had rather an empty taste. More than 4,000,000 Jews were already in ashes, and until an effective instrument could be fashioned to save Hungarian Jewry, over 1,000,000 additional Jews would lose their lives. The four years that it had taken to remove the operation from the State Department were crucial. The time lost could not be regained, nor could the dead be brought back to life.

Analysis: Negative

Furnished with a brief description of what transpired within the Roosevelt administration during the Holocaust years, we are now prepared to make some general observations and draw some conclusions, not about victims but about third parties.

We begin by observing that after the failure of the first phase of the rescue effort, which, as we have seen, contributed to Berlin's decision to liquidate European Jewry, the possibility of large-scale rescue became more remote. In a sense, the battle was lost in the first round. After January 1942, it would have taken an inordinate passion to save lives, a huge reservoir of good-will to achieve mass rescue. Such good-will was not forthcoming. There was no crisis of will; there was simply an absence of it. The energy and organization that went into the administration's rescue effort, even after the establishment of the WRB, never remotely approached the expenditure Berlin was willing to make to see the Final Solution through to the bitter end. Even after Miklós Horthy's amazing offer to halt the deportation of Hungarian Jewry in July 1944 and Heinrich Himmler's remarkable change of mind, there was an Adolf Eichmann to make certain that the ovens of Auschwitz were well stocked. The operation of the Final Solution had achieved a momentum of its own in 1944 that not even Berlin could stop.

Once it is understood that rescue required a commitment and a price that Roosevelt was unwilling or unable to make, the puzzling activities of the administration become comprehensible. Roosevelt and many in the administration wanted to rescue Jews—if only the price were not so high and the possibility so remote. In the absence of active measures, humanitarian rhetoric was substituted for action. Virtually every action taken before the establishment of the WRB— the Evian and Bermuda conferences, the search for resettlement areas, the liberalization of the visa procedures, and even the establishment of a temporary refuge haven in Oswego, New York, in August 1944—should be viewed as humanitarian gestures without serious intention of carrying them through. There is a double irony here; for although London and Berlin soon learned to dismiss the American initiative as a political gesture made for domestic consumption, American Jewry rarely directly questioned the sincerity of Roosevelt. They preferred to attack the State Department, which was being used by Roosevelt as a foil. It was one of the few instances in which Roosevelt found some use for the department. Roosevelt, in fact, had been fully briefed on the rescue issue and knew precisely what was happening. Like all love, the Jewish "love affair" with the New Deal showed a distressing tendency to be blind.

Then, there is the question of Breckinridge Long. I have never heard historians attribute anything to simple *finster mazel* (black luck), but here is certainly a case that deserves examination. Long, an early admirer of Hitler and Mussolini, a charter member of the American version of the Cliveden set, came to head the special Problems Division of the State Department almost by accident. He actually was considered as a possible replacement for Joseph Kennedy in London or for Hugh Wilson in Berlin. It was the caprice of this single individual that could make the difference between life and death. He was utterly devoted to foiling the rescue effort and was everywhere successful until Morgenthau was activated as a countervailing force within the administration. During the seventy-sixth, seventy-seventh, and seventy-eighth Congresses, dozens of antialien bills were introduced, which had the effect of reinforcing Roosevelt's sensitivity to the restrictionist element in Congress. Roosevelt thought his hands were tied by the continued strength of the restrictionists; and in case he forgot, Long was always there to remind him because Long himself was on very friendly terms with this group and able to suggest to them the legislation he considered necessary to plug the loopholes in the immigration law. Much of the initiative for the alien registration and other security laws emanated from Long.

Roosevelt, of course, had other problems besides the real or imagined strength of the restrictionists. He was a superb politician and prided himself on his fine political touch. His political antennae were astute, and when the label "Jew Deal" began to be heard across the land, he may have overreacted. Roosevelt was reputed to have appointed more Jews to high places than any previous president. He had stuck his political neck out for the appointment of Felix Frankfurter to the Supreme Court. But the "Jew Deal" label nettled and had its effect on the rescue initiative. The rescue of a foreign minority, whose coreligionists in the United States were not overly popular, represented a distinct political risk. The "political refugee" label, which gave Berlin considerable help in disguising the nature of the Final Solution, may have been maintained to avoid an overclose association with a Jewish problem and, therefore, not prove counterproductive for rescue purposes. In 1938, there was in fact a sizable minority of non-Jews in the refugee stream, so that this policy had some justification. But Roosevelt continued to insist on the interdenominational image even when it was clearly no longer feasible. Thus, when Rublee returned to the White House with the Statement of Agreement, Roosevelt expressed regret at the specific mention of the unmentionable—Jews. Before he made public his intention to establish a temporary haven in Oswego, Robert Murphy, his agent in North Africa, was given specific instructions to select a "good ethnic mix." One may read the memoranda in the State Department archives on the Holocaust and never know that the whole tragic business had something to do with Jews.

Less explicable is the administration's reluctance to use psychological warfare techniques, such as threats of retribution. A statement by Washington that the massive raid on Hamburg in July 1943 was in retribution for Treblinka or Auschwitz would have contributed substantially to opening a dialogue on the Final Solution. As it was, the cattle cars rolled to Auschwitz amidst an eerie silence. Crimes against Jews were consistently omitted from war-crime statements. Not until March 1944 could Roosevelt be prevailed upon to make some correction in the Moscow statement on war crimes, which promised dire vengeance for crimes against Cretan peasants but not specifically against Jews. Ostensibly, the silence was maintained for fear that such threats would actually lead to a Nazi escalation of terror. Berlin, it was believed, was fully capable of exacting retribution on the people of occupied Europe for what was being done to her from the air. It was a game in which Berlin held all the cards. But for European Jewry, at least, one is hard pressed to imagine what greater terror than Auschwitz might have been conceived. And the consequences of the policy of silence were tragic. Men like Joseph Goebbels fully believed that the Allies approved or were at least indifferent to the fate of the Jews. When one reads Anthony Eden's reference to "surplus people" in the State Department archives or Lord Moyne's infamous reply to Joel Brand when informed about the possibility of rescuing the Jews of Hungary ("Save a million Jews? What shall we do with them? Where shall we put them?"), Goebbels was after all not so far off the mark. At one point, for example, Breckinridge Long argued vehemently against relief shipments to the camps because that would relieve Berlin of this responsibility and thus help their war effort.

Bombing the crematoria and the rail networks leading to the camps would have gone even further in making clear Allied opposition to genocide. More important, it could have disrupted the actual killing process, which was everywhere dependent on a fragile coordination between available transportation and the capacity of the crematoria. But here, too, there was a strange reluctance to proceed. John J. McCloy, then assistant secretary of war, dismissed a joint request by the World Jewish Congress and the WRB to bomb the crematoria on the grounds that he could not divert needed air power on projects of such "doubtful efficacy." Moreover, it might "provoke even more vindictive action by the Germans." The refusal to consider such bombings marks a separate calamity within the larger tragedy of the Holocaust. The Hungarian rescue case establishes beyond doubt that the mere threat of bombing that emanated from within Hungarian underground sources was sufficient to frighten Budapest half to death and was instrumental in leading to the halting of the deportations. The satellites were sensitive barometers to how the winds of victory were blowing. After Stalingrad (February 1943), the need to dissociate themselves from the Final Solution must have been fairly apparent.

A word should be added concerning the role of American Jewry. When the catastrophe descended, the deep fissures between its "uptown" and "downtown" elements had barely been bridged. Jews, anxious above all to move into the mainstream of American life, did not accept the mantle of leadership, ensconced for centuries in Europe, with alacrity. American Jewry was divided and hesitant about exerting pressure through its *shtadlanim*. One has only to read Long's description of the numerous Jewish delegations, each representing another set of clients, to realize how tragic its posture was. It is, of course, easy to talk from hindsight. The role that fell to American Jewry was a difficult, perhaps an impossible, one to fulfill. They had the unenviable task of trying to change the administration's rescue ground rules, which were frozen solid by an immigration law thought immutable, and which, incidentally, a majority of American Jews had supported in 1938. They had to counteract a hysterical fear of the prowess of German espionage. No hyphenate group had ever been faced with the prospect of total annihilation of its European brethren, and although there was great urgency to use its influence, the instruments for doing so had to be developed from scratch. Moreover, the delivery of a voting bloc, the most potent weapon in any political arsenal, was practically denied to the Jewish leadership. The Jewish "love affair" with Roosevelt had, in contrast to other ethnic groups, become more ardent after the election of 1936. Jewish leadership could not gain leverage by threatening the withdrawal of votes and, therefore, was forced to depend on the less-certain rewards for political loyalty. As in the international arena, American Jewry lacked political organization and power. Jews loved the New Deal because of its humanitarianism, and ironically, it would be Jews who would require most evidence of its authenticity. For the most part, this evidence was denied to them. The most interesting facet of Arthur Morse's *While Six Million Died* is that he still reads the New Deal as did the Jews of the thirties. Most of American Jewry still does. The assumption is that the New Deal, *especially* the New Deal, ought to have been able to make a more humane response to the Holocaust. It is forgotten that there was the internment of the Japanese, an action that bears some parallels to Berlin's treatment of the Jews.

Something needs to be said also about the posture of American Zionism. Its startling growth as the catastrophe reached its apogee led its leaders to believe that the Jewish community should be unified under its auspices. But other organizations stubbornly refused to follow the Zionist lead and protected their organizational integrity against a real or imagined assault. For the Zionists, the rescue issue posed a special dilemma. The emergency had given the old territorialists a renewed lease on life. Roosevelt, we have seen, was specially taken with visionary resettlement schemes. For Zionists, a national homeland in Palestine was so clearly the answer to the refugee-rescue problem that to consider resettlement elsewhere was viewed as criminal heresy. The merest suggestion by the Bergson group that the rescue goal and the national commonwealth goal were working at cross purposes to the detriment of both, brought storms of invective from the Zionist leadership. Yet, a decision to divert some support to resettlement schemes outside of Palestine might have made a difference. The Zionist movement had, after all, fashioned the only major successful mass resettlement experiment in the twentieth century. It possessed the zeal and the pioneering skill that would have helped overcome the serious demographic difficulties that interfered with resettlement elsewhere. Many more might have been rescued had there been more Sosuas, and more Sosuas might have been developed in Latin America had there existed an ability to pioneer. For the Zionists, the decision was an agonizing one. Resettlement outside Palestine was even under the most favorable circumstances only remotely possible, while, in contrast, the *Yishuv* was firmly established. Palestine was the logical area for resettlement, they reasoned, and to divert funds and energy from it would have been a liability to the pioneering operation. An agonizing choice had to be made. There were not enough resources and energy to do both; and yet, for mass rescue to become a reality, not only would both have had to take place but, in addition, a massive campaign to encourage infiltration to established states would also have been necessary. The Zionist movement made the only choice it could make and in doing so left itself open to the charge of complicity.

Unfortunately, the strife between Zionist and other groups did not remain merely academic. The makeshift, largely Zionist-organized rescue operation that had been established on the periphery of Nazi Europe was often plagued by bickering between the different agents. Almost always the issue was who should get the credit for rescuing the handful that were brought out. The bitter recriminations that could be heard in Lisbon, Ankara, Stockholm, and even Bern possess an irony all their own; for although Berlin endlessly projected a picture of a well-coordinated international Jewish conspiracy, the rescuers were plagued by questions of which Jews should be saved and who should get the credit.

Mitigating Considerations

Our picture would be incomplete if the mitigating circumstances that contributed to the failure of the Roosevelt administration to become a more energetic rescue agent were not given mention. Some of the realities of the American political scene during the war have already been described, and the crucial importance of the rescue failure between 1938 and 1942 has been highlighted. Between 1942 and 1944, the possibility of mass rescue was severely circumscribed by Berlin, so that one can give no assurance, even had Washington acted, that the Final Solution could have been entirely prevented. Two variables were never under Allied control: Nazi determination to liquidate European Jewry and physical control of the scene of the depredations. The potential for rescue varied from country to country and was dependent on the degree of Nazi control. Jews directly under the Nazi heel, like those in the *général-gouvernement*, had far less opportunity for rescue than those living in the cobelligerent states like Italy and Hungary or favorite satellites like Denmark. One is hard pressed, for example, to discover a way in which the Jewish community of Poland might have been rescued even under the most fortuitous circumstances.

Admittedly, one feels wary about quibbling over legal technicalities when an operation of mass murder is in question, but there can be little doubt that legal questions played a crucial role in the posture of the third parties. Arthur Morse assumed that the Roosevelt administration was not true to its humanitarian precepts when it undertook only a listless rescue effort. Even if this assumption about the New Deal were fully acceptable, it would have only a peripheral significance as far as mass rescue of European Jewry is concerned. Few nation-states are able to muster concern about the fate of a foreign minority. They have enough trouble making human responses to their own minority problems. On the foreign scene, nation-states, if they do have souls at all, are probably more demonic than saintly. We tend to forget that even the American government under Roosevelt was a human-made institution, not human itself. It had no natural soul and little concern about morality. But things were entirely different when there was a clear legal responsibility to do something. Hungary did protect Hungarian Jews living in France from deportation and even protested their having to wear the telltale yellow star. Turkey and Spain gave similar protection to their Jews. The American government went to considerable lengths to protect the property of American Jews in Germany. When the nation-state had a clear legal responsibility, it could act. Sometimes, the knowledge of this possibility could be used for rescue. Often, Latin American legal papers made the difference between life and death, for, paradoxically, even the Nazis in the midst of their bloody operations retained certain legal niceties.

Perhaps, if a broader segment of the American people had joined in the agitation, the Roosevelt administration might have responded sooner. But here, too, rescue advocates were persistently stymied by a failure to gain credibility. The idea that a mass-murder operation, using modern production techniques, was in progress simply beggared the imagination. It played havoc not only with the victims, who could not bring themselves to believe the unbelievable, but with the rescue agents as well. How does one react to such a datum except by asking over and over again whether it is true? A Roper poll taken in December 1944 showed that the great majority of Americans, although willing to believe that Hitler had killed some Jews, could not accept the idea that a mass-murder operation in which millions had died, had occurred. Apparently, there is such a thing as a saturation point as far as atrocity stories are concerned. In the American mind, the Final Solution took its place beside the Bataan death march and the Malmédy massacre, in which seventy US prisoners of war were killed by Germans. It was just another atrocity in a particularly cruel war. It was a supremely difficult task to break through the curtain of disbelief, and the role of the State Department in suppressing the details of the story did not make the task easier.

Then, too, the Roosevelt administration was but one of many components that had to be activated for a successful mass-rescue operation. There were also the Vatican, the Committee of the International Red Cross (CIRC), the neutrals, the other Allied governments, the governments-in-exile, and the people in the occupied areas. A more energetic leadership from Washington would have invigorated the flagging rescue effort, but no one can be certain to what extent. All maintained their own measure of commitment and did not necessarily follow Washington's lead. that was especially true in the case of resettlement in the Latin American republics, the unsuccessful Taylor mission to the Vatican, and the failure to activate fully the International Red Cross until mid-1944. In the case of the Vatican and the CIRC, even after Washington stopped saying "do as I say, not as I do," the two rescue components remained reluctant to participate fully. The existence of so many independent components made for problems of coordination and unity. The IGC, which was established after the Evian conference, was supposed to furnish such coordination, but, as we have seen, it became instead the first casualty of the general lack of will and ultimately was used by the State Department and Whitehall as a foil for rescue. The early rescue effort was literally strangled in a sea of red tape, which itself was a reflection of the lack of will. The classic example of this is the diplomatic game played between Britain and the United States over the resettlement question. They played a game that might be called "who has the moral onus now?" The need to have a collective effort meant in practice that no one really felt the responsibility to do anything. Collective failure, like collective guilt, has an allure all its own. It is far easier to bear.

Finally, even if all the problems that beset the rescue effort had been magically solved—if Breckinridge Long had been converted to the cause of rescue, if London had abandoned its inhumanely political attitude toward Palestine, if the divisions within American Jewry had been healed, if the pope had spoken out, if the CIRC had had been more courageous in interpreting its role—we still have no guarantee that mass rescue could have been realized. Certainly, more might have been saved, especially in the satellites. Something like such a miracle took place in Hungary in 1944: virtually all the components of a complete rescue effort were fully activated. Yet, within full view of the world and when Berlin knew that the war was lost, the cattle cars rolled to Auschwitz as if they had a momentum all their own. Over half of Hungary's Jewish community went up in smoke.

Apparently, even the passionate will to save lives was not enough. Something else was also required, something to soften the hearts of those in Berlin who were in physical control of the slaughter. The production of such a miracle was never in the hands of the Washington policymakers. Perhaps it was in the realm of a higher kingdom. Its strange indifference has become the overriding preoccupation of the theologians.

6

Could Mass Resettlement Have
Saved European Jewry?

THOUSANDS OF EUROPEAN JEWS went to their deaths believing until
the last moment that they were being resettled. How did the term
resettlement, a benevolent word with connotations of renewal, become a code word for the implementation of the Final Solution? At
least part of the answer lies in the fact that between 1938 and the
German invasion of the Soviet Union in June 1941, Nazi authorities
considered making the Reich *Judenrein* by means of resettlement,
rather than by mass murder. Best known to us are the plans for
Jewish reservations in Madagascar and Lublin. These schemes, however, never viewed resettlement in a positive sense, and in practice,
resettlement by the Nazis turned out to be a precursor to liquidation
or, as occurred in many instances, merely another form of the Final
Solution. "There is no question of a Jewish state," warned Alfred
Rosenberg, in reference to the Madagascar project, "but only of a
Jewish reservation."[1]

The term *resettlement* was also used extensively by the Allies.
One of the solutions considered during the refugee crisis was the
organization of agricultural communities in unused lands—as opposed to the admission of single refugees or families into hard-
pressed existing communities. Such schemes called for the establish-

This essay appeared originally in *Rescue Attempts During the Holocaust: Proceedings of the Second Yad Vashem International Historical Conference, April 1974* (Jerusalem:
Yad Vashem, 1977), 123–81, under the title "Roosevelt and the Resettlement Question."

ment of settlements that ranged in size from those involving hundreds to new nation-states involving millions.

Eventually, a bridge developed between the two contrasting conceptions. Thus, during the early months of 1939, both sides involved in the refugee chaos—the receiving nations bordering on the Reich and the National Socialists who were responsible for the crisis—agreed upon a solution that was primarily based on resettlement. Providing empty spaces was one of the major tasks assigned to the receiving nations by the Statement of Agreement, which was the product of the Rublee-Schacht and Pell-Wohltat negotiations.

As things turned out, few Jews who survived the Holocaust owe their lives to resettlement projects. In fact, there was actually only one partially successful colonizing venture, and those who did escape were saved mostly by their timely flight. Moreover, hope of rescue through resettlement became increasingly remote as the Nazi *Drang nach Osten* brought larger numbers of Jews under Nazi hegemony.

An examination of the James G. McDonald papers at Columbia University confirms what other manuscript collections have already made abundantly clear. A large number of the rescue schemes proposed by the Roosevelt administration during these early years were based on resettlement. Dozens of schemes were brought to the attention of the administration and the refugee advocates on the President's Advisory Committee on Political Refugees, which acted on its behalf. This chapter will include a brief survey of these schemes and a description of Roosevelt's thinking on resettlement. It will then focus on the four schemes in which the administration played a role: Alaska, Mindanao, British Guiana, and Santo Domingo. Finally, I will discuss why resettlement, in which so many well-meaning persons invested so much, failed to fulfill its potential as a means of rescue. Indeed, I want to answer a more basic question. Was resettlement ever a viable alternative to solve what Roosevelt called the problem of the political refugees and what the Germans simply referred to as the Jewish problem?

From the moment that the Roosevelt administration unexpectedly issued an invitation to thirty-two nations to meet at Evian to try and solve the refugee problem, it was compelled to rely heavily on the idea of resettlement. Because the administration considered its stringent immigration laws immutable, the invitation stated that no nation would be expected to alter its own immigration regulations. Once at Evian, however, it quickly became apparent that the participants, especially the delegates of the Latin American republics, were reluctant to admit any immigrants whatsoever. One by one, the delegates rose to make known their nation's unwillingness to open their gates. "Nations loath to give asylum to Jews," read the headline of the *Christian Science Monitor*.[2] Roosevelt's initiative, which had received an unexpected amount of press coverage, was going nowhere.

The imminent failure of the conference was undoubtedly one of the factors that forced the Roosevelt administration to direct itself in earnest to the resettlement alternative. James G. McDonald had been appointed chairman of the President's Advisory Committee on Political Refugees when the invitation to Evian had been extended. PACPR was supposed to be the administration's quasi-official clearing house on refugee matters. It was also supposed to coordinate the work of the private refugee agencies, and as it turned out, it became the body that screened the various resettlement proposals. In November, McDonald, who sometimes suspected that Roosevelt had forgotten that he had created such a body, received one of his rare invitations to the White House. Once there, he was urged to speed up the committee's efforts to locate resettlement havens, especially in Latin America.[3]

Shortly thereafter, George Warren, the executive secretary of the PACPR, suggested that the Latin American delegates be approached informally at the forthcoming Lima conference. The refugee issue had already been placed on the agenda at the suggestion of Helio Lobos, the Brazilian delegate at Evian, but Warren was convinced that in private the Latin American officials would be more magnanimous in accepting refugees, especially if they could be assured of receiving immigrants who would be able to help in the development of agriculture and local industry.[4] Officials at the State Department informed Warren that they placed little hope in the informal approach, and as it developed they were right.[5] The participants at the conference rejected the pro-refugee resolution. Things had not changed two years later, when Cordell Hull went to the Havana conference with instructions from Roosevelt "to consider the possibility of saying something in regard to the ancient principle of political asylum."[6] Roosevelt preferred to think of the refugee crisis as a political one and of the Jews involved as "political refugees." In the midst of the crisis, however, the Latin American countries on which the Roosevelt administration had placed much hope, closed their doors to most refugees.

In November 1938, Roosevelt met with a group of State Department officials at his Warm Springs, Georgia, retreat in order to engage in a thorough examination of the resettlement alternative. Among those present were William Phillips, ambassador to Italy, George Messersmith, temporarily an assistant secretary of state, and Hugh Wilson, ambassador to Germany, who had been recalled from Berlin by the administration in response to *Kristallnacht*. Before he left Washington, the president had informed journalists that he was giving a great deal of thought to the refugee question, but the time was not yet right to make his thinking on the subject known.[7] At his request, Sumner Welles forwarded all the department's files on resettlement to Warm Springs.[8] The Warm Springs discussions triggered several probes on the resettlement front.

Roosevelt's sudden interest in resettlement was partly based on the fact that his Evian initiative had opened up a diplomatic Pandora's box and partly on his vision of himself as a wise, humanitarian statesman. At Roosevelt's behest, a new international immigration agency had been established in addition to those already in the field that the administration chose not to use. The Intergovernmental Committee on Political Refugees, which was created at the Evian conference, was directed by George Rublee, an old friend of the president's. The negotiations that Rublee conducted with Reich officials concerning the refugee problem unexpectedly began to bear fruit in the early months of 1939. The success of the talks would largely depend on whether a haven could be found for the resettlement of the Jews of Germany. Both Rublee and his successor Robert Pell urgently pleaded with the State Department for concrete proposals with which to spice their negotiations. Palestine, which might have been the administration's most logical choice, was placed off limits at Whitehall's insistence. In addition, there were problems in the Middle East that the administration had no desire to aggravate.

The idea of resettlement also struck a responsive chord among the general public and political leaders. Was America not the fruit of a successful resettlement effort in the seventeenth century? "The shores of New England offered a refuge for the Pilgrim fathers, and the shores of our country have ever since been a haven for the oppressed," read one of the hundreds of suggestions received by the PACPR.[9] (The second assertion had, of course, not been true since

1921.) Similarly, the Baruch-Hoover scheme to establish a "United States of Africa" raised the hope that the refugees would "build in Africa a new country like America."[10] The latter suggestion was more appealing because it did not dredge up the embarrassing reminder that the nation's interior could no longer play its traditional role.

The analogy to colonial America was sometimes taken to ridiculous extremes. Thus, the resettlement prospects in British Guiana, ten degrees above the equator, were believed by one administration official to be identical with the conditions faced by the early settlers in Virginia and "therefore suitable for a Jewish pioneering effort."[11]

Roosevelt's personal proclivities for geography and nation building also played a significant role. During his stint as assistant secretary of the Navy in the Wilson administration, he had some peripheral connection to the writing of a new constitution for Haiti, and in the 1920 campaign he blew the matter out of all proportion by boasting that he had written the constitution.[12] In addition, during the 1920's, he had submitted a peace plan (to win the Bok prize) in a contest sponsored by the *Ladies Home Journal*. His love of sailing and travelling had given him a firsthand knowledge of geography that was further cultivated by his hobby of collecting stamps from faraway places. Moreover, his administration already had some experience in resettling people. In the spring of 1935, a Resettlement Administration had been established to move Americans from unproductive soil to areas more suitable for agriculture. Resettlement, albeit of a different sort, was thus already part of the working policy of the New Deal.[13]

Roosevelt believed that the outbreak of war would aggravate the refugee problem, and this belief reinforced his tendency to think in terms of nation building. The forthcoming meeting of the officers of the IGC, which was scheduled to be held in Washington in October 1939, offered an opportunity to make his thinking on the problem known. He therefore rejected all suggestions to cancel the meeting. The war had only made the refugee problem more urgent.

The meeting was convened on October 16 in an atmosphere of despair. Six weeks of war had demonstrated that the Nazi war machine was formidable, perhaps even invincible. The fate of the Jewish refugees seemed unimportant to the delegates, who faced the possibility that their own homelands would soon be overrun and that they themselves would become refugees. What was so special about the Jews? Sir Herbert Emerson, the new chairman of the IGC, informed the conferees that Britain would be forced to withdraw her generous offer of aid for resettlement in British Guiana.[14] The war had changed the situation, and British resources were hard pressed.

The climax of the meeting was the president's long-awaited address. He began with a pessimistic prognosis. The problem that the delegates presently faced was minor compared to what the future held in store. He predicted that, after the war, the refugee problem would encompass from 10,000,000 to 20,000,000 persons. In view of this fact, Roosevelt believed that the IGC, which was a product of his own imagination, was thinking on "too small a scale." They must "clear the decks" of the piddling refugee problem they now faced, Roosevelt urged. Massive resettlement ventures using "modern engineering techniques," that would capture the imagination of the world had to be undertaken. An altered version of Emma Lazarus's poem "The New Colossus" ended the remarkable display of New Deal rhetoric: "Let us lift a lamp beside new golden doors for the poor, for the huddled masses yearning to breathe free."[15]

The delegates were stunned. They had not succeeded in finding havens for a few thousand refugees, and here the president was talking in terms of millions. He had presented a grandiose vision, but not a single suggestion about how that vision might be realized. A few weeks later, Roosevelt elaborated further. The occasion was a memorandum from Paul Van Zeeland, the former prime minister of Belgium, who had been appointed to head the Coordinating Foundation charged with implementing the Statement of Agreement with the Reich. Van Zeeland outlined a detailed resettlement program that called for small agricultural and industrial projects whose financing would be arranged "on a strictly business basis . . . as investors not as dispensers of charity." That was necessary, he thought, because of the paucity of offerings and the lack of available funds. Each project would be financed separately; and after an initial period of dependence on a parent holding company, it would be expected to operate at a profit.[16]

Roosevelt did not approve of Van Zeeland's scale of planning, as it did not "stimulate the imagination," and "missed the psychology necessary for success." According to Roosevelt, "this [was] not the time to speak of small settlements . . . the picture should be in terms of millions of square miles occupied by a coordinating self-sustaining civilization." "I could raise money on that," boasted the president, "far quicker than if I talked in terms of individual communities . . . overall planning on [an] enormous scale is essential."[17]

Ironically, this statement was made in December 1939, and at that point not a single project supported by the administration had borne fruit. Roosevelt understood what had to be done and understood the importance of size. When it came to supporting a scheme for resettlement in Alaska, however, we shall see that he did not dare assume the political risks involved in supporting the project. At a critical juncture, he preferred to switch to the postwar problems that offered a suitable platform for his grandiose ideas.

In 1940, in fact, FDR took steps to implement his postwar program. Henry Field, an anthropologist, was called to Washington and put to work on a secret project to research possible resettlement havens. By 1945, the "M" project, as it was known, had produced 666 classified colonization possibilities. Roosevelt even entertained plans to make the North African desert bloom by using desalinated water and building air-conditioned cities.[18] These plans, however, had no bearing on the refugee crisis; they were earmarked for postwar problems. The thinking of Alex Hŕdlička of the Smithsonian Institution also caught the attention of Roosevelt. In contrast to Bowman's generally pessimistic outlook, Hŕdlička was convinced that Latin America could absorb a large number of immigrants. But his advice that the administration establish an "immigration nucleus," was reasoned to death by the State Department.[19]

Thus throughout the crisis, Roosevelt's thinking was visionary and out of touch with the facts of the case. He did not acknowledge that the refugee problem primarily involved Jews and was unwilling to take the political risks involved in contributing to a solution.

On the grass-roots level, however, resettlement continued to be considered a real alternative. Virtually every refugee group had its favorite resettlement scheme. In addition, private persons, many of them undoubtedly refugees, were attracted to the idea. The archives are full of detailed schemes written neatly in European script and excessively formal language that outline some plan to save the refugees by colonization. Private companies like Ford and Birdseye Foods also momentarily entered the picture. The most fertile source for ideas were the private Jewish agencies. At times, one particular area suddenly became very popular. Before Berlin became interested in Madagascar, it had been investigated by a Japanese survey team in 1929, the Polish Lepecki Commission in 1937, and the French in 1939. In fact, the dream of Madagascar was not discarded until May

1941, when a highly confidential report by the Research Institute on Peace and Post-War Problems finally delivered a definitive report that noted the island's deficiencies as a resettlement site.[20] Yet, islands and tropical rain forests in which troublesome minorities could be tucked away continued to have an allure of their own. Before Charles Liebman, president of the Refugee Economic Corporation (REC), became enraptured with Mindanao and the Dominican Republic, he was attracted to Cyprus. One scheme, submitted through Albert Einstein, suggested that refugee intellectuals be settled in the Belgian Congo and other "unsettled" areas in Africa.[21] Even the Soviet experiment in Birobidzhan did not escape perusal. The suggestion to send Jewish refugees there, however, was rejected by the Soviet authorities.[22]

The number of schemes received by the administration increased sharply after *Kristallnacht*.[23] A proposal submitted by Kurt Battsek, quoted generously from the Bible and presaged the actual arrangement finally reached with Berlin. Battsek suggested the establishment of a Jewish resettlement corporation with a capital of £50,000,000 which he assumed would partly be contributed by Lord Victor Rothschild.[24] A Dr. Stolper hit upon the same idea.[25] Charles S. Dewey, formerly assistant secretary of the Treasury (1924–1927) and financial adviser of the Polish Government (1928–1930), submitted an elaborate scheme that linked the solution of the refugee problem to the outstanding debts still owed to the United States. According to his plan, the debtor nations would be allowed to repay their debts by furnishing havens in their colonies or other forms of aid. A meeting of the Brookings Institution held on February 10, 1939, seriously pondered the possibilities of implementing Dewey's scheme.[26]

Some of the proposals to solve the refugee crisis might serve as comic relief. Thus, Julia S. Hotchkiss of Westport, Connecticut, assured McDonald that her suggestion was delivered "from an unprejudiced point of view" because "she had not, nor [had] any of [her] relatives a drop of Jewish blood." She began by suggesting a "ship of freedom" to be sponsored by the forty-eight states, which would transport the refugees out of Europe. Unfortunately, she had not yet decided where the vessel would deposit its human cargo. Eight months later, she thought of a solution and hastened to submit it to McDonald under the rubric "A New Solution to the Jewish Problem." Seemingly totally unaware of what Jews had been doing for generations, she proposed that Palestine be purchased from the Arabs and when the purchase was completed that a "Temple of

Peace" be erected in Jerusalem. As a token of Britain's good faith, Jacob's Pillar, a statue then apparently housed in the British Museum would be "surrendered" and placed in the temple. Mrs. Hotchkiss, it seems, was also an art lover.[27]

The idea of rich Jew purchasing a haven, much the way one purchased a newspaper, also occurred to William Randolph Hearst, who thought that the Belgian Congo was a suitable piece of real estate. The authorities in Leopoldville quickly denied, however, that the Congo was for sale.[28] The proposals to buy a solution to the crisis are interesting because they were as popular in Washington as they were in Berlin and were apparently based on an anti-Semitic caricature of rich Jewish bankers in control of the world's money markets. James McDonald made good use of this notion when he visited Latin America in 1935. In his talks with Latin American officials, he frequently conjured up the image of Jewish money following Jewish refugees.[29]

In some cases, resettlement schemes emanated from friendly sources within the administration. Such, we shall see, was the genesis of the Alaska scheme. In December 1938, the press reported a "vast refugee plan" in the works at the Department of Labor. It called for the retraining of young Jews from Central and Eastern Europe and their systematic emigration and also guaranteeing the security of the rest of the Jewish population.[30] Frances Perkins refused to reveal the details of the plan, but it appears to have been one of the ideas that was included in the agreement with Berlin. No doubt she eventually realized that retraining was futile if the refugees had no place to practice the new skills.

The retraining process was essential if Jews were to be able to do pioneering work, and this may have been the reason that so many Jewish groups sponsored such programs. Not only the *Reichsvertretung* but also the various local and regional organizations of German Jewry supplemented training that the Zionists had given on their *hachshara* farms for years. In Vienna, where the refugee problem became acute following the *Anschluss* in March 1938, a special group, the League of Jewish War Veterans, established a retraining project on the banks of the Danube.[31] The Germans did not disturb the project, but the group's plan to settle in Australia, Kenya, or Rhodesia never materialized.

One of Roosevelt's favorite potential resettlement sites, the Orinoco Valley in Venezuela, was suggested by Antonio Gonzalez, former Venezuelan minister to the United States.[32] Although Isaiah

Bowman frowned on the idea and the Venezuelan delegate at Evian spoke of his country's need to establish a "demographic equilibrium," which, freely translated, meant a refusal to admit refugees, interest in Venezuela continued and was ultimately transferred to the Orinoco Plateau.[33] In 1941, Samuel D. Phillips, who maintained a long-term interest in resettlement in Venezuela, became convinced that the local authorities had changed their minds and were now ready to accept refugees. The PACPR was informed, but nothing developed.[34]

In September 1938, a suggestion was made that refugees be settled in Mesopotamia, and in December the first probes were made regarding resettlement in Ecuador. The latter became a favorite project of Colonel Walley Cohen, a member of a group in England, headed by Anthony de Rothschild, which play a role similar to that of the PACPR. For a while, the Viennese veterans group also appeared interested in the project, and it was rumored that the Nazi authorities in Vienna would make an exception in the case of these veterans and would allow them to leave with the equivalent of £50 each, rather than in the usual penniless state. The veterans planned on a grand scale. They would settle 100,000 Jewish families over a twenty-year period.[35] That was in February 1939, however, and war was only months away. Despite the cooperation of the Anglo-Ecuadorian Land Company and the Anglo-Ecuadorian Oil Fields Ltd., little could be achieved. The Roman Catholic Church was especially strong in Ecuador, and thus the special attention given by the Ecuadorian authorities to the International Hebrew-Christian Alliance, a new group representing non-Aryan Christians, was understandable.

In April 1939, two delegates from Quito arrived in London authorized "to negotiate an agreement for agricultural settlements to be established in different regions of the country." Eventually, a proposal to settle 1,000 refugees was presented to the London group. However, the motives of one of the negotiators, Frederico Vottelez, who it appeared was a German refugee anxious to supervise the planned resettlement projects, aroused suspicion. Moreover, the negotiators failed to appear in New York to present the details of their scheme.[36] In the interim, the plan became increasingly farfetched. A cable from Anthony de Rothschild raised the number of refugees to be resettled to 10,000 and urged the PACPR to send commission to that country. Warren turned to the State Department for advice.[37] The communication ends there, and few Jews were admitted to Ecudador.

In December, interest was suddenly aroused regarding resettlement in Canada, where the province of British Columbia was ostensibly interested in receiving refugees. However, the French in
Quebec, whose representatives held the balance of power in the Ca-
nadian Parliament, refused to agree to such proposals.[38]

The prospect of resettlement in the Mexican province of Lower
California, which was also introduced in December, was the brain-
child of Frederick Cox among others. He had formerly been British
consul in Costa Rica and was something of an amateur geographer.
McDonald, however, was skeptical.[39] Unless a way could be found
to obtain the approval of Lazaro Cardenas, the Mexican president
who had expropriated American and British oil interests a few
months earlier and was contemplating selling his oil to boycotted
Germany, the situation was hopeless. Nevertheless, in January, Alfred Jaretzki, Joseph A. Rosen, Charles Liebman, and McDonald
conferred with a Mexican representative and drew up an official request to Cardenas concerning the resettlement of refugees in Lower
California.[40] McDonald recalled that Rublee had served as Dwight
Morrow's assistant in Mexico, when the latter had literally charmed
President Plutarco Calles not to enforce ARTICLE 17 of the constitution, which gave the Mexicans subsoil rights. Perhaps Morrow and
Rublee could be called on for a repeat performance with Cardenas in
order to convince him to do something for refugees.

In June, PACPR received an affirmative report on Mexico from
the Mexican undersecretary of foreign affairs. Frank Aydelotte of the
American Friends Service Committee (AFSC), and Bernard Kahn of
the American Jewish Joint Distribution Committee (JDC) consulted
with Cardenas in August 1939,[41] and preparations were made to resettle two hundred families. The liaison with Cardenas was to be
Professor Frank Tannenbaum of Columbia University, whose book
Peace by Revolution: An Interpretation of Mexico, written in 1933, en-
deared him to Cardenas. In its final form, the plan called for the
resettlement of 2,500 refugees, who would be selected from among
German and Spanish loyalist refugees, and Mexicans, who were to
be repatriated from the United States. The first stage was supposed
to be a trial settlement of two hundred families.[42] The inclusion of
Spanish refugees among the settlers complicated things, however,
and the PACPR, owing to its status as an unofficial agency of the
American government, thought it the better part of wisdom to break
off contact lest it arouse controversy. The families ultimately selected
for resettlement in Mexico were primarily Polish and Spanish Catholics rather than Jews.

Haiti and Dutch Guiana (Suriname) received some attention in the early months of 1939. The former excited the mind of Anthony de Rothschild but never received the support of the State Department, whose officials at first considered the republic too unstable to absorb refugees and later rejected it on the grounds that it was too close to the Panama Canal to admit German-speaking refugees who might be spies.[43] The situation in Suriname was not much better. The initiative came from a newly organized group, headed by Daniel Wolf, that was affiliated with the Jewish Colonization Association. The group enlisted the help of the director of the Royal Colonial Institute of Amsterdam and it was decided to survey the area. The help of the British Guiana Survey Commission, which was organized by the PACPR, was requested,[44] but the State Department was uncertain whether the Wolf group had the support of the Dutch government. An inquiry soon revealed that the group was not backed by the Dutch authorities, and the PACPR hastily rejected the offer for a joint survey. Similarly, the PACPR rejected the offer to participate in a British survey of Northern Rhodesia.[45]

The State Department was also skeptical regarding resettlement possibilities in Bolivia. Its doubts were borne out in 1941, when the Bolivian legislature considered a resolution to prohibit "Jews, Mongols and Negroes" from entering the country.[46] For a time, the admission of refugees to Costa Rica was advocated by Leo Sach, the former American ambassador to that country, but his argument that resettlement would strengthen the security of the Panama Canal was hardly acceptable to the security-minded State Department, whose officials suspected refugees of being enemy agents.[47] The proposals for resettlement in Chile met a similar fate. The State Department feared that any discussion of the refugee issue in the Chilean parliament would excite "violent partisanship."[48] Chile, it must be recalled, possessed a sizable German minority and did not intend to declare war on the Axis.

There were several reasons why Latin America's largest and potentially wealthiest republic became the administration's major hope for resettlement. In contrast to Argentina, with whom the United States competed on the world market, Brazil had always been especially close to the United States. After the Evian conference, Helio Lobos, the Brazilian delegate, was offered the vice-chairmanship of the IGC in the vain hope that the honor would encourage the Brazilian authorities to open Brazil's vast interior to settlement.[49] Lobos, however, rarely attended the subsequent meetings of the IGC. Moreover, Brazil steadfastly resisted all attempts to induce her to accept refugees. When James McDonald and Guy Inman visited Latin America in 1935 to encourage a more liberal immigration policy, he found Brazil the best hope for refugee absorption and an "extremely hard nut to crack."[50]

That observation was borne out by the manner in which a remarkable offer by Henry Ford was handled. We first hear of Henry Ford's interest in the refugee problem in the crucial month of December 1938. After a meeting with Rabbi Leo Franklin in Dearborn, Ford, who had never bothered to halt fully the distribution of the *Protocols of the Elders of Zion* even after his public apology for his earlier anti-Semitic tirades in the *Dearborn Independent*, advocated the admission of Jewish refugees to the United States. He told reporters that although the Jewish workers in his plants did not as a rule stay long, he felt they possessed "special adaptability in the fields of production, distribution and agriculture." They demonstrated marked "ability and loyalty," and he would do everything in his power to encourage the Jewish back-to-the-land movement which he thought would solve all the world's problems.[51] This was quite a remarkable display from a man who was not known as a friend of the Jews and who had recently accepted a medal from the Nazi government.

In the interim, the PACPR had also begun to focus on Brazil. Isaiah Bowman, who had been retained by the committee, set to work examining the resettlement possibilities in various regions of Brazil. He had previously written that the climate, high cost of housing, scarcity of food, and primitive market conditions in the Amazon region would make it difficult to sustain colonies.[52] The intercession of Pope Pius XI, however, had softened the attitude of dictator Getulio Vargas toward non-Aryan Christians, and it was announced that three thousand such refugees would be resettled in St. Catharina, Minas Gerais, and Sao Paulo.[53] Perhaps a similar concession could be obtained for Jewish refugees?

In the early months of 1941, Ford again became involved in the refugee problem. McDonald received word regarding Ford's interest in using his plantations in Brazil for the resettlement of refugees, and he hastened to Dearborn to meet with the mogul. According to McDonald's version of the events—related in a confidential memorandum—it was a strange meeting. McDonald spent most of his time speaking to Harry Bennet, Ford's right-hand man. He was given a detailed description of Fordlandia, one of the larger plantations in the Amazon. McDonald experienced some difficulty in discerning the purpose of the Ford offer, which was never stated explicitly. Finally, Ford himself appeared; and McDonald, deciding to take the bull by the horns, described the problem and outlined a plan in which the Ford plantations would be used as the basis for large resettlement ventures. He proposed a large-scale settlement that would be established jointly by Brazil, the United States, and Ford. Ford momentarily showed interest when he heard of the possibility of dealing directly with governments but shortly thereafter returned to his favorite topic, the causes of the war and its relation to money power. "Nothing was settled definitely," but McDonald contacted the State Department to learn the official American position and to establish communications with the Vargas government.[54] Welles replied that the Ford offer was firm enough, but he also informed McDonald that the news from Brazil was not hopeful. Convinced that Jews would not be pioneers in the Amazon and afraid that they would pose "endless difficulties," the Brazilian government rejected Ford's offer.[55]

It was only natural that the Roosevelt administration would first focus on Latin America, just as the British naturally focused on their possessions in Africa. However, following the realization of the British Guiana scheme, about which more presently, an interesting reversal occurred. Roosevelt's enthusiasm appeared to grow the further away such projects were from the Western Hemisphere and London became firmly wedded to a scheme in Latin America.

The most intriguing of the administration's African schemes was the so-called big idea, which sometimes also bore the name of Bernard Baruch. Deceptively simple in its outline, the plan called for Jews to contribute a tithe of their resources so that $300,000,000 could be raised to establish the new republic. The nation would be carved out of a "sufficiently large" section of Kenya, Tanganyika, and Northern Rhodesia and would be open to all those who needed a haven. Baruch planned for the new nation to be "under the sovereign control of England" because England "will have nothing but a democratic government."[56] That Britain had an imperial claim on the territory may also have had some bearing on that decision. Once the new republic was established, Baruch envisaged 10,000,000 of "the strongest and most courageous people" resettling there to escape "from these over-regulated, goose stepping civilians of Russia, Germany and Italy."[57] Trouble was foreseen with the British, who would have to cope with the opposition of the British settlers already in the area. Moreover, it would serve as an alternative to the British Guiana scheme on which the Colonial Office had become fixated. "If

Mr. Chamberlain and Mr. Baldwin want to fully solve the problem, there it is," said Baruch.[58]

Lewis Strauss, who had helped enlist the support of his mentor, Herbert Hoover, for the project, was a little more realistic and understood how visionary such a proposal was. Nonetheless, he agreed with Baruch that mass immigration was a key to development of Africa and that it would be accompanied by an increase in world trade. Strauss believed that the project would act like a Keynesian pump primer as he was convinced that periods of prosperity were directly correlated with periods of immigration.[59] For Baruch, the important thing was not to confine the new state to Jews, as such a policy would be self-defeating. Samuel Rosenman, the president's speech writer, agreed. "It is no solution," he informed Roosevelt, "to create a world ghetto instead of many local ones."[60] The bubble of enthusiasm did not finally burst until Strauss broached the idea to Malcolm MacDonald and hit a stone wall.[61]

For a while, Roosevelt displayed keen interest in the establishment of an entire new nation with the help of American planning and Jewish largess. Thus, when Hamilton Fish Jr. was dispatched to investigate and enlist support for the idea, Roosevelt was annoyed that he had not been informed of the move. Fish, a Republican, represented Roosevelt's own Dutchess County district in the House of Representatives, and he served as a constant reminder to the president that he rarely carried his own district. During the campaign of 1940, Fish, who also headed the Interparliamentary Union, became part of Roosevelt's alliterative slogan "Martin, Barton, and Fish." No love was lost between the two. "I wish this great Pooh Bah would go back to Harvard and play tackle for the football team," Roosevelt wrote, "he is qualified for that job."[62]

Not everyone involved in the efforts to solve the refugee problem shared the administration's enthusiasm for large visionary schemes. Isaiah Bowman had earlier warned the administration that "talk of empty spaces in Africa and Latin America belongs to a species of thinking we call geopolitical" and was "fundamentally misleading."[63] The more Bowman examined these areas, the more convinced he became that Roosevelt had been taken in by a dangerous myth. By 1941, he had prepared several reports for the administration, the PACPR, and the Refugee Economic Corporation; and his team had participated in the preliminary surveys of British Guinea, Santo Domingo, and Mindanao. Bowman had also organized special field studies in Southwest Asia together with the Institute of Pacific Relations and in Australia and New Zealand. Surveys had been prepared, or were in preparation, for the former German colonies in Africa, as well as for Costa Rica, Lower California, Bolivia, Chile, Peru, Ecuador, and Columbia.[64] In short, the Bowman group was among the most experienced in the theoretical aspects of colonization. Although Bowman was generally pessimistic about the possibilities for large-scale resettlement, his assessment of specific areas showed considerable variation. Thus, for example, his opinion regarding Angola, on which the administration's attention focused momentarily, was relatively positive.[65] Portugal had successfully launched a colonization project of its own on the plateau, and Bowman felt that the area was "well suited to settlers of European stock."[66] Thus after London's rejection of the "United States of Africa" scheme, the plans for large-scale resettlement naturally moved to other areas. Angola had never belonged to Germany and so it did not offend Jewish sensibilities, nor did it interfere with Berlin's vision of someday repossessing her African territories.[67]

The administration's shift of focus from the British possessions to Angola can be attributed mostly to Sumner Welles. "The possibilities of Angola appear of such importance," he informed Roosevelt in January 1939, "as to warrant heroic efforts to overcome political obstacles."[68] One such obstacle was Antonio Salazar, the authoritarian prime minister of Portugal, who did not take kindly to the idea of foreigners establishing colonies in Angola. Moreover, Portugal had not been invited to the Evian conference and was therefore not a member of the IGC. A method would have to be found to court Lisbon. Because Britain was Portugal's traditional mentor, it was decided to approach London. A message was sent to Chamberlain that, among other things, mentioned the possibility of developing Angola as an alternative to Palestine. "I cannot emphasize too strongly," wrote Roosevelt, "the importance which I attach to the creation of a supplemental Jewish homeland as a step essential to the solution of the Jewish problem or my belief that Angola offers the most favorable facilities for its creation."[69] In Roosevelt's mind, Baruch's idea had become attached to another one so that the nondenominational character that Baruch desired was no longer present. Yet, the basic vision was still there. Roosevelt had simply dangled some bait before the British government, which was increasingly hard-pressed regarding its "inhumanly political" policy of restricting Jewish immigration into Palestine. "Even if the political difficulties could be overcome," Roosevelt confidentially informed

Chamberlain, "it is doubtful whether Palestine could absorb and maintain the necessary influx of population."[70] Salazar could be won over to the idea by the promise of increased prosperity and the prospect that "he would become the greatest figure in the history of his country and our time."[71] There were also some precedents for welcoming outsiders to Angola. The Boers had established a successful colony there in 1900, and the Jewish territorialists had given it serious consideration in 1912. When a group of German-Jewish pioneers inquired about settlement opportunities in 1931, however, they were discouraged by the authorities.

Neither the British nor the Portuguese were very enthusiastic about Roosevelt's proposal. Lord Herbert Emerson, chairman of the IGC, berated the idea as "utopian" and "unrealistic," and his assistant Earl Winterton, chided Myron Taylor about his "dream of Angola." Taylor was actually as opposed to the idea of a "new Palestine" in Angola as Winterton, but for different reasons. He had become convinced that most Jewish refugees wanted neither Palestine nor Angola as a haven but instead some established community where they could live out their lives in peace.[72]

Chamberlain, already near the end of his term, briskly rejected Roosevelt's inquiry about Angola, and suggested that the normal diplomatic channels be used. A second letter by Roosevelt emphasized that he considered the matter important and "that we have no intention of letting the matter drop,"[73] but it too was ignored by Whitehall. Private probings in Lisbon, however, were more successful. After five months of negotiations, Jacques Politis, a member of the French branch of the Rothschild family, obtained permission to purchase land and the unconditional acceptance of a limited numbers of refugees.[74] A representative of the Baruch-Bernard Ittleson- Julius Rosenwald group joined the survey team. Meanwhile, however, Roosevelt had become peeved at Baruch's premature leakage of the "Washington Secret." Late in 1939, therefore, official contact was established through Paul Van Zeeland, who was an old friend of Salazar. He cautioned the State Department "not to indulge in subterfuge when dealing with the Portuguese authorities."[75] As we have seen, Van Zeeland preferred the more practical, small-scale, self-sustaining projects. He need not have worried, however, because the war that broke out one month earlier put an effective end to the administration's grandiose schemes for creating a new America in Africa that might take the place of Palestine.

Interest in Angola, however, continued into 1943. Most persistent were Dr. M. Kirschberg and Rabbi Jacob Rosenheim. The former had been advocating settlement on the Angola plateau since the early thirties and continued to hope that the Nazi authorities would send camp inmates to settlements in West Africa.[76] The latter, a leader of Agudas Israel, informed McDonald in 1943 that his group had obtained the "sympathetic interest" of an important Portuguese cabinet official.[77] Nothing, however, ever came of the idea.

Italian-occupied Ethiopia served as a kind of counterpoint theme to Angola. It was apparently one of the many notions discussed at the Warm Springs conference that was attended by Ambassador Phillips. The Italian people for the most part never understood the animus against the Jews, nor did they wish to emulate the German example in this respect. Thus, one of the solutions proposed by the Fascist Grand Council was to resettle the Italian Jews in Italy's new colony. In this manner, two problems would be solved. Ethiopia would be settled by Italian subjects, and at the same time, Italy would be made *Judenrein* in keeping with the Nazi model. The only problem was that Italian Jews were reluctant to leave the homeland for the wilds of Ethiopia.[78] They were equally reluctant to resettle in Palestine, an alternative that the Mussolini regime also encouraged for a time.

As in the case of Salazar, the administration's approach to Mussolini was not successful. The dictator suggested that Brazil, Russia, or the vast interior of the United States offered better opportunities for the refugees.[79] As in the case of Angola, private individuals proved to be more persistent in their efforts than was the government. The most notable in this respect was a Dutch Protestant minister, Frank van Gildmeester, who entertained hopes of establishing the world's greatest Jewish city on the shores of Lake Tana. His group, the International Committee to Aid Jewish Refugees (ICA), however, was no more successful in convincing the Fascist government than was Ambassador Phillips. The resistance of Italian Jewry to resettlement, the unpopularity of settling in an "occupied" area, the lack of financing, and rumors concerning van Gildmeester's collaboration with the Gestapo put an end to the hopes of founding a great Jewish metropolis on Lake Tana.[80]

This plan was replaced by an even more visionary project—the idea of an autonomous Jewish republic in the province of Harar. In 1942, rumors circulated that Mussolini was willing to make this province part of an autonomous Jewish state, provided that British and French Somaliland contributed some territory to the province to make it viable. The scheme was denounced as a trap by the American Jewish Congress, but a "Harar Council for the Autonomous Jewish Province in Harar" was nevertheless established by Erwin Kraft.[81] Kraft, who was apparently a German refugee, had previously been involved in refugee schemes. One of his plans was connected with an organization by the name of The American *Kulturkampf* Association, which he founded in March 1939 to counteract Nazism.[82] Needless to say, he failed to realize any of his objectives.

Mussolini's reference to the interior of the United States as a suitable location for resettlement highlighted the embarrassing vulnerability of the Roosevelt administration. Roosevelt, unwilling to tangle with the restrictionists in Congress, had long since given up the notion of bringing masses of refugees directly to the United States, and that was the major reason for the search for resettlement havens elsewhere. The idea of bringing refugees to America, however, had never been totally abandoned by refugee enthusiasts. There was, moreover, a specific Jewish tradition of agricultural colonization in the United States. In 1825, for example, Mordecai Noah, the Tammany Sachem and prominent Jewish political leader, had organized the ill-starred Ararat scheme near Grand Island, Buffalo, where, he hoped, Jews would "be gathered from the four quarters of the globe . . . to resume their rank and character among the governments of the earth."[83] Earlier, an evangelistic preacher, W. D. Robinson, had come to the astounding conclusion that "Jewish towns and villages adorning the banks of the Mississippi and Missouri" would not only "ameliorate the unfortunate state of this class of human beings"[84] but would also be an asset to the development of the country. With the arrival of the East European Jews, several agricultural colonies were established with the help of the Baron de Hirsch Fund. Some were peopled with recruits from the *Am Olam* movement who, like the early *Biluim* of Zionist fame, were motivated by populist Tolstoyan back-to-the-soil notions. But the colonies that had been established in the Sicily Islands of Louisiana; Cremieux, South Dakota; New Odessa, Oregon; and Beersheba, Kansas, had failed within the first decade of their founding. A group of agricultural settlements had stubbornly clung to life in Southern New Jersey, aided by their proximity to Philadelphia. They were still operating in the thirties, albeit in a different form, and were asked to help out during the crisis. A training farm for German-Jewish refugees was established in the vicinity, and the infusion of refugee farmers helped give the colonies a new lease on life, as the newcomers played a role in the establishment of the lucrative poultry industry.[85]

The efforts to found Jewish agricultural settlements in the United States were continued by the Refugee Economic Corporation, which founded a new agricultural colony in Van Eden, North Carolina.[86] The massive resettlement schemes in the interior of the country, however, such as those suggested at one point by Paul Baerwald, chairman of JDC, could not be realized as long as the restrictive immigration laws were in effect.[87] For resettlement projects to succeed in the United States, a way had to be found to circumvent the law. The scheme to settle refugees in Alaska in 1940 did not succeed; but in 1944, when millions of European Jews had already been murdered, the laws were finally circumvented.

In June of that year, the administration implemented the "free ports" project, or as Roosevelt preferred to call it, temporary havens project. The concept of "free ports" was popularized by Samuel Grafton, a columnist for the *New York Post*, who ingeniously combined several elements from previously existing plans. "A free port," he wrote, "is a place where you can put things down for a while without having to make a final decision about them. . . . We do it for commercial cans of beans . . . it should not be impossible to do it for people."[88] The administration charged the War Relocation Authority with establishing a temporary haven at Fort Ontario, an obsolete army facility in Oswego, New York, and 983 refugees, of the "proper Jewish-Christian mix" were admitted outside the immigration quota on the condition that they would return to their homes after hostilities had ended. Strictly speaking, the temporary havens project was not a resettlement scheme. It simply stored people away for the duration. An earlier proposal to implement a similar scheme on the Virgin Islands, which had the support of Harold Ickes and Governor Lawrence Cramer, was bitterly opposed by Breckinridge Long, who viewed it as an attempt to sneak refugees, some of whom might be enemy agents, into American territory without subjecting them to the elaborate screening process that he had been instrumental in establishing.

The major attempt to alter the immigration law and thus enable the settlement of masses of refugees on American territory took place in 1940. In that year, refugee advocates combined with people from the Department of the Interior and others who sensed an opportunity to develop Alaska to put the administration's intentions to a major test. That Alaska would someday come to the attention of refugee advocates was a foregone conclusion. The territory possessed an estimated 100,000 square miles of unused arable lands and was inhabited by only 30,000 white settlers. It seemed like a "virgin empire" that badly needed population and development. Most important, its suitability for resettlement had already been tested by the administration itself. In 1935, the Federal Emergency Relief Administration had resettled some 170 families from drought-stricken areas in Michigan, Wisconsin, and Minnesota in the Matanuska valley in the Pacific coastal region of the territory. Three years later, the colonists, who had organized themselves into the Matanuska Valley Colonization Association, were producing a bumper crop. Not all Alaskans were happy about the colony; but in 1937, the Governor of Alaska, John W. Troys, called for "more colonies like Matanuska."[89]

The PACPR asked the administration about Alaska even before the Evian conference, but the results had been discouraging. George Brandt, then the State Department's liaison with the PACPR, informed its members that Alaska clearly fell within the purview of the immigration law, and any attempt to circumvent the quotas would surely backfire.[90] Brandt's reply was bad news for refugee enthusiasts because changing the law was considered to be virtually impossible. They reasoned, however, that Alaska was a special case because it clearly needed the refugees as much as the refugees needed it.

Interest in the territory was therefore maintained by refugee advocates. In August 1938, McDonald communicated with Carl L. Alsberg, the author of a new report on Alaska, and inquired about the absorption capacity of the territory. Perhaps the answer was infiltration rather than resettlement?[91] Private groups were also attracted by the possibilities in Alaska. One of the earliest of these seems to have been the Alaskan Resettlement Corporation for Refugees founded by Robert G. H. Tallman of Denver in early 1939. In his first mailing, he cited Alaska's Report for the Annual Fiscal Year (ended June 30, 1937) as proof that the territory needed additional inhabitants. Tallman, moreover, had a plan. He urged the issuance of special low-interest Refugee Colonization Bonds to finance resettlement. The immigration law would be amended to permit the entry of those immigrants accepted by the corporation after screening. Such an influx, he argued, would do a lot to stimulate the territory's sluggish economy as well as keeping "alive these aspirations and achievements of freedom and democracy."[92] The cry was next taken up by Democratic Congressman Charles Buckley, of a heavily Jewish district in the Bronx. To the chagrin of the State Department, he offered to introduce a measure for refugee settlement in Alaska.[93] The PACPR's interest in the idea also continued.[94]

Sometime early in the development of the idea to make Alaska a resettlement haven, Harold Ickes and Henry Wallace, the secretary of agriculture whose department could conceivably have contributed the know-how to make any resettlement project a going concern, were won over to the scheme. For a time, even the Army and Navy departments became interested because an empty Alaska posed a serious defense problem for them.[95] In August 1939, the Department of the Interior released a report entitled, "The Problem of Alaskan Development," written by Harry Slattery, the department's under-secretary. The major thrust of the report was that Alaska's development required people. Without an increase in population, the territory would remain an economic backwater indefinitely. Slattery considered the existence of refugees, many of whom were experienced businessmen with some capital behind them and an empty Alaska with a stagnating economy, nothing less than a divinely ordained confluence of circumstances that it would be sinful not to use. His plan for financing settlement, however, differed markedly from Tallman's. He called for the establishment of a federally chartered public-purpose corporation to develop the lumber, mineral, fur, and fishing industries. The primary concern was to develop the territory's economy and, in the process, help the refugees. Like Tallman, he envisaged a suitable modification of the quota system. Once refugees settled in Alaska, they would be compelled to remain there for five years, after which time they would have to go through the regular process to obtain a visa for the mainland.[96]

With the assistance of Felix Cohen, the department's assistant solicitor, the Alaskan Development bill, encompassing the major provisions of the Slattery report, was drawn up. In February 1940, H.R. 5971 was introduced in the House by Frank R. Havenner and S. 3577 by William H. King and Robert F. Wagner in the Senate. A special pressure group, the Alaskan Development Committee, headed by Erwin Klaus, busily organized public support for the measure. "The plan of developing Alaska," Klaus wrote to McDonald, "is in keeping with the American pioneering tradition and can be the answer of a democracy to totalitarian forces." In addition, he claimed to have the endorsement of 84.5 percent of the 340 newspapers who bothered to comment on the bill.[97]

Despite the public relations campaign and the firm support of the Department of the Interior, which had reissued the Slattery report in April, the chances of passage were not good. Much depended on an endorsement from the president. For a moment, it seemed as if such support might be forthcoming. The president was preparing a statement on refugees for the forthcoming meeting of the officers of the IGC, which at the president's insistence had been scheduled for October. Harold Ickes had forwarded a copy of the Slattery report to the White House with a strong recommendation for approval and a suggestion that it be placed before the IGC.[98] Both Sumner Welles and Cordell Hull reacted negatively to Ickes's suggestion, however, because they feared that it would stir up too much excitement and raise false hopes. Roosevelt wavered. "Do you think I should sign this?" he inquired of Welles.[99] The reply came back in no uncertain terms, as it had a year earlier to Buckley's untimely proposal.

Thus, precisely at the moment when Roosevelt addressed the officers of the IGC urging them to think in "grander" terms, he had a proposal in hand that, if passed by Congress, would have met all his requirements. He did not give the proposal his support. When the chips were down, Roosevelt reverted back to empty rhetoric regarding the postwar refugee problem and nation-building schemes in Africa, that were preferable because they involved no political risk and there was little chance of their ever being realized.

It should be noted that the president had more than a vague idea of what was involved. When Ickes met Roosevelt in November, the president seemed fully aware of the content of the Slattery report and even offered some interesting amendments. He would move 50,000 immigrants into Alaska over a five-year period. Half of the newcomers would be natives and the other half would be made up of aliens admitted outside the quota but whose nationalities would be in accordance with the quotas prescribed by the existing immigration law. To avoid the criticism that would surely arise "if there were an undue proportion of Jews," their percentage of the group should be limited to 10 percent.[100] Roosevelt had apparently not yet realized that the problem of those he insisted on labeling as "political refugees" was in fact a problem of unwanted Jews.

Despite the absence of administration support and opposition from domestic restrictionists and leading Alaskans, many of whom were convinced that the object of the King-Havenner bill was to "dump" unwanted Jews in Alaska, Ickes introduced the measure to Congress.[101] On May 13, 1940, hearings began before the Senate Committee on Territories and Insular Affairs. Harold Ickes led off with a strong statement in favor of the bill. He was followed by some of the proposal's prominent supporters, such as Clarence Pickett, executive secretary of the AFSC, Vihljalmur Stefanson, the Arctic explorer, Alvin Johnson, director of the New School for Social Research, and Frank Bohn, a noted authority on land settlement. Only three witnesses testified against the bill.

Behind the scenes, however, opposition to the King-Havenner bill was gathering force. It emanated not only from the still-powerful restrictionist element in Congress, which considered the measure little more than an ill-concealed attempt to bring refugees into the country "by the back door," but also from some of Alaska's leading political figures, such as Anthony J. Dimond, the territory's congressional delegate, Ernest Gruening, director of the department of the interior's division of territories, and Don Carlos, the major of Seward, Alaska. Their arguments ran the gamut from skepticism regarding the financial aspects to the suspicion that refugee advocates were using the notion of Alaskan development as a screen to conceal their real objective, which was to find a haven for refugees. In order to refute this charge, the King-Havenner bill stipulated that at least 50 percent of any new jobs created would be given to American citizens. These stipulations, however, were ignored by those opposed to the measure, and the King-Havenner bill was never reported out of committee.

In January 1941, Congressman Samuel Dickstein disinterred the measure, emphasizing his favorite gambit, the use of the unused places in the quotas of the previous six years. For good measure, he also stressed the security factor involved in populating Alaska. Again, the same forces of opposition were aroused, and the measure never reached the floor of Congress.

In contrast to the King-Havenner bill, the plan to resettle refugees in the Philippines was not opposed by the restrictionists. Under the provision of the Tydings-McDuffie Law, the Philippines had become virtually a self-governing commonwealth in November 1935 and was to be completely independent after a ten-year transition period. The government of the island, led by Manuel Quezon, could decide for itself whether it would accept refugees. For that reason, the proposal to establish a resettlement colony on the island of Mindanao seemed more likely to succeed and was supported by the administration.

The idea of resettlement on Mindanao, which was proposed by

refugee enthusiasts in mid-1938, was not new. The Philippine authorities, aware of the deteriorating situation in the Pacific, had been concerned about the composition of the population of that island and considered colonizing it with its own citizens. (In 1937, it was estimated that about 14,000 Japanese resided on the island. Most lived in the province of Davao, where they dominated the hemp-growing industry.) From $8,000,000 to $10,000,000 had been earmarked for public improvements on the island.

Thus, REC officials were positively impressed when they established contact with Philippine government officials in November 1938.[102] Philip Frieder, a merchant who did business in the Philippines, met with Quezon, and the president spoke of the possibility of absorbing millions of refugees and of his government's willingness to sell land on very reasonable terms. Quezon had requested that the REC delegation wait until the matter could be communicated to the State Department. The delegates' enthusiasm knew no bounds, and they were convinced that they had found the answer to the refugee problem. "If this plan goes over," Frieder wrote to his brother, " . . . it will be a bigger project than Palestine. The land is more fertile than Palestine, there are more minerals, timber—as a matter of fact, it is the richest land in the Philippines—virgin soil. This is such an enormous proposition that one can hardly visualize potentialities of same." Frieder was already thinking of a Hoover dam "which can supply electricity and current for all of Mindanao." At the same time, he was a little worried and asked Quezon why the area had not been more thickly settled.[103]

In fact, other refugee enthusiasts had discovered the island before the REC. In August, Paul V. McNutt, the American commissioner, had received an inquiry from the State Department regarding the possibility of settling two hundred refugee families. After a hasty survey, McNutt optimistically reported back to Welles that ten times that number could be absorbed and possibly an additional 5,000 families could be resettled at a latter date.[104]

The refugee agencies were quite excited at the new development. The details of a large-scale resettlement project were being planned by McNutt and Quezon.[105] It was believed that a settlement of 30,000 Caucasian refugees on Mindanao would go far to counteract the Japanese threat to the island. When the final plans became known, however, the enthusiasm waned. The Philippine offer was actually carefully circumscribed and left many unanswered questions. The first contingent of refugees would be limited to 1,000, barely enough to make a dent in the refugee problem. Also, the economic prospects, which had appeared so rosy, were now uncertain. In order not to compete with domestic producers of staples, who had only limited access to the American market, the settlers would not be allowed to raise sugar, hemp, or coconuts. A committee of the Filipino legislature had recommended that the settlers limit their crops to rubber, citrus fruit, and vegetables. In effect, the settlement would be limited to sustenance farming, which meant that the settlement could never become financially independent. How could a large settlement with virtually no hope of ever showing a profit be financed? George Warren desperately tried to redeem the situation by suggesting that the settlement be based on small industry rather than agriculture,[106] but that suggestion was considered impractical.

Nevertheless, the REC, acting jointly with the PACPR, made plans to send a survey commission to Mindanao. By now, the State Department was far more reserved about the plan, and the planners were cautioned not to publicize the offer, lest the market price of land rise and domestic opposition be aroused. Moreover, Emilio Aguinaldo, the venerable independence fighter, had already spoken of the need to resettle Filipinos rather than alien refugees.[107] Meanwhile, a remarkably optimistic report had been prepared by Isaiah Bowman. "Mindanao," the report began, "seems to offer sufficient possibilities to guarantee a successful future for selected groups of European settlers."[108] In July, an optimistic report on Mindanao, the second largest island in the Philippine archipelago, was in the hands of the State Department. The commission had seen two tracts of arable land that they believed were suitable for colonization, but one required an access road that would cost an estimated $400,000. A more likely site, one that was accessible by national highway, was located on the Bukednon plateau. This area, however, was under private grazing and agricultural leases that had twenty-five years to run and had an option for renewal.[109] The optimistic reports regarding Mindanao's emptiness now appeared in a different light. True, the island had only 1,265,000 inhabitants in 1935 and only 6 percent of the land of any province was under cultivation, but these lands were in the most accessible areas of the island. The final report of the survey commission, issued one month after the outbreak of war, recommended the leasing of 100,000 acres in the Bukednon area for an eventual settlement of 100,000 refugees. It also prescribed noncompetitive crops to be grown for the home market.[110] The State

Department, anxious to publicize an "American" solution to the refugee problem, prepared to transmit the news to the IGC in London.

The director of the project would be Charles J. Liebman, the well-known agricultural expert who worked with both the REC and Agro-Joint, while the actual on-the-spot control of the project would be in the hands of Stanton Youngberry. Within a few months, a program for selecting and retraining refugees was initiated. Several Jewish refugees who had found a precarious haven in Shanghai had already requested to join the settlement,[111] and care was taken to maintain good relations with the Philippine authorities. When Mc-Donald expressed greater hope for the resettlement scheme in Santo Domingo, he received an exasperated communication from Liebman cautioning that such statements might offend Quezon and endanger the project.[112]

Unaware of the fate awaiting the Jews of Europe, those in charge of the project developed it at an excruciatingly slow pace, which made it virtually impossible to rescue Jewish refugees while there was still time. The survey had taken an inordinately long time to complete, and the selection and retraining of refugees, the clearing of the sight, and the building of houses took even longer. The location of the Philippines caused transportation and communications problems, and not until the spring of 1941 was the site ready for the absorption of the refugees. By then, however, it had become extremely difficult to get them out of occupied Europe. And almost before the project could get underway, the islands were occupied by the Japanese.

We turn next to two schemes that claimed much of the Roosevelt administration's limited energy for refugee rescue. They are the projects for settlement in British Guiana and Santo Domingo.

There is some reason to believe that the idea for resettlement in British Guiana began in the deep recesses of the British Foreign Office, where there was a concern, not so much about the fate of the Jewish refugees, but about muting the outcry regarding the restriction of Jewish immigration to Palestine. British Guiana was first officially mentioned as a possible resettlement site by Chamberlain in a speech before the House of Commons on November 21, 1938. The scheme offered the advantage of being located in the Western Hemisphere rather than in Africa, where settlers had already made known their opposition to plans to resettle Jewish refugees.

The PACPR was asked to participate in a survey of the area to locate a likely site. At the same time, Robert Pell and Theodore Achilles of the State Department were apprised of developments within the government by Anthony de Rothschild, whose role on the British scene was similar to that of James McDonald. They, in turn, transmitted the information to the PACPR with a strong recommendation that it participate in the venture. It was advice that the State Department would have cause to regret. Much of the preliminary planning for the mixed survey commission was done by Joseph Rosen and E. C. Bataille of the Jewish Colonization Association and Mortimer Kahn, an anthropologist associated with the Cornell Medical Center. Kahn had made nine previous trips to the Guiana highlands, which it was believed offered the best prospects for resettlement.

From the outset, the selection of the members of the commission was controversial because the members of the Jewish Colonization Association who participated on the commission were considered to be unobjective regarding settlement possibilities.[113] The PACPR itself came into possession of previous surveys whose findings were mixed. Sir Alfred Sherlock, who participated in the British survey conducted in 1927 as part of the preparations for the settlement of Assyrians, did not believe, "owing to the nearness of the equator," that white men could inhabit the area. Sir Geoffrey Ebans and a Brigadier General Browne concurred with that report, especially as it concerned commercial viability: "[Settlers] might scrape along on a bare existence. There is no market whatever for their products and there are no means of communication." The report concluded by stating that "any money which was spent in this country for this purpose would be better spent elsewhere."[114] In addition, the resettlement of 20,000 Assyrians by the League of Nations had been a dismal failure.

British enthusiasm for the British Guiana scheme, it should be noted, was not unanimous. In December 1938, there was a minor controversy over the technical feasability of the project in the pages of the London *Times*. A letter by a former settler, who had lived in the colony for twenty years, challenged virtually every affirmative assertion made by another former settler, L. H. T. Ashburner. "Why think of British Guiana," asked the reader, "when there are millions of acres in Canada and Australia crying out for settlers."[115] It was the same question many Jewish refugee advocates were asking.

More bad news came from the preliminary reports composed by Isaiah Bowman and Mortimer Kahn,[116] both of whom emphatically rejected the British Guiana scheme. Bowman pointed out that not only had the Assyrian settlement failed but so had numerous other ventures in similar areas. Bush-yaws, yellow fever, and other tropical diseases would surely decimate the ranks of any group of settlers in short order. Settlement, he argued, might indeed occur anywhere, but supporting such a venture would be expensive. Settlement in the hinterland of British Guiana "would be like a city in the South Pole. Civilization could maintain it, but the cost would be prohibitive."[117]

Despite such reservations, the PACPR proceeded with the organization of the commission, aware that the entire project would be damaged if Britain were to drop out as she threatened to do.[118] On January 31, 1939, it issued a press release announcing the names of the members of the survey commission that would leave for Georgetown on February 8 and remain there for three months. In other words, the commission's trip coincided with the crucial negotiations about to take place in London regarding the formation of the Coordinating Foundation, the agency that was to be established, upon Berlin's request, to bail out German Jewry. The announcement of the names of the members of the survey commission, especially that of Joseph Rosen, whose association with territorialism made him anathema to Zionists like Stephen Wise, created difficulties. Even Bowman agreed "that it would be rather easy to forecast what he [Rosen] would say on Palestine or British Guiana."[119] Wise also expressed the "profoundest doubts" about British Guiana and linked it to the White Paper about which he was "heartsick."[120]

Yet, the urgency of having some resettlement project on the road before Robert Pell returned to Berlin to continue negotiations could hardly be denied. "The essential point remains," wrote Anthony de Rothschild, "that for political and other reasons we must take the necessary steps to get some schemes working if only on an experimental scale."[121] In addition, the Rothschild group was being pressured by the colonial secretary, Malcolm MacDonald, who had told them that there was no alternative to British Guiana.

Despite pressure from the upper echelons of the British government, the realization of the project never seems to have proceeded smoothly. In April, on the occasion of the publication of a preliminary report by Rosen, controversy broke out anew. His primary argument, one that previewed the final report, was that Guiana was the best that could be expected. As far as the actual possibilities of resettlement, he avoided committing himself. "It does not require any extensive investigation to readily concede that British Guiana is not by any means an ideal country for large-scale settlement," read the introductory sentence of the preliminary report.[122] He acknowledged that there were soil, climatic, transportation, and potential racial problems. Nonetheless, there were no "good" areas, and the problem of refugee rescue was so urgent that the mere political availability of Guiana was, according to Rosen, a strong point in its favor. "The problem reduces itself," he concluded, "to a consideration as to whether British Guiana, in spite of the obvious disadvantages, offers any feasible potential possibilities for development of refugee settlement on a suitable scale."[123] Rosen also noted that the project would be expensive, and he estimated that it would cost $1,500 to $2,000 to resettle each family or approximately $3,000,000 to resettle 5,000 people.[124]

The final report, which was made public in May, faithfully reflected Rosen's reasoning. The territory "would not be considered suitable for *immediate* large-scale settlement," but the potential of British Guiana justified a "trial settlement."[125] Rosen defended the report against its detractors.[126] The health and sanitary conditions, "provide no insurmountable problems," he told members of the PACPR.[127] Prospects for the success of a trial settlement were also good. The main thing was to begin work and keep in mind the urgency of the refugee problem. Not everyone agreed with Rosen's appraisal however. Bowman, for example, pointed out that the trial settlement would not be an experiment at all, but an "artificially sustained enterprise." "I am bound to say," read the last sentence of his response to the commission's report, "that I think the money that is proposed to invest in such a trial settlement could be better expended in other places."[128] It was an argument Bowman and others had made many times before.

Such controversy, however, hardly put a crimp in the plans of the British authorities. They were determined more than ever to wrap things up in a neat package. The British Guiana scheme was firmly linked in their minds to the Coordinating Foundation. On May 12, 1939, Prime Minister Neville Chamberlain appeared before Parliament to announce his government's formal acceptance of the British Guiana report. The government would slightly expand the land offer and encourage inquiries into the possibilities of industrial development. In addition, it would provide the necessary arterial communication between the coast and the interior provided adequate private capital was forthcoming to make the venture a success.

Once that occurred, the government would grant the colonists a measure of autonomy, although they would not, of course, control such matters as revenue, customs, and security.[129]

All these concessions would be granted providing that the funding came from other sources—the private, primarily Jewish, refugee and self-help agencies, such as the JDC, or the American government. This was the key to the problem. The leaders of the JDC hesitated to support the Coordinating Foundation and opposed linking it with the British Guiana scheme. Thus, there was no response to Anthony de Rothschild's urgent pleas to raise large sums of money. Wealthy Jews like Baerwald, Ittleson, Jaretzki, Felix Warburg, and others were not the only ones opposed to the British maneuvering. The State Department was chagrined at the diplomatic coup that enabled the British to exploit the refugee crisis in order to get money from private American sources for the development of a remote area of the British Empire by means of a project that simultaneously earned them headlines for their humanitarian efforts on behalf of refugees, pushing the news of the White Paper into the background.[130]

The British tactics did not work, however, particularly because their success was dependent on Jewish funds. The leaders of the JDC had long since become convinced that the task of resettling thousands, and eventually perhaps millions, of refugees could not be achieved solely by private philanthropy. Also, when the British linked the plans for British Guiana to the Coordinating Foundation, it automatically earned the animosity of those elements in the Jewish community who opposed having any dealings with Berlin regarding the "ransom" of German Jewry, such as the American Jewish Congress, the Jewish Labor Committee, and the boycott committees. Abba Hillel Silver, chairman of the United Palestine Appeal, cut off his organization's subsidy to the PACPR and was firmly opposed to contributing to the Coordinating Foundation. When he was told of the less militant attitude of Stephen Wise, Silver asserted that "Rabbi Wise does not represent the Zionists on the President's Committee . . . [and] nothing Rabbi Wise said or promised binds anyone else."[131] A member of the PACPR concluded that "Dr. Silver's attitude is in part at least explained by a conflict of personalities and organizational politics."[132]

The supporters of the anti-Nazi boycott adamantly opposed the transfer plan to which the British Guiana scheme had become attached. Angered by the fact that no one had bothered to find out how the Jews felt about the plan, Joseph Tenenbaum, a leader of the boycott movement, pointed out that London had "closed the only remaining haven in Palestine and substituted for it the wilds of British Guiana, which at best, could only accommodate 5,000 Jews in the next few years at considerable cost and sacrifice."[133] The paramount problem, argued Tenenbaum, "is not how to get the Jews out of Germany, but where to settle them."[134] British Guiana was certainly not the answer. The German transfer proposal, in which Rublee and Pell had placed so much confidence, was in reality "a preposterous scheme of extortion." The statement was made in July, and war was but a few weeks away.[135]

That was the state of affairs when Helmut Wohltat, Schacht's successor at the talks, arrived in London, ostensibly to attend a conference on whaling. The American leadership had not been able to decide on their support of the Coordinating Foundation and certainly not its link to the British Guiana scheme. They also had various objections concerning organization and funding. Wohltat, however, evinced no interest in the question of organization or resettlement, which he considered to be the business of the "outside Jews." He simply wanted to know if sufficient capital to convince the führer was involved.[136] If not, there was no point in talking. Sensing that an opportunity was slipping away, the British Foreign Office and, to some extent, the Roosevelt administration, showed signs of impatience at the reluctance of the Jews to participate. As Herbert Emerson described it, "The trouble with the whole refugee affair was the trouble of the Jews and most eastern people. There was always some other scheme in the background for which they were prepared to sacrifice schemes which were already in hand."[137] Threats to withdraw the offer of British Guiana began to be heard from Whitehall.[138]

The JDC finally succumbed and agreed to finance its share of the cost, but the linkage of British Guiana to the establishment of the Coordinating Foundation continued to pose problems. Joseph Tenenbaum and Adolph Held, chairman of the Jewish Labor Committee, asserted that the Rublee plan was not the answer to the burning question of the day. "Where will the immigrants supposedly helped by the Rublee plan go?"[139] Held urged the JDC to reverse its decision on funding the Coordinating Foundation. Caught betwixt and between, the JDC leadership decided to stall, and requested that the agreement be altered to make the Coordinating Foundation appear as a secretariat rather than the agency that would provide capital for the transfer of goods.[140] When Lewis Strauss cabled from London that the $500,000 appropriated was inadequate, he received the following cable in reply: "JDC AS YOU KNOW UNDER ATTACK FOR FINANCING NEW CORPORATION STOP BESIDES PALESTINIAN FRIENDS ALWAYS SUSPICIOUS GUIANA SCHEME."[141]

The French authorities were, if anything, even more adamantly opposed to the participation of French Jews in financing the Coordinating Foundation. Henry Bérenger at one point threatened to resign from the IGC if the negotiations with the Germans continued. "The French Jews were not stupit little fish," he explained excitedly, "Robert de Rothschild was not a stupit little fish. Mr. Taylor could have his trap. He could put his head in it." He, Bérenger, would not permit the "gaunt prophet" (Rublee) and the "romantic acolyte" (Pell) whose "fonction" was "apparently to go to Berlin every week or so and salute Hitler's, or is it Goering's behind," to seduce French Jewry.[142]

Nevertheless, the JDC decided that it could not permit such a rescue opportunity to slip by, and it would therefore go ahead with plans for a trial settlement of 250 refugees. A complex financing arrangement was thereupon worked out whereby funds left over from the colonization ventures of Agro-Joint in the Soviet Union would be added to the funds in ICA's possession. Also, if the Czech fund was added to the contribution of the British and French groups, there would be sufficient capital at least to start the project. In addition, the British promised at the last moment to make some funds available under "certain conditions."[143] Roosevelt's invitation to the officers of the IGC to meet with him in Washington convinced some British officials that a major American-sponsored breakthrough, perhaps an offer of a haven in Alaska, perhaps the promise of matching funds for resettlement, was imminent. Strauss suggested that it was time to seek the help of powerful congressional leaders, such as Senators William Borah, Lyndon Johnson, and Gerald P. Nye.[144] The decision was taken on July 20, 1939. War was barely six weeks away.

When the war did break out, the plans that had taken over one year to prepare were radically changed at one stroke. The Roosevelt administration began to move toward more stringent visa regulations, and the British withdrew their offer of reasonable provisions for land title and financial assistance in British Guiana. The matter of resettlement havens was thrown back to the private refugee and Jewish self-help agencies, who had previously demonstrated that the solution of the refugee problem was beyond their resources. For a time, momentum carried them forward. They continued to select young Jews who had the potential to become pioneers, but the necessary support of the governments was now directed elsewhere. Britain and France were preoccupied with their own survival, and Roosevelt chose to take off on a visionary excursion of nation building in a territory he never bothered to mention. Soon, other victims would feel Hitler's lash and compete with the refugees for a share of world concern.

In 1938 and 1939, the Roosevelt administration became involved with dozens of resettlement schemes only one of which, the Dominican Republic project, bore some fruit. The project presents an opportunity to examine what might have been had resettlement been undertaken earlier. Moreover, the failure of other projects to get underway tended to focus more attention on Santo Domingo than the project really deserved.

The first we hear of resettlement in Santo Dimingo was at the Evian conference in July 1938, where the idea was mentioned, albeit informally, as a prospect. Early in August, the proposal was officially confirmed by President Rafael Trujillo, and the subject was discussed on several occasions by the PACPR. In December, after due consultation with the State Department, the PACPR sent Alfred Houston to meet with Trujillo. He took a letter of introduction from Sumner Welles, who wielded considerable influence in the Caribbean republics, but this did not mean that the department was enthusiastic about Trujillo's largess. It had reservations about resettling German-Jewish refugees in the Caribbean and was skeptical about Trujillo's claim that 100,000 could be absorbed by the tiny republic.

After several interviews with the dictator, Houston attained confirmation of the offer and details regarding the admission of the refugees. Trujillo promised to provide public land as well as some of his own private estate to settle as many as 100,000 refugees. There would also be no entrance fees for the refugees. It all seemed too good to be true. Trujillo mentioned only one indispensable requirement. "Refugees may be of any race or religious belief, provided they are of Caucasian races, namely white."[145] For Jews escaping the Nazis, conditions of this sort might have seemed a refreshing change. We shall presently see, however, that this racial requirement had an irony all its own.

Once again, a survey commission was formed. Information on

markets, soil, and types of agriculture had to be gathered before-hand. The task fell primarily to James N. Rosenberg, chairman of Agro-Joint. Soon, however, there was disturbing news from Paris. Dominican Republic authorities had extended a similar offer to 1,000 Czech refugees, and Spanish refugees from southern France had also been contacted. It looked as if the tiny republic would become a "dumping ground" rather than a haven for refugees.

In March, the survey commission, which included Atherton Lee, director of the Agriculture Department's experimental station in Puerto Rico, and B. Washburn, a public health expert, examined the proposed site. Predictably, their report was favorable. Sosua, the area surveyed, was part of Trujillo's personal estate and consisted of 26,000 acres of good land in the northern part of the island east of Puerto Plata.

The State Department, however, which was reluctant to have refugees settled in the Caribbean owing to its concern about the po-litical stability of the island republics, began earnestly to urge cau-tion.[146] The matter of publicity was particularly problematic. On the one hand, it might raise the price of land and offend others, such as Quezon, who had also made offers. On the other hand, as time went on, it became apparent that the Dominican scheme would be the only project that the administration could adduce to prove its good intentions. Sosua became for the Roosevelt administration what British Guiana was for London—evidence of its efforts on be-half of the refugees. Moreover, the Americans soon discovered that the project could serve other purposes as well. Thus, it was continu-ously cited by the State Department in answer to Pell's urgent re-quests that he be given some concrete evidence that resettlement was a reality so that he could conclude his negotiations in Berlin. When Roosevelt addressed the officers of the IGC in Washington, he again made reference to the project. He hoped it would be "the fore-runner of many similar projects in other countries."[147] One year later, Robert Pell again communicated with George Warren regarding the delicate matter of publicity. He was informed that Rosenberg had retained Rebecca Reyer for public relations purposes. Her press re-leases soon appeared in the Herald Tribune, Daily Mirror and Jewish Telegraphic Agency Bulletin, and a special booklet on the project was prepared.[148] Pell soon felt that a saturation point had been reached: "The trouble now is," he informed McDonald, "as a consequence of the arrival of Spanish refugees in that country, that we are having too much publicity."[149]

As in other projects, the actual process of resettling the refugees was painfully slow. The Dominican Republic Resettlement Association, Inc. (DORSA) was not established until January 1940. It was incorporated in New York State under the directorship of James N. Rosenberg, and the occasion of the incorporation served as an opportunity to focus public attention on the project. The officers of DORSA as well as some IGC and State Department officials appeared on the island to celebrate the signing of the contract between DORSA and the government of the Dominican Republic. The colony's charter guaranteed the settlers' full economic and civil rights, and the corporation was granted a tax exemption. Two months later, the first sizable contingent of a proposed total of five hundred settlers arrived on the island. It would take sometime for the colony's complement of settlers to be filled. The figure of 100,000 refugees had long since been abandoned.

Almost from the beginning, the settlement was plagued with unpredicted troubles. As a result of the entrance of Italy into the war in June 1940, a group of settlers from that country was unable to reach the Dominican Republic. And after the initial publicity, the administration showed almost no interest in the colony. When McDonald requested a congratulatory telegram for the celebration of the colony's first anniversary in January 1941,[150] Welles rejected the idea as such a message "might possibly appear to be more than was required to indicate our abiding interest in the project."[151] Also, the idea of creating a model refugee project in the Dominican Republic that other Latin American states might emulate did not materialize. Instead, the republics firmly closed their doors to Jewish refugees. Fortunately, they chose not to examine the results of the Sosua experiment too closely. Had they done so, they might have discovered that the results of a major expenditure of time, effort, and money were meager indeed.

The colony became enmeshed in internal problems and in the administration's security psychosis. A confidential FBI report found in the State Department archives describes the refugees as "allergic to work" which, according to the observer, was being performed by the natives while the refugees lounged half-naked in shorts. The report also suggested that the Jewish refugees were signaling and feeding German submarine crews operating in the Caribbean.[152] Social problems among the settlers also plagued the project. One could be retrained to do agricultural work, but retraining for collective living was another story. The internal harmony in the colony was sometimes wrecked by intense personal animosities. Meanwhile, leadership and administrative problems compounded Sosua's difficulties, and financial support for the project began to fail.[153] It was apparent that the project would not develop beyond its first phase. In January 1943, one Jewish journal expressed doubt whether the project would survive.[154] What ultimately happened to the family life of those Central Europeans thrown willy-nilly into a Caribbean ambience that featured a far less rigid sexual code would make an interesting theme for a dozen novels. DORSA apparently fulfilled only Trujillo's goal.

With this admittedly incomplete survey as background, we are ready to seek a preliminary and necessarily tentative answer to a key problem in Holocaust research: Was resettlement ever a viable rescue alternative? The question is crucial, especially if one accepts the notion, as I do, that the Final Solution was not presaged in the historical development of Nazism. In other words, there was a period between 1938 and mid-1941 when the possibility of resettling the Jews of Europe might have served, even for the Nazis, as an alternative to mass murder.

One is bound to say at the outset that had Alaska, Mindanao, British Guiana, Sosua, and the dozens of other projects mentioned here been able to get underway rapidly, thousands, perhaps millions of Jews, and especially those in Western Europe, might have survived the Holocaust. The projects were not started quickly enough because they required inordinate will, energy, and financial resources, none of which were available to the rescue advocates who thought in terms of resettlement. That more could have been rescued in this way is only theoretically true, just as it is theoretically true that more Jews might have been saved had the railroad system of Europe broken down. In practice, there was very little chance of ever realizing the resettlement schemes.

Two separate sets of problems were involved in the resettlement projects. One stemmed from the resettlement process itself and from those who were involved in it; the other concerned those nations-states who sought to use it for their own purposes. We have seen that beyond the term of resettlement, which refers only to the movement of people, there existed a series of technical problems that had to be solved before a settlement could actually be founded. One could not simply remove people of all ages and backgrounds to some remote corner of the world and hope that they would thrive. The quality of the soil, climate, transportation, market conditions, access to markets, and other problems had to be examined by experts. In the case of British Guiana, climate and accessibility were crucial factors on which the experts found it difficult to agree. This was also the case in Mindanao, where the government was willing to extend generous terms, except that it denied the colony the all-important right of producing for the commercial market. By limiting the settlement to sustenance farming, all the other assets were cancelled out, and the colony was relegated to economic limbo.

When the hope of profit vanished, so too did the hope of raising the funds necessary to finance the projects. Financing, we have seen, could not be provided by private philanthropy alone, and there was precious little opportunity to obtain funds from governments who were either at war or did not feel any responsibility toward a minority of another nation's citizens. Considering the conditions of the world markets in 1939, it seems highly unlikely that such resettlement schemes could ever have loosened the purse strings of private investors. Without commercial viability, the settlements would have become little more than warehouses to store unwanted people for the duration. Now, one can argue that at least in that way they could have remained alive and that it was rescue after all, not profit, that was the key consideration. As it developed, however, the creation of such projects depended in the long run not on humanitarian sentiments, of which there were precious few in the world of the thirties, but on the promise of returns on capital investments. Had it been possible to guarantee a profit and harness the forces of the market, resettlement havens might have materialized more rapidly and in greater numbers.

The alternative was somehow to compel the nations to accept responsibility for supporting the refugees. In view of the British White Paper and the Roosevelt administration's attitude toward resettlement in Alaska, that was hardly likely to happen. Nonetheless, some great philanthropic effort might have enlisted the sympathy of the smaller nations. In this respect, Roosevelt's visionary scheme was in reality far more practical than those of such professionals as Rosen, James N. Rosenberg, Liebman, and Van Zeeland. He understood at an early stage that the dream of small, commercially profitable settlements envisaged by the planners of the Coordinating Foundation was chimerical. It was not big enough to attract international sympathy, nor was it a significant step toward solving the refugee problem. Moreover, the projects were far too expensive. In 1938, the Jewish Agency, one of the most experienced colonizers, estimated that it cost £1,200 to resettle one family,[155] and other estimates were approximately the same. The Coordinating Foundation thought in terms of $10,000 per family, and an estimate to settle three hundred settlers in British Guiana came to $3,000,000.[156] The lowest estimate came from Waley Cohen, who, as was mentioned earlier, was a member of a British group interested in settlement in Ecuador. He estimated £52 per person, but that did not include the cost of transportation.[157] The matter of financing was of crucial importance because it was common knowledge that a primary cause for the failure of resettlement schemes was a lack of funds. Yet, even if Roosevelt had not been so visionary in proposing large-scale resettlement, there was a more serious criticism that one might level against him. He was never able to produce an area where such a large-scale resettlement project might be realized.

Chaim Weizmann once noted with chagrin that, of all the territories being considered, "none could be found in the temperate zone."[158] Climate, however, was a primary consideration, not only in terms of what geographers called "biological optimums" but also in terms of soil and other factors.[159] Thus, Bowman's argument that British Guiana's "political availability is not going to change the climate" had a great deal of truth to it.[160] Joseph Rosen's effort to defend the scheme by arguing that Jews, as a Mediterranean people, were "apt to acclimatize under tropical conditions more easily than others," was no answer at all when one considers that Jews, having resided in Europe for millennia, possessed no built-in talent for pioneering in the tropics.[161]

The demographic and social profile of those who had to be resettled militated against colonization anywhere. Having no agricultural tradition to speak of, the Jewish population of Europe was perhaps least suited for resettlement in agricultural colonies. Thus, for example, 73.7 percent of the German Jews, the primary candidates for resettlement, were over forty. In fact, had the Nazis waited a few generations, the Reich would have been practically *Judenrein* by the turn of the century owing to the low birthrate, natural attrition, and high intermarriage rate among German Jews. Only 1.7 percent were employed in agriculture, whereas a whopping 52.5 percent were involved in trade and commerce.[162] Moreover, the high degree of urbanization intensified during the Weimar period as the sources of livelihood in the smaller towns and villages were liquidated. Almost one-third of German Jewry and one-half of the Jews in Prussia lived in Berlin. The Jewish communities in the provincial capitals, Breslau, Cologne, and Frankfurt, also grew apace.[163] In addition, the most qualified candidates for colonization had, in many cases, already immigrated to Palestine.

To be successful, pioneering required zeal, optimism, willingness to uproot oneself, and physical stamina. These are attributes possessed by youth and idealists; they must come from within. The Pilgrims, the Mormons, the *chalutzim*, and the settlers of Birobidzhan and the Crimea, all had a sense of mission generated by an ideology. They willingly assumed the challenge of colonization. The story is quite different when resettlement is imposed on a group, when it is a reflection of their impotence. Average Jewish refugees could muster little enthusiasm for any of the resettlement schemes. They merely wanted to survive in a world that gave no quarter. After years of observing the refugee chaos, Myron Taylor became convinced that what the Jewish refugees really wanted was "to get into settled countries where they can set up their lives in existing communities . . . in commercial and industrial activities."[164] Undoubtedly, that accounted for the "drift back" phenomenon in Latin America. Refugees admitted as farmers soon moved to the cities, where they competed with the indigenous merchants. According to Brazil's chief of immigration, Jewish refugees were not admitted because of "their unwillingness to [follow] a pioneering life."[165] Two years later, when the Henry Ford offer came up for consideration, that view had not changed. "It is the view of the Brazilian government," stated Welles, "that such refugees would not remain in the Amazon region and in these unsettled times the Brazilian government would, consequently have 'endless difficulty' with them."[166]

The attitude of the Brazilian authorities was dictated by something more than anti-Semitism. Isaiah Bowman made a similar observation. "The migrant in 1937 wants civilization to follow him because the homeland is comparatively rich and safe in contrast to the meagerness and limited security of life on the frontier."[167] Nonetheless, anti-Semitism was certainly an important factor, and it at least partially accounts for the failure of the various resettlement projects. Thus, for example, the "endless difficulties" foreseen in Brazil were apparently confined to Jewish settlers. Brazil's attitude toward non-Aryan Christians, who were allowed to infiltrate by the thousands, was obviously entirely different.[168] They were preferred by the Brazilian authorities, just as the American Congress preferred non-Jewish British children to Jewish refugee children from France. The same held true of Mexico and Ecuador, which preferred uprooted Catholics to Jewish merchants and professionals. The latter were anathema on two counts—they were Jewish and they were merchants. In practice, however, the economic profile of baptized Jews was not very different than that of those who had not converted.

The anti-Jewish sentiment in Latin America was first evidenced at the Evian conference. Francisco Calderon, the delegate from Peru, had not "forgotten the teachings of Nietzsche, that Jewish influence, like leaven or ferment, is of value to all nations." Peru, however, had quite enough ferment, and her immigration laws, like those of her northern neighbor, were designed to protect the racial composition of the nation.[169] Most of the Latin American republics followed a similar pattern. When Stephen Wise and Nahum Goldmann planned a trip to Latin America in the final months of 1940 for the purpose of mobilizing the local Jewish communities for the difficult tasks that lay ahead, they were cautioned by Adolf A. Berle, then an assistant secretary of state and later to become ambassador to Brazil, that their activities "might energize the anti-Semitic feelings" of the natives.[170] The anti-Jewish sentiment was particularly strong in Mexico, where the Federation of Mexican Farmers urged stricter immigration laws against Jews because "almost all of them came in under false pretenses and did not engage in work as they promised. They have all become merchants and gangsters."[171] Also, if Jewish refugees could not be classified as "merchants or gangsters," then subversives would do as well. That was a common assumption of Latin American security agencies. Mexico, after all, was the only major Latin American republic actively to support Loyalist Spain. Paradoxically, when Jewish refugees were not accused of being Communists by their unwilling Latin American hosts, they were being accused of harboring spies by the American security agencies and the State Department. In Latin America, some of the regimes, such as that of Getulio Vargas in Brazil, had taken to mimicking the rhetoric of the "wave of the future" emanating from the Continent. They were aided in this endeavor by the pro-Nazi ethnic Germans who lived in Brazil, Bolivia, Argentina, and Chile.

Anti-Semitism, it should be noted, was not confined to the receiving nations of Latin America. The government of the Union of South Africa was naturally reluctant to admit refugees because they might disturb the country's apartheid pattern of development.[172] In British Guiana, according to Joseph Rosen, the variation on the racial theme was unique. There blacks were "outspokenly in favor of Jewish immigration, because they were convinced that it would raise their living standards, but their Indian neighbors were far less so inclined and the white planter class of the interior, like their peers in Rhodesia, Kenya, and Tanganyika, could muster very little enthusiasm for the admission of Jewish refugees."[173]

Most ironic was the fact that the same Jews who were expelled from the Reich because of their religion were desired elsewhere because they were white. It is one of the bizarre aspects of the Holocaust that the Jews who went to the Dominican Republic to escape one racist gehenna were able to do so only because Trujillo was convinced that their blood was desirable to improve the indigenous breed.

The Trujillo regime was not the only government that was interested in resettlement for ulterior motives. The same was true of the United States and Great Britain. By linking the British Guiana scheme to the Coordinating Foundation, Whitehall was able with one stroke to pass the responsibility for further action to private organizations and thus, simultaneously, to relieve the public pressure generated by the White Paper. At the same time, the British Colonial Office could look forward to having Jewish capital and human resources develop a particularly remote and hopeless outpost of the British Empire. The scheme was perfect. Its advantages did not escape C. G. Vickers, a partner in the London law firm retained by Lewis Strauss to draw up the charter for the Coordinating Foundation. "It will be ironic," he wrote to Harold Lucas, "if we succeed in developing the Empire with Polish Jews, having failed to do so with Englishmen."[174] British Guiana, however, was mostly intended to deflect pressure from the British Government. DORSA came to play a similar role for the Roosevelt administration. In fact, it was mentioned endlessly as evidence of what might be done, even after it had become evident that Sosua was not a particularly successful venture.

One of the primary reasons why resettlement never became a practical hope for rescue was that several years were required before any refugees could actually be settled. One had to wait for offers to materialize, then a suitable site had to be selected by a survey commission that examined the feasibility of settlement by checking such factors as the soil, market conditions, and health facilities. Next, a contract had to be signed with the local government. After that was done, prospective pioneers had to be selected and retrained so that they could be farmers. Only then was the group transported to the site, where they were housed and fed until the settlement became self-sustaining. Often, roads had to be built and financial arrangements negotiated. There were a myriad of details that had to be resolved before resettlement on any scale could occur. The case of Mindanao is a good illustration of this lengthy process. The idea materialized in mid-1938, but settlers were not actually ready to begin colonization until three years later. Roughly the same amount of time was necessary in Sosua and British Guiana. Events, of course, did not await feasibility studies. The outbreak of war in September 1939 caught most of these ventures only halfway completed. It interfered with transportation and the selection of pioneers and especially with financing. Most important, it focused the attention of governments on their own well-being. After September 1939, official enthusiasm for resettlement diminished considerably.

The question might be asked why the projects were not implemented with greater urgency. Why the process was not speeded up? One ought to recall that, between 1938 and 1941, few were aware of the consequences of failure. The relationship between the German concept of resettlement and annihilation was not fathomed by those involved in resettlement, just as it was not understood by the victims themselves. The credibility factor, the inability to believe that Hitler meant to kill all the Jews, plagued not only the victims but also their would-be rescuers.

Aside from the Zionists, who were unenthusiastic about resettlement for their own reasons, only one person consistently reminded the administration and rescue advocates of the futility of thinking in terms of mass resettlement. Few people, however, could allow themselves to hear the voice of Isaiah Bowman because to accept the notion that there were simply no longer any empty spaces in the world where one could embark on grandiose nation-building schemes meant giving up a good part of the rescue effort. There were few alternatives. Bowman had warned in the introduction to his work *Limits of Land Settlement* that "new land will accommodate too slow and small a stream of civilization to be of real importance."[175] Pioneering had changed radically since the great age of colonization in the seventeenth, eighteenth, and nineteenth centuries. At that time, settlement was voluntary rather than coerced; and most pioneers, convicts and indentured servants excepted, were convinced that a better life awaited them in the New World. Although they were often disappointed, and commercial factors often joined together with idealistic ones, there was sufficient motivation for settlers to move to the colonies of their own volition. Moreover, these pioneers came from countries where the economy and society were based on agriculture. By the 1930s, however, there had been a considerable change. Society had become urbanized, and even agriculture was well on the road to being commercialized. It required retraining to teach the would-be pioneers what their ancestors knew as a matter of course. It also required management ability and a knowledge of marketing, which were relatively new variables in colonization. Emigrants in previous centuries were bound for lands that, in terms of soil quality and climate, offered better conditions than those of the homeland. That has hardly true in the thirties, when resettlement sites were frequently located in underdeveloped lands in torrid climates.

Yet, it is possible to entertain some doubt regarding Bowman's pessimistic prognosis, which was primarily based on physical factors and ignored ideological ones. The most successful resettlement venture of the late nineteenth and twentieth centuries, the Jewish settlement in Palestine, was, after all, achieved by practically the same human material, or an East European variation thereof. The Jewish pioneers in Palestine faced incredible difficulties in regard to the soil and climate, not to mention the unsympathetic attitude of governments and the hostility of the native population. Nonetheless, a nation-state was established with the kibbutz settlements serving as one of the pillars of the new society. "If one wills it," said Theodor Herzl, "it is no legend." Had there been a will and a sense of urgency, many of Bowman's reservations might have been overcome in time. We have seen, however, that that was far from being the case.

Might an infusion of Zionist pioneering skill and zeal have made resettlement more feasible? The situation is stated eloquently by George Backer, a JDC official who appealed for a more active rescue effort at the Bermuda conference. He claimed that "the general feeling was that the Zionists had sabotaged efforts to find other places for Jews." "They thought," according to Backer, "that if there were pressure on America, and by Americans on Britain the doors of Palestine would be opened. But they were naïve in this. If the Zionists had helped in leadership," Backer asserted, "perhaps tens of thousands would have been saved." "It is horrible to think," he concluded, "how responsible we were for all that happened. The ships were there and the people were not saved."[176]

Backer's accusation, like many indictments made in retrospect, contains just enough truth to make it appear reasonable. Its underlying assumption that Zionist zeal and resources were transferrable was mistaken, however. Zionism was, after all, organically focused on Palestine as Zion, not on British Guiana, which was, in effect, a competing venture. It was only natural that the Zionist movement regarded such substitutes with ambivalence.

By 1930, the Zionist movement, helped by the crisis, had captured the center stage of world Jewry. Nonetheless, we have seen how London and Washington gave the old Zangwillian territorialism, Zionism without Zion, a new lease on life. Roosevelt's idea of a "supplemental national home" and the outlines of the British Guiana scheme bore a remarkable resemblance to the old vision of the territorialists. In fact, the signs of territorial revival were to be found everywhere during the thirties. Not only did dozens of groups (such as the group of Austrian veterans and the Daniel Wolf group in The Hague), spring up as a result of the crisis but in 1935 the Freeland League for Jewish Territorial Organization, a successor to ITO (Jewish Territorial Organization) was founded in Poland. In 1938, the International Jewish Colonization Society, an umbrella organization, came into being. These organizations supplemented existing groups, such as the Refugee Economic Corporation and Agro-Joint, which had sponsored colonizing ventures in Argentina, Russia, and other areas. Whereas territorialism seemed to be infused with new energy, the Zionist enterprise became hopelessly enmeshed in big power politics, and it was never able to acknowledge that the movement did not possess the political leverage necessary to extricate itself.

In 1939, to acknowledge the fact that London could at one blow compromise a movement that had taken decades of agonizing effort to build up would have constituted a breach of faith. Such a course of action was not permissible after most Jews had finally become convinced that Palestine was the necessary solution. Zionists were compelled to reason that if refugees were barred from entering Palestine as a result of a political decision, then that decision would have to be undone politically. Thus, the primary thrust of Zionist agitation during the war was to have the White Paper revoked and to establish the Jewish state. For actual rescue, an underground network, called *Aliyah Bet*, was established.[177]

Several American Zionist leaders in fact shifted their position on resettlement once the extent of the catastrophe became known. When Tanganyika was considered early in the crisis, Rabbi Stephen Wise's reaction was purely emotional: "I would rather than my fellow Jews die in Germany than live somehow, anyhow, in the lands which bear the imprint of yesterday's occupation by Germany, in lands which may tomorrow be yielded back . . . to Germany."[178] This statement was made, however, in November 1938, when few were able to fathom the fact that the alternative was in fact death. Later, Wise could not muster much enthusiasm for the Alaska scheme or the temporary-haven idea. As a Zionist, he found it difficult to transfer his allegiance to schemes that offered so little hope of fulfillment. Nonetheless, he never directly opposed such ventures when they held out promise of rescue. As early as 1937, he appeared willing to settle for Kenya and Uganda. "Being a Semite," he wrote to his friend Pesach Rosenblatt, "I would be willing to do a little bargaining with Britain."[179] Again, when the question of partition came to the fore in 1938, he wrote, "If we must have a limited Palestine [then give the Jews] some additional English colony."[180] The abrogation of the White Paper and the establishment of a commonwealth remained uppermost in his mind, but in 1943 he urged that the Allies prepare "temporary refuge and even permanent asylum" for those who may not wish to return to the lands of "famine and slaughter" after the war.[181]

Although Abba Hillel Silver would not appropriate a penny for the Coordinating Foundation lest Palestine "get the short end of the bargain" and even cut off the PACPR, by 1943 he had somewhat altered his attitude. At the Bermuda conference, held in April of that year, the World Jewish Congress came preciously close to advocating resettlement when it suggested setting aside "uncultivated areas . . . with a view toward agricultural settlement."[182] It should also be noted that not all Zionists opposed separating the rescue issue from that of the White Paper and the establishment of a Jewish state. The Revisionist group, headed by Peter Bergson (Hillel Kook) and active in the United States, counseled early that the goals of rescue and statehood were working at cross purposes and ought to be separated. As early as May 1942, the *Jewish Forum*, an Anglo-Jewish monthly, argued that it would be "folly to think of establishing 100,000 Jews a year in Palestine and ignore the crying needs of millions of other Jews."[183] In June, the magazine sponsored a discussion on "Palestine and Auxiliary Immigration Stations." The idea of resettlement never gained the wholehearted support of the Zionists, but as we have seen, neither did it win the support of most of the Jewish community or even of those who were candidates for resettlement. During the years under consideration, most Jews did not succeed in reconciling themselves to the injustice that had befallen the Jewish people. Resettlement seemed to compound the felony.

It has been argued that the resettlement alternative might have proven more effective as a rescue alternative had suitable areas been offered. There was a great deal of bitter truth in Weizmann's observation that "the world is divided into two groups of nations—those that want to expel the Jews and those that do not want to receive them."[184] Had a proper offer been made and been backed by the powers, the situation might have been different. But no such offer materialized, although many likely places were mentioned. The most promising areas—Alaska, Angola, Kenya, or Northern Rhodesia—were rejected by the powers. Had resettlement havens been developed in these countries, thousands of Jews might have been rescued.

In summation, one conclusion seems compelling. Many more Jews might have been saved had resettlement been pursued energetically in the period between 1938 and 1941, but the concept lacked whatever was necessary to generate the enthusiasm and passion needed to ensure its success. During this period, resettlement was imposed by one group upon another. In such cases, resettlement more than likely constitutes a form of community dissolution. That was certainly true of the Nazi concept of *Umsiedlung*. When carried out in the West, the idea of tucking away a despised minority in some tropical wilderness was only slightly less lethal.

7

The American Effort to
Save the Jews of Hungary

WITHIN THE TRAGEDY that was the destruction of the Jews of Europe, there is a special chapter, more poignant and perhaps more keenly felt. After almost having survived to witness the downfall of the architects of the Final Solution, Hungarian Jewry was at the last moment forced to share the fate of other Jewish communities. President Roosevelt gave some indication that he finally understood the tragedy of the Holocaust when he warned, shortly before the ghettoization program in Hungary, that it would be a "major tragedy" if "these innocent people, who have already survived a decade of Hitler's fury should perish on the very eve of triumph over the barbarians."[1] The efforts of the Roosevelt administration notwithstanding, the major portion of Hungarian Jewry did perish in the final agonizing moments of the war. Examination of the circumstances of that rescue failure is the subject of this chapter.

New Deal Holocaust Posture

Until January 1944, the concern of the Roosevelt administration about the Holocaust was minimal and lacked credibility. There were always officials like Harold Ickes, secretary of the interior; Henry Morgenthau, secretary of the treasury; Sumner Welles, under secretary of state; Francis Biddle, solicitor general; and others in the mid-

This essay appeared originally in *Hungarian Jewish Studies*, ed. Randolph Braham (New York: World Federation of Hungarian Jews, 1969), 211–59, under the title "The Roosevelt Administration and the Effort to Save the Jews of Hungary."

dle echelons of the administration, who knew precisely what was happening and were profoundly concerned. The rescue question, in fact, was an integral part of the series of issues that sparked often bitter animosities within the administration. In the absence of a certain mandate by the president, actual rescue policy was determined by the struggle between those who favored and those who opposed a more active rescue policy. Thus, the periodic announcements from the White House that the visa procedure had been liberalized were effectively canceled at the consular level where, by a quirk in the immigration law, the final decision on an application for a visa was made. That the quotas were consistently underissued despite the dire emergency was owing to the well-known reluctance of many of these consuls to make visas available to Jewish refugees.

It was probably the influence of rescue advocates like Dorothy Parker that led Roosevelt to take the unexpected step of calling a special conference on refugees in March 1938.[2] Subsequent events proved that here, too, those opposed to rescue were easily able to neutralize this effort. The Intergovernmental Committee on Political Refugees that was created at the Evian conference was ineffective from the moment of its inception. Eventually, the State Department's assistant secretary in charge of the special problems division, Breckinridge Long, attempted to use the defunct agency to assuage the growing agitation that swept the American Jewish community in 1943.[3] An agency designed to help refugees was used ultimately to confuse and clutter the rescue effort.

At least part of the reason for the irresoluteness of the early rescue effort could be traced to the strictures of the immigration law. Although Roosevelt's instinct to do the humanitarian thing might impulsively have led him to call an emergency refugee conference, a no-less-keen political sense soon made him wary of the political price entailed in trying to circumvent the immigration law. Senator Robert Reynolds, a North Carolina Democrat, spared no effort in keeping the administration properly attuned to restrictionist sensibilities in Congress.

A similar inconstancy could be discerned in the effort to rescue refugees prominent in the arts, sciences, and politics. At the time of the Evian initiative, the president also created a quasi-official advisory committee to help in coordinating the efforts of the several private organizations involved in refugee work. The committee soon served as a conduit between the private organizations and the State Department in compiling lists of prominent refugees for special visa

consideration. By mid-1941, Long, by arguing that Berlin had infiltrated the refugee stream with agents, was able to bring this program to an almost complete halt. Thereafter, the security gambit was
used effectively in all cases involving the rescue of refugees and was
eventually to play a key role in closing the doors of Latin America.
Moreover, until 1944, the State Department insisted on the use of
the euphemism "political refugees," when it was apparent that the
thrust of Nazi genocide was aimed primarily at Jews. Nor was a
distinction between normal immigrants and refugees ever made in
administering the immigration law. Small wonder Goebbels was
convinced that Washington and London looked with favor on the
Final Solution.[4]

Mass resettlement, a prospect for mass rescue, did not fare
much better in the hands of the administration. Official policy maintained throughout the crisis that Palestine was within the British
sphere of interest with which the administration could not interfere.
Instead, a search for alternate "supplemental national homes" was
begun. One such scheme, generated by Bernard Baruch, came to be
known within the administration as the "big idea." The scheme, a
virtual reenactment of America's colonial experience, envisaged the
establishment of a "United States of Africa," where all the unwanted
people of the world could be safely tucked away. The sincere belief
in the pertinence of the American experience to the refugee problem
and perhaps, too, his love for things geographical may account for
Roosevelt's being completely captivated by the idea. The more visionary the resettlement scheme, the more the president was likely
to favor it. He would rebuke Paul Van Zeeland, former prime minister of Belgium and director of the official agency concerned with
finding resettlement havens, for not thinking big enough. "This is
not the time," insisted Roosevelt, "to speak of small settlement . . .
the picture should be in terms of a million square miles occupied by
a coordinated self-sustaining civilization . . . overall planning on an
enormous scale is essential."[5] But in fact, there was little that could
be planned for because the only tangible offer that was made was by
the dictator of the Dominican Republic, Rafael Trujillo. It was on a
parcel of land donated by the dictator located in the northern part of
the island east of Puerto Plata that the Sosua experiment in resettlement was eventually undertaken. It was virtually the only such experiment to get off the ground.

The unavailability of suitable areas did not dampen the president's enthusiasm for a solution of the refugee-rescue problem by

mass resettlement. This remained true even after his principal advisor on resettlement, Isaiah Bowman, the most prominent geographer in the nation, repeatedly cautioned that the idea of tucking a troublesome minority away in some remote area was no longer possible in the twentieth century.[6] The administration's visionary search brought contact with strange bedfellows like Salazar and Mussolini, who insisted on pressing embarrassing questions concerning the vast interior of the United States. The republics of Latin America, on whose land area the Roosevelt administration focused first, were also never able to fathom how a request for such areas could be made of them while Washington kept its own gates tightly shut. The administration's rejection of resettlement in population-starved Alaska and the Virgin Islands, both of which were pushed by Harold Ickes, did not pass unnoticed.

After Pearl Harbor such rescue activity as existed came almost to a halt. Soon a "curtain of silence" hid the fate of Europe's Jews from public notice. It was precisely at this juncture that Berlin chose to begin its Final Solution of the Jewish question in earnest. It was only after the war that the public learned that at least part of the eerie silence in the West was owing to a deliberate policy of suppressing confirmed reports of the actual operation of the Final Solution.[7] But despite the State Department's attempt to silence Leland Harrison, the American minister in Bern who was the conduit for the first eyewitness reports of the genocide operation, the enormity of the operation soon led to its discovery.

In the early months of 1943, enough evidence on the extent of the catastrophe had accumulated to make some form of public reaction, especially among American Jews, inevitable. On March 1, 1943, public agitation culminated in a giant rally that filled New York's Madison Square Garden to overflowing. Held under the slogan "Stop Hitler Now," the sponsors demanded an entirely new rescue policy, including a special government agency with the specific mission of rescuing Hitler's victims. The no-less-intense agitation that swept British Jewry forced the British Foreign Office to make some kind of response that took the form of arranging for a new conference on refugees. The State Department reluctantly went along with London's transparent scheme to head off the agitation before more decisive steps might have to be taken.

In April, a second refugee conference was held on the inaccessible island of Bermuda, which was from the outset a fiasco for London and Washington. Choosing to grapple with the problem of refugees rather than the far more urgent problem of rescue, the conferees turned down virtually all the suggestions made by the advocates of a more active rescue policy. Viewing the Bermuda conference as a thinly veiled subterfuge, the rescue advocates intensified their agitation for action. The Emergency Committee to Save the Jewish People of Europe, the name finally settled on by a new organization on the fringes of organized American Jewry, demonstrated a special flair for publicity. It publicized its "action not pity" campaign with full-page ads in popular newspapers, and through its liaison in Congress, succeeded in having introduced in both houses special rescue resolutions that recognized not only the specific anti-Jewish character of the Nazi genocide program but openly suggested that the time had come to organize a new rescue agency that might negotiate with the enemy where lives could be won without impeding the war effort.

The resolutions set off a series of events that changed the direction of the flagging rescue effort. The testimony of Breckinridge Long at the hearings of the House Foreign Affairs Committee proved enough to identify him finally as the source of much of the administration's stalling. Containing errors on the number of refugees admitted and fabrications on the possibilities of negotiating with Berlin under his own operation, the testimony was used as a lever by rescue advocates to remove Long from the rescue operation and to create change within the administration. The instrument used to achieve that change was Henry Morgenthau, whose special file carefully documenting the deliberate sabotage of the rescue effort by the State Department was now delivered to President Roosevelt, whose regard for the State Department was so low that he did not need much prodding to create a new rescue agency. To what extent Roosevelt used the State Department as a foil to absorb rancor that might otherwise have been directed at the White House is difficult to determine. There can be little doubt that the State Department played this role in the rescue operation and that Roosevelt gave up this shield only when it was no longer useful.

The War Refugee Board

On January 22, 1944, the president issued Executive Order 9417, which established the War Refugee Board. Included in the order were many of the features requested by the rescue advocates. The special anti-Jewish character of the Final Solution was recognized, and the new agency was given special powers to cut through the labyrinth of red tape with which the Department of State strangled the rescue effort. The director would report directly to the president and was given the power to negotiate with the enemy through intermediaries when lives could be won without impeding the war effort. Although legally the board was a joint venture of the State, War, and Treasury departments, in practice it was almost exclusively a Treasury department operation. Its director, John Pehle, and much of the staff were drawn from the group of bright young men whom Morgenthau had gathered around himself. The effort to breathe new life into the dormant rescue operation began almost immediately. The increasingly ominous news from Hungary promised that it would be the area where the new agency's mettle would be tested.

Reasons for the Survival of Hungarian Jewry

The survival of Hungarian Jewry in the heart of Nazi Europe may be attributed to the proprietary interest that Budapest maintained toward "its" Jews. It jealously guarded its sovereign right to handle its "Jewish problem," and its position as a cobelligerent rather than an occupied area or satellite gave Miklós Horthy the legal leverage needed to thwart the designs of Berlin. That did not mean that Hungary cherished its Jews. When Budapest's version of the Nuremberg laws were put into effect, they proved in some instances to be harsher than those of the Reich. Nor was its guardianship extended to Jews inhabiting the newly acquired areas. There, thousands of Jews were unceremoniously pushed into Nazi-occupied territories in eastern Poland, where they subsequently perished.

As it became apparent to Berlin that the war was lost, the existence of nearly one million Jews in the heart of Europe was a source of unending frustration. "They mark out Jewry as a more dangerous and greater enemy than any other adversary,"[8] observed Döme Sztójay, then Hungary's ambassador in Berlin and hardly a friend of the Jews. It seemed as if Berlin were turning with a special vengeance to wrest a final victory from the one "enemy" it could still master. The Final Solution in Hungary was to have the highest priority. Nowhere were the deportations to be fiercer and more swiftly executed and with less concern about the sensibilities of world public opinion.

The Complexity of Rescue in Hungary

On the surface at least, the prospects for rescuing the Jews of Hungary seemed good. The back of Nazi power was broken in 1944, and there existed in Romania and Yugoslavia two fairly accessible escape routes. More important still was the posture of the rescue advocates. By 1944, the rescue agents, neutral nations, the International Red Cross, the Vatican, and the private rescue organizations appeared ready to follow the United States, whose organization of the WRB signaled a call for more energetic efforts at rescue.

But when the crisis was upon them, these circumstances played almost no part. The speed with which Eichmann was able to establish the destruction apparatus outpaced the ability of the rescue agencies to act. The deterioration of the position of Hungarian Jewry was signaled in mid-March 1944 by a tightening of reins on Budapest. On March 21, 1944, the Eichmann *Sondereinsatzkommando* made its debut in Hungary. The private rescue agencies, which under the new scheme were able to work closely with the WRB, urged that Hungarian Jewry be warned to destroy all community lists, avoid special registration, and the wearing of the telltale yellow star.[9] The suggestions, made primarily by the World Jewish Congress, embodied a wisdom learned at a dear price in the Netherlands, Poland, and elsewhere. Such steps inevitably preceded actual concentration and deportation. Although such suggestions could be made from abroad, the actual power to coerce the Jews was in the hands of Eichmann, who was able to organize the Jewish Council in record-breaking time. In Hungary, as elsewhere, the council became an instrument in organizing the Jews for deportation.

The lack of a physical presence on the scene was a major roadblock that was only partially solved by the WRB request to enlarge diplomatic missions in Budapest. Nor could one physically extricate Hungarian Jewry. Even if it were possible to get some out, as would later be the case, the problem of where to put them was no closer to solution in 1944 than in 1939, when German Jewry found itself in a similar position. The failure to find a resettlement continued to plague the rescue effort.

It was these circumstances that forced the WRB to fashion a strategy designed to secure the safety of the Jews in Hungary itself. They would attempt to encourage the people of Hungary to dissociate themselves from the operation of the Final Solution in Hungary. If the Hungarian populace and government did not cooperate, the implementation of the Final Solution would become infinitely more difficult.[10]

A steady stream of appeals to humanitarian instincts and threats of retribution against those who cooperated were beamed at

Hungary. Knowledge that the Hungarian government was aware which way the winds of victory were blowing made John Pehle and his group perhaps overoptimistic about the success of such a strategy. Early in March, Budapest and several other satellites were cautioned that "any continuation of these policies of Hitlerite persecution is viewed with great seriousness by this government and will be kept in mind." A second warning was given at the end of March.[11] It was hoped that Hungarian officialdom might, by this means, be cajoled into noncooperation. Such hopes, it was soon discovered, were based on illusion.

The WRB also succeeded in involving the president personally in the campaign to change attitudes. Pehle and Morgenthau had spared no effort to keep him well informed on the developments in Hungary as well as the growing dissatisfaction felt by many toward his administration's handling of the catastrophe.[12] On March 24, their efforts were crowned with success. The president, whose prestige was at an all-time high, abandoned hope that London would join in a statement and issued a ringing declaration on the situation of Hungarian Jewry. Hoping to fill the void left by the failure of the Moscow Declaration on War Crimes (November 1943) even to mention crimes against Jews, he appealed to Hungarians not to cooperate with the deportation program, to give succor to the Jews where possible, and above all, to "record the evidence" so that justice could eventually be done.[13] Neutral nations were urged to open their doors to refugees, and the likelihood of compliance was buttressed by a clear promise that America would "find the means of maintenance and support until the tyrant is driven from their homelands."[14] It was the first clue that a change was impending in the administration's policy toward the admission of refugees. It was the apprehension that they would be stuck with large numbers of refugees for which they would have to foot the bill for maintenance that played havoc with the infiltration possibilities in Spain, Portugal, and Switzerland. Now the president's promise would help keep these doors open.

The Office of War Information (OWI), heretofore strangely silent on the matter of the Final Solution, gave the president's appeal the widest circulation. No such change of heart could be detected in London, where official policy remained for the time adamantly opposed to such emotional declarations. Only a noticeable intensification of public agitation and an open appeal from Washington finally caused Eden to succumb and issue a similar declaration.

Enlisting the Aid of the International Red Cross
and the Vatican

More distressing than London's attitude was the reluctance of the International Red Cross to become involved in a matter that it viewed not in its "traditional and conventional competence."[15] Not until the crisis was several months old did a Red Cross emissary appear in Budapest and then only after urgent appeals by Pehle.[16] There was no suggestion of the important role it would play in the final months of 1944 in this early period.

The efforts to enlist the aid of the Holy See by the WRB were considerably more complex. An attempt had been made in the earliest phase of the Holocaust by sending Myron Taylor, former president of US Steel, to the Vatican as the president's personal emissary in December 1939. Roosevelt, always a supremely good salesman, took the political risk involved because he was convinced that the major difficulty in the refugee and related resettlement problem was the failure to dramatize their humanitarian aspects properly. He confided to Hull that he hoped to "place the whole refugee problem on a broad religious basis, thereby making it possible to gain the kind of worldwide support that a mere Jewish relief setup could not evoke."[17] But despite Roosevelt's special effort, the Vatican proved wary of being formally drawn into the rescue operation.[18] Thus, Pehle's renewed effort could not be viewed hopefully. Nevertheless, an approach was made through the apostolic delegate in Washington in which it was tactfully suggested that "His Holiness may find it appropriate to express himself on this subject."[19] Together with pressure from other neutrals, such tactics eventually succeeded in wringing a statement on atrocities in Hungary and Slovakia from the Vatican. But such statements were kept general and could therefore have little effect. Concrete rescue activity, when it occurred, was sponsored by individual bishops rather than the official church. What was true of Cardinal Roncalli, later Pope John XXIII, in Ankara or Cardinal Van Roey in Belgium was true to some extent of Cardinal Serédi in Hungary. When the first deportations began in mid-May, Cardinal Serédi, apprehensive about the number of converts and mixed marriages in his flock, addressed a mild note of concern to the authorities but hastened to assure them that he was not doing so from a "false sense of compassion."[20] Many Hungarian Jews were saved by the possession of baptismal certificates, but the church had precious little influence in convincing its flock, especially those in key government positions, not to cooperate with the deportation procedure. Raoul Wallenberg, a member of the Swedish diplomatic mission and a key rescue figure in Budapest, observed that "eighty percent of Hungary's metropolitan population are quite unmoved."[21]

Neither the International Red Cross nor the Holy See nor the Catholic hierarchy in Hungary were ever able to muster a determination and enthusiasm for saving lives that could compare favorably with Eichmann's determination to take them.

The Deportations and the Cry for Bombing

Eichmann's design of the deportation procedure reflected a diabolic shrewdness learned from special experience. He would begin with the newly annexed areas closest to the advancing Soviet army and save Budapest for last, thus avoiding any great "crisis of conscience" among Hungarian officialdom when it came to deportations from Hungary proper. Hungarian gendarmes cooperated fully, and with their help the deportations were carried out so quickly that the kommandant of Auschwitz, Rudolf Hess, rushed to Budapest to complain personally to Eichmann about the severe overburdening of the crematoria facilities.[22] The WRB was also outpaced by the fast-moving operation.

As the news of the deportations reached American shores, feelings of despair shook the entire community of rescue advocates. Patrick Malin, the executive secretary of the IGC, reflected sadly that "there is almost nothing one can do . . . it is a terrible and brutal fact."[23] But others turned to bombing as the answer. "Hungary," cried one Jewish weekly, "must be taught a lesson similar to Berlin."[24] Such demands, increasingly voiced since March 1943, were given fresh impetus during the crisis by a request from within Hungary, relayed through Bratislava to Bern, for precision bombing of key agency locations involved in the Final Solution and rail junctions on the line to Auschwitz.[25] It was hoped that such bombing might slow down the deportations. Moreover, there was growing evidence that fear of such raids was manifest in all satellite capitals. On June 28, 1944, for example, the Bulgarian minister in Ankara parroted the Goebbels line on the barbarism of the bombings but added parenthetically that some compliance with the rescue effort might ensue after the bombing was halted.[26] The dread of bombing was especially prevalent in Budapest, where the interception of the request for bombing message from Bratislava triggered the series of events that led to the countermanding of the deportation order by Horthy. The Budapest regime literally frightened itself to death after several isolated raids on the capital at the end of June. Ironically, Pehle was unable to get the army to see the need for such bombing.[27] The reply of John J. McCloy, assistant secretary of war, is perhaps one of the most tragic documents to come out of the Holocaust:

> Such an operation could be executed only by the diversion of considerable air support essential to the success of our forces now engaged in decisive operations elsewhere and would in any case be of such doubtful efficacy that it would not warrant the use of our resources. There has been considerable opinion to the effect that such an effort, even if practicable, might provoke more vindictive action by the Germans.[28]

What possible "more vindictive action" than Auschwitz remained the secret of the War Department. There can be little doubt today that such bombing would have succeeded at least in opening up the whole question of the Final Solution to public scrutiny. As it was, the question was barely touched during the war. The fear of an escalation of terror, an old standby excuse often used by the administration for its inaction, made even less sense in 1944, when the means of retribution were at hand. The Final Solution continued to be carried out amidst an eerie silence on both sides. Even in 1944, it continued to have far higher priority in Berlin than did rescue in the Allied capitals.

New Techniques in the Continuing Rescue Effort

Faced with almost complete failure in its attempt to influence Hungarians in key positions to sabotage the deportation effort, the WRB sought desperately to find new tactics for rescue. One such idea was to request all neutrals to increase the size of their diplomatic missions inside Hungary "in the interest of the most elementary humanity."[29] It was hoped that an actual physical presence on the scene and an increased surveillance of Hungarian officialdom would be more effective in minimizing collaboration with the Eichmann *Sondereinsatzkommando*. At the suggestion of the World Jewish Congress, increased pressure was focused directly on the regime. Budapest was requested to state clearly its "intentions with respect to the future treatment to be accorded to the Jews in ghettos and concentration camps."[30] The message, relayed through Bern, contained a sharp warning that the United States intended to see that full justice was done.

An opportunity to remove at least small numbers of Jews from Hungary was also used to some advantage. Financial support was extended to several small operations, conducted primarily by the Zionist Hechalutz organization, which relayed small groups to Romania, Slovakia, and Yugoslavia.[31]

At the same time, the Hungarian-American community was enlisted in the campaign to convince their countrymen not to cooperate with Berlin's design. An appeal by such a group, urging a return to Christian precepts while wearing the yellow star, was beamed to Hungary by the Office of War Information. Perhaps even more impressive was the campaign sponsored by seventy-three prominent Americans headed by the former governor of New York, Al Smith, to mobilize Hungarian public opinion against the depredations. The OWI, which did not at first accept the idea of using its facilities for rescue propaganda, eventually broadcast the rescue resolutions of the House Foreign Affairs Committee and the Senate Foreign Relations Committee, Roosevelt's speech initiating the temporary refugee program, and several appeals by Cordell Hull encouraging people in occupied areas to help Jews.

The WRB and the Rescue Activities of Raoul Wallenberg

One result of the WRB's request of the neutrals to enlarge their diplomatic missions deserves special mention because it resulted in the saving of at least 20,000 lives. It led to the enlistment of a member of a patrician Swedish family, Raoul Wallenberg. He was first approached by Herschell Johnson, the American minister in Stockholm, at the suggestion of Hilel Storch and Chief Rabbi Marcus Ehrenpreis, both agents of the World Jewish Congress. After some hesitation, Wallenberg became convinced that he could play an important humanitarian role in Hungary. He received a detailed briefing from Iver Olsen, the agent of the WRB in Stockholm who was to finance many of his activities. Olsen gave him a carefully prepared list of Hungarian officials who it was felt might cooperate with the rescue effort. Various rescue plans, such as contacting the Danube skippers and the railroad workers along the Budapest-Mohács line, were also discussed.[32]

Once in Budapest, Wallenberg soon proved to be a one-man

rescue operation. He was able to save thousands by the relatively simple means of extending Swedish diplomatic protection and necessary documents to Hungarian Jews, many of whom had only the remotest connection with Sweden. He leased blocks of houses for his clients and placed them under the extended protection of the Swedish mission. His determination to save his clients was so great that on one occasion, when troops of the *Sondereinsatzkommando* arrived at the quarter to begin deportations, Wallenberg physically intruded his own body, stating defiantly to the officer in charge that they would have to shoot him first before a soul would pass from under Swedish protection. When later the Germans did succeed in sneaking six of his clients out of the quarter and placed them on a cattle car bound for Auschwitz, Wallenberg raced madly by auto to the border, intercepted the train, and removed the victims.[33]

Wallenberg became Olsen's eyes and ears in Budapest and a veritable thorn in Eichmann's side. Before he vanished under mysterious circumstances, he wrote a letter of appreciation to Olsen through whom much of the financing of Wallenberg's rescue work was arranged: "Mr Ollsen [sic] believe me your donation in behalf of the Hungarian Jews has made an enormous amount of good. I think they will have every reason to thank you for having initiated and supported the Swedish Jewish action the way you have in such a splendid manner."[34] Unfortunately, the WRB did not succeed in getting many men like Wallenberg on the scene. His success was the exception rather than the rule.

Eichmann Versus Berlin

From Eichmann's point of view, the first wave of deportations was highly successful. Throughout May and June, the cattle cars rolled uninterruptedly to Auschwitz, carrying approximately 12,000 victims a day. Over 400,000 Hungarian Jews perished.[35] But no number of mock victories at Auschwitz could alter the fact that the Reich's days were numbered. *Festung Europa* was successfully breached on June 6, 1944, at the peak of the Hungarian deportations. The continual broadcasts from the BBC and the OWI beamed at the occupied areas that warned of the accounting that was to come now took on added meaning. Indeed, cracks in the fanatic determination to carry out the Final Solution began to appear in Berlin roughly paralleling the waning enthusiasm already noted in the satellites. The most notable case of "conversion to Christian mercy" was that of

Reichsführer Heinrich Himmler, a prime architect in the Final Solution. In a matter of weeks, he moved from a strong proponent of biological destruction to an arranger of ransom deals. Joachim von Ribbentrop, foreign minister and heretofore an uncompromising advocate of genocide, was quick to echo Horthy's plea for evacuation of certain categories of Jews; and even Hitler did not, as formerly, lose his temper at such suggestions. The führer now preferred to cite technical difficulties and the failure of the Allies to provide havens as being the cause for the continuance of the Final Solution.[36] The German Foreign Office showed renewed sensitivity for world public opinion when, at the outset of the second phase of the deportations, it urgently requested that some subterfuge, such as Jewish attacks on policemen or sabotage activity, be found before the action took place.[37]

As the leaders in Berlin allowed the spirit of 1942 and 1943 to flag and returned full cycle to the practical business approach that marked their earliest dealings with the "Jewish question," Eichmann's enthusiasm for the venture grew, if anything, more intense. Such a change in policy must have been unsettling to him because it removed the moral underpinnings from his bloody work and made it appear like mass murder. Paradoxically, his testimony at his trial in Jerusalem in 1960 indicates that Eichmann, perhaps more than most men, was concerned with matters of morality, albeit of a perverse sort. He viewed with ill-concealed contempt the series of ransom offers that emanated from Berlin in the final months of 1944. He complained bitterly to Berlin that if Horthy's order halting the deportations was allowed to stand, "important biological material" would escape his net.[38] He rushed to Berlin to plead his case in person; and when everything else failed to change the minds of his superiors, he took matters into his own hands and smuggled out an extra transport from the detention camp at Kistarcsa some seventeen miles outside of Budapest.[39] In the hands of such a zealot, the Final Solution had achieved a momentum of its own.

Halting the Deportations

While the Horthy offer to halt the deportations and release certain categories of visa-holding Jews dismayed Eichmann, it caught the rescue advocates by surprise. The last minute reprieve occurred on July 6, 1944, just as the deportations were about to zero in on Budapest. Horthy had, of course, never been an advocate of genocide and had in fact done much to thwart Berlin's plans to liquidate the Jews of Hungary. But with the formal occupation of Hungary on March 19, 1944, Horthy, whose leverage in Berlin was based on Hungary's position as cobelligerent, was subject to the same direct coercion as were other occupied areas. What suddenly gave Horthy the will to thwart Berlin's design was doubtlessly related to the invasion of Europe and the attempt, in July, on the life of Hitler. Perhaps more directly involved in Horthy's decision was the growing pressure by neutrals, spurred on by the renewed vigor of the American effort, to get Budapest to dissociate itself from the Berlin-sponsored genocide program. Especially telling was the personal intercession of King Gustaf of Sweden and the Vatican. Constant threats of retribution that emanated from the WRB also convinced Horthy to make the break. He was able to use these threats in warning Berlin of his impending action in June. Mention of the fear of increased bombing and an imagined threat on the lives of Hungarian Americans did not visibly impress Ribbentrop, who on the surface maintained a strong front on the need to solve Hungary's Jewish problem quickly. It was not until Sztójay played his trump card that Berlin relented. He presented the aforementioned intercepted messages, which emanated from Bratislava, and urgently requested precision bombing of certain key buildings in Budapest that were involved in the anti-Jewish operations and destruction of the key rail junctions on the route to Auschwitz.[40] It remains one of the great ironies of the Hungarian catastrophe that a threat originating from within the helpless Jewish community, a threat that the Allied command would not carry out, became nevertheless a temporary instrument of salvation for Hungarian Jewry.

The Horthy offer to release all Jews holding visas to other countries or Palestine certificates proved embarrassing for London and Washington because it revealed once again that resettlement remained the key rescue roadblock. London was especially anxious about such offers ever since the Romanians had offered to release thousands of Jews in 1943. It tended to bring to the fore the issue of resettlement in Palestine that London wanted to keep out of the picture. Involved in the Hungarian proposal were about 9,700 families and an additional 1,000 children below the age of ten, a total of about 17,000 to 20,000 people. Berlin had already agreed to allow these Jews to pass through its domain, and all that was needed was assurances that such Jews would be resettled in neutral or allied territory.

The offer was transmitted to the WRB through Alfred Zollinger, Washington representative for the International Red Cross (IRC), who attached an urgent request that the administration accept the offer immediately and publicize the number of such persons it planned to admit. Budapest needed a "visible sign of a favorable reaction to their decision to cease their persecution of Jews."[41] But no immediate response could be forthcoming; the administration had not foreseen a test of its sincerity.

Pehle, for whom the Horthy offer was welcome proof of the effectiveness of the WRB strategy based on changing attitudes, had always been a strong advocate within the administration for the need to buttress with rescue deeds the administration's rescue policy. Even before the Horthy offer, he had achieved considerable success in getting the administration to relax the tight anti-infiltration policy that Breckinridge Long had established in Latin America.[42] Visa policy was relaxed so that nonquota preference could be given to relatives of citizens and aliens already in the United States. The private rescue organizations were again enlisted to provide lists of such persons. On July 1, 1944, the administration offered to revalidate all visas issued up to July 1941 and not claimed. But such steps, while welcome, were not sufficient to convince London, the neutrals, and especially the Budapest regime of the sincerity of the administration's rescue intentions. It would be necessary to find a way to circumvent the immigration law.

The Idea of Free Ports

The opportunity to circumvent the immigration law lay with the revival of an idea as old as the refugee rescue crisis itself, temporary havens where refugees could be maintained. First, suggested by prominent German refugees in 1938, it was popular currency in almost every non-Zionist rescue proposal up to 1944. It received prominent mention at the Bermuda conference and was incorporated into the executive order that established the WRB. But until Samuel Grafton, popular syndicated columnist of the *New York Post*, presented it under the rubric "free ports," no one had conceived of a way in which the idea of temporary havens might lend itself as an instrument to finally circumvent the strictures of the immigration law that had, from the beginning, played havoc with the rescue effort. Grafton's logic was compelling: "A free port," he wrote, "is a place where you can put things down for a while without having to make a final decision about them." Why not have such a port for refugees of the Nazi terror? "We do it in commercial free ports for cases of beans," observed Grafton, "it should not be impossible to do it for people."[43] Indeed, there was good reason to believe that such a scheme might be within the purview of the law at least as it was administered by the State Department Visa Division. Rescue advocates had for some time shown intense interest in Breckinridge Long's scheme to rid Latin America of thousands of unfriendly aliens by interning them in the United States. If these unfriendly aliens could be admitted outside the quota laws, why not refugees? In its anxiety to keep refugees out and in its overreaction to the problem of security, the department had inadvertently given an important weapon to the rescue advocates.

An alternate scheme that was based on a possible parallel between the admissions of POWs and refugees was being advocated by Sam Rosenman and Eleanor Roosevelt. The common denominator of both plans was the idea of some temporary shelter where people could be maintained while not legally admitted to the United States. Franklin Roosevelt, aware that Congress had passed resolutions in favor of temporary havens in November 1943, nevertheless displayed no desire to tangle with the restrictionists in an election year. But he could not long withstand the persuasive arguments of Henry Morgenthau, who had been completely won over by the idea.

Predictably, opposition to the scheme soon manifested itself. Within the WRB, Secretary of War Henry Stimson, echoing Senator Robert Reynolds in the Senate, strongly insisted that the president simply did not have the power to act unilaterally on something that "concerns a very deeply held feeling of people."[44] What if Berlin used the opportunity to dump thousands of starving refugees in our laps, argued Stimson, in a familiar echo of the British Foreign Office.

Meanwhile, Pehle tried to muster public sentiment behind the measure. At a specially scheduled news conference, he revealed some of the reasoning that ultimately convinced Roosevelt to go through with the idea: "The necessity for unilateral action by this Government lies in the fact that we cannot expect others to do what we ourselves will not do and if we are to act in time we must take the lead."[45] The American effort, argued Pehle, must at long last be given credibility. At the same time, he lightened the blow by holding out the hope that geographical and time factors would make the possibility of large numbers of refugees coming to the United States slim.

Nevertheless, Roosevelt felt that careful groundwork had to be laid before such a bold step could be taken. The preparation for a temporary haven here offers an almost classic example of the Roosevelt political style. He wished above all to avoid the impression that he was concerned with an exclusively Jewish problem. The charge of "Jew Deal," frequently heard in 1938, still nettled. The instructions given to Robert Murphy, the president's special agent in North Africa, were quite specific about the matter. He was to select a group of refugees making certain to "include a reasonable proportion of various categories of persecuted minorities."[46] At a news conference, he hinted that he did not expect temporary havens to be confined to the United States.[47]

As the administration was making its careful preparations, the idea of free ports itself showed signs of picking up considerable public support. During the months of March and April, hundreds of letters from Jewish and non-Jewish organizations and individuals flooded the White House. Most indicated support of the free-port idea. The *New York Times* assured its readers that "the plan has nothing to do with unrestricted and uncontrolled immigration. It is simply a proposal to save the lives of innocent people."[48] The publicity-wise Emergency Committee to Save the Jewish People of Europe ran a full page ad in the *Washington Post* under the caption "TWENTY FIVE SQUARE MILES OR 2,000,000 DEAD—WHICH SHALL IT BE?"[49]

A few days later, the president finally revealed that he had ordered the preparation of certain "obsolete" facilities for refugees but hastened to add that he personally felt that bringing refugees to the United States would be wasteful.[50] At a third news conference on July 9, in the midst of intense public interest in the successful invasion of Europe, the president casually announced that a temporary haven was being prepared in Oswego, New York. Even then, the order was carefully hedged by limiting it to 1,000 refugees. The announcement also revealed that Cyprus and Tripolitania would also serve as sites for temporary havens.[51] Three days later, Congress was formally faced with the *fait accompli*. Using jointly arguments stressing humanitarian aspects of the operation and arguments of expediency, Roosevelt tried desperately to disarm beforehand the opposition that he knew was destined to come from the restrictionist Congress. Pointing out that refugees in the war zone would interfere with the war effort, he reminded Congress that "we must not fail to take advantage of any opportunity, however limited, for the rescue of Hitler's victims. We are confronted with a most urgent situation."[52]

Indeed, with Horthy's offer to release certain categories of Jews, the situation had taken on a special urgency. Although the circumvention of the immigration law was in fact only a token one, it could serve to give the WRB the necessary support needed to convince the neutrals and London of the credibility of the rescue effort being sponsored by the administration.

But London, feeling its position in the Middle East still threatened, proved difficult to convince; and without its cooperation, the most accessible escape route from Hungary to Romania to Turkey to Palestine, would prove useless. Pehle, anxious to get joint action on the Horthy offer and convinced that speed was essential in having more Palestine certificates made available, urged London to cooperate. "It might prove tragic," he observed, "if the fullest advantage of the present opportunity were not (repeat not) taken."[53] In July, Morgenthau and Josiah Du Bois Jr., formerly the secretary's right hand man, flew to London to press their case personally, but they found that the attitude of the Foreign Office remained "inhumanly political."[54] Eden simply repeated the argument he had used while visiting Washington in March 1943. What would London do with so many refugees? Its attitude did not visibly soften until the Foreign Office was informed that the Roosevelt administration would proceed to act on the Horthy offer. Then London accepted the offer with qualifications. By the time cooperation had been wrung from London, and the Latin American nations and neutrals had been apprised of the latest developments, a precious month had passed. It was August and events were again taking an ominous turn in Hungary.

On August 11, Pehle was finally able to inform Budapest that "this Government now repeats its assurances that it will arrange for the care of all Jews permitted to leave Hungary in the present circumstances who reach United Nations or neutral territory and will find such temporary havens of refuge where they may live in safety."[55] Within the administration, some apprehension had developed regarding Budapest's interpretation of the American response. Would the Hungarians view the acceptance a go-ahead sign to permit those Jews who were not exchanged to be otherwise disposed of so that the Jewish problem in Hungary could be considered officially solved? The administration requested clarification.[56] More disturbing was the word that Berlin was again shifting positions. On the pretext that Jews making their way from occupied Europe to Turkey would disturb German-Arab relations, Berlin now limited the offer to those Jews bound for Britain or the United States. If safe passage was to be offered, such names would have to be given to Berlin beforehand.[57] At one stroke, the offer was limited drastically and made unsafe. Apparently, Berlin preferred to "sell" the Jews rather than simply to let them go. Of the "special category" Jews, 1,200 prominent Hungarian Jews were sent to Strasshof in Austria and thence to Bergen Belsen, many eventually reached Switzerland as a result of the later ransom negotiations, an additional 15,000 were kept "on ice" in Austria and 600 others were confined in Budapest.[58]

Rescue and the Ransom Option

The several ransom offers for Hungarian Jewry that marked the *Götterdämmerung* period, marked a return, full cycle, to the business-mindedness of the first phase of the Holocaust. At that time (winter 1939), the protracted negotiations between George Rublee, Hjalmar Schacht, Robert Pell, and Helmut Wohlthat resulted in a "Statement of Agreement" that really amounted to a German offer to ransom German Jewry. Thereafter, individual ransom deals, such as that arranged for the family of Baron Weiss in Hungary, were not uncommon. There was never a scarcity of "businessmen" like Dieter Wisliceny, from whom Gizi Fleischmann was able to buy time for the Jews of Slovakia, or Kurt Becher, who was actually a skillful business agent for the SS. Nazi idealism that devised the Final Solution was often matched by a keen commercial instinct that sought to sell the Jews.

The "blood for trucks" offer carried by Joel Brand and the protracted negotiations of Saly Mayer, Kurt Becher, and Rudolf Kastzner that continued the first offer mark the principal ransom proposals of the Hungarian catastrophe. The details of that first offer are too well known to be gone into here. Less well known is the dilemma posed by the offer in the allied capitals. For Washington, the basic problem was how to use the offer without giving succor to the enemy. There was a great deal of suspicion about Berlin's motivation. Was this an attempt to split the Allies? Was Berlin making a last-minute attempt to implicate the Allies in the Final Solution?[59] How serious was the offer and from where did it emanate? Was it intended as a peace feeler?

It was clear from the onset that, for London, the offer was unwelcome. The Foreign Office could never bring itself to share or even believe Washington's new-found enthusiasm for rescue. It tried to kill the ransom offer in the bud by prematurely publishing an indignant refusal in the London *Times*. Nor was London's opposition confined to the Foreign Office. Churchill also expressed adamant opposition to ransom and preferred a declaration that everyone connected with the atrocity "will be hunted down and put to death."[60] Almost before the rescue advocates could determine how to handle the new rescue opportunity, the doors were being closed on it.

London's contention that the offer was not bona fide were at first shared by the WRB. But instead of allowing the matter to rest there, Pehle dispatched Ira Hirschmann, a New York department store executive and a highly successful WRB agent in Turkey, to interview Brand. After overcoming Lord Moyne's attempt to head off the interview, Hirschmann finally succeeded in talking to Brand on June 11, 1944. Apprehension about the authenticity of the offer was put to rest as a result of Hirschmann's report. He observed that although the offer might have been "pulled out of a hat," it originated with the highest authorities in Berlin and that there could be no question of Brand's absolute sincerity.[61] His advice paralleled that of the Jewish Agency: Don't refuse the offer out of hand but keep the doors open. "Though the exchange proposition may be mere eye wash and the possibility of ulterior motives must be assumed," cabled Moshe Shertok to Nahum Goldmann, "it is not impossible that even preliminary negotiations might result in salvation of substantial numbers."[62] Goldmann had, in the interim, convinced Edward Stettinius, the new under secretary of state, that the "Germans must be made to think that we take it seriously."[63] As had happened so many times before, London and Washington appeared to be on opposite sides on the rescue question.

But this time, the British held the trump card; for in order to convince Berlin that the offer was being seriously considered, Brand had to be returned to Budapest. This the British would not do despite desperate pleas to bring them into line. Chaim Weizmann, the most renowned of all Jewish leaders, implored Eden to send either Joel Brand or Menahem Bader, Jewish Agency agent in Istanbul, back to Budapest with a suitable reply. Morgenthau and Pehle pleaded the same cause before Roosevelt.[64] The Jewish Agency appealed to the president "not to allow this unique and possibly last chance of saving the remains of European Jewry to be lost."[65] A *quid pro quo* was suggested whereby the Allies would negotiate further provided that Berlin promised to halt all deportations. When this also brought no response, the Jewish Agency attempted to keep the offer alive through Joseph Schwartz, JDC agent in Lisbon, who was in touch with Freiherr Von Schroeder, head of the SS Main office.[66] But the British remained opposed to using dilatory tactics to extend the talks, plagued as they were by the fear that the "dumping" of Jews would create a "Jewish problem" at home and aggravate the already tense situation in Palestine. Nor were they convinced of the sincerity of Berlin's motivations.

Indeed, the motivations of the "blood for trucks" offer are still obscure. At the time, some saw in it a last minute attempt by some Nazi officials to make profit before they went underground. Others saw a last minute attempt by Himmler to ingratiate himself so that he might be considered a possible conduit to end the war. The most popular view at the time was that the offer did, in fact, originate on the highest level of the Reich and represented a "psychological warfare" effort to split the Allies. This accounts, according to this theory, for Eichmann's oft-repeated assurances that such military hardware would be used only on the eastern front.[67] Many Germans had no doubt swallowed their own propaganda line and believed that a split in the "strange alliance" was not only possible but imminent. The offer carried by Joel Brand was merely designed to help things along. This is what the administration suspected when they hastened to inform Moscow of the offer on June 9, 1944.[68] The Soviets, always true to type, reacted with extreme suspicion and informed the State Department that they did "not consider it expedient to carry on any conversations whatsoever with the German government."[69] The administration hastened to assure the Soviet authorities "that neither this Government nor the British Government have been deceived as to the character of this alleged offer. . . . (They) were convinced from the outset that the offer is part and parcel of the German psychological warfare effort."[70] But continued Soviet suspicion combined with London's opposition put a damper on any fruitful rescue opportunities that might have come through the ransom offer.[71]

Despite the optimistic manner with which rescue advocates welcomed the ransom offer, whether there was, in fact, a real opportunity for rescue is an open question. Despite promises to the contrary, the mills of Auschwitz kept grinding throughout the Brand mission. We have seen that, at the level of operation where Eichmann reigned supreme, there was opposition to such backsliding. Such fanaticism made a great deal of difference once it became apparent that the government apparatus of the Reich was beginning to disintegrate. The Final Solution had achieved a momentum and a life of its own apart from the Berlin government.

The Szálasi Regime

In Hungary, too, a ray of hope turned quickly into gloom. In late August, Horthy, interpreting the breakthrough of the Soviet army as a hopeful sign, deposed the collaborationist Sztójay regime and replaced it with one headed by General Géza Lakatos. A request for the removal of the *Sondereinsatzkommando* that followed came none too soon, for Eichmann's plans to remove the Jews of Budapest were scheduled to take place within the next few days. For the moment, Berlin chose to comply with the request; for as one Nazi newspaper put it, "pressure from enemy and neutral countries has become so strong that those circles in Hungary that are friendly to Jews . . . influence the Hungarian Government to prevent any further measures against the Jews."[72] The influence of the WRB seemed at last to be felt even in Berlin. But when it was suspected that Lakatos was moving toward a separate peace with the Allies, its reasonableness vanished. The respite had given Wallenberg and others an opportunity to do their work, but now with a German panzer division occupying Budapest, the Lakatos regime was toppled. In the wings waited Eichmann, prepared this time to finish the job. Otto Skorzeny's movie scenario operation of kidnapping Horthy's son proved sufficient to break the dictator's spirit. Ferenc Szálasi, head of the fascist Arrow Cross Party, was made the new prime minister. Dreaded news of new concentrations of Jews in open fields or empty factories outside Budapest soon reached the WRB.[73] New inquiries were made concerning these measures against Jews but the "new order" in Budapest proved far more insensitive to pressure from abroad. Its response included the story that Hungarian Jews were being integrated into the German economy or were being settled outside Budapest to protect them from Allied bombing and the imminence of Soviet invasion.[74] A renewed threat of retribution was made by the WRB: "None who participate in these acts of savagery shall go unpunished . . . all who share the guilt shall share the punishment."[75] There were intercessions by the IRC and the papal nuncio. But these measures availed little. By mid-October, Eichmann had succeeded in rounding up 22,000 Jews, who were to be marched to Germany. Reports of depredations along the route of march, in which hundreds were shot, reached the WRB. Especially gruesome were Wallenberg's reports to Olsen.[76] Not even Himmler's express order countermanding Eichmann's foot marches could halt the final ordeal of Budapest's Jewry.

The Mayer–Becher–Kasztner Negotiations

Even as this last ordeal was occurring, a rescue hope, based on Berlin's willingness to continue ransom negotiations, still existed. After the WRB discouraged the Schwartz-Von Schroeder meeting at Irun on the Portuguese-Spanish border, there arose the possibility of continuing negotiations through Saly Mayer, the Swiss representative of the Joint Distribution Committee. As a Swiss citizen, Mayer would have far more maneuverability than a citizen of a belligerent nation. The Mayer-Becher-Kasztner negotiations that followed lasted through the final months of 1944 and were in a sense a substitute for the fruitless Brand venture. Berlin, completely taken in by its own propaganda, simply assumed that the London rejection was a ruse to fool the Soviets.

We have seen that the rescue advocates wanted to participate in such negotiations primarily to buy time. It was hoped to delay the destruction process until the time that the war in Europe would be over. Behind the German willingness to bargain lay not only the old commercial instinct that was always an integral part of the war against the Jews but also the enigmatic figure of Rudolf Kasztner and his relationship to Kurt Becher. It was Becher who convinced Himmler of the utility of using the captive Jews as a bargaining wedge against the Allies, and it was Kasztner who was instrumental in keeping the idea of negotiations alive after the defunct Brand mission.[77]

The negotiations began auspiciously in August 1944 with the arrival in Basel of a transport of 318 orthodox Jews from Bergen Belsen. Thereafter, Mayer and Becher would meet at the Swiss border town of St. Margarethen to discuss, according to Kasztner who was a frequent witness to the negotiations, "the price of abandoning the gassing."[78] Before the talks were over, Mayer succeeded in getting the Germans to abandon this brutally inhuman business approach in favor of a more acceptable one. For the moment, the price remained the same as in the "blood for trucks" offer. It had been made abundantly clear in the Allied capitals that such a transaction could not take place. Mayer's task was doubly difficult because he had to convince Becher to abandon this position while still holding out bait that some other form of profit would accrue to Berlin. The urgency of keeping the talks going increased with the news that Slovakian Jewry, relatively secure heretofore, was being concentrated in preparation for annihilation.[79] Even more grim was the news that Eichmann had returned to Budapest on September 13, 1944. It was to these deportations from Slovakia that Mayer first addressed himself in the hope of getting them postponed for the duration of the negotiations.

In the meantime, it became imperative to develop some gambits by means of which the talks could be stretched out. It was thought that every day won in this way might mean the difference between life and death for thousands. The Germans were therefore requested to spell out precisely what type of foodstuffs and technical goods they desired. This meant that Becher had to consult with his superiors, which took time. But by September both Mayer and Roswell McClellan seemed to have run such tactics to their limit. "My personal opinion and that of Saly Mayer also," McClellan informed Pehle, "is that all the time possible has now been gained and that in all probability the Gestapo has lost patience so that these negotiations can be considered as having lapsed, negotiations which were after all ultimately doomed to failure,"[80] Despite such pessimism, Pehle, strongly influenced by news of an impending change for the worse within Hungary, encouraged Mayer to keep talking. In mid-October, McClellan met personally with Becher and his assistant at the Savoy Hotel in Zurich. He came away from the interview so discouraged that soon thereafter he recommended that the talks be terminated.[81] Pehle again urged that the negotiations continue. But such an extension was proving difficult without talk of money; and because the WRB policy on placing funds in blocked Swiss accounts had hardened, it was doubly difficult to offer Becher suitable bait. Once again, Pehle's judgment proved wise; for in December Mayer finally succeeded in getting Becher to abandon bargains based on material aid to Berlin. Instead, the Allies would simply take over the material needs of those still in their hands provided the killing stopped. It was a hopeful development because such a program fell within the purview of the newly established WRB policy of delivering food packages, through IRC channels, to the camps. In early December, a second reward of lives was also made by Berlin to show good faith. On December 6 and 7, 1944, a transport of some 1,355 souls arrived in Basel. Soon thereafter, a further development gave the talks a new lease on life. After McClellan suggested that blocked funds be made available for bargaining purposes, the WRB relented and again allowed such money to be deposited in blocked Swiss accounts.[82]

In the final death agony of the Reich, such ransom probes increased in frequency and culminated finally in Himmler's order to deliver the surviving inmates of the camps to the Allies.[83] The order was countermanded by Hitler when he heard that the liberated prisoners of Buchenwald were plundering Weimar.

Evaluation of a Failure

For Hungarian Jewry, the thousands saved by negotiations and other means barely gave solace for the enormity of the tragedy that befell it. Of the approximately 745,000 Jews in prewar Hungary, barely 180,000 survived.[84] In any terms therefore, the rescue operation in Hungary was a failure. The key question that historians must face is how much greater that failure would have been had there occurred no change in the ground rules of rescue policy fashioned by the Roosevelt administration in January 1944.

The failure of the Hungarian rescue operation, unlike previous rescue failures, cannot be attributed to the absence of will but rather to the inability to make that will effective on the scene. Washington was forced to act by remote control while Berlin, through its actual physical control of Hungary, had in its hands the primary requisite to wreak destruction. Even when it became apparent that the will to destroy the Jews was waning in Berlin, the determination to see the operation through remained strong on the operational level, where Eichmann reigned supreme. He seemed to be anxious to show the Allies that nothing could stop him. He gave the following reason for organizing foot marches: "I wanted to show these Allies my hand, as if it were to tell them: Nothing will help; even if you bomb and destroy, I still have my way to the Reich."[85] In the face of such zeal, only a physical deterrence might have saved the situation. With the exception of bombing, such a deterrence was simply not available. It is from this point of view that the decision not to bomb stands out as an especially tragic one for Hungarian Jewry. The evidence that the Hungarian government was amenable to pressure to comply with the rescue effort under the threat of bombing is irrefutable.

The need to coordinate with London also had a depreciating effect on the potential success of the operation. It was London's recalcitrance that contributed to the delay of one precious month in dealing with the Horthy offer. The number of rescued might have been greater had the offer been accepted with alacrity. The wait allowed Berlin's confused priorities on the disposition of the Jews to crystallize further around the idea of ransom. Once ransom became the primary means of rescue, the possibilities of saving lives actually grew more remote because the Allies, especially the Soviet Union and Britain, found the idea of dealing with Berlin particularly repugnant; and in Washington there was actually a tightening of the liberal interpretation of the "trading with the enemy" regulations during the Hungarian episode.[86]

One rescue variable that was never in control of the WRB was the posture of the victims toward rescue. The actual concentration-deportation-liquidation procedure was managed by a relatively small administrative nucleus that required not only the collaboration of the local police force but of the victims themselves. The slightest resistance by any element in the operation could be enought to upset it. The speed with which the Hungarian deportations were carried through reflects Eichmann's success in getting the cooperation of all concerned to create a "smooth" operation. He was able to organize the Jewish Council in record-breaking time; and for various reasons, the countless warnings to destroy community lists and discard the yellow identification stars beamed to Hungarian Jewry were disregarded. The failure to convince key officials and the Hungarian gendarmes not to cooperate with the deportation procedure also contributed notably to Eichmann's success.

But what of the role of the Jewish Council? It is probably safe to assume that Hungarian Jewish leadership, rather than consciously betraying the community, as some would maintain, reflected the powerlessness of the divided Hungarian Jews.[87] In the hands of Eichmann's *Sondereinsatzkommando* they were no longer able to give leadership but simply had to follow orders. The leadership of the provincial communities remained uninformed of the real meaning of the measures taken against them and fell easy prey to the highly developed German camouflage techniques. Many no doubt entered the cattle cars fully believing that they were destined for Germany to alleviate the labor shortage. This may account for the compliance, noted by German observers, of most Jews when the Romanian or Slovakian borders, which offered relative safety, were close by. Wallenberg's observation of "total lack of courage" is more readily understood when one realizes that the dissolution of all local and regional Jewish institutions and the capture of existing Jewish leadership left the Jews a disorganized mass, incapable of resistance.[88] Once such disorganization is present, the only response possible is fear and terror. Indeed, Wallenberg also observed that "the Jews are so terrified that they are simply hiding in their own houses."[89] After the dissolution of the Jewish community, each victim felt that he faced the full onslaught of the murder apparatus alone. The irony that although Berlin endlessly attributed to the Jews remarkable feats of international organization and conspiracy, the very first thing to disintegrate in the face of the Nazi onslaught were the delicate strands that bound Jews together.

When the efforts of the Roosevelt administration in the Hungarian aspect of the Holocaust are compared to its previous efforts, a remarkable improvement in the will and instrumentation to save lives must be noted. Yet, the most it was able to achieve was to mitigate the disaster rather than prevent it. That some survived at all can be attributed in part to the energy that Washington breathed into the effort in 1944. The fate of Hungarian Jewry might have been more tragic. What was true of the Holocaust in general was especially clear in the case of Hungary. The energy, organization, and instruments for mass rescue developed by the Allies did not remotely match the will and energy to destroy the Jews developed by the Nazi Reich.

8

Governmental Response to Human Crisis

FOR THE HISTORIAN of the Holocaust, the role of witnesses poses the greatest problems. The witnesses are assumed to have had options: They could resist, they could be indifferent, or they could even collaborate. The assumption that there was a choice gives moralists an entrée. They demand to know why Roosevelt, the Pope, the neutral nations, and the International Red Cross did not do more to save the Jews. Because there can never be an adequate answer to this question, a series of pseudo-historical works have appeared, that are in reality thinly veiled indictments.[1] What I would like to demonstrate in this essay is that the model of conspiratorial indifference hardly encompasses the complexity of motives behind the inaction of witnesses. that is especially true of Roosevelt's America to which other witnessing nations and agencies looked for an example. A blanket indictment conceals more than it reveals about the problem of rescue itself, about the fairly broad spectrum of opinion on what ought to be done, about the intractability of the credibility problem, and about the difficulty of assigning humanitarian objectives to nations at war.

I will focus primarily on decision-making elites in the United States. The Roosevelt administration played the classic role of the witness, but from what we know, the complexity of motivation, the gap between intent and policy were no less manifest in London and

This essay appeared originally in *The Holocaust: Ideology, Bureaucracy and Genocide,* ed. Henry Friedlander and Syvil Milton (Millwood, N.Y.: Kraus International, 1980). 245–59, under the title "The Governmental Response."

Vatican City. Let us turn first to a fuller examination of the problem of the witness.

For the historian anxious to avoid moralistic fulminations, the primary question is not why more was not done but what was possible to do and what actually was done. We are well on the way to answering the second question, but the first continues to pose difficulties.[2] The researcher soon discovers that it is nearly impossible to determine possibilities of rescue and that in examining the Final Solution we are faced with a catastrophe of such enormous magnitude that no matter what was done to rescue the victims, it would never have been enough. Indeed, the question of rescue possibilities actually reverts to the bitter debate of the Holocaust years, which revolved precisely around what was possible. We are not much closer to resolving that conflict today. Given Nazi fanaticism, how possible was it for witnessing nations to rescue Jews in the death camps in 1943? The problem can be seen clearly when one considers the Hungarian episode. There, the rescue effort reached its apogee. Led by the War Refugee Board, all the components for rescue were in place. The witnessing nations had enlarged their diplomatic legations, a sustained psychological warfare campaign suggested by the World Jewish Congress was aimed at the Hungarians, money was funneled to underground sources, and the Vatican and the International Committee of the Red Cross were encouraged to play a more active role.[3] Yet, it hardly balanced Berlin's zeal to win this last battle against the Jews. In full view of a world that now understood what the Final Solution meant and even though Nazi decision makers knew that the war was lost, the cattle cars rolled to Auschwitz as if they had a momentum of their own. More than half of Hungary's Jews were gassed. Those who controlled the actual slaughter determined possibilities for rescue even at that late date. Until there is some agreement on rescue possibilities, the tendency to assign witnesses a responsibility their power to influence events did not match will remain strong, and the gap between polemics and history will remain wide.

It seems clear today that the greatest possibilities for rescue existed during the first phase of the crisis, from November 1938 to June 1941. During that phase, the Nazi leadership was uncertain about the ultimate disposition of the Jews. While the murderous rhetoric emanating from Berlin openly suggested mass murder, the bureaucracy actually worked within the context of emigration and forced extrusion to achieve the much-desired goal of making the

Reich *Judenrein*.[4] That policy is best symbolized by a remarkable Statement of Agreement that resulted from the secret negotiations between George Rublee, director of the Intergovernmental Committee on Political Refugees, Robert Pell, Rublee's technical adviser assigned by the State Department, Hjalmar Schacht, president of the Reichsbank, and Helmut Wohlthat, an official of the ministry of economic affairs. It called for the phased ransoming of German Jewry over a period of three to five years by "outside" Jews, and the finding of a resettlement haven. It is possible to make certain judgments regarding rescue during this phase. Clearly, had there been a will among receiving nations to take in the penniless refugees from the Reich, more might have been saved. But that policy was enormously difficult, and it required considerable goodwill. Germany had only 500,000 Jews, but in the wings stood Poland and Romania with 4,000,000. The situation seemed impossible for the receiving nations, and the ground rules of indifference and moral obtuseness were established during that first phase. They were not changed again until 1944, when it was all but too late.

It is not necessary to recount here the now well-known story of the Roosevelt administration's action and inaction in relation to the Holocaust. What needs to be understood is the existence of a broad spectrum of opinion on the issue among decision makers (broader among political leaders than the public at large), the complex intertwining of personalities, domestic politics, and conflicting views of the world, which fed into the policy-making arena on the question of the Holocaust. A case study of three leading personalities will best illustrate these points. I have selected Henry Morgenthau Jr., secretary of the treasury and Roosevelt's close friend, who became the most powerful advocate of rescue in the administration; Breckinridge Long, director of the State Department's Special Problems Division, who became the most adamant foe of rescuing the Jews; and finally Roosevelt himself, perhaps the only political leader alive at the time whose actions might have drastically changed the course of events.

Breckinridge Long made his debut in the State Department during the Wilson administration.[5] In the 1920s, he gained a considerable reputation as an attorney specializing in international law. He returned to the State Department during the New Deal. As in the case of Laurence Steinhardt, it was a political appointment; he had made a considerable monetary contribution to Roosevelt's campaign. Steinhardt ended up as minister to Switzerland, and Long ultimately became ambassador to Italy. Long loved the glamour of the position, but a series of mishaps led to his removal and to what may have been a nervous breakdown. Long was extremely ambitious, a careerist who poured out his frustrations—and there were many—into his diary at night. He thought that he deserved at least to be undersecretary and, failing that, perhaps ambassador to the Court of St. James. Instead, he was made head of a potpourri of operations assembled under the newly organized Special Problems Division. Little did he understand that his appointment to a position that would make him responsible for visa policy implementation was as unfortunate for rescue advocates as he thought it was for his career.

For historians, the crucial question about Long is to what degree his blocking activity was motivated by anti-Semitism. Despite revealing passages in his diary, it is difficult to answer this question with certainty. Long was typical of those bureaucrats who resented the intrusion of Jews into the upper echelons of the civil service, which occurred at an accelerated pace during the New Deal.[6] But Long rarely spoke about Jews as such. He preferred code words such as "New York liberals." His attitude confirms what every Jewish aspirant sensed about the State Department: Jews were not welcome. Long wrote about his attendance during the oral part of the foreign service examination.[7] He frankly stated that he preferred the boys from his Princeton alma mater to the "pushy" candidates from the city colleges. But for Long, it was a matter of gentility and class. One rarely sees evidence of strident anti-Semitism. He missed the character, the social ambiance, and the grace of the department under the Wilson administration, when it was a playground for the sons of the rich established families of America.[8] His resentment of the "new men" who had made their debut under Roosevelt knew no bounds, although only a small proportion of these were Jewish. Ironically, he recognized in Roosevelt a fellow patrician, and throughout the crisis, successfully gained the president's consent to administratively block the inflow of refugees. To build what the historian David Wyman called a "paper wall" to keep refugees out, Long capitalized on what I have called a security psychosis, an intense fear that Germany had infiltrated the refugee stream with agents. During the crucial years between 1939 and 1941, increasingly stringent security procedures were employed, so that by June 1940, it was no longer possible to issue a visa to anyone with a "close relative" under Nazi control. This rule meant that a good number of the refugees were subject to rejection. Indeed, so successful were Long's gambits that only in 1939 was the combined quota for Austria and Germany filled. The security procedures of a neutral United States were as rigid as those of wartime Britain, and one historian maintains that, considering comparative absorptive capacities, Britain's refugee admission policy before September 1939 was more generous.[9] Yet, although one can safely say that the congressional rejection of the Wagner-Rogers bill, which would have allowed the entry of 10,000 mainly Jewish children in 1939 and 10,000 in 1940 for a total of 20,000—while the admittance of thousands of British children, non-Jewish victims of the 1940 blitz, was greeted with enthusiasm—was anti-Semitic, one can have some doubts that the security screening was simply anti-Semitism translated into policy. Long was genuinely convinced—as was his friend Martin Dies—that there was a conspiracy to breach American security and that there were spies in the refugee stream. There were magazine stories to support such a belief, and of course the FBI had files. When Stephen Wise pointed out to him after the SS Struma episode that German intelligence could surely find a safer means to transport their agents to America, Long thought he was being facetious. Even Roosevelt spoke about fifth columns and Trojan-horse techniques that must be guarded against. Indeed, so effective was Long's strategy that it was practically impossible for any political leader to oppose the measures without calling his own loyalty into question. And that was the last thing Roosevelt wanted to do after the unsuccessful radical left turn taken by his administration after 1936. When combined with the dislocation caused by the depression, and the popular opposition to refugees at a time of unemployment at home, Long's use of the security gambit was virtually irresistible. Keeping refugees out had not only a popular mandate, but it seemed to be in consonance with the national security interest as well. It was a combination few decision makers cared to oppose.

A second policy, that of suppressing news of the Final Solution, is not so easily rationalized. The story of cable no. 354, which instructed Leland Harrison to cease forwarding reports of mass murder, is well known. Suffice it to say that the department not only conspired to conceal news of the Final Solution but also attempted to cut off at the source any additional news emanating from Harrison in Bern. According to one source, this ploy went a long way in creating the "wall of silence" that rescue advocates found almost impossible to penetrate.[10] The paucity of authenticated information on the implementation of the Final Solution, when combined with the incredibility of the story, is one of the key factors used to rationalize the inactivity of all witnessing nations and agencies. Long doubted the stories and attributed them to atrocity mongering by the Jewish leadership.[11] It is important to note, however, that he was hardly alone in his skepticism. Some Jewish leaders could not believe it either. In the American context, there was a special reason for such doubts. One of the principal arguments of the revisionist school of history during the 1930s was that the United States had been duped into entering World War I by the skillful atrocity mongering of the British.[12] It was believed that Lord Bryce, Wilson's favored scholar, had sacrificed his academic career to further the British interest in the United States.[13] For those who saw World War II as merely a recapitulation of World War I, and for members of Congress who, in the 1930s, had legislated a series of neutrality laws designed to prevent a situation like that of the pre-World-War-I period from arising, the idea of atrocity mongering was not so far-fetched. Even the Jewish leader Stephen Wise, who had been the recipient of the message from Gerhard Riegner (agent of the World Jewish Congress in Switzerland) giving the first confirmed gruesome details of the slaughter and the use of prussic acid, feared that such a story would not be believed. For confirmation, he gave the message to Undersecretary of State Sumner Welles, who was considered friendly to the rescue cause. Indeed, the question of credibility deserves a book in itself. It plagued even those stationed in the listening posts around the periphery of occupied Europe, who found it difficult to believe such stories. It plagued the victims, who did not want to believe it, and the witnesses, who found it too incredible to believe. A poll taken in December 1944 showed that most Americans estimated Jewish losses at about one hundred thousand.[14]

The label "Roosevelt administration" with its implication of collectivity and unity also poses certain problems for the researchers. There were in fact men in the administration who recognized the problem and wanted to do more. Harold Ickes, the secretary of the interior, put up a strong fight to get Alaska considered as a refugee haven. Attorney General Francis Biddle fought Long at every turn, also over the question of the internment of the Japanese, which Long predictably favored. Long wondered how a man with so "much courage and determination" could place himself in the camp of those with "tender hearts."[15] James McDonald, who headed the president's Advisory Committee on Political Refugees, a quasi-official agency whose task it was to monitor the crisis, compiled special visa lists, and investigated resettlement suggestions. His conflict with Long over visa lists even reached the Oval Office. But Long had little difficulty convincing the president that McDonald's plea for refugees was "sob stuff." McDonald lost his battle despite the strong support of Eleanor Roosevelt, who put herself at the service of rescue advocates and acted as a direct line to her husband.[16] Among the Catholic hierarchy, the strongest advocate for rescue was Archbishop Joseph Rummel of New Orleans.[17] His stance was directly opposed by men like Archbishop Michael Curly of Baltimore, who refused to make a judgment on Nazi Germany because it was 3,000 miles away. But most decision makers were simply indifferent to the issue, and in that stance they reflected general American public opinion. We tend to forget that, during the refugee phase, the Jewish question was a small side issue in the great debate between isolationists and interventionists; and after the United States entered war, the rescue issue was subsumed by the overriding objective of winning the war. Jewish leaders were told that the fastest way to save their brethen was by victory, and nothing must be allowed to interfere with that—not even the rescue of their brethen.

The case of Henry Morgenthau Jr. has a special irony.[18] Roosevelt sometimes tried to use Morgenthau as a liaison to the Jewish community. He was asked to head the PACPR but rejected the idea, informing the White House that he was not interested in philanthropy. Morgenthau was rather taken aback when, in the early months of 1939, he was asked to compile a list of the richest Jews in America to finance a visionary resettlement project favored by the President—the United States of Africa scheme. The president slipped easily into notions that there were rich Jews who might actually fund such a proposal. Morgenthau came rather late to the question of rescue. In 1940, he brought Isaiah Bowman, a noted geographer and resettlement expert, to Roosevelt's attention; but after that we hear little of his activities. When he finally did take an interest in the final months of 1943, it was caused as much by a spin-off from his long-standing rivalry with the State Department as it was by news of the fate of his coreligionists in Europe. But his involvement changed when he learned from his non-Jewish assistants— Randolph Paul, the general counsel of the department; Josiah Du Bois, his assistant; and John Pehle, head of the Foreign Funds Control Division—that the State Department had deliberately suppressed news of the Final Solution. Then Eleanor Roosevelt observed that he began to play a new role in the inner circle of the administration: the president's conscience.[19]

On January 13, 1944, Morgenthau's assistants had ready a report on the State Department's blocking role entitled "A Report to the Secretary on the Acquiescence of this Government in the Murder of the Jews." Morgenthau thought the title was too strong and changed it to read "A Personal Report to the President." He delivered it on January 16.[20] Possibly, it had the desired effect for two reasons: its contents were political dynamite, and 1944 was an election year. It set in motion a new effort to save the Jews. The War Refugee Board was established with seed money from Roosevelt's slush fund, and it initiated a new and somewhat imaginative program to save those Jews who might still be saved. A few months later, in April, a second breakthrough occurred when rescue advocates convinced Roosevelt to circumvent the immigration laws by establishing a temporary refugee haven in Oswego, New York. It was the high point of the administration's rescue program.

Morgenthau paid dearly for his open action in favor of his coreligionists. Accusations that his loyalties were ethnic rather than American were soon heard, and were partly responsible for bringing his political career to an abrupt end.[21] Once involved, Morgenthau sustained his interest. Undoubtedly, it was his knowledge of what the Germans had done to Jews that led to his conception of the Morgenthau Plan for the treatment of postwar Germany. It was a "hard" plan, calling for the pastoralization of that country, and the secretary convinced Roosevelt to make it America's official policy. But there was opposition from the State and War departments. When it was pointed out to him that 15,000,000 German workers would likely starve to death if his plan were ever implemented, Morgenthau's response was bitter: "Why the Hell should I worry about what happens to their people? . . . We didn't ask for war, we didn't put millions of people through gas chambers, we didn't do any of these things. They have asked for it."[22] After leaving office in July 1945, he wrote *Germany Is Our Problem*. It was published at the historical juncture when many Washington decision makers were becoming convinced that "our problem" lay further to the east, in the Kremlin.

We come finally to the case of Roosevelt himself, who throughout the crisis hovered somewhere between the positions of Long and Morgenthau. What emerges from the growing record is that the president, so beloved by American Jewry, did not have the spiritual depth to fathom the crucible being experienced by European jewry, the historical insight and intelligence to understand the meaning of Auschwitz for his time in history. It was at once a failure of mind, spirit, and will.

We must attribute the vacillating, contradictory character of America's rescue activity to Roosevelt himself. The State Department, which he never trusted and bypassed at every opportunity, was used as a foil to absorb the ire of the Jews as well as other components of the liberal urban-ethnic coalition that sometimes helped to amplify the Jewish voice. There developed a "policy of gestures," composed of the rhetoric of humanitarianism and an occasional insignificant step while, at the same time, the State Department conceived and implemented increasingly restrictive measures to curtail the influx of refugees. After the *Anschluss,* Roosevelt announced dramatically that he was combining the German and Austrian quotas in order to prevent the loss of the latter. (The step entailed an indirect recognition of the annexation.) Other such steps were the extension of visitor's visas and the calling of the Refugee Conference at Evian with the clear stipulation that none of the participants would be required to alter their immigration laws. That meant of course that the conference would accomplish little to mitigate the refugee chaos. Meanwhile, the State Department was carrying out a policy candidly articulated by Long, calling for delay and postponement of the granting of visas by the consuls.[23] That was precisely what was done. By September 1940, we hear him gloating over his success on the granting of special visas. "The list of Rabbis has been closed and the list of labor leaders has been closed and now it remains for the President's Committee to be curbed."[24] The department went on to rule out the possibility of Alaska as a resettlement haven; finally, it even tried to conceal news of the Final Solution.

In the case of rescue, Roosevelt was clearly more the fox than the lion. Undoubtedly, he wanted to do more, but doing so would have entailed a price he was unwilling to pay. It meant thwarting a very clear political consensus that Jewish refugees were not welcome. Paradoxically, Washington's failure in the crucial first phase of the Holocaust was a classic example of democracy at work.[25] Public opinion was adamantly opposed to tampering with the restrictive immigration laws so that a distinction between immigrants and refugees *in extremis* could be made. To be sure, he was impressed with the caliber of refugees coming from the Third Reich.[26] One of his most farsighted acts was to heed the advice of Albert Einstein and Leo Szilard concerning the potential for building an atomic bomb.[27] But he did not allow that positive impression to interfere with political reality. He rejected the idea of a refuge in Alaska, and he did nothing to support the Wagner-Rogers bill to bring 20,000 Jewish refugee children to the United States. Instead, he turned to a strategy that would avoid both political conflict at home and confrontation with London. He proposed visionary and grandiose resettlement schemes in Africa and Latin America. (The British used much the same gambit when they proposed settling the Jews in British Guiana with American financing.[28]) At the same time, Roosevelt seemed anxious to conceal the Jewish character of the crisis. Thus, while Berlin spoke incessantly about Jews, and converted all enemies including Roosevelt to that faith, his State Department reconverted them to a bland category called "political refugees" and insistently stuck to that classification as late as the Bermuda conference. The president was dismayed when George Rublee mentioned Jews directly in his agreement with Schacht.

The reasons for his distress are not difficult to discern. The depression had released intense inter-group tensions. The anti-Semitic Right pictured Jews in Nazi images. They considered them a "paramount menace to American values and tradition." They prattled about "Judeo-Bolshevik conspiracies." This was not exactly new; it merely re-echoed the nativist-restrictionist line of the 1920s, but something new had been added on the political scene. The aberrant Right, men like Charles E. Coughlin, Gerald L. K. Smith, William Pelley, and Fritz Kuhn, had been successful in linking themselves to the tide of isolationism that amplified their voice and cloaked them with the mantle of legitimacy.[29] The link between anti-Semitism and isolationism was sealed with a golden spike by no less an American hero than Charles Lindbergh, who in September 1941 warned America that Jews and Anglophiles were pushing the nation toward war with Germany, a war he was convinced would be catastrophic for the national interest.[30] Roosevelt, the supreme politician, would not risk the consequences of having his administration labeled a "Jew Deal." He had appointed Felix Frankfurter to the Supreme Court, he had surrounded himself with Jewish advisers, and Jews were flooding the enlarged Federal Civil Service. To push for Jewish refugees against popular opposition required him to run the political risk of overly close association with an American Jewry that was not winning medals for popularity.[31] That kind of political courage was simply not in the Roosevelt arsenal. The Jewish voting bloc had moved closer to him after 1936 while other hyphenates had cooled their ardor. The Jewish "love affair" with Roosevelt remained unrequited.

Politically, Roosevelt—like Stalin—wanted to avoid making World War II a war to save the Jews. That was true despite the fact that Nazi cosmology pictured it in precisely those terms.[32] Yet, political considerations only partly explain Roosevelt's indifferent showing. Oliver Wendel Holmes once described him as possessing a third-rate intellect but a first-rate temperament.[33] In the case of the Holocaust, that observation is borne out by the president's failure of mind. He never remotely understood the meaning of Auschwitz. His thinking on the rescue question had an above-the-battle quality. A refugee conference is proposed without any serious effort for a solution or follow up, and the British soon dismiss it as "intuitive."[34] Resettlement havens of immense proportions are sought without any serious consideration of the enormous difficulties involved in such nation-building schemes. In October 1939, he proposes a massive refugee absorption plan to delegates of the IGC meeting in Washington who feared above all that they would soon become refugees themselves. Roosevelt was a visionary who knew what he wanted to do in the abstract, even while his State Department was implementing quite another policy on the administrative level. That accounts for the duality of Washington's policy on the Holocaust that some less kind observers have labeled duplicitous. There is always a gap between a policy and its administration. But in the case of rescue policy, its administration actually refuted the ostensible humanitarian intentions of the administration. That is perhaps what Roosevelt desired, a policy that made political points at home but risked very little. The irony is that every other witnessing nation soon understood the game being played by the Roosevelt administration and planned its own actions accordingly. But, with only a few distinct exceptions, American Jewry seems never to have understood that it was being manipulated.

For Roosevelt, it was politics as usual. In other areas, New Deal rhetoric was also a far cry from performance. The gap between policy and implementation on the rescue question was therefore not atypical. But the saving of lives is qualitatively different from such issues as unemployment or rural electrification. Ultimately, the yawning gaps and contradictions between the rhetoric of humanitarian concern and actual policy may have to be explained by an examination of Roosevelt's psyche. Some of the required data are already available. They speak of Roosevelt's emotional superficiality. The historian Paul Conkin observes that "few men were more attuned to people and less attuned to ideas," but he actually loved people only in groups and rarely fathomed the travail of any single person. "He loved the adoration and attention of people, even when elementary privacy was violated. With consummate art he played for his audience and won their plaudits. Some grew to love him and projected onto him their hopes and joys and deepest longings. They invested so much in the relationship; he invested so little and invested so broadly."[35] That is the way it seems to have been between the Jews and the Roosevelt administration.

Finally, one cannot escape the conclusion that the will and mind-set required to save the lives of the victims was simply not present among the witnesses who might have acted. Decision makers never had the support of an aroused public opinion that might have compelled them to take more active steps. Yet, we should note that, in the case of the Roosevelt administration and in the case of London and the Vatican as well, there were always notable exceptions, leaders who realized what was happening and were anxious to do more. Although they did not often succeed, they might serve today to redeem our fallen image of humankind. If one had to give a primary reason for the failure of the witnessing governments to act, then the inability of rescue advocates to gain credibility and to pierce the "wall of silence" would have to be placed close to the top.

Linked to the problem of credibility one can identify a certain failure of mind. Roosevelt shared with the general public the sense that what Berlin was doing to Jews was merely another atrocity in a particularly cruel war. He never remotely fathomed the meaning of Auschwitz and the centrality of the Jewish question to the war. Most leaders did not. We are just now, more than fifty years after the event, beginning to understand the centrality of the Holocaust to the enigma of what World War II was all about. It is true that Hitler began and ended the war with statements about the need to destroy the Jews, but Allied leaders at the time were convinced that the Jewish question was peripheral and ordered their priorities accordingly. Rescue of the Jews had a low priority because that was not what they thought the war was about. Even today, few historians go as far as Lucy Dawidowicz in viewing the war as one against the Jews. In that context, the conflict over rescue was really a conflict over priorities. Policymakers felt that the first order of business should be to win the war. Saving the Jews would be accommodated only as it fit into that priority. It usually did not. It is likely that no amount of pressure—whether on London with regard to the White Paper or on Roosevelt with regard to admission of refugees—could have changed that. The historical problem of the role of witness cannot be resolved until we find an answer to the larger problem of what World War II was all about. Yet even today, most historians do not recognize the destruction of the Jews as a central event in that war.

Lastly, one should note that, even had Washington's priorities been successfully reordered, there would still have been almost insurmountable roadblocks. The mass slaughter of the Jews was focused and coordinated by Nazi authorities who possessed total power and a bureaucracy noted for its efficiency. The effort at mass rescue on the other hand, could not be coordinate because it involved various witnessing nations and agencies, each of which retained its own conception of its priorities on the Holocaust question. Latin American nations, for example, rejected exhortations to be more generous about accepting Jewish refugees and offering havens for mass resettlement. Roosevelt's private emissary to the Vatican, Myron C. Taylor, could not convince the Pope to speak out. Salazar, the dictator of Portugal, could not be convinced that Angola was ideally suited to accept Jewish refugees.[36] Most British Commonwealth nations were as reluctant as the United States when it came to opening their gates.[37] Britain would not abandon her White Paper policy, which limited immigration to Palestine, because she viewed her interest in the Middle East and the exigencies of the war as having a far higher priority than the rescue of Jews. The International Red Cross thought it would lose its effectiveness as an absolutely neutral agency if it were overly bold in interpreting its role vis-à-vis the incarcerated Jews.[38] And so it went. Ironically, the Intergovernmental Committee on Political Refugees, whose purpose it was to coordinate the refugee effort and, after the Bermuda conference, also the effort to rescue Jews, became itself an early casualty of this fragmentation and general lack of will. The early international effort, like the national efforts, was strangled in a sea of red tape, which in itself reflected the lack of will. Collective responsibility, like collective guilt, has an allure of its own. When everyone is responsible or guilty—no one is. Throughout the crisis, the Nazis were in physical control of the slaughter. Given their fanaticism on the Jewish question, it probably would have required a physical intrusion to remove their hand from the throats of the victims. Such an intrusion was not in the power of the witnessing policymakers who were, at least for the first years of the war, concerned with their own survival. The suggestion to bomb the camps and the rail lines to them came rather late in the crisis and could not be achieved until advanced air bases in Italy were secured. Moreover, allied leaders feared that it would lead to an escalation of terror, such as the retributive slaughter of war prisoners and hostages.[39] The Allies, it was thought, could never match the Germans in their ability to implement such steps of escalating terror.

One comes away from the examination of the role of witnesses with some skepticism regarding the assigning of humanitarian roles to nation-states who bear witness to human-made catastrophes like the Holocaust. The instrument of slaughter was, after all, the nation-state itself. Nation-states are human institutions, not humans themselves. They possess no souls, no conscience, and are not the containers of the spirit of civilization. When they act at all, it usually is to assure little else than their own continuance. Can we assign to them a humanitarian mission? One wonders if the assumption that we can is warranted by the history of the twentieth century.

9

PBS's Roosevelt

Deceit and Indifference or Politics and Powerlessness?

IN APRIL 1994, the Public Broadcasting Service (PBS) aired a film documentary provocatively titled "America and the Holocaust: Deceit and Indifference." Sponsored by public television's WGBH (Boston) in cooperation with WNET (New York) and KCET (Los Angeles), Martin Ostrow, its producer, based the documentary entirely on David Wyman's popular *The Abandonment of the Jews* (1984). Wyman also was the principle "scholar/talking-head," a role that has become customary in historical documentaries. PBS's Roosevelt is essentially Wyman's, and it is that fact that makes the documentary problematical.

The documentary rekindled a debate among historians about how the Roosevelt administration's posture during the Holocaust should be viewed. At present, that debate is a minor contretemps in Holocaust historiography, but it may soon develop into an American version of the *Historikerstreit* that continues to wrack the fraternity of German historians. So stung were some Roosevelt enthusiasts by the tone and content of the documentary that they have collected a series of articles, soon to be published by St. Martin's Press, to respond to it.

A shorter version of the essay appeared in *Dimension* 8, no. 2 (1994): 9–14, under the title "Roosevelt and Europe's Jews: 'Deceit and Indifference' or Politics and Powerlessness."

The Historiographic Context

That collection and the critical reaction of the noted historian Arthur Schlesinger Jr. in *Newsweek* should not come as a surprise to the producers because the Wyman approach has been a source of sharp controversy since his book first appeared in 1984.[1] His contention that it was possible to mobilize American public opinion to put pressure on Roosevelt to mount a more energetic rescue program was challenged by Lucy Dawidowicz, author of the prize-winning *The War Against the Jews* (1975).[2] There were also differences regarding the genesis of the War Refugee Board in January 1944 and the evaluation of the role of the dissident "Bergson boys" whose version of events Wyman accepted almost without exception. In all these cases, what nettled was not Wyman's research, which was impeccable, but his historicity. He was writing about the Roosevelt administration and American Jewry, not as they were, but as he thought they should have been. Predictably, few players in the historial drama were able to satisfy his standards.[3]

In fact, the debate between historians who hate Roosevelt and those who love him is as old as the New Deal itself. Only this phase concerning Roosevelt and the Holocaust is comparatively new. In 1967, Arthur Morse, a journalist who worked with Edward R. Murrow and then with Fred Friendly at CBS, called attention to Roosevelt's indifference to the fate of European Jewry. His book *While Six Million Died* went into three printings, leaving Roosevelt's rosy image, especially among Jewish readers, in tatters. It was followed in 1970 by my own *Politics of Rescue*, which was the first attempt to view the problem from a nonpolemical perspective.[4] Since the publication of these early works, there have been at least five additional books and dozens of scholarly articles on that subject. "America and the Holocaust" is actually the second documentary to deal with the subject. The first, "Who Shall Live, Who Shall Die," by Laurence Jarvik, attacked primarily American Jewish leaders like Stephen Wise.

The special interest of Jewish researchers in this area is understandable. The Holocaust may not yet have gained much interest in world history but its importance in the Jewish corner of the historical canvas is truly extraordinary. The massive bloodletting that stole the lives of two-thirds of European Jewry could not help but change the character and direction of Jewish history. An assumption, however, that there is an ideological and sectarian dimension to the emerging debate, one which pits liberal Jewish against conservative Gentile historians, is unwarranted. Wyman is the grandson of a Protestant minister; and Richard Breitman and Alan M. Kraut, the two historians who have felt that anti-Semitism has been overstated as a cause for the administration's indifference to the fate of European Jewry, are Jewish.[5]

Still, aside from the fact that it happened to them, there is an additional reason for a special Jewish interest—it concerns the Jews' relationship to the Roosevelt administration. Judging from the high percentage of Jewish voter support given to Roosevelt, no ethnic group "loved" Roosevelt with such ardor as American Jewry. Only African Americans come close. Roosevelt's New Deal had a special meaning for Jews. Especially those with a social democratic leaning saw in the welfare state the fulfillment of their long-awaited dream of the humane, caring state. In New York State, a third party, the American Labor Party, had been organized largely through the efforts of the Jewish Labor movement. Some observers explain the aspiration for a "caring" government as inherent in Judaism. The various versions of democratic socialism, to which many Jews of the second generation were committed, was but a secular incarnation of that ancient religious concern. That is what is echoed by Rabbi William F. Rosenbloom, of New York City's Temple Israel, who viewed the Episcopalian Roosevelt as "the Messiah of America's tomorrow" and also in the rhetoric of Rabbi Stephen Wise, who prayed for Roosevelt's "immortality."[6]

What is remarkable about Wyman's approach is that he reads Roosevelt the way the Jewish voters of the thirties did and then, like them, is outraged when he discovers that Roosevelt did not live up to his high expectations. Forgotten is the political context in which Roosevelt and American Jewish leaders were compelled to operate. For example, after the Quarantine address (September 1937), which was not received with great public enthusiasm, Roosevelt became a huge disappointment to interventionists, who feared that he was now lagging behind public opinion. That speech was part of the emerging "great debate" between isolationists and interventionists in the two years before Pearl Harbor, of which the rescue of refugees was a small blip on the monitor. The lineup of political forces in that debate was virtually the same as on the question of the rescue of largely Jewish refugees. Those who counseled "America First" were not likely to welcome refugees. No historian can ignore the fact that, until the attack on Pearl Harbor, interventionists never fully convinced the American public that German aggression in Europe posed a danger to the nation. When Roosevelt's inaction on the refugee front is considered apart from its prewar historical context, it assumes a more uncaring character than it had in reality. An indication of that point is that the refugee issue, which we can see today as a harbinger of the Holocaust, did not, during those crowded years, arouse the kind of stormy protest, even among Jews, as did the British White Paper (May 1939) that limited Jewish immigration to Palestine.

We will not soon have a certain answer about whose view concerning the Roosevelt administration and the Holocaust will prevail. Such historical debates have a way of swinging back and forth from generation to generation. Wyman's view seems dominant today, but already his negative assessment of Roosevelt as a wartime leader is being challenged. Viewing Roosevelt's role from the perspective of his effectiveness in holding the fragile wartime alliance together, while fashioning overall war aims designed to secure postwar peace, Warren F. Kimball, a Rutgers history professor, emerges with a highly affirmative judgment.[7] In fact, the Roosevelt administration's witness role during the Holocaust need arouse neither ex post facto love nor hate. In the fifty years that have passed, researchers have gotten a far better handle on how governments behave when faced with crisis in which their survival is at stake. Such a history of the American role during the Holocaust, viewed from within the context of the total war in which it occurred, would be more balanced and less accusatory than this film documentary.

The Issues of the Debate

At heart, the debate between idealists and realists (let us call them that for the moment) is about standards of behavior for governments, international organizations, and political leaders like Roosevelt. The historian's dilemma lies in the difficulty of determining how much and what kind of action by these agents in the historical drama would have been sufficient to satisfy the claims of morality. In a human-made, willful catastrophe on the scale of the Holocaust, it is difficult to imagine that enough could ever have been done to save the lives of all who needed saving. The historian's judgment of sufficiency ultimately rests on an estimation of rescue possibilities that are difficult to make because they also involve a judgment of how much power there was available to the actors in the historical drama. How much power did Roosevelt or American Jewish leadership have to discharge the responsibilities we assign them? Not only is it difficult to trace the flow of power in a democracy but even to define it and to distinguish it from influence is problematical. There are dozens of other variables to consider. Power also includes something as undefinable as will; the Nazi will to annihilate the Jews and the Allied will to prevent it. The "Jewish question" was the centerpiece of Nazi cosmology. Clearly, that fact made Berlin's urgency to kill the Jews far greater than the will of the Allies to save them.

The problem of gaining credibility, which plagued rescue advocates, also has to be included in the historian's judgment of rescue possibilities. So surreal was the vision of a modern nation-state placing the liquidation of an ancient people at the center of its public policy and actually using crucial facilities and resources in the midst of a war of survival to do so, that it beggared the imagination. It seemed incredible that attempts to tell the story of the death camps inevitably were associated with the "gruel" propaganda that many Americans viewed as part of British manipulation to get them to enter World War II.

What we need to understand is that the rescue of Jewish refugees, on which we focus here, and the possibility of rescuing the Jews in the camps thereafter, had only limited prospects of success. What was required, after all, was to extricate the victims from the clutches of a bureaucracy, supported by a powerful totalitarian state, utterly intent on genocide. Rescue possibilities were far more promising during the refugee phase of the Holocaust (1933–1941) than afterward during the extermination phase. But in neither period was there much cause for hope.

The Case of the Refugees

We encounter all these difficulties when we examine the core plot of "America and the Holocaust," which deals mostly with the refugee problem. The "should have" proposition here is that the Roosevelt administration should have mounted a far more energetic attack on those restrictionist/antialien elements in Congress and in its own State Department who spared no effort to keep desperate refugees out of the country. That is an especially telling part of the anti-Roosevelt indictment because it is conceivable that, had a "solution" been found to Berlin's "Jewish problem," either through infiltration into receiving nations or through mass resettlement of

German and Austrian Jewry before the outbreak of war in September 1939, there might never has been a Final Solution. The failure to find a place to settle European Jewry during the refugee phase of the Holocaust meant, in effect, that the rescue struggle was lost in the first round. After Pearl Harbor, rescue possibilities became much more remote. It is difficult to imagine how the over 10,000,000 Jews of a Europe made *Judenrein* all could have found haven elsewhere.

Roosevelt's critics assume that he was aware that the Nazi intent was genocide from the beginning, although Nazi leadership itself may have had no such awareness. The Final Solution was implemented with assurance only after the physical and ideological wars were joined with the invasion of the Soviet Union in June 1941. The requisite administrative coordination for such a massive project was not fully in place until after the Wansee conference of January 1942 in Berlin. There is little agreement among historians concerning the precise date of the decision, but generally Karl Schleuenes's observation that the road to Auschwitz was in fact improvised and not preplanned has gained considerable acceptance.[8]

One of the most successful parts of the PBS documentary is the story of how Kurt Klein, a young German Jewish refugee, after having negotiated an incredible bureaucratic maze, finally collected the massive number of forms and papers required to save his parents, who have, in the meantime, been deported to Gurs, a detention camp in Vichy France. But at the last minute, there is a bureaucratic snafu; and instead of coming to America, they are transported eastward, where they die a nameless death. It is a heartrending story, probably repeated thousands of times. That personalizing of the refugee plight allows the viewer to see that, behind the statistics and impersonal regulations, there were real lives, parents who wanted to care for their children and children who needed their parents. That situation is something that viewers understand. Still, it makes our need to call attention to the political realities that shaped Roosevelt's lethargic response to the refugee crisis seem obscene.

But inappropriate or not, the economic and political realities in the United States influenced decisions. One of these realities was adamant public opposition to the admission of the refugees. At the same time in the international arena, Roosevelt faced the unprecedented barbarism of the Nazi regime, with governments like Poland and Romania threatening to follow suit. It did little good to appeal to Berlin's humanitarian conscience. Had such a conscience existed, the heartless policy of extrusion of penniless Jews would not have developed in the first place. We tend to forget that, in the years immediately preceding the war, the tone and standards of behavior in international relations reached a very low level. It is, for example, difficult to imagine a more callous act than the Schacht-Wohlthat proposal literally to "ransom" German Jewry. Together with the "blood for trucks" offer to ransom the Jews of Hungary in 1944, these proposals serve as bloody bookends for the Holocaust. Yet, the negotiated Statement of Agreement to fund resettlement of European Jewry between a US delegation headed by George Rublee and German officials in 1939 was taken in stride by the diplomats. Roosevelt even hoped that the Jewish leaders would comply.

There was little help that could be expected from other potential refugee-receiving nations. France and Britain believed that they already bore a disproportionate share of the refugee burden. Berlin had pointedly not attended the Evian conference in the spring of 1938, the most important initiative dealing with the refugee crisis taken by Roosevelt. At the conference, only the Dominican republic offered to take some refugees. Most of the republics of Latin America, on whom Roosevelt had counted, made no offers. After Evian, Roosevelt must have realized that the refugee problem promised only to be a liability for his domestic program and that little prospect of amelioration could be expected from abroad. At the same time, events pushed the refugee crisis off center stage, where *Kristallnacht* had momentarily placed it. Hitler's march into the rump of Czechoslovakia in March 1939, after stating that Germany had no interest in gathering non-Germans to the Reich, marked an even lower point in international morality. A highly successful nation-state, created by the international community with strong American support, was allowed to succumb to open aggression. Not a finger was raised to help the Czechs. Indeed, with the outbreak of war in September, it looked as if the leadership of potential receiving nations in Europe would themselves join the refugee stream. By 1940, all but those in Britain had. Could one then realistically expect help for the Jewish refugees? Within the context of the onrushing crisis that was leading to war, what was happening to Jews was considered minor. If Roosevelt paid it any attention at all, he probably saw it only as additional evidence of the world's spinning out of control.

Schacht's ransom proposal also posed problems for the leaders of world Jewry, most of whom never viewed it as an opportunity for rescue. Not only were the enormous sums required not available but compliance also would reinforce a central assumption of the anti-

Semitic imagination that there was such a thing as "international Jewish finance." Moreover, the idea behind the offer, which would have made each fleeing refugee a forced salesman for German capital goods, originated with the Transfer agreement (*Ha'avara*) between Germany and the *Yishuv* (Palestinian Jewry). The agreement had become a bitter source of acrimony between the World Zionist Organization, which welcomed German Jewish capital for development, and the supporters of the international boycott, who fantasized that Nazi power could be toppled and better treatment for Jews wrung through economic pressure. The boycott campaign, which became worldwide in 1934, had a cathartic affect on groups like the Jewish War Veterans, who felt a need to strike back at the Nazi tormentors. But the bitter conflict over the boycott was also a harbinger of the divided response of Jews to what was happening to their European brethren.

It was a disunited, frightened Jewry that was called upon to act, only to discover that it was a community in name only. During the refugee phase of the crisis, the leaders of American Jewry avoided a concerted Jewish/liberal effort to confront the restrictionists in Congress. Jewish representatives in Congress, like Samuel Dickstein and Emanuel Celler, were convinced that such an effort would boomerang and produce an even greater avalanche of anti-alien bills. In the case of the Wagner-Rogers bill, which would have allowed 10,000 Jewish refugee children to enter outside the quota, the ball during the committee hearings was carried by non-Jewish refugee advocates. Jews remained in the background. In retrospect, that seems a sensible strategy. Between 1933 and 1944 the restrictionist congressional block represented an overwhelmingly popular consensus that could not have been circumvented. Not until the spring of 1944, when the movement for free ports came to fruition and brought over nine hundred refugees to Fort Ontario, an army relocation center in Oswego, New York, was it possible for Jews to challenge congressional restrictionists. By that time, all signs of the depression had been replaced by the economic boom generated by the war, and the light of victory could be seen at the end of the tunnel.[9]

Still, the circumvention of the supposedly immutable immigration laws by executive order leads one to wonder whether such a direct presidential intrusion could have been made earlier. It was, after all, Roosevelt's own State Department that, using a rationale popularized by the Dies committee that spies had infiltrated the refugee stream, was imposing increasingly stringent directives to the consuls to halt the flow of refugees. The policy of deliberate blocking of those who might legally have come was articulated by Breckin-ridge Long, the assistant secretary of state in charge of the Special Problems Division in June 1940:

> We can delay and effectively stop for a temporary period of in-definite length the number of immigrants into the United States. We could do this by simply advising our consuls to put every obstacle in the way and to resort to various adminisrative ad-vices which could postpone and postpone the granting of the visas.[10]

It was probably the bureaucratic labyrinth created by that policy that trapped Kurt Klein's parents. Here, there was a clear case of deception; and one needs to ask why Long and his cohort of State Department officials were not kept on a shorter leash by the presi-dent. There is no easy answer, except to remind ourselves of the context. A massive increase in the size of government occurred dur-ing the New Deal. The power of bureaucracy had, in some cases, taken on a life and interest of its own, especially in the State De-partment, which many considered a playground for the rich and wellborn. Controlling that department particularly on an issue of secondary importance, was far removed from Roosevelt's free-wheeling style of administration. He rarely micromanaged the im-plementation of policy, preferring to give his appointees free rein. In the case of the State Department, which he considered hopeless, he simply bypassed it and used it as a foil.

Resettlement

It was to avoid the shoals of the refugee question at home and the White Paper issue abroad that helped convert Roosevelt into a staunch proponent of mass resettlement of Jews outside of Europe. He spent hours consulting with Isaiah Bowman, president of Johns Hopkins University and a well-known geographer, Henry Field, an anthropologist at the Chicago Museum of Natural History, and Ales Hrdlička, a geographer at the Smithsonian Institution, hoping to lo-cate an undeveloped region that might at once absorb sizable num-bers of Jews, who would also act as developers for such areas. Roosevelt fully shared the notion that Jews could raise the required development capital. Many places were scrutinized, including Mindanao, British Guiana, and the Belgian Congo. The nearer to the equator, the more attractive they seemed to become. "The Jews are after all an oriental people," one expert observed.

After much hesitation, the State Department took advantage of an offer made by Trujillo, the caudillo of the Dominican Republic, at the Evian conference in July 1938. But Sosua, the name of the area near Puerto Plata, became a haven for fewer than six hundred Jewish refugees, who were soon accused of exploiting native labor and feeding German submarine crews at night.[11]

The enormous expense of resettlement and the unsuitability of the highly urbanized, aging European Jewish population for pioneering, made mass resettlement an unrealistic solution for the refugee crisis. At most, it offered an opportunity to save a handful of Europe's 10,000,000 Jews. The rescue of all of European Jewry would have required the developed receiving nations to absorb the greatest portion, and at the same time, making Palestine available to absorb some share. Even then, collective action would also have been necessary to stay the Nazi regime from liquidating the millions of Jews who, for various reasons, would have been compelled to remain in Europe. Also, there were those who considered resettlement a cruel illusion that deflected needed resources and energy from more practical responses to the crisis. But for political reasons, Roosevelt seized upon it as a doable option. It was risk free.

The Roosevelt administration did mitigate the plight of some special refugees. Emergency procedures were established to permit prominent political, labor, and cultural leaders easier access. One such group, the Emergency Rescue Committee, sent Varian Fry to southern France, where between August 1940 and September 1941, he managed to rescue almost 1,000 prominent artists and writers. Other lists were gathered by organized labor; church organizations, especially Quakers and Unitarians; and various rabbinic groups. After persistent complaints about the rigidity of consuls in certain cities, a "special care" directive was issued by the White House. But in toto, fewer than 5,000 were brought to the United States by these special programs. The special lists aroused the ire of State Department officials. Under the guise of prevention of infiltration of spies, they imposed increasingly stringent security-screening procedures to stop the refugee stream at its source. It was this same group that later tried to cut off news of the Final Solution emanating from the World Jewish Congress agent in Bern, Switzerland. The policy outlined by Long was so rigorously applied that even those who might have legally entered could no longer scale the "paper wall" that the State Department erected. Only in 1939 were the relevant quotas fully used. Unable to find haven in America, Kurt Klein's parents, together with thousands of others, were "resettled in the east." That was the euphemism preferred by Berlin to conceal their fate. Rather than realizing its promise, *resettlement* became the first code word for the destruction of European Jewry.

Mitigating Circumstances

The death of the Kleins is all the more poignant because they might have been so easily saved had there been a will to do so. But the historian who must find a balance between what he thinks in his heart should have been done and the reality of what was actually possible finds no easy answers. The possibility of simply doing the humanitarian thing was circumscribed by an over-whelming popular consensus that opposed admission of refugees. That verdict was yielded by the democratic process that Jewish rescue advocates cherished.

Should they have nevertheless confronted the American people? Would it have made a difference had they done so? Researchers in this area rarely speculate about such questions because they know there was no timely way to disarm antirefugee sentiment, reflected in Congress by the deluge of antialien measures, especially after the severe 1937 downturn in the economy. As late as *Kristallnacht* (November 9–10, 1938) it was not yet clear, even to Jews, that the fate of European Jewry hung in the balance. To rescue advocates, the immigration laws and codes seemed immutable. At the time, most expert observers of the domestic political scene agreed with that appraisal.

Similarly, Roosevelt could not be convinced to expend scarce political capital on the refugee question; nor did he have to. In the election of 1940, the Jewish vote was his. His political clout could best be used to prepare a reluctant nation for war. He had learned in prior elections, when the "Jew Deal" label had been affixed to his administration, that even the appearance of an excessive concern with a Jewish interest could be a political liability. The cry of Judeo-Bolshevism, endlessly sounded by Nazi propaganda, had resonance among powerful professional anti-Semitic interests at home.

It was not merely that there was a scarcity of political courage in the Oval Office. The president's action in exchanging "overage" destroyers for British bases in the Western Hemisphere (September

1940) indicates that, on the larger issue of keeping Britain in the war, Roosevelt could daringly step out in front of public opinion. But allowing the largely Jewish refugees easy access could endanger weightier foreign-policy concerns. Taking up the cudgels on the refugee issue and the later question of the fate of European Jewry entailed a price. It could hamper the mobilization of the American people for a war they did not yet want to fight. Although World War II would become a war against racialism and anti-Semitism, it could not, in 1939, be presented to the American people as a war to save the Jews. German propaganda was already projecting the war as having been started by Jews in defense of Jewish interests.

The signing of the Atlantic Charter in August 1941, three months after the invasion of the Soviet Union, marked the limit to which Roosevelt could bring a resistant nation into the war. Had Berlin not honored its treaty obligation to Japan and declared war on the United States, the indifference of the American people to the war in Europe would have continued beyond Pearl Harbor. The inwardness of the American people was Roosevelt's real problem. What appears to the producers of this documentary as "indifference and deceit," turns out, on closer scrutiny, to be something less evil and more politically driven.

Yet, one can hardly resist Wyman's passion. It is true that the refugees and the victims in the camps were not legally America's concern. It is also true that there was political risk in opening the gates of America. But if Washington had shown more humanitarian concern, if it had warned and cajoled Berlin, if it had set an example for other potential receiving nations—in a word, if it had led, certainly more lives might have been saved. But surely by this time the reader recognizes that the entire democratic world sounded that complaint in the prewar years. But while there was still time, the plea to stop Hitler was not heeded in Washington. What chance then had a plea for the hapless Jewish refugees?

American Jewry

There is little about the posture of American Jewry in this documentary. Yet, it is a crucial variable without which the American role in the Holocaust remains incomprehensible. For the most part, Wyman follows Peter Bergson's (Hillel Kook) view, which castigated American Jewish leadership for their lack of militancy and imagination. By 1944, Bergson proposed that the rescue objective should be

separated from the Zionist-inspired "homeland" goal, first proposed
in the Biltmore program established at the Zionist convention meeting held at the Biltmore Hotel in New York (May 1942).[12] That strategy finally made the Bergson group totally irreconcilable with the
mainline Zionist organizations that viewed rescue and a Jewish
homeland in Palestine as inextricably bound. For Zionists, Palestine,
which they increasingly projected as an autonomous Jewish commonwealth, was the logical and preferable place to resettle the unwanted Jews of Europe.

To this day, it is difficult for researchers to determine with the
kind of certainty that Wyman does whether the "Bergson boys"
were an asset or liability to the rescue cause. Clearly, they had an
earlier and more realistic view of Nazi intentions and demonstrated
great talent and energy in alerting American Jewry to the mortal
danger faced by its brethren. Their well-honed talent for getting the
story out went far in breaking through the curtain of silence that
surrounded the workings of the Final Solution. But these activities
in the public-relation sphere must be balanced against the fact that
the group aggravated the disunity and strife that characterized Jewish organizational life and prevented American Jewry from speaking
to Roosevelt with a single coherent voice. Self-appointed and foreign
born, the leading members were linked to the right-wing Irgun faction of the Revisionists in Palestine. The Bergson group's organization and activity ran counter to the democratic style that had been
introduced by the American Jewish Congress with much passion in
1918. Bergson rejected Rabbi Wise's offer to become part of American Jewry's loose communal governing structure in turn for being
bound by its decisions.

The split with the Bergson group was just one of several that
divided American Jewry during the Holocaust. That division less-
ened the ability of the American Jewish leadership to influence refu-
gee/rescue policy. With the exception of the United Jewish Appeal
(UJA), which finally unified American Jewry's far-flung philanthropy network in 1938, the major Jewish organizations never succeeded in finding a common basis for action. The four attempts to
unify in the face of the crisis were ignominious failures. American
Jewry seemed more anxious to tear itself apart than to mobilize its
resources to rescue its brethren. Modernity had robbed it of a common language, culture, and experience that might have served as a
basis for joint action. The crisis revealed that there were actually
several separate Jewish communities, each with its own dearly held

ideology and interest; each with its own priorities. Not even a crisis that threatened the existence of every Jew proved sufficient to bridge the gulf that divided Jew from Jew.

It is left for the historian to determine what effect that disunity had on the rescue cause. The steps taken by the Roosevelt administration to ameliorate the refugee crisis—the "special care" directive, the combining of the Austrian and German quota, the invitation to the Evian conference, the creation of the War Refugee Board, and the opening of the free-port shelter at Fort Ontario in Oswego would probably not have occurred had Jewish and non-Jewish groups not exerted pressure. Had Washington had its druthers, it would gladly have ignored problems that were not its legal responsibility. We cannot consider Roosevelt's response therefore without also considering the community called upon by kinship to exert such pressure. Some would go as far as linking the weak response of the Roosevelt administration to the failure of American Jewry to project sufficient pressure. That is surely what Wyman concludes. But is he assigning it a role that it could not fulfill and then flailing it for its failure? We have noted that the very notion that there existed a united, coherent community that agreed on what had to be done and, welded together by the crisis, was prepared to do it, is a figment of the imagination.

The argument that American Jewry should have come together in the face of the crisis is based on an aspirational reading of modern Jewish history or no reading at all. Historians like Wyman wish that American Jewry were something other than it was and is. It is an argument with what history has made modern American Jewry. There is no possibility for satisfying such longing, except perhaps to note that, even had American Jewry been more unified, there is still no assurance that there would have been an appreciably different outcome on the refugee issue. The occasions when an ethnic group successfully pulled foreign policy away from what was believed to be the national interest are rare in American diplomatic history, and nonexistent during wartime.

Anti-Semitism

Finally, my discussion of Roosevelt's action and inaction would be even more incomplete if I did not return to what one scholar recently characterized as a "real and ignoble part of America's heritage,"—anti-Semitism.[13] Its virulence was especially evident during

the thirties. I have already noted how it affected the political atmosphere in which decisions regarding Jews were made. That was an
indirect impact. But it is far more difficult to establish a direct influence of anti-Semitism on refugee policy. Based on rumor and occasional random comment, some maintain that Roosevelt was not free
of the malady. He is purported to have sympathized with visitors to
the White House who complained that German Jewry had become
too prominent in the professions and as redactors of German culture. Roosevelt supposedly agreed that quotas to limit Jewish influence in these areas were necessary. Yet, although he probably
shared the anti-Semitic sensibilities of his class, there is no evidence
that either anti- or philo-Semitism (he was more frequently accused
of the latter) played a role in his approach to public policy. There
were officials in the State Department like Breckinridge Long, whose
diary contains evidence of a general dislike of Jews, particularly the
activities of Jewish leaders like Rabbi Stephen Wise.[14] But one did
not have to be an anti-Semite to oppose the influx of Jewish refugees. Many in the opposition were genuinely concerned with security and the ability of the economy to absorb the refugees.

Roosevelt was a supremely political animal, and it can be assumed that he was aware that his administration had become the
foil for the virulent anti-Semitism of the depression years. There was
not a national election between 1936 and 1944 that did not feature
some untoward judeophobic incident, usually in a minor key.
Frances Perkins, his secretary of labor, was accused of being a concealed Jewess; and Sidney Hillman, a Jewish labor leader and presidential advisor was accused of being a concealed Communist.
Sometime, Roosevelt himself stood accused of being a Jew. In 1935,
there were over 120 professional anti-Semitic organizations. Before
1940, there could be little doubt that financial and ideological support of the German-American Bund came directly from Berlin.

A favorite motif was to picture Jews as dominating the administration and pushing it toward war. That was the thrust of Charles
Lindbergh's address in Des Moines in September 1941. Jews had
indeed become more visible in Washington. They were a loyal and
important constituency and received their share of the spoils of office. Newly minted Jewish lawyers, who, despite their often high
university ranking, could not hope for a position in a Wall Street law
firm, sought appointments in the new federal regulatory agencies.
Too frequently, they were appointed to "friction" agencies that dealt
directly with the public. In conservative circles, they were viewed as

the policemen of the hated New Deal. But although they were more visible, the appointment of Jews was not disproportionate to their share of the qualified candidates for such positions. During the interwar period, the Jewish work force upgraded its skills and increased its professionalization. There were already a disproportionate number of practicing Jewish doctors and lawyers.

In the case of appointments to the judiciary, Roosevelt did not exceed the number of Jewish judges appointed in the Hoover administration. But that reality mattered little to anti-Semitic orators like Father Charles E. Coughlin, Charles Sylvester, William Pelley, or Fritz Kuhn. In the case of successful dissidents like Huey P. Long or Upton Sinclair, Roosevelt played a skillful waiting game until these demagogues destroyed themselves. But such a strategy could not be employed with those who made anti-Semitism the centerpiece of their politics. Undoubtedly, Roosevelt had concluded after the failure of the Evian conference that giving priority to the refugee crisis played into the hands of the professional anti-Semites. It gave them ammunition. Life could be made easier if the Jewish question were muted.

The full impact of the heightened anti-Semitism of the thirties could be seen among the Jews. Their apprehension was noteworthy enough to be reported in the press.[15] They observed with cold fear what was happening to German Jewry, then considered the most advanced and secure Jewry in the West, and worried if the same could happen here. They were haunted by the spector of a fully emancipated, well-situated Jewry, not unlike themselves, at one stroke of the pen being deprived of all rights of citizenship, as German Jewry was by the Nuremberg Laws (1935). It was another reason why they hesitated to take the lead on the refugee issue that they understood was part of Berlin's strategy to spread the virus of anti-Semitism to other countries. They did not require the survey research available to contemporary scholars to inform them that they were not popular. But there was little agreement on what to do. American Jewry was not fully prepared to accept the mantle of leadership that European Jewry was now compelled to pass on. They faced the onrushing crisis divided, fearful, and alone.

The remarkable fact about American anti-Semitism is that, at the historical juncture when the nation became involved in a life-and-death struggle with an enemy whose primary objective was to rid the world of Jews, its own anti-Semitism was reaching new heights of intensity. Unlike the war against Japan, American public opinion was not fully attuned to the meaning of the war in Europe.

The hatred of the "Japs" knew no bounds. The aim of the war was simple. The Japanese had mounted a sneak attack on Pearl Harbor, and they would be made to regret it. But Auschwitz was not Pearl Harbor. It did not threaten the nation directly. It would take time to educate the American public to understand the insidious threat to American pluralism posed by the racialist ideology of National Socialism and to approve Roosevelt's "Europe First" strategy.

It is probably wishful thinking to assume that the mysterious decline of anti-Semitism after 1944 marks the historical juncture when the American people understood what the war in Europe was all about. Whatever the case, by helping to defeat Nazi Germany, the nation was willy-nilly also delivering a mortal blow to the anti-Semitism it expounded. But we cannot forget the pre-1944 reality that America had to be dragged kicking and screaming to mobilize for war against Germany. Mobilization would have been infinitely more difficult to achieve had it been portrayed as a war to save the Jews.

For our purposes here, we need to recall that during a bloody total war with a strong racial component, anti-Semitism was also a weapon of war that, if it could be incited and fueled, could do serious damage to the war effort. Democracies are not perfect societies but only in the process of becoming what they should be. There is no guarantee that they will produce humane decisions or even group tolerance. During a war that, much more than World War I, was fought to "make the world safe for democracy," America did not itself always act the way a democracy should. That much the Japanese inmates of our wartime detention camps and the segregated soldiers in our armed forces can attest to.

Anti-Semitism affected rescue policy not because the actors who shaped policy were under its influence. Its impact was usually more subtle than that. It colored the political and social environment. Roosevelt and Jewish leaders might have acted sooner and more vigorously had they not had to take it into account.

Conclusion

I have confined this discussion to only a small segment of the Holocaust—the refugee crisis. Examining even so delimited an aspect of the Holocaust suggests that PBS's indictment barely touches all the historical considerations that are required to create a balanced account of America's relation to the Holocaust.

That fuller historical account awaits some agreement among

students of the Holocaust regarding standards of behavior of by-standers. What could reasonably have been expected from the states and agencies that witnessed this disaster? What would have been sufficient? That determination, without which historical responsibility cannot be assessed, depends, in turn, on finding some agreement on the question of power. How much actual and usable power was available to the actors in the historical drama? What were the possibilities of rescue at every stage of the crisis? To assign responsibility when power to shape events did not exist produces, at best, bad history and, at worst, endless flagelation. Yet, power is extraordinarily difficult to define and measure. To what extent did American Jewry's rapid acculturation and assimilation affect its communal cohesiveness and coherence, on which its political power or influence was dependent? We have seen how lack of unity affected its ability to project pressure. Finally, the judgment of the historical weight, or valence, of the Final Solution by the actors in the historical drama is crucial to explain their action or inaction. If Roosevelt had seen the Holocaust as the shaping event of his time in history rather than merely another atrocity in a war full of atrocities, he might have done more to save European Jewry. The Roosevelt administration gave highest priority to winning the war. The rescue of Jews was not considered a special problem deserving its own priority. It would be achieved by defeating the Axis as quickly as possible. Nothing would be allowed to detract from that goal, not shipping food parcels to the camps, nor infringements of the "trading with the enemy" regulations, nor bombing the gas chambers and the rail lines leading to them.

    The underlying problem of most caring observers is that they find it difficult to reconcile their notion of what America stands for and the fact that the rescue of Jews was assigned such a low priority. They expect much more from this nation, perhaps too much. Yet, it is an expectation not totally rooted in unreality. Even if we accept that Roosevelt's highest priority had to be winning the war, the State Department's sabotage of rescue activities during the refugee crisis appears to go beyond what was necessary. It first created a bureaucratic "paper wall" to prevent even those who might legally have reached an American haven from doing so. It then tried to cut off news of the Final Solution. Finally, it blocked some rescue possibilities until the administration's hand was forced in the preelection months of 1944, which allowed for the establishment of the War Refugee Board and the circumvention of the immigration laws. Rescue advocates finally won their battle, but only when it was all but too late. These are facts not likely to become less damning with the passing of time.

Some judge the greatness of leaders by how well they understand and confront the defining crisis of their time. By that measure, Roosevelt does not come out well. He did not understand that the death camps represented such a defining event. With all our explanations of mitigating circumstances, it seems clear that Roosevelt was simply not fully on top of the refugee crisis or the Holocaust generally. Still, there is emerging a historiography that sees the Holocaust in much the same terms as did Roosevelt. It is viewed in the context of the war, particularly the bitter ideologically fueled war against the Soviet Union.[16] Waging that war had to receive the highest priority. In that context, Roosevelt's primary responsibility was to keep a nation, riven with class and racial strife, together so that a war of survival could be waged and won. That goal he achieved. He was forced to operate in a domestic political arena that was ignoble at best and an international arena dominated by a Darwinian code, unprecedented in its brutality. If that often base domestic political and international environment within which the American aspect of the Holocaust story was played out is omitted, there is distortion. There was deceit and indifference during the refugee crisis, but there were also many other things that a balanced account should mention. Principally, there were the almost half a million American soldiers who became causalties in the war. And there was politics and its driving force, the play for power, which hardly provide a conducive environment for the forces of justice and goodness to prevail.

When such contextual factors are considered, the terrible plight of the refugees tends to be muted. But it cannot for that reason be ignored. The producers of this documentary must, at some point, have become aware that the rules that make for good theater can come into conflict with those that make for good history. When that happens, as it does in this documentary, a balance between the demands for truth and for drama has to be searched for and found. PBS's "America and the Holocaust" fails to do that.

PART THREE

American Jewry and the Holocaust

10

Was There Communal Failure
Among American Jews?

THE AMERICAN JEWISH RESPONSE to the Holocaust has become a central question in the group's historiography and has produced a plethora of books and articles that question not only the effectiveness of that response but the character of the leaders who organized it.[1] I suspect that there is much more to the story than merely noting that the second and third generations had become uncaring Jews.[2] American Jewry's prior record of reaction to overseas crises was after all a good one. Calls for help from abroad had elicited a generous Jewish response during the Damascus blood libel (1840), the Mortara kidnapping (1858), the Dreyfus affair (1894), the Beilis blood libel case (1903–1907), and the Kishinev pogrom (1903). Including the familiar mass protest ritual and the quest for government diplomatic intercession, the community response to these crises were neither notably different from what Jews were doing in the thirties and forties nor more effective. Were the researchers who found American Jewry indifferent to the fate of their European brethren imagining a Jewry that they wanted to exist rather than contending with the one that was? I suspect that the best clues to explain the behavior of American Jewry during the Holocaust is hidden in its experiences during the interwar years. Specifically, the roots of the Jewish response could be found in the individual and group identity changes of the postimmigrant generations, which made them at once freer of

This essay appeared originally in *American Jewish History* 81, no. 1 (Autumn 1993): 60–80, under the title "Was There Communal Failure? Some Thoughts on the American Jewish Response to the Holocaust."

communal constraints and less able to identify with a worldwide Jewish interest.

There was also a qualitative difference between these former crises and the one that began in 1933. The crisis faced by Jewish communities everywhere as a result of the advent of National Socialism threatened the survival of Judaism as a distinct religious civilization. It threatened the Jews collectivity as well as hundreds of Jewish communities. There had been during former crises no modern nation-state that had made anti-Semitism an intrinsic part of its public policy. Other conditions were also different during the thirties. There was a worldwide depression that heightened extremism at both ends of the political spectrum. Although the impending disaster threatened to be of unprecedented scale and ferocity, few were able to foresee a movement to annihilate the Jewish people. Clearly, the inability of the modern imagination to envision the world of Auschwitz affected the early Jewish response to the Holocaust. But these factors cannot account for the loss of communal cohesiveness that became discernible as the crisis unfolded. During the Roosevelt era, American Jews were more politically active than ever before, and they had achieved a place in the Roosevelt administration; but throughout the crisis, they remained a divided community wracked by bitter internecine strife. What could account for it? Had the bonds between them become so weak that they could not hold?

The picture of American Jewry that emerges is complex and yields no easy answers. Ultimately, the historian must question whether a Jewish community in the accepted sense—a group bound by common culture, language, experience, and religion—was still functioning during the interwar years. Historical forces associated with modernization and acculturation, which American Jewry experienced simultaneously and which were superimposed on a reenergized anti-Semitic movement, reshaped the consciousness of American Jewry. I confine my observations to the impact of anti-Semitism superimposed on a people caught in transition and to how a people insecure and afraid that "it might happen here" responded to the deepest crisis in postemancipation Jewish history, perhaps in all Jewish history.

Anyone examining this period in the American Jewish experience cannot escape the impression that anti-Semitism was the most constant source of concern for Jews. But to note simply that there was anti-Semitism in the twenties and thirties, even of a particularly virulent variety, is like observing that there was a cycle of seasons.

Anti-Semitism can, after all, be found in every epoch of postexilic Jewish history. Even those who observe that it was especially severe during the interwar years must also note that the series of incidents and practices that composed it were not cut from the same cloth and that their impact on Jewish well-being varied considerably. The rantings of Henry Ford's *Dearborn Independent* or Charles Coughlin's post-1938 radio addresses may have seared the collective Jewish spirit, but they hardly affected the conditions of daily Jewish life. Second- and third-generation Jews did not spend every waking moment worrying about anti-Semitism. Members of the aging immigrant generation may, in fact, have found the American brand of anti-Semitism mild compared to what they had experienced in Europe. Indeed, for the growing number of Jews who were in the process of severing their links to the community, anti-Semitism probably meant little and may in some cases have hastened that separation. Curtailment of employment or housing opportunities, which impacted directly on the material conditions of life, were usually far more telling. The rantings of such anti-Semitic publicists as Burton J. Hendricks or the Reverend George Simons fed the deep underlying wellsprings of anti-Semitism. Their poisonous effect on public morality was cumulative, although they did not directly affect access to the American dream, which had a great impact on the way Jews shaped their lives. But the minor blood libel in Massena, a small town in New York State, placed these Jews directly in danger's path. Local authorities, including the mayor, held Jews for questioning; the threat was here and now, palpable and frightening. Similarly, the Harvard enrollment limitations case affected only a handful of Jewish students but impinged on the interests of Jewish elites in formation. Leaders such as Louis Marshall, who played an active role in the campaign to undo the limitations policy, understood that access to the highest positions in the country was involved because Harvard established the conventions of the American university culture. For practical and historical reasons, Jews placed enormous value on higher education. If Harvard's quotas stood, Jewish goals would be limited; if they fell, young Jews could aspire to almost any position. Still, the case baffled less acculturated Jews who could not understand why anyone would want to be in a place where they were not wanted.

In the most serious case of public anti-Semitism during the twenties, the restrictionist immigration laws of 1921 and 1924, we encounter difficulty in determining where a specific anti-Jewish animus begins and general "Nordicism" ends. The immigration laws had the greatest potential impact on American Jewry, for if they had been aimed exclusively at Jewish immigrants, the result would have been a case of political anti-Semitism such as existed in nineteenth-century czarist Russia or the Germany of the thirties. With the exception of General Order Number 11 (1862), such political anti-Semitism was virtually unknown in the American Jewish experience. In the case of the restrictionist immigration laws of 1921 and 1924, there is no question that lawmakers were especially concerned about a "flood" of Jewish immigrants from eastern Europe, which they imagined was poised to burst forth on America. But there is also evidence that the arrival of masses of penniless Jews was not the only fear of restrictionists. Potential Jewish immigrants shared the status of "undesirable" with immigrants from southern and eastern Europe whose quotas were accordingly limited on the basis of national origin. If there was an exclusive desire to keep out Jews, it was difficult to prove. Congressman Emanuel Celler, who represented an almost all-Jewish district in Brooklyn, noted that there was contempt for all "new" immigrants. He realized, finally, that "they simply didn't want any more 'wops, dagoes, Hebrews, hunkies, bulls.'" As one House immigration committee member put it in response to an accusation made by Gedaliah Bublick, editor of the Orthodox *Tageblatt*, that the law was anti-Semitic in intent—there would have been no restriction had the Jews taken care to have been born in Scotland.[3]

Paradoxically, these laws, whose anti-Semitic intent was embedded in a general distaste for the people of eastern and southern Europe, would have a formidable impact on retaining in the United States a distinctive ethnic culture based on Yiddish. They meant that the infusion of cultural and religious energy from abroad, on which American Jewish communal and religious life was in some measure dependent, would be throttled. Only approximately 71,000 Jews were able to enter the United States between 1921 and 1929, a far cry from the hundreds of thousands who entered in the first decade of the century. Deprived of a steady stream of consumers, the Yiddish press and theater as well as numerous institutions for cultural transmission declined markedly during the twenties. Of course, there were those like Cyrus Adler, who insisted that "if three and a half million Jews in America cannot maintain Judaism without a constant stream of immigration then they are unworthy of Judaism."[4]

During the twenties, few were prescient enough to realize that, by permitting no distinction between refugees in dire need of haven and ordinary immigrants, the quota laws would become lethal during the refugee crisis of the thirties when Hitler sought to make the Reich *Judenrein* by forcing German Jews and later the Jews of Austria and Czechoslovakia to emigrate. The strict implementation of the laws by the Hoover administration, especially the LPC (likely to become a public charge) provision, made it virtually impossible to gain access to America. Only in the year 1939 were the relevant quotas fully used. If one had a taste for historical symmetry, one could note that the ideology of "Nordic supremacy" behind the quota system was the same as Hitler's notions of racial purity embodied in the mystique of Aryanism. During the interwar years, America would not welcome Jews for much the same reason that Berlin wanted to get rid of them.

As raucous as the anti-Semitic rhetoric of the twenties often was, as troublesome as it could be for Jewish job seekers, as limiting as the immigration laws would prove to be for the continuance of Jewish culture, anti-Semitism hardly put a crimp in the second generation's drive to achieve middle-class status. More than anything else, it was that aspiration which marked Jewish life during the decade of the twenties. More energy and concern were expended on the private drive to achieve than on any public endeavor in Jewish American life. American Jews were an extraordinarily ambitious, some might say driven, group. It was as if the freedom of America had caused the release of a steel coil pent up for millennia behind confining ghetto walls. Their campaign to open government civil service to merit furnished more and better employment, especially in teaching, but it also incurred the wrath of the Irish, who had grown to think of municipal civil service as their own fief. There were complaints in the *Brooklyn Eagle* that few Irish names could be found on the new civil service lists. But Jews were delighted with the merit system. Their children did well in school and on such tests, which above all required good reading comprehension. The *American Hebrew* boasted that the list of regent scholarship winners in New York State "reads like a confirmation roster at a temple."[5] Indeed, the second generation reached the ivy-covered halls of academe fully one generation before other groups in the post-1890 immigration.

That Jews shared fully in the prosperity of the twenties is demonstrated by the continued growth of the Jewish ethnic economy. By 1937, two-thirds of the 34,000 factories and 104,000 wholesale and retail establishments in New York City were owned by Jews. A similar pattern was discernible in other large cities.[6] The twenties were also a period of self-improvement and professionalization of the Jewish work force. A finisher in the garment industry might strive to become a cutter, a bookkeeper an accountant, a teacher a principal. Jews were prone to using their limited capital to invest in the human capital of themselves. The entire family often shared the expense of sending a son to college and then for professional training. Medical and law schools were flooded with Jewish applicants, who seemed to redouble their efforts when blocks were placed in their path. When housing in desirable neighborhoods was restricted, Jewish developers built their own. They did the same when Jews were rejected for membership in college fraternities and country clubs. Anti-Semitism was real, but it could be fought as in the Ford and Harvard cases. If that seemed too remote a goal for impatient Jews at the grass roots, it could be circumvented as in the case of the young Jewish job applicant who obtained a note from the local minister testifying to the fact that she was not Jewish so that she might get a position with the telephone company. "Would going around jobless and having to come to her father or mother for a dollar be better?" queried the chagrined mother.[7] Name changes and other subterfuges to conceal Jewish origins were sometimes resorted to by those who refused to suffer for a faith whose tenets they no longer observed.

Such strategies might gain one employment, but they could not shield from the more virulent anti-Semitism of the thirties that attacked Jews collectively. Ford's rantings, the Rosenbluth trial, the Harvard quota case, and the dozens of other anti-Semitic incidents of the twenties were part of the nativist xenophobic atmosphere of that decade, which also produced the reenergized Ku Klux Klan and the dozens of patriotic societies that agitated for immigration restriction. This atmosphere was more indigenous and less target-centered on Jews who shared the antiforeign animus with other ethnics of the "new" immigration. But after the advent of National Socialism in Germany in 1933, there was a steady infusion of financial and ideological support from Berlin and Rome to specific anti-Semitic organizations. Like the National Socialists, the Fascist Party of Italy sought to bring Italian Americans closer to the regime. "Italian consuls do nearly everything but administer the fascist oath to Italo-Americans," wrote one observer.[8] Berlin viewed anti-Semitism as a heightened form of political consciousness and spared no effort to energize the existing anti-Semitic organizations with money and propaganda. That infusion gave indigenous anti-Semitism a new stature and virulence. It was now part of a worldwide movement that everywhere produced cadres of professional anti-Semites. Over 120 professional anti-Semitic organizations were active during the thirties, producing anti-Semitic literature, organizing rallies and boycotts of Jewish businesses, and offering a full social life based almost entirely on a distaste for Jews.

Such right-wing organizations as Fritz Kuhn's German-America Bund, William Pelley's Silver Shirts, and ultimately Father Charles Coughlin's Social Justice movement seemed to possess the potential for becoming popular mass movements, as had already happened in Germany. That possibility haunted American Jewry, which watched in disbelief as the highly integrated Jews of Germany were restricted in the professions and finally lost their civil and political rights as a result of the Nuremberg Laws (1935). The physical attack on Jewish persons and property known as *Kristallnacht*, which occurred on November 9–10, 1938, may have shocked American Jews more than their German compatriots because they were totally unprepared to believe that the rights of citizenship associated with emancipation could be withdrawn. Small wonder that *Fortune* magazine began its special issue on American Jewry in 1936 with the observation that there was a need to quiet "Jewish apprehensiveness," which had reached pathological dimensions.[9] Particularly worrisome for Jews was the possibility that the right wing of the isolationist movement represented by the "American First" committee might gain the upper hand in the political arena. It was the members of that movement who often openly echoed Berlin's Judeophobia. When the popular folk hero Charles Lindbergh warned in his Des Moines address (September 1941) that Jews should not push the nation to war because they would be the first victims, it sent shivers down the American Jewish spine. The speech echoed the warning Hitler had made in an address before the Reichstag in January 1939. Though the public did not take well to Lindbergh's speech, Jews feared that the wall between isolationism and anti-Semitism was being breached. Just nine months later, on June 21, 1942, the House Un-American Activities Committee secretly questioned a professional anti-Semite who, according to Martin Dies, stated that he favored "not the persecution, but execution of the Jews."[10]

Small wonder that, as the war approached, American Jewry's sense of security seemed badly shaken. The cumulative effects of indigenous anti-Semitism of the twenties had been heightened during the depression by the virulent brand that had made its debut in Europe. In the beleaguered perception of the second and third generations, it seemed that the next step would be the appearance of a "Jewish question" on the American political agenda, in the form of how much power and wealth Jews should be allowed to have. Private anti-Semitism would be transformed into a far more dangerous political anti-Semitism. The result was fear in the Jewish population and paralysis among its leaders. No understanding of the American Jewish response to the crisis in Europe is possible without knowing the context in which that response had to be organized. A shaken, insecure American Jewry had become more uncertain than ever of its place in America.

For the players on the historical stage, perception and reality are indivisible; but with hindsight there can be a gap between the two. Did American Jewry overreact to the anti-Semitism of the thirties? That there was a heightened anti-Semitism in the thirties and forties few will dispute. As late as 1944, 65 percent of Americans believed that Jews had too much power. But survey research is not particularly reliable in measuring the depth of anti-Semitism and often yielded contradictory results. Some polls indicated that only 12 percent of Americans were actually classifiable as anti-Semitic during the thirties. After *Kristallnacht*, a strong "spectator sympathy" for Jews developed. Ninety-four percent of Americans disapproved of Nazi anti-Semitic depredations, which became a cause for concern in Berlin.[11] At the height of isolationism, there was probably little danger of a Jewish question becoming part of the political dialogue; and in 1944, the year when anti-Semitism reached its zenith, Americans were far more concerned with winning the war than with worrying about whether it was a war to save the Jews. The nation, after all, waged war against an enemy that placed anti-Semitism at the center of its ideology. Such anti-Semitic demagogues as Fritz Kuhn, Gerald L. K. Smith, William Pelley, Gerald Winrod, and Robert Edmondson were not a particularly impressive lot who might fit comfortably into the mainstream of American politics. Moreover, the general influence in politics of such ethnics as German and Italian Americans, groups in which an imported anti-Semitism might have been planted, had declined considerably as they acculturated. Just as in the case of the Yiddish press, there was a parallel decline in the readership of the American ethnic press and in membership in its fraternal organizations. Anti-Semitism remained an isolated, largely inchoate force.

Most important, America's entrance into the war against Germany in December 1941 militated against a racist world view held by the Axis powers.

Clearly, the Jewish perception of danger went beyond the reality. America was not Germany, and the ability of organized anti-Semitism to insert itself into the political process was limited by its aberrance and its alienation from the American mainstream; yet, the Jewish perception of the imminence of such a thing's happening is understandable. This perception was built on the experience of anti-Semitism during the twenties and its increased bitterness during the thirties, which witnessed a fallout of interethnic hostility stemming from the depression.

The Jewish perception of anti-Semitism, or perhaps better, the misperception of it, serves as background noise in the environment in which the American Jewish response to the Holocaust was fashioned. The factors directly affecting the quality of that response were the subtle alteration of the mind-set and self-image of second- and third-generation American Jews. These changes gradually deprived them of traditional cohesiveness and self-understanding. In the free atmosphere of America, the divisions that everywhere characterized postemancipation Jewish communities were exacerbated. It was not that secularizing Jews felt less Jewish but that they no longer felt exclusively so. The American Jewish identity was multileveled. Jewish citizens functioned in a professional public arena and in a private one, they responded to crisis both as Jews and as Americans. The freer secularized communal structure made unified action more difficult to achieve because there was no one to order Jews to their Judaism or even to mute their ideological differences in order that they might act together. The four efforts between 1938 and 1944 to create an institutional mechanism for unified action to rescue European Jewry came to nought. The only recorded instance of successful co-ordination came in the important area of fund raising when, pressured by the newly established Council of Jewish Federations and Welfare Funds (October 1932), the United Jewish Appeal attained a fragile unity in 1939. It raised $124,000,000 between 1939 and 1945, insufficient for the need at hand but a remarkable feat when compared to organized fund raising in other areas of American society. During the depression, a period of heightened political activism for Jews, their talents and energy continued to flow in traditional fund-raising philanthropic channels. It was only after the war that Jews qua Jews became fully involved in the political process.

By the thirties, total communal unity was probably no longer achievable, even in the face of the murderous threat emanating from Berlin. On the one hand, the traditional sources of unity—religion, a common language and culture, and a common interest and world view—had grown weaker. On the other, ideological and political diversity had grown stronger, so that one generation could barely recognize much less find something in common with its successor. Listen to one writer ruefully describing the distinctions between first-generation Jews who settled on the East Side of Manhattan and their successors who had moved to the new neighborhoods in the Bronx and Brooklyn:

> It's the second generation Jew with all the outward characteristics minus beard and mustache, playing baseball, great fight fans, commercial travelers, clean-shirted, white-collared, derby-hatted, creased-trousered. The women are stylish and stout, social workers, actresses, stump-speakers, jazz dancers with none of the color and virtues of the erstwhile bewigged parents, and a few vices of their own acquisition. But they bathe frequently.[12]

Something was lost in the passage from the first generation to the "clean-shirted creased-trousered" second that went beyond appearance. The "bewigged" first generation continued to generate a fairly strong sense of Jewish identity. It was strong enough so that even as "uptown" German Jews may have looked down upon their brethren from eastern Europe, they nevertheless supported a liberal immigration law and dozens of programs and institutions to ameliorate their condition. But in the second generation, the weakening of the religious and ethnic bonds that bound all Jews together had become more noticeable. By the thirties, it was the bewigged Jews that would appear to be aberrant. To be sure, synagogue building and membership in congregations actually rose during the twenties; and the Yiddish theater flourished until 1927. But the traditional sources of strength and unity, rooted in the family and the Yiddish-based secular culture, were weakening. The acculturating second generation was establishing new behavioral norms that were often in conflict with traditional ones. For example, the matchmaker (*shadkin*), who helped negotiate the path to marriage in the older generation, was being replaced by new courting patterns based on the notion of romantic love that, in turn, was based on a more liberated position of women. Going to a matchmaker, complained one young woman, was "like going on the slave market . . . to be weighed and measured like a cow at a fair."[13] The laws of family purity that guided the behavior of religious Jews were especially difficult to adhere to in the hedonistic culture of the twenties. The result was generational conflict, which sometimes became the subject of Yiddish plays and *romanen* published in the Yiddish press.

But only a few contemporaries, such as Mordecai Kaplan, who in 1921 founded the Reconstructionist movement, perceived what was happening as a massive survival crisis. It was manifested in the weakening of corporate group identity. Inherent in the secularization process was a strong drive for individuation and autonomy, which led ultimately to detribalization. That process was an inevitably product of living in a free secular society. Matters of religious law such as *kashrut*, which formerly could be enforced by rabbinic or community sanction, no longer could be in a complex and free urban environment. To the extent that traditional behavioral norms still applied concerning relations between the sexes or in business, they were adhered to voluntarily. Compliance with religious practices came to depend on the individual Jew finding a balance between the new life goals, which placed a high value on self-realization and becoming American, and the ethnic and religious tenets of the Jewish tradition. Many modified such practices, and some abandoned them altogether. The second-generation American Jew remained recognizably Jewish, but he was now also influenced by behavioral norms and goals that prevailed in the majority culture. The generation that reached maturity in the twenties possessed less knowledge of the traditional religious culture from which such values stemmed; the generations that followed would know even less. A ramshackle, ineffective Jewish education system and a family preoccupied with achieving material success or simply making a living meant that the traditional agencies for transmitting Jewish knowledge and values had lost influence. At the same time, widespread use of the public school system meant that familiarity with secular American culture increased at the juncture where knowledge of the traditional culture waned. The second-generation Jews no longer learned *yiddishkeit* or the religious culture with their mother's milk. A special effort and new institutions were required to teach the culture. People were increasingly free to shape their own relationship to the community, which could be expressed through philanthropy or culinary habits or simply by insisting that Judaism was something heartfelt. The strong individuation inherent in the culture of self-realization would be reflected in a more diverse and weakened community structure. It was that internally weakened community that was called upon to respond to the impending catastrophe facing European Jewry.

Thousands of Jews retained their linkage to the community through voluntary organizations and fraternal orders. During the interwar years, the 4,228,000 Jews of America developed the richest organizational infrastructure of any American ethnic group. It consisted of 17,500 organizations of forty-nine different categories ranging from community service agencies, such as the Hebrew Immigrant Aid Society (HIAS), to multicountry agencies, such as the American Jewish Joint Distribution Committee (JDC). Eighteen percent of these organizations were associated with religious concerns, the bulk of which were a growing number of congregations that were establishing themselves in areas of second settlement. Defense organizations, service organizations, and fraternal orders provided their memberships with medical insurance and cemetery plots and even vacation resorts at reasonable prices. There were dozens of Zionist organizations, each representing a different ideological stripe, and a growing number of federations whose goal it was to bring order into the chaotic fund-raising activity. But programming for Judaism, which these organizations did, proved no substitute for living it. Hadassah or the dozens of organizations to which a second-generation Jew might belong could generate great acts of devotion, but they did not create communities of faith.

During the twenties, philanthropy became an important way for secularizing Jews to continue their community connections. It also added a new dynamic factor to Jewish communal life, especially after growing Jewish affluence dramatically increased the sums raised. Now the millions of dollars collected yearly represented real "spoils," whose allocation would be bitterly contested by the various political factions. The conflict over the allocations formula between Zionists and non-Zionists during the interwar period warrants a separate book. It became particularly bitter during the Crimean resettlement venture undertaken by the JDC after 1924. Zionists felt that such funds should go to build up the *Yishuv* (prewar Jewish settlement in Palestine), whereas the "Joint" argued that resettling Jews where they were was cheaper and more practicable. The Arab riots of 1929 reinforced that argument, which predictably also won the support of the Communist element in the community. The alliance between the wealthy Jewish "philanthrapoids" and the Kremlin is one of the strangest episodes in American Jewish history.

The proliferation of Jewish organizations should not be confused with the existence of a tightly bonded community, for the reverse proved to be the case. The innumerable political and ideological divisions actually caused the organizations to multiply. Each ideology, even a shading of an ideology, tended to produce its own organizational expression. Lack of flexibility, which ideological commitment tended to bring in its wake, created dividing walls between the various factions of the community during the years of the Holocaust, making it almost impossible to find a middle ground. The huge sums of money involved compounded the problem. Except for the federations, which tried to play a bridging role, as in the case of the reformation of the UJA in 1939, there was little to hold the Jewish community together.

By the late 1930s, the reenergized American Zionist movement might have played such a binding role. Its failure to do so warrants special comment. After the divisive Cleveland convention of the Zionist Organization of America (ZOA) (1921), led the Brandeis-Mack faction to give up its leadership, the movement entered a period of decline. That was reflected in the difficulties of the United Palestine Appeal, the fund-raising arm of the Zionist movement, in achieving its goals and a decline in membership. By 1931. its principal umbrella organization, the ZOA, had about eight thousand shekel payers, the requisite token payment for membership. When the Nazis took power in January 1933, the American Zionist movement was in the humiliating position of advocating grandiose goals of nation building while having neither the finances nor the organizational coherence to realize them. It seemed as if the American Zionist movement was moribund.

Yet eight years later, this sad picture of decline and disarray was completely reversed. ZOA's membership rose to 55,000 in 1939, and membership in the World Zionist Organization rose to almost 250,000. Zionists also finally penetrated the American Jewish fund-raising apparatus. What had happened? American Jews had begun to view the crisis of German Jewry in Zionist terms. They came to Zionism, not through the esoteric ideology of Zionist thinkers who spoke of the "renaissance of the Jewish people," but through the refugee crisis. Few nations welcomed the Jewish refugees being forcibly extruded from the Reich in order to make itself *Judenrein*. They understood in simple terms that what Jews required was a refuge, a piece of land, where they could find a haven should it become necessary.

But the American Zionist movement was ill-prepared to receive the human bounty cast out by the events in Germany. Ironically, although some leading Zionist thinkers had warned about the untenability of Jewish life in the Diaspora, the Zionist movement generally was late in evaluating the crisis befalling European Jewry and therefore was slow in making a transition from a group of loosely held-together organizations devoted to philanthropy into the political agent of American Jewry. Its leadership was old and driven by personal ambition, and the movement was divided into factions that reflected the riven state of the world Zionist movement. The thin line of settlements in Palestine, which had become the pride of all committed Jews, concealed an economy that was developing painfully slowly and would not be prepared for years to absorb all the Jews who needed to find a new home.

Most important, the solutions the Zionist leadership sought in the face of the crisis either ran counter to the effort of Jews to mobilize themselves or were too narrowly conceived to be effective for the primary task of rescuing Jews. During the twenties, the movement's efforts were hampered by a low ebb of organizational energy. It never fully recovered from the bitter internal conflict between the Americanists, led by Brandeis, and the Palestinianists, headed by Louis Lipsky. The victory of the latter meant that the bridge to the "uptown" philanthropists, whom Brandeis sought to link to the development of Palestine on a project-by-project investment basis, was weakened. Rabbi Stephen Wise, the Zionist leader who was president of the American Jewish Congress, might give vent to his frustration regarding the power of these philanthropists by declaring that one Haim Bialik, the beloved Jewish writer and poet, was worth more than one hundred Felix Warburgs, the leading Jewish philanthropist of the interwar period.[14] But the reality was that the major portion of funds required to manage community affairs was still raised by such "philanthrapoids." In the years between 1921 and 1925 the Zionist organizations launched four "appeals" but raised only $6,000,000, a paltry sum when compared to the $20,800,000 raised by the JDC in the same period. The JDC's sponsorship of Jewish resettlement in the Crimea demonstrated that, in the Jewish community, the monied piper still played the tune. The expansion of the Jewish Agency to include American philanthropists in 1929 did not resolve the problem.

As in the World Zionist movement of which it was part, the American Zionist leadership was forced by the crisis to make terrible choices between its own development and the need to rescue European Jewry. The choice did not, of course, appear that way to Zionists, who were convinced that the best way to rescue European Jews was to allow them to settle in Palestine, whose economy would thereby be strengthened. During the thirties, the Zionist movement placed the development of Palestine's economy above the boycott of German goods. There was relative prosperity in Palestine during the depressed thirties because Hjalmar Schacht, the president of the Reichsbank, had reached an agreement with the Bank of Palestine whereby a portion of blocked German Jewish assets could be transferred in the form of capital goods. But by participating in the transfer agreements, the Zionist movement inevitably faced a bitter confrontation with the militant Jews who had organized a boycott of German goods, the first Jewish communal effort to hit back against its tormentors.[15] Similarly, after the 1939 British White Paper limited the number of refugees allowed to enter and the amount of land that could be purchased in Palestine, the Zionist movement, led by David Ben Gurion (who then headed the Jewish Agency), mounted a campaign to change British policy. Ben Gurion was convinced that sufficient pressure could be brought to bear to do so. But the contest between the British government and the Zionist movement was from the outset an uneven one and grew more so as the war progressed. The energy and resources spent on trying to mobilize public opinion against the White Paper were of no avail. All attempts to change British policy failed. At the same time, the Zionist leaders were unwilling to expend precious resources to settle European Jews elsewhere. Thousands of Jews who would have settled anywhere for the moment in order to save their lives were instead transported eastward for Berlin's version of "resettlement," which usually meant death. Zionists could neither easily transfer their skills in resettling Jews nor expend the necessary resources to develop such areas as British Guiana or Mindanao without short-changing their own enterprise. There were not sufficient resources to do both, and the prospects for developing the over six hundred areas searched out by the Roosevelt administration were not good. The hapless refugees fell between two chairs.

Might things have happened differently had the world Zionist movement, and especially its American wing, focused exclusively on getting Jews out of Europe? After decades of resistance, American

Jewry seemed ready to follow Zionist leadership during the Holocaust. But it discovered that the movement was badly split and that its rescue strategy was focused on safeguarding the development of the *Yishuv*, and only through it on rescuing the millions. Disunity was nothing new in the world Zionist movement, but the crisis rather than healing old conflicts exacerbated them. The conflict with the Revisionists, which began in 1926 when the followers of Vladimir Jabotinsky left the movement, exploded with a vengeance in the United States after a small group of Irgunists led by Hillel Kook (Peter Bergson) capitalized on the compelling idea of organizing a Jewish army to fight the Nazis. For a victimized people, the notion of having its own army to fight its enemies proved to be irresistible. It catapulted the Bergson group into prominence, and their skillful use of public relations kept them there.

Throughout the conflict, the Irgunists remained a thorn in the side of the mainline Zionist organizations, refusing all offers to bring them into the fold. In some measure, the popularity of the "Bergson boys," which belied their small number, was related to the fact that American Jewry, especially its now-weighty Zionist component, was radicalized by events in Europe. That radicalization led the Zionist convention meeting in the Biltmore Hotel in New York in May 1942 to accept the idea of establishing a Jewish commonwealth, a euphemism for a sovereign Jewish state in Palestine. The Biltmore program became in itself a new source of disunity. Tamar de Sola Pool and others on the left end of the political spectrum did not agree with Ben Gurion, who had counseled the delegates of the Biltmore convention that "Palestine would be as Jewish as the Jews will make it."[16] They argued that the resolution brought rescue no closer and it needlessly antagonized the Arab world. In 1943, when the American Jewish Conference approved the commonwealth resolution, which caused the American Jewish Committee and the Jewish Labor Committee to leave the conference, Judah Magnes, rector of the Hebrew University and leader of a group who favored a binational state in Palestine, warned that the commonwealth declaration was "a declaration of war by Jews on the Arabs."[17] More disturbing for rescue advocates was the fact that the commonwealth resolution did not directly confront the issue of rescue because few European Jews could get to Palestine. A new division between maximalists and conciliators was now superimposed on the myriad preexisting divisions of the Zionist movement, which remained hopelessly divided throughout the crisis.

Ironically, the American Zionist movement had achieved a new high point in political effectiveness by the time the divisions within the community had become unbridgeable. Mobilized by the reorganized American Zionist Emergency Committee (AZEC), which became the political arm of the American Zionist movement, its four hundred local emergency committees would soon be able to flood the Oval Office or Congress with ten thousand telegrams within hours of the announcement of a need to do so. But despite such prowess, the Zionist movement proved too weak to change Roosevelt's Middle East policy, which was not inclined to challenge British dominance in Palestine during the war. Despite strong support in Congress, the Wright-Compton resolution (HR 418) and the identical Wagner-Taft resolution (SR 247), in which the commonwealth resolution and the anti–White Paper policy were embedded, were easily defeated by the Roosevelt administration by the simple strategy of questioning the propriety of passing such resolutions during wartime. The blame for that failure does not belong exclusively to the Zionist movement. American Jewry simply did not possess the power to change foreign policy priorities during hostilities.

A divided American Zionist movement thus failed to unify American Jewry; but even had it been able to do so, it could not have broken Roosevelt's hold on the Jewish voter. In the election of 1944, Jews continued their love affair with Roosevelt despite his weak rescue policy and his failure to support the idea of a Jewish homeland. Roosevelt, after all, was the leader who led America into a war against the arch enemy of the Jewish people. Jewish leaders could not hope to threaten the administration by removing the Jewish vote. They did not have that kind of control of the maverick, heavily ideological, Jewish voters who viewed themselves as patriotic American citizens rather than victimized Jews. There is a lesson in the election of 1944 for those who see an all-powerful Jewry ready to serve a Jewish cause exclusively and able to dictate public policy. They need only observe its ignominious failure to unify itself and project influence on the Roosevelt administration during that crucial year.

America's entrance into the war, a war to defeat National Socialism first, rekindled Jewish confidence and a sense of solidarity with the nation. Earlier than most Americans, Jews were convinced that Hitlerism posed a threat to civilized world order, not only to Jews. By 1941, American Jews were virtually unanimous in their support for America's entry into the war, which they viewed as a just one. The Roosevelt administration's argument that a quick victory was the best way to save the Jews was not directly challenged by American Jewry. Given the patriotic fervor of American Jewry and fear of the accusation that Jews were fighting for an ethnic rather than a national interest, it was difficult for Jewish leaders to oppose the administration's argument. For most American Jews, winning the war—not the rescue of their brethren—received priority. The two objectives did not seem in conflict because few understood until 1944 that, by the time victory came, European Jewry would be in ashes. The ferocity of the assault on European Jewry eluded them. The warning that nothing must be allowed to interfere with the war effort sent the Wright-Compton Resolution for a Jewish commonwealth in Palestine down to defeat, and it also cast suspicion on Morgenthau's "hard" plan for the postwar treatment of Germany.

During the war, American Jews were also preoccupied with their own security. Even as they mobilized all communal resources to help achieve victory, the fear persisted that the still-powerful anti-Semitic elements would single Jews out as draft dodgers and war profiteers. With the anti-Semitic allegations made during World War I still etched sharply in their memories, Jewish leaders would be prepared this time. Jewish defense organizations planned to wage a separate battle to deflect the expected attacks, which did in fact materialize. In October 1941, the Jewish Welfare Board established a Bureau of War Records to assure that the Jewish contributions to the war effort were made known to the American public. Eventually, the bureau informed the nation that 550,000 Jewish men and women served in the US armed forces, 8 percent above their proportion of the population. Every person who won a medal for valor and every casualty was duly registered and publicized by the bureau.

What the historian observes in the interwar years is that the elements on which traditional Jewish communalism was based had become weaker, with the result that it becomes increasingly difficult to speak of a single American Jewish community. It was left for anti-Semites, whose organizations proliferated during the thirties, to imagine that American Jewry was a unified, conspiratorial tribe. The erosion of the religious tradition and the loosening of ethnic ties, both traditional pillars of cohesiveness, left American Jewry a divided confederation. American Jewry had to find a new base for unity in the face of crisis. In the mid-thirties the strongest hope that such unity might still be achieved lay within the growing dominance of the American Zionist movement. But that movement, too, was beset by strife, and its rescue strategy was limited by what its leaders imagined to be the needs of the *Yishuv*. Its aspiration, to compel Britain to open the gates of Palestine, was far beyond what it could achieve. For ideological and financial reasons, it could not wholeheartedly support the temporary resettlement of European Jews elsewhere. Only with the movement to establish the Jewish state was a new foundation for unity set in place.

The task faced by American Jewry between 1933 and 1945 was forbidding. It first required Jews to persuade the American people to liberalize their restrictionist immigration policy in the midst of a severe depression and then to convince the Roosevelt administration to change wartime priorities to allow for the rescue of European Jews. The kind of political influence required to change such basic public policy was simply not available to American Jewish leaders, whose position, despite the rantings of anti-Semites regarding the "Jew Deal," was in fact only marginally enhanced during the Roosevelt era.

Nevertheless, Jews probably overestimated the danger posed by organized anti-Semitism during the thirties. They knew there was a financial and informational link between the reenergized anti-Semitic organizations and Berlin. The huge rallies staged by Fritz Kuhn's German-American Bund had a suspicious "made in Germany" look. When they shared the "hit list" with other minority groups, American Jews showed that they understood this was not the Ku Klux Klan of the twenties. The Klan had in fact lost most of its steam by the thirties. Many concluded that what had happened in Germany might very well happen here. Insecure and fearful, the second and third generations reacted with enormous apprehension. Until America entered the war, they felt they were alone in facing a powerful foe bent on destroying all Jewish civilization.

American Jewry also faced the Holocaust as a riven people. Caught between a demanding acculturation and secularization process, which called for alteration of the group's ethnic and religious identity but left them uncertain that making such changes would yield complete access to the promise of America, Jews were unable to determine where history had positioned them. The depression radicalized much of its younger generation, who believed that the way to save the Jews was to join in the fight against Fascism. During the war, it was difficult for secular, Americanized Jews to perceive a specific Jewish interest apart from an Allied victory.

Some people indict American Jewry for what it was becoming, as if it had the power to halt the historical forces that were transforming it. There are, however, few instances in history when a people have been able to reverse such processes in order to meet better the needs of the moment. Had Jews by some divine intervention suddenly possessed the power to transform themselves, they probably would have rejected the opportunity to reclaim their Judaism, especially if they believed that it would mean abandoning their success in the private realm, which was where modern American Jewry's primary interest lay. There was no assurance that such an abandonment would have meant a greater achievement in the public realm where rescue policy was made.

It develops that those who are convinced that the second and third generations of American Jewry, who determined the shape of Jewish life during the interwar years, performed the way they did during the Holocaust because they were indifferent Jews, see only the tip of the iceberg. It was, after all, the same Jewry that, a few years later, was able to move mountains to win diplomatic recognition for the newly established Jewish state. The war and the Holocaust accelerated the process of reshaping American Jewry. It became an organized, effective community finally able to carry fully the mantle of leadership formerly held by European Jewry. The historian must take great care not to read this later coherence and effectiveness back into the interwar period. Those words do not apply during those fateful years.

11

Jewish Leadership
During the Roosevelt Years

THINKING ABOUT THE RELATIONSHIP of the Roosevelt administration to American Jewry entails no ordinary difficulty. Compelled to develop new ways to confront depression and war, that administration possessed a high degree of complexity. Similarly, American Jewry's unique organization and its resistance to normal patterns of acculturation, makes it no ordinary subculture. And if these two variables alone were not yet sufficiently complex, the Holocaust, which is today at the center of Jewish sensibility, is emerging as an event of extraordinary historical valence. It reminds us that the relationship between Roosevelt and the Jews was but the most recent episode in the continuing encounter between Judaism and the West, between Jerusalem and Rome. Some are ready to link the loss of 6,000,000 Jewish lives to a failure of concern by the Roosevelt administration and that idea also generates a special intensity, that of lovers betrayed. It is not the same as the relationship between Italian Americans or even Japanese Americans and Roosevelt. There is no blood to account for, and they did not adore him the way the Jews did. Given that feeling of betrayal, the indictment that insists on assigning to the Roosevelt administration a task it did not want to assume and to American Jewry a responsibility not matched by its power to discharge is understandable.

Yet, it cannot produce sound history. Instead, it leads to an-

This essay appeared originally in *Modern Judaism* 8, no. 2 (May 1988), 101–18, under the title "Crisis and Response: American Jewish Leadership During the Roosevelt Years."

other important endeavor, an attempt to measure the extent and nature of Jewish power in the thirties, without which there can be no reasonable judgment on what might have been done. The indictment against Roosevelt and American Jewry is itself a characteristic of American Jewish political culture. The same habits and assumptions brought into the political arena that have shaped the relationship between the Jews and Roosevelt have generated the indictment today. That is, those who hold these habits and assumptions assign to the political process the imperative of mission and also deal with politics, not as it is, but as they think it should be. The Armenians, whose slaughter by the Turks haunts the Holocaust, make no assumptions about the humanitarian concern of governments or their own power to alter the course of events. They do not assign to themselves and to others such awesome tasks. How did a fragmented and disunited subculture, no longer accustomed to thinking of itself as a single unified political entity, assume such an awesome responsibility? How did it use its supposedly enhanced power? Did the prominent secular Jews in the Roosevelt entourage fathom what a human, not necessarily an ethnic response, required? How atuned was the occupant of the Oval Office to hear and sympathize with a plea for special action? What follows is a preliminary probe for the answer to these questions.

It is difficult to avoid the conclusion that American Jewish political culture was peculiarly ill-suited to discharge the responsibility history and kinship assigned to it. Roosevelt required a simple direct request for action, delivered by a recognizable, coherent constituency, reinforced by a normal political transaction. Jews were able to furnish none of these. What Roosevelt heard instead, when he bothered to listen at all, was a cacophony of sound and fury from a subgroup whose internal political life was so raucous as to be uncivil.

Yet despite its lack of coherence, a penchant for activism, a comparatively rapid emergence from the depression, and a growing level of formal education and professionalization created the impression during the New Deal that the Jewish voice was louder than warranted by its 3.6 percent of the population.[1] That American Jewry projected any power at all is remarkable when one recalls how reluctantly the East European Jewish immigrants entered the political arena. There were better things to do with one's time than to partake in a game that lacked transcendent purpose. Politics, they believed, was to bring the new day, not a means of self- or group aggrandizement. Jews had a tendency to ideological intensity, a characteristic that would become more pronounced during the depression. Since World War I, the Jewish vote had particularly demonstrated an uncontrollable maverick tendency. It had twice veered to third-party candidates, favoring Eugene V. Debs with 24 percent and Robert M. La Follette with 17 percent.[2] Moreover, although Jews were continuously condemned for separatism and clannishness, their vote demonstrated paradoxically an inability to cohere ethnically. Jews preferred to vote for a "constellation of values" rather than a candidate of flesh and bones and incidental rewards.[3] When the Jewish political club finally made its debut in the twenties, it reflected the preference of its individual voters for ideological issues. Jewish voters also switched to the Democratic Party during the twenties and have remained a loyal constituency ever since. Al Smith's "Brown Derby" campaign drew their enthusiastic support, more because of their notion that religious preference ought not to disqualify for any office than for the fact, well known to Jewish voters, that Jews like Belle and Henry Moskowitz, Samuel Rosenman, Joseph Proskauer, and Robert Moses had gained prominence in the Smith entourage. It was the coalition fashioned by Al Smith, in which Jews had a role, that was inherited by Roosevelt in 1932.[4] But the relationship of Franklin Roosevelt and the Jews was not precisely new. They had shown a preference for James Cox, Roosevelt, and the League of Nations in the election of 1920. They had preferred Roosevelt for governor over Albert Ottinger (former attorney general of New York) who spent some energy defending himself against the charge that he was a "bad" Jew. The election of 1928 was the first evidence Roosevelt had of his peculiar attraction to Jewish voters. By 1930 the switch to the Democratic Party was complete. Six of the eight Jews elected to Congress were Democrats, a complete reversal of the election of 1920, when ten out of the eleven Jews elected to Congress were Republicans. The eleventh was a Socialist.[5]

If one had to single out one prominent characteristic of the Jewish political persona, it would be its overriding concern for the welfare of Jews abroad. Even before the establishment of a Zionist consensus in the late thirties, it tilted outward almost as if better to hear the cries for help from its beleaguered brethren. There was frequent opportunity to request diplomatic intercession on behalf of their coreligionists; yet the results of such intercessions, especially in the case of Romania and Russia, were more apparent than real. Like Nazi Germany, these governments were peculiarly immune to moral suasion, especially when it concerned Jews.[6] Frequent requests for such intercession allowed for accretion of experience in the foreign policy arena, but it also created the precedent of response by meaningless gestures to assuage Jewish opinion. By the time of the Roosevelt era, there existed a kind of ritual in which Jewish leaders requested some gesture of support that those holding power, sensing that it cost nothing and earned political points, granted willingly. The nature of the crisis faced by Jews during the years of the Holocaust make the "politics of gestures" developed by Roosevelt seem particularly inappropriate in retrospect. But in making them, Roosevelt was adhering to a political precedent established at the behest of former Jewish leaders.[7]

Once they were part of the New Deal urban ethnic coalition, Jews were also distinguishable by their unerring support for the conception and implementation of the welfare state. That affinity has been traced back to the tenets of Judaic religioculture and to their more recently adopted secular social democratic proclivities.[8] They supported Roosevelt more enthusiastically than other ethnics, especially after the start of the so-called second New Deal that swung to the Left. In his turn, Roosevelt was aware and properly appreciative of the solidity of Jewish support, especially during the election of 1940, when the enthusiasm of other elements of the New Deal coalition began to wane.[9] Yet from a political perspective, that certainty given to Roosevelt regarding the Jewish vote diminished the political leverage available to Jewish leaders. In political terms, it made it virtually certain that the Jewish "love affair" with Roosevelt would be an unrequited one. On a personal level, those who unreservedly loved Roosevelt suffered a not dissimilar fate.

Yet another distinctive facet of the Jewish political persona during the Roosevelt era was its consistent interventionist posture. There was no mistaking where American Jews stood in the "great debate"; and for those who had missed it, there was a preachment of Charles Lindbergh in his famous Des Moines address (September 1941) to remind them. The polls show that Jews were less inclined to accept a common characteristic of the isolationist imagination that American entrance into World War I had been an error. They were predictably among the first to perceive that Hitler would become a dire threat to world peace. They opposed the Ludlow amendment, which sought a national referendum before a declaration of war was passed, and the neutrality laws of the thirties. They favored aiding the Spanish loyalists. They largely opposed the appeasement at Munich. And as the war they feared approached, Jews favored the destroyer-bases deal, Lend-Lease and the convoying of ships to Britain, and after June 1941, to the Soviet Union.[10] Given the fact that Hitler had target-centered their brethren for a special ordeal, Jewish attitudes were understandable, even predictable. But Jewish interventionism went far beyond reflecting an ethnic impulse. A humanitarian universalist proclivity, adopted by many secularized Jews, was also involved.[11] In fact, the interventionist posture may have been strongest precisely among these Jews. The poll data indicate that the Jewish rank and file was not nearly as interventionist-minded as was generally believed. A sizable Jewish minority favored the isolationist position.[12] Moreover, Jews were themselves sharply divided on the admission of Jewish refugees in 1937 and 1938. They "grossly underestimated" the length to which anti-Semitism would be taken by the Nazi regime.[13] There are two conclusions one can draw from these polls: Jews, like all Americans, experienced some difficulty in abandoning the privatism created by the depression to confront the threat from abroad; and it was possible in the thirties for a small group of highly secular spokesmen to preempt the Jewish voice.

It was not merely the enthusiasm of the Jewish public for Roosevelt that stoked both the anti-Semitic and Jewish imagination. There were also several largely, but not entirely Jewish, bridging elites who formed a supplemental link to the Roosevelt administration. The most important of these were the dozens of Jewish lawyers who, when unable to secure positions in prestigious law firms, went to Washington to staff the newly established regulatory agencies dealing with the government's expanding role in providing welfare benefits.[14] From these citadels, they gave battle, perhaps with unseemly passion, to their counterparts whose proper religious and class credentials allowed them to represent the interests of the private sector, which were now required to submit to regulation. That sub-rosa conflict may give us a separate reason for the excessive hatred of Roosevelt and the growing popularity of the "Jew Deal" pejorative. Roosevelt was aware of the special intellectual and spiritual capital represented by these lawyers. "Dig me up fifteen or twenty youthful Abraham Lincoln's from Manhattan and the Bronx to choose from," he instructed Charles Burlingham, "grand old man" of the New York bar and an old chum from Harvard Crimson days.

"They must have no social ambitions."[15] That final caveat may have been triggered by Roosevelt's concern that his administration had flooded the capital with "pushy" Jewish lawyers. Adlai Stevenson, destined one day to become the recipient of a similar Jewish adulation, wrote to a friend that "there is a feeling that Jews are getting too prominent and many of them are autocratic."[16]

A second bridging elite was anchored in the community of scientists and technocrats whose ranks had finally been penetrated by Jews in the twenties. The group was then further enriched by refugee scientists, many of whom were Jewish. Ever since the whirlwind tour of Chaim Weizmann and Albert Einstein in April 1921, who were everywhere overwhelmed by mobs of enthusiastic Jewish admirers, it was clear that science would soon join medicine as a favorite Jewish endeavor. By the 1930s, the influence of a scientist like Einstein matched that of the orator-rabbi, and among secularized Jews, probably surpassed it. The fact that the refugee scientists had experienced Nazi depredations personally often allowed them to play a balancing role against those many Jewish intellectuals who were pacifists. For American society and government, these scientists possessed skills and knowledge not only useful for industrial development but also crucial for the national security that the keenest minds in the administration knew would be threatened by the ominous events in Europe. It was an elite whose power stemmed directly from knowledge.[17]

Yet a third group heavily represented by Jews were the intellectuals. It was they who furnished a rationale for the often inconsistent countercyclical measures of the Roosevelt administration. Many of their ideas were first resonated through the Jewish community, which took ideas seriously and supported an independent intellectual strata with its own press. The New York intellectuals are important, not because they pressed a Jewish cause, for they were usually unable to distinguish a Jewish interest apart from the interests of humanity at large, but for their power as opinion leaders. Throughout the thirties, a special stream of thought and opinion, often embodying unmistakable Jewish concerns and passions, emanated from the New York intellectuals to form an important part of the national dialogue. It sharpened and articulated the liberal position.[18]

The relatively new profession of social work, a popular choice of career for earnest and committed young Jews, was the last of these bridging elites. Beginning with the professionalization of Jewish philanthropy and community work in the twenties, social workers became prominent in many Jewish communal agencies during the thirties. They formed a group with administrative skills who, by the very nature of their work, maintained a direct link with the "masses." There was for them a traditional link to the Oval Office through the generalized tie of upper-class Protestants who had been involved in Jewish settlement house work since the turn of the century. The conduits included not only the Morgenthaus, who supported the Henry Street settlement house, but Eleanor Roosevelt, Harry Hopkins, and others who had begun as social workers. Belle Moskowitz, the woman behind Al Smith, served as a kind of prototype.[19]

The precise extent of the influence of these elites is difficult to measure. They did not use a direct political channel, to which Roosevelt was attuned, nor did they necessarily plead Jewish causes. More likely, they mobilized Jewish support for such favorite domestic causes as emergency relief, public housing, social security, and the entire panoply of welfare-state legislation. It was precisely these domestic programs that won Jewish hearts, creating the illusion of a general confluence between the Jewish and the New Deal agenda. But eventually, it became apparent that no such mutuality existed when a strong, separate Jewish need developed, such as a more generous refugee admission policy. The administration's lack of support for the Wagner-Rogers bill, which would have admitted 20,000 mostly Jewish children to the country outside the quota, was a reflection of what could be expected when a specific Jewish need entailed a price. Roosevelt tolerated Eleanor's support but would himself have nothing to do with it. His approach was highly political, and even the special fate of children made no difference.[20] The fate of the act itself serves as a kind of paradigm, not only of Roosevelt's relationship to the Jews but also of the role of Jewish leadership and agencies during the refugee crisis. They were divided and uncertain, preferred to let non-Jewish agencies take the lead, and were virtually paralyzed by a fear of the new strident domestic anti-Semitism released by the dislocation caused by the depression and orchestrated partly from Berlin.

Yet, politics could not sustain itself on only negation. Roosevelt occasionally did make a gesture aimed specifically at the Jewish problem. There was an extension of visitor's visas followed by a statement of concern after *Kristallnacht*. But the actual liberalization of the visa procedure was canceled out by the State Department at the consular level. Throughout the crisis, the State Department maintained its own level of concern so that the gestures emanating from the Oval Office were not implemented at the grass roots. As with all of Roosevelt's administration, the gap between policy and implementation was wide, nowhere more so than in the case of Jewish refugees.[21] Roosevelt did maintain an elaborate party apparatus to deal with the ethnic constituencies that were carefully monitored, and sometimes, when it was thought necessary, deep intrusions were made into their internal political life. But the purpose of this interest was not to allay suffering but to ensure continued political support and the delivery of votes.

Communication between ethnic subgroups and power holders is conducted through ethnic leaders. But the process of selecting them and giving them authority had become a source of bitter conflict in the Jewish community at the turn of the century. By the 1930s, no adequate system had yet emerged, so that American Jewry, in the midst of the crisis, possessed no agreed-upon formal leadership. Given the strife within the community, it is doubtful whether such a stratum could ever have become functional. Yet without such a formal mandate, the voice of the community could be, and frequently was, preempted by those who insisted they spoke in its name. Lack of cohesiveness inevitably led to lack of coherence. Whether boycott or bombing, the Jews did not find agreement on a single issue during the Holocaust. But even had they done so, the problem of speaking to Roosevelt would, in the absence of a formal communications channel, have remained formidable. Roosevelt was not compelled to transact business with the Jews directly and probably preferred not to do so. When contact could not be avoided, he exercised the prerogative of selecting his own agent to the Jewish community. It could be Morgenthau Jr. or Frankfurter or any "house Jew" who happened to be handy. The Jews so chosen were not comfortable in the role, but they were nevertheless standing evidence that leadership could be imposed on that strife-ridden community merely because Roosevelt preferred them and that such leaders did not require a standing in the community.

By the 1930s, the single stratum of leaders, at one with their Jewishness and armed with a sense of service, had given way to a bifurcated one who could not agree on what the Jewish interest required. Closest to Roosevelt was a group of secular Jews who had achieved prominence in one of several power bases of American society—the labor movement, the university, the legal profession, the political party, finance and banking, journalism, professional politics and business. Men like Morgenthau Jr., Frankfurter, Hillman, Rosenman, Cohen, Lubin, Niles, Baruch and many others were only remotely affiliated with organized Jewry and usually viewed their identity in religious rather than ethnic terms.[22] A few had vague organizational ties; Rosenman belonged to the American Jewish Committee, Morgenthau contributed to the Joint Distribution Committee, Hillman retained some links to the Jewish Labor Committee, Frankfurter and Cohen retained a loose affiliation with the Brandeis wing of the American Zionist movement, and Baruch, whom Roosevelt did not admire, occasionally contributed to Jewish philanthropy. All were highly assimilated Jews who, while not denying their Jewishness, were anxious to be known as something more than merely Jews. Paradoxically, all had at some point in their public careers been forced to suffer the slings and arrows of anti-Semitism for a Jewishness that had become an unimportant aspect of their lives. They were not Jewish men of influence but rather men of influence who remotely and, one suspects sometimes unhappily, happened to be Jewish.

The second group, more difficult to characterize, were those who attained leadership positions within the Jewish community as heads of Jewish organizations, prominent rabbis or prominent lay leaders.[23] But men like Wise, Adler, Proskauer, Henry Monsky, Morris Waldman, Warburg and others did not display a uniform way of coming to grips with the fact of their Jewishness. Joseph Proskauer's identification and general value system would have made him much more comfortable with the first group of influential Jews noted above than the rabbis in his own. But in no case did they have direct access to the Oval Office. For that, they often had to call on men like Frankfurter. The day when men like Schiff and Straus were recognized by Jews and secular authority alike as representing Jewish interests had disappeared into the past.

The first group that earned the Roosevelt administration the "Jew Deal" perjorative was imagined to have enhanced Jewish power. But the real picture that emerges indicates that they were not activated to serve a Jewish interest during the crisis and did not generate an interest on their own volition. Frankfurter, whose influence was in some measure based on his talent for recognizing, cultivating, and finally acting as a broker between talent, especially legal talent, and power holders, preferred to keep his Jewish interest well in the background.[24] He was far more circumspect than his mentor Brandeis in pressing a Jewish interest. When his favorite uncle, a chief librarian in Vienna, was encarcerated by the Nazis, he turned for help, not to Roosevelt, but to Lady Astor, whose statements regarding Jewish ownership of the press brought forth only a long, didactic but mild letter that sought to correct her misconception.[25] When the Frankfurters adopted two children in 1940, they were refugees of the London Blitz, not the Jewish refugee children stranded in France, whom the Wagner-Rogers bill vainly sought to bring to an American haven. Brandeis had recruited him for the Zionist movement in America, and he had done yeoman work at Versailles in its behalf. But as Weizmann and others often observed about the group around Brandeis, they were only part-time Zionists and not even part-time Jews. Frankfurter claimed that Zionism gave him "a fresh psychological relationship to other Jews and Gentiles."[26] It furnished a means of coming to some kind of terms with his Jewish background, but the point where it came to rest seemed to allow precious little space for commitment. His marginal Zionism became the sum of his Jewish identity. It was sufficient for him occassionally to attempt to establish contact between the Zionists and Roosevelt. It was not necessarily a rewarding exercise. In June 1942, Roosevelt pinned his ears back when Frankfurter tried to pave the way for Chaim Weizmann and Ben Gurion to meet him.[27]

Paradoxically, Frankfurter was convinced that some of the opposition he faced was motivated by anti-Semitism. He was not part of the Columbia University oriented "brain trust"; but the bad feelings that existed between him and Adolf Berle, his former student, he suspected were based on Berle's dislike of Jews.[28] He sensed that Hugh Johnson also disliked him because of his Jewishness. Frankfurter had enough personal quirks so that there was no need to turn to anti-Semitism as a reason for disliking him. But the great fear among many Jews of arousing anti-Semitism almost played a spoiling role in his own advancement to the Supreme Court. Arthur Sulzberger, the Jewish publisher of the New York Times, gave precisely that reason to Roosevelt for opposing the appointment. Morgenthau Jr., simply favored the appointment of James Landis because he found Frankfurter distasteful.

Frankfurter's appointment to the Court may prove that, contrary to the popular imagination that conceives of such appointments as evidence of influence, the reverse was true. Roosevelt did need to muster political courage to make the appointment, but its effects actually diminished potential Jewish influence in the administration. It deprived American Jewry, especially its Zionist component, of a major conduit to the Oval Office. To be sure, even after the appointment, Frankfurter continued to advise Roosevelt. But on Jewish matters, the pattern of never allowing a direct link between the Jewish and national interest to exist, established by Brandeis in 1916, would be followed. Before he established his behind-the-scenes leadership of the American Federation of Zionists, Brandeis was roundly condemned by Judah Magnes and the *New York Times* for impropriety.[29] Frankfurter became so remotely connected with the Jewish enterprise that when the Polish underground courier presented him with a precise description of the systematic murder process in the Belzec death camp, Frankfurter would not believe him, although those who cared to could have learned the gruesome details of what was happening in these camps as early as October 1942.[30]

In some sense, the Jew Roosevelt felt most comfortable with was Henry Morgenthau Jr., whom he appointed secretary of the treasury. In fact, the Morgenthaus and the Roosevelts were not only neighbors but friends, or at least what passed for friendship for the Roosevelts.[31] Both were members of a patricianate with strong mercantile origins; both were interested in politics; and in young Henry, Roosevelt found a Jew who was not fast and clever, but completely loyal, devoted, and willing to make up by hard work what he lacked in quick wits. The president, acting like an older brother, teased Morgenthau mercilessly, so much so that on one occasion Morgenthau turned in desparation to Eleanor for redress. He was, of course, unaware that Eleanor had even better reasons to complain about Franklin.

Yet in retrospect, Frankfurter's characterization of Morgenthau as a "stupid bootlick" who was ashamed of his Jewishness was unfair and inaccurate.[32] Without question, he was the bravest Jew near Roosevelt, the one who was finally activated to appeal personally to Roosevelt for special action to rescue the Jews. When Samuel Rosenman signaled fear and resistance to Morgenthau's idea that he, Ben Cohen, and Morgenthau take the facts of the State Department's blocking activities to the president, Morgenthau told Rosenman: "Don't worry about the publicity. What I want is intelligence and courage—courage first and intelligence second."[33] He was the first directly to confront Breckinridge Long, the assistant secretary of state who single-handedly sought to block any rescue attempts, with the charge of anti-Semitism. He pushed through the granting of licenses when rescue opportunities developed in Romania and Bulgaria. He convinced Roosevelt to establish the War Refugee Board, a federal agency charged with the rescue of European Jewry.[34] Finally, utterly convinced that the only way to assure peace was to dissolve Germany as an economic entity, he conceived and promoted his "hard" plan for the postwar treatment of that country. Ultimately, the Morgenthau plan placed his political career in jeopardy and may have brought it to a premature end. There was a feeling that it was prompted by an ethnic rather than a national interest. There was no doubt that the impact of what the liberation revealed of the death camps had a profound impact on him. When he defended his plan, he spoke emotionally of dynamiting "every mine, every mill and factory and wreck it . . . just close it down" because the Germans had put millions through gas chambers.[35] In Morgenthau, we see a secular but rather marginal Jew occupying a position of power in the Roosevelt administration who became radicalized by the Holocaust and who did in fact use his influence for a Jewish purpose, which, some will argue, should have been a universal one.

But the Morgenthau model was the exception. Ironically, in most cases, the Jews nearest to Roosevelt who could be called upon to act in the Jewish interest, at a critical juncture in Jewish history, were no longer able to feel specifically empassioned by what was being done to their brethren in Europe. They no longer felt themselves Jewish at all and could not identify with European Jewry. They had laid aside their Jewish identity as part of the transaction for social status. Those of the second group who had gained leadership positions within the Jewish community were compelled to activate and to act through the first group. When Roosevelt established the WRB in January 1944, it was at the urging of Morgenthau, who was alerted to what was happening within the administration by three assistants and to the affects of the Final Solution by several sources, including the Bergson group of Revisionist Zionists.[36] But by and large, Jewish power in Washington was not enhanced because the prominent Jews near Roosevelt were reluctant to act and did not automatically pave the way for the leaders within the community to make their voices heard.

The most likely leader of this group was Rabbi Stephen Wise. He was a Reform rabbi who defied the classic position of that branch to become a pillar of the American Zionist movement. His position among Jews rested, in some measure, on his oratorical talent. Speaking eloquently counted for much among first- and second-generation American Jews. He had also early developed as an activist in secular politics, where he staunchly supported progressive causes like honesty in government and better treatment for the American worker. He was a kind of unofficial spokesman and agent for the Jewish community to other religious denominations and to secular power holders.[37]

Yet in relation to Roosevelt, his power had been undermined by lingering too long in the Smith camp after his defeat in the election of 1928. Wise had, together with his daughter, been very outspoken regarding the corruption of the Jimmy Walker administration in New York City. Before Governor Roosevelt's hand was forced by the ensuing Seabury investigation, Tammany Hall was an important mainstay of his administration in the state Assembly. Wise did not get fully back into the good graces of the Roosevelt camp until the campaign of 1936. Thereafter, Wise, who at first harbored serious doubts about Roosevelt's ability and integrity, was totally won over by the aura and the program of the president. He was flattered when a phrase he had suggested concerning treatment of minorities in Germany found its way into the second inaugural address.[38] It was a sign that he was indeed accepted. Yet, his access to the Oval Office was rarely direct, nor did he develop into the "pope of the Jews" Roosevelt might have wished to substitute for the several Jewish factions, each with its own program and its own clients for rescue. Wise worked through Frankfurter, who had been instrumental in paving his way back to Roosevelt's entourage, and through Eleanor, with whom he shared speaking platforms for liberal causes.

Wise's "hot" ideological cargo sometimes prevented him from seeing the entire political picture, but in the case of sensing the threat to world peace posed by the development of National Socialism, it allowed him to become aware of danger far earlier than other Jewish leaders. He spoke about the threat it posed in the 1920s and actually attempted to call Jewish leaders together to make contingency plans in 1932, before Hitler came to power. After the *Machtangriff*, Wise's activities to alert America against the Nazi danger and to devise tactics to resist and control it became more intense. He brought a reluctant American Jewish Congress to support the anti-Nazi boycott and organized numerous mass protest rallies.[39] The American Jewish Committee was convinced that such emotional displays achieved little. But it gave Wise a platform from which to speak out against the Nazi menace. It made his name anathema in Berlin but increasingly beloved by the Jewish public who found itself without any other response but that of crying out. In retrospect, the calumny recently heaped on him seems peculiarly ill-placed, especially when his activities are compared with those of other Jewish leaders. After all, it was Wise who most frequently gained the animosity of State Department officials like Breckinridge Long for his gadfly activities.

There is also evidence that under the influence of those secularized Jews closest to Roosevelt, Wise increasingly reined in his passion and allowed his voice to become silent.[40] It may have been the price he paid for access to power. The "Jewish question," an incessant preoccupation in Berlin, was not recognized and not openly discussed in Washington. He explained in 1944, "The truth is, in the midst of war, it is very difficult to make anyone see that we [Jews] are most particularly hurt. These wounds are deeper and sorer than any other wounds inflicted."[41] Earlier, his own universalist instincts prevented him from fully understanding the depth of the "deeper" wounds Jews were bearing in comparison to other groups under the Nazi heel. "The greatest crime against the Jewish victims of Hitler," he wrote in 1940, "would be to treat the crimes against the Jews differently from the treatment of the crimes against the Czechs or Poles or Greeks."[42] But in two short years, he would be forced to ask the administration to recognize that Berlin's objective of totally liquidating the Jews of Europe constituted such a difference. He failed to convince the Roosevelt administration and the prominent Jews around Roosevelt that a special response was warranted, indeed required.

Wise was sixty-nine years old in 1943, the year when the last delicate bridges that still connected American Jewry collapsed. On the one side, there was a new radicalized young Zionist camp formed by those around Abba Hillel Silver and supplemented by the Bergson group of Revisionists. The first favored the immediate establishment of a Jewish commonwealth in Palestine. The second wanted the separation of the rescue goal from the Jewish commonwealth in Palestine. A third group had withdrawn from Jewish organizational life and organized the Council for American Judaism. It was totally opposed to the idea of a Jewish homeland in Palestine. Wise must have realized that there was no way to bridge the gulf between these three positions. In 1940, in a vain attempt at creating

unity, he had made his peace with Chaim Weizmann, only to discover that other gaps were opening up. It was a low point in his
public life. Years of strenuous activity in Zionist politics, known for
its roughness, had taken its toll. Wise was never one to show openly
his despair; yet what was happening in Europe and the response in
Washington surely placed all his assumptions regarding progress
and the existence of a caring spirit in the world, in doubt. Moreover,
the normal practices of speaking out in beautiful mellow tones no
longer seemed to work. He spoke to 10,000 Jews who needed no
convincing at Madison Square Garden rallies. Roosevelt spoke to
millions on the radio, but rarely mentioned the fate of European
Jewry. The nation's priorities were focused on winning the war. It
was clear that not only could the rescue of the Jews not be accommodated to that goal but that Roosevelt was wary of being maneu-
vered by Berlin into making the war one to save the Jews. Fully
aware of the crucible of European Jewry, aging and seriously overex-
tended, challenged by younger radicalized Zionists, Wise in 1943
had good reason to despair.[43]

We come finally to Franklin Roosevelt with whom the business
of rescue had ultimately to be negotiated. One can hardly avoid the
conclusion that even had the moment in history been more suitable
and not colored by the urgency of depression and war, had the political and decision-making process lent itself to a more effective
response, had it been possible to arouse public opinion, Roosevelt's
response to the processed murder of the death camps would still
have been muted. He was not emotionally equipped to fathom fully
the meaning of the liquidation of the Jews for his time in history. It
is inaccurate to speak of a low priority given to the rescue of the
Jews. It had no priority at all and was simply not considered. The
rescue issue does not appear on the agenda of any of the wartime
conferences; Washington decision makers preferred a euphemism
like "political refugees" to mentioning Jews directly. The camouflage
terminology designed to conceal what was happening to European
Jewry was generated in Washington as well as in Berlin.[44]

Like most Americans, Jews were heartened by the buoyancy,
the "boisterous good humor" of the Roosevelt leadership style.[45] It
inspired confidence. But beneath that confident exterior, Roosevelt
was somehow inured from fathoming the profound tragedy repre-

sented by the mania for genocide. He may not even have fully understood his own tragedy. It was more the character of Eleanor and Louis Howe that was deepened by the crippling attack of polio, than Roosevelt's. Alice Roosevelt Longworth dismissed as "absurd" the notion that the president's illness had in any way deepened his character. "He was what he always would be!" she observed of him after the illness struck. "He took polio in his stride."[46] Roosevelt did love and need people; but throughout his life, remained insulated from "intimate involvement," even with his own family.[47]

Roosevelt, most agreed, was bright, but his intelligence was not characterized by a fondness for sustained thought or the ability to make careful distinctions. He was unable to distinguish the crucible of the death camps from other wartime atrocities. He was supreme in the manipulation of people, perhaps ultimately a more important form of intelligence for a president. Rather than confronting an unpleasant issue, he liked to join it with others and disarm it by obfuscation. The refugee crisis was subsumed beneath the greater problem of the depression and then became a minor facet of the "great debate" between interventionists and isolationists. The problem of rescue, which followed as a matter of course from the failure to resolve the refugee crisis, was subsumed beneath the greater problem of winning the war. In neither case could anything significant be done from Roosevelt's perspective. It is unlikely that his mental set would have changed had the inconceivable case of an aroused American public opinion developed and called for action in 1943.[48]

More important, American Jewish leaders brought their special burden to Roosevelt when the drastic downturn in the economy in 1937, coupled with the politically disastrous scheme to "pack" the Supreme Court, dissipated his aura as a leader, on which his power was based. At the same time, the fast-breaking crisis in Europe and the Far East distracted Roosevelt. The Roosevelt of 1938 was a far cry from the confident and buoyant Roosevelt of the "one hundred days." The Jewish delegation who visited the Oval Office on December 8, 1942, to present their case and to request some action, found there a manipulative president, sympathetic to their plight to be sure, but able to give them only a few minutes to convince him.[49] It was one of several delegations scheduled to see him that day. The crisis at home and abroad overshadowed their special cry for help. They were pleading for their brethren who were legally not the responsibility of the United States, and the request was put forward by the leaders of a group whom the polls indicated were an unpopular minority in America.[50] Given these circumstances, the fact that the refugee and rescue problem received little attention was predictable. Had it been otherwise, had it received a sharper focus, Roosevelt would not have been comfortable with it. His currency was, after all, people and politics, not pain.

These then are some factors historians will want to consider in assessing the interaction of Roosevelt with the most loyal and loving of his constituencies, American Jewry. They impinge on the nature and play of power in American society. On the face of it, American Jewish power seemed to have been enhanced during the Roosevelt era. It was reflected in the increased number of Jews who found positions in the higher levels of federal government. In assigning a noble mission to government, the New Deal was peculiarly in consonance with the assumptions that informed Jewish political culture. It concealed from view American Jewry's relatively short experience with practical politics. The Jews were a highly active constituency, but they were also unpredictable and divided by cultural, class, and ideological differences. When the crisis was upon them, they did not view themselves as a single, unified political community. As the crisis developed, it was clear that the thing they had most in common was an extreme sense of insecurity, triggered by a new strident anti-Semitism here and abroad, and a love for Roosevelt.

Jews took pride in the number of their kind that found a place in Roosevelt's entourage. Paradoxically, they were probably as much convinced that this signified an enhancement of their influence as were those anti-Semites who conceived of the "Jew Deal" label. Both ignored the fact that these individuals were primarily Jews in name only; and most could not recognize a specific Jewish interest, much less support one. They had long been involved in a transaction with secular society that traded ethnic identity for a full measure of professional success and esteem. Yet, the urgency of the historical moment required those who gained leadership positions within the community to make their case for action through them because they had better access to the Oval Office. They were largely disappointed; ultimately, it was the activation of one of these Jews, Henry Morgenthau Jr., who broke through to convince Roosevelt that specific action was required. Morgenthau's belated success, followed by a successful circumvention of the immigration laws, opens up an agonizing question for survivalists. Was enough done to convince prominent Jews near Roosevelt of the need to use their influence to save their European brethren? Could men like Frankfurter and Rosenman have convinced Roosevelt to act earlier? These are not ordinary historical questions, but then the Holocaust is not an ordinary historical problem.

12

Rescue and the Secular Perception

THE INEFFECTIVENESS of American Jewry during the Holocaust represents something of a paradox for the historian. Like other Diaspora communities in the West, American Jewry has a good track record in nurturing beleaguered Jewish communities abroad. During the Colonial period "Messengers" who collected *chaluka* found American Jews generous.[1] As early as 1840, the small Jewish community requested diplomatic intercession from the Van Buren administration to help the libeled Jews of Damascus. In 1958, their protest over the kidnapping of Edgar Mortara was so vehement that it earned the antagonism of the American-Irish, who felt that Mortara's baptism was a good thing. After the Civil War, Jews requested and received from the State Department "statements of concern" for the hard-pressed Jews of Morocco, the Swiss cantons, Russia, and Romania. Similarly, one Jewish historian recently found that the Dreyfus affair created almost as much stir among American Jews as it did in Europe. The State Department archives are full of anxious letters from American Jewish communities and congregations written after news of pogroms in czarist Russia reached them.[2] The Kischinev pogrom triggered such a hysterical reaction and such a plethora of new relief organizations that the establishment of the American Jewish Committee, its major defense agency, was founded in channel the unrest in what the patricianate called "the congested quarter." Its charter grandiloquently charged it with preventing "the

This essay appeared originally in *Organizing Rescue: Jewish National Solidarity in the Modern Period*, ed. Sylvan Troen and Benhamin Pinkus (London: Frank Cass, 1992), 154–66, under the title "Rescue and the Secular Perception: American Jewry and the Holocaust."

infraction of civil and religious rights of Jews *in any part of the world*."[3] Between 1908 and 1914, Louis Marshall, the president of the AJC, tried to fulfill that charge by orchestrating a campaign to abrogate the Commercial Treaty of 1832 with Russia in the hope of wringing better treatment for the Jews of that benighted country. So skillful were his strategies that the abrogation campaign still stands as a model of how to project influence on American foreign policy.[4] There may be some alive today who recall the outpouring of American Jewish philanthropy to the *Yishuv* and Eastern Jewries during and after the First World War. That generosity hardly exhausts the list and does not include the much heralded advocacy role of American Jewry, without which the Jewish state could not have been established in 1948.[5] Moreover, the financial aid granted freely to Israel thereafter is nothing short of remarkable because it was frequently given at the expense of its own institutions and infrastructure.

Then what happened during the Holocaust? Is it possible to imagine that precisely at that crucial historical juncture American Jewry abandoned the nurturing posture toward its brethren by which it virtually defined itself? I would like in the next few pages to examine one unheralded aspect of that lapse that centers on the impact of the twin forces of secularization and acculturation on its ability to respond to the crisis. Clearly, during the decades of the twenties and thirties there arose such an intensification of these twin processes that what emerged was a community, if one could call it that, whose organization and leadership structure were altered beyond recognition, whose cohesiveness was weakened, and whose perception of itself in relationship to other Jews was changed. I must hasten to add that this is only one aspect to explain American Jewry's failure during these critical years, not even the most important one. But the problem this essay probes may turn out to be a crucial one: Can Jewries in the process of modernization in a particularly benevolent and absorbent culture respond adequately to crisis in the world Jewish enterprise? For obvious reasons, our colleagues in Israel ought to be particularly interested in this case.

Let me begin with a remarkable datum rarely confronted by researchers. The American Jews recruited for the Lincoln Brigade, the military unit organized to fight Franco during the civil war in Spain, came to approximately 30 percent of all American volunteers. (Jews were 3.7 percent of the population in 1935.) When combined with Jews in the contingents from other European states and Palestine, the Jews in that International Brigade might have gone down in history as the first sizable Jewish army since Bar Kochba's time.[6] Yet, they fought and bled in a country that four centuries earlier had expelled its Jews and for a cause that could only be viewed as part of a Jewish interest by a stretch of the ideological imagination. But in 1940, half a decade later, when Jabotinsky made his appeal for the formation of a Jewish army to be composed of Palestinian and stateless Jews, a call taken up by the Bergson group, the response among American Jews was almost nil. Moreover, British reluctance to form such a contingent was matched by American Jewish leaders who were aware that American Jewry could no longer understand the reason for such a formation.[7]

That strange juxtaposition tells us at a glance something about the attitude of an important part of American Jewry. The case of the Lincoln Brigade could be supplemented by the disproportionate number of young Jews in the peace movements of the thirties or the high percentages whose enthusiasm for the labor movement of the New Deal welfare state program far outweighed their support of specifically Jewish causes or their apprehension about a specific danger facing European Jewry.

Theirs was a universalist perception in which Jews were only one of several victimized groups. That perception was abandoned only with great reluctance when it became clear that a very specific, ultimately murderous, intent was aimed at the Jews. Stephen Wise, whose interest in the Jewish dilemma was often overshadowed by such preoccupations as the Sacco and Vanzetti case or the corruption in the Jimmy Walker administration of New York City during the New Deal or the progress of the newly formed Congress of Industrial Organization (CIO), was fairly late in accepting the idea that the Jews were to be singled out among all Hitler's enemies.[8] In 1940, he rejected the idea that a special case had to be made for the rescue of European Jewry. His letters tell of his embarrassment at speaking in the Oval Office of the special crucible of the Jews when the entire world was in flames. He was exasperated that some Jews did not understand the dilemma in pleading such a special case before the power holders.[9] It was his secular universalist outlook that made Wise an activist, and he did not abandon it lightly. It was for the reverse reason that groups like the Agudath and the Bergson boys, the latter composed primarily of Palestinian Jews, were so much better able to imagine the disaster and propose solutions more appropriate for the specific Jewish need. Both groups were not locked into the prevailing secular universalist perception. They wanted simply to save Jews qua Jews. The new more secular, more American perception had a disarming impact in other areas as well.

We now have five studies on the relationship of the Roosevelt administration and the Jews of America.[10] They differ considerably in their estimates of the possibility of rescue. But all agree on the forlorn posture of American Jewry that remained conflicted over issues that, given the desperation of the situation, appear today to be appallingly irrelevant. There can be little doubt that they squandered the opportunities for speaking to power holders with one voice. They were unable to put aside their differences to build a unity based on the desperate need of European Jewry.

Those divisions are well known and need not occupy much of our time. They were structural, cultural, and above all ideological and superimposed on all was the fragmentation of the religious community that in some aspects, was as bitter in the thirties as it is today. No single group was ultimately able to impose its will on the whole. The Zionist consensus that had developed by 1939 was itself too weak and locked in internecine strife to persuade other agencies to surrender their organizational sovereignty for the good of the whole. Rather than unifying American Jewry, the crisis seemed to exacerbate the things that divided it. The relationship between Jewish organizations lacked the basic civility that might have permitted them to act together even for limited objectives.

Virtually every issue became the subject of acrimony. Even their perception of the nature of the threat posed by the advent of the National Socialist regime in Germany differed markedly. The more established sections of the community at first shared the conventional assumptions that power would somehow mature and tame Hitler.[11] The powerful left-wing elements knew better. But what to do? In 1933 and 1934, the boycott movement triggered endless debate when it came into conflict with the transfer agreement. Should Jews press for a less stringent administration of the immigration laws that the Hoover administration had imposed at the outset of the depression? The cognoscenti who knew popular and congressional sentiment and had become alarmed at the rise of restriction and anti-Semitic sentiment, argued against it. Refugee advocates who wanted the "golden doors" opened a little more widely could not even be sure that they had the support of the Jewish grass roots, who were as concerned about the effects of immigration on the unemployment situation as other Americans.[12] Jewish leaders preferred to let non-Jewish rescue advocates argue for the admission of a total of 20,000 Jewish children outside the quota system in 1939 and 1940. After the war began, the question of mass resettlement of Jews outside of Palestine, favored for obvious reasons in Washington and London, tore American Jewry apart. Most American Zionists could not conceive that resettlement in British Guiana or the Dominican Republic could replace Palestine, which they saw as the only clear answer to the refugee plight. If Palestine was being denied by political fiat, then they would fight it politically. They would struggle against Nazis as if there were no White Paper and against the British as if there were no Nazis. But in truth, they could barely hold their own on one front. In late 1943, the resettlement alternative, which paradoxically never approached reality, was accepted by the Bergson group, which proposed separating the homeland goal of the Biltmore platform from the immediate need to rescue Jews.[13] Soon, the bitter conflict between the Revisionist Bergson group and the mainline Zionists was waged in the public press, and all this while thousands were being led to their death every day.

Yet in the traditional field of philanthropy used by wealthy secularized Jewry to maintain a connection with the community, a fragile coming together did occur. The United Jewish Appeal began again in 1939 and this time survived the rocky road to organized professional fund raising.[14] It was one of the things that American Jewry could see eye to eye on. Paradoxically, the only other thing one could point to was the almost universal Jewish adoration of Roosevelt. The highly secularized Jewish patricians, notwithstanding Joseph Proskauer and Abba Hillel Silver, were for him.[15] And so were left-wingers who formed the American Labor Party in New York State in 1936.[16]

How can one explain such disunity that, in the case of American Jewry, seemed to go far beyond the normal diversity of postemancipation Jewish communities? When the migration of Eastern Jews began, the German Jews held their noses, but they helped. Now, the children of these same Eastern European Jews did not seem to be able to muster the interest and energy to repay in kind. It was partly the triple layers of immigration that formed the community caused the lack of the requisites for unity—common experience, common language, and a common vision. American Jewry was more than simply disunited. In 1943 after the breakup of the American Jewish Conference and the establishment of the Council for American Judaism, it looked very much as if American Jewry was more anxious to tear itself apart than to help its brethren in Europe.

I would suggest that the impending crisis caught American Jewry in a dilemma. The inability to react collectively was part of the process of modernization with its intense individualization and voluntarism. Jews were in the midst of the dissolution of the old form of communalism and the new had not yet taken shape. There was no longer anyone who could order them to their Judaism. Leaders could not lead because followers would not follow. Superimposed on that process was the accelerated acculturation of the thirties that occurred at different rates among different strata of the Jewish population. And if that were not sufficient, there were the intensely privatizing effects of the depression. Most Jews in the thirties were preoccupied with problems of *parnossah*—making a living. When the depression did activate people politically, it was over the question of domestic economic policy, the welfare state. That policy had after all been incubated in the Jewish Labor movement and had a special appeal for many Jews. There was then a Jewish kind of isolationism in the thirties that was related directly to the privatizing effects of the depression.[17] The news reports about the depredations against their European brethren had first to work their way through a layer of consciousness about their own plight.[18] And until September 1939, the news they heard was largely stories about German Jewry, which some still believed, like their parents before them, was competent enough to take care of itself. Most important, the free secular atmosphere of America had for over two decades led to a process of fragmentation; it tended to act as a solvent on Jewish corporateness. Increasingly secular-achieving Jews—lawyers, professors, doctors— were committed to professional advancement. If they related to Jewishness at all, it was merely one of several loyalties, and not necessarily the most important one. When the crisis called them back, they were becoming less Jewish and more self-involved.

Nowhere is that fragmentation and resultant loss of coherence more apparent than in the development of a dual leadership rather than the single stratum of leadership that customarily made the Jewish agenda known in the American political arena. There had always been a small group of Jewish officeholders and achievers who had political influence. But in the early decades of the century, they served only as a supplementary representation of the Jewish community. Congressman "Silver dollar Smith," a Jewish barkeeper who represented his district in Congress under the auspices of corrupt Tammany Hall, was not considered by Jews to represent their interests generally, although even he could be called upon to help, as was Congressman Henry Goldfogle during the abrogation struggle.[19] Primary issues such as immigration policy or the depredations in Russia were represented by Jews like Jacob Schiff, Louis Marshall, Oscar Straus, or Mayer Sulzberger, who, by dint of personal fortune and belonging to the same "crowd," were recognized by Theodore Roosevelt and William Taft as Jewish spokesmen. Their role went beyond mere *shtadlanut* because the American system permitted, and even encouraged, the projection of influence directly on the electorate. Indeed, the American Jewish Committee spared little to influence American public opinion on the Russian depredations. The struggle to abrogate the Commercial Treaty of 1832 with Russia and the way Jacob Schiff, by means of the financial leverage available to him, tried to influence the outcome of the Russo-Japanese War still serve today as models of how special interests can influence American public policy.[20] Once recognized and legitimated by the administration in power, the "Jewish masses" went along, albeit increasingly reluctantly. The result was a measure of coherence. Everyone knew who spoke for the Jewish community and through whom to speak to it.

By 1933, two things had happened to alter that simple workable system. The class that produced such leadership types, people willing to place fame and fortune at the service of the community, had experienced enormous attrition. It lost much influence after the death of Louis Marshall. The cry for democratization in Jewish life, first sounded by the "illustrious obscure" who proposed a congress movement, made the interior political life of the American Jewish community far more raucous and ultimately far more universalist. Democracy, which is itself a secular/modern concept, rarely encourages blind submission to authority. Despite the two internal elections by the American Jewish Congress, the community structure had, in fact, become more amorphous and in that sense less effective; that is, less able to project a coherent voice in the political arena. Franklin Roosevelt, we shall see, was not slow to capitalize on the altered situation, but he often had occasion to envy the simple situation faced by his uncle. He sometimes wished that the divided Jewish community would have a pope like the Catholics.[21]

During the New Deal, American Jewry no longer transmitted its agenda through a leadership cohort recognized by both sides.

There were now secular Jews who had risen to the top through various different power centers: the university (Felix Frankfurter), organized labor (Sidney Hillman), the law establishment (Ben Cohen, Isador Lubin, Sam Rosenman), the business community (Bernard Baruch, Herbert Lehman), who were located near political power and often were coopted into politics as advisors and managers. They did not see themselves merely as Jews, much less as spokesmen for Jewish causes, although some had a tenuous connection with Jewish organizations, especially the American Jewish Committee.[22] As a shorthand, we can refer to them as the "Jew Deal," the pejorative used by anti-Semites at the time to express their hostility to the proliferation of Jews in the top echelons of the Roosevelt administration. For the most part the "Jew Deal" was composed of "new" men whose loyalty was to career. They were not Jews incubated in a holistic Jewish environment who turned to the east wall three times daily as if by Pavlovian conditioning. Such totally Jewish environments were, with the exception of a few insular communities, no longer influential in generating the Jewish outlook. For these men, when a Judaic influence played a role at all, it was merely one of several influences. They were Americans who happened to be Jewish. Nor were they scions of the uptown "crowd." Felix Frankfurter was a descendant of Viennese *galitzianer*; Sol Bloom, who played the *shabbes goy* role at the ill-fated Bermuda conference; Isador Lubin; Ben Cohen; Sidney Hillman; and David Niles were of Eastern European Jewish descent. And Bernard Baruch, for whom Roosevelt found little use, stemmed from Sephardic Jews.[23]

Not only did these "new" men not inherit the tradition of service of the older Jewish patricianate, but their Jewish identity formation was so confined by other influences that, if they perceived the Jewish interest at all, it was through a universalist or an American prism. They were either out to improve the world or American versions of Walter Rathenau—patriotic and utterly loyal to the nation they served. That explains the disproportionate Jewish recruitment during World War II or Frankfurter, Lubin, and Cohen's brilliant legislative engineering of the New Deal domestic program. The question of rescue for such men, when it was perceived at all, served as a disturbing counterpoint to the public business with which they were involved. Their assumption was naturally that the Jewish fate was linked to the fate of America. The Jews would be saved if America won the war. Therefore, nothing could be done to impede that victory. That was the same argument used by political leaders in Washington. For many Jews, it had a compelling logic even though it meant, in effect, that their brethren would not survive the war. They never remotely understood that it was being used as a ploy to avoid the rescue question. After 1943, bombing concentration camps would not have changed wartime priorities, just as sending food to Greece throughout the war did not alter them.[24] It was only when one of the members of the "Jew Deal" saw through the ploy that serious rescue activity could be mounted. But even in the exceptional case of Henry Morgenthau Jr., the risk to his political career caused by his activities in the rescue cause occurred only after it was clear that the light of victory could be seen at the end of the tunnel. Only then did it become possible to tamper with virtually sacred war priorities that were ordered on the assumption of victory before everything else.[25]

The "Jew Deal" held one of the crucial keys to rescue. It was through it that leaders like Stephen Wise and others had to act. The route to the Oval Office was through the conduit that these marginally Jewish men offered. No effective advocacy could be conceived without them. The tragedy was that, unlike their predecessors, they were *of* the Jewish community but no longer exclusively *for* it. One can argue, as David Wyman does, that the best road to rescue was through an aroused public opinion.[26] But in the context of the availability of the "Jew Deal," that seems a far less possible course of action. Most feel that it would have been impossible for an organized Jewish community to mobilize general American public opinion in the interest of Jewish rescue in 1943 and 1944. Some feel it would have been dangerous to do so. Most important, whether even such a mobilized public opinion would have led a preoccupied and inured Roosevelt to change his mind about the Jews is a highly dubious proposition. Even if that were possible, an effective advocacy role would still have required the mobilization of these highly placed Jews who could no longer recognize, much less act in, a specific Jewish interest. The interesting fact for us is that the Holocaust itself served to mobilize most of these same Jews in the cause of establishing the Jewish state barely three years later, and it is such Jews who play a leading role in the United Jewish Appeal and the federation today. The transition to a new form of communalism has been made.

Lest we imagine that the failure to rescue European Jewry was the fault of American Jewry who failed to exercise their power, let us imagine the following: The burden of its historical development had been magically lifted from American Jewish shoulders; that rather than variation and pluralism that everywhere follow upon freeness, there was instead coherence and unity; that rather than projecting a cacophony of sound, they were able to speak to power with one voice; that their Jewishness somehow remained intact and allowed for a better perception of the impending disaster; that Jewish leaders could be assured that free autonomous Jews would follow—in a word, that the myriad factors and conditions of modernity that interfered with a more effective response could be magically cancelled. Would it have made an appreciable difference?

After many years of working with this problem, my conclusion is that what American Jewry did and did not do is perhaps 5 percent of the problem. It is simply not true that the US government, acting under Jewish pressure, would have allowed the Second World War to become a war to save the Jews. Those who imagine otherwise assign American Jewry an influence on events that views it in the same power terms as the anti-Semitic imagination. There is, in the first place, an inherent structural and ideological limitation on how far a special-interest group can pull foreign policy in its own direction. In the second place, there is an even greater unwillingness on the part of governments who seek to persecute Jews to allow themselves to be persuaded by moral pressure. During the case of the depredations of czarist Russia or Romania, a better organized, more coherent Jewry did not bring better treatment of its religious brethren, even when the American government was willing to act on its behalf. The Hitler regime gave the destruction of European Jewry a comparatively high priority and probably could not have been dissuaded merely by moralistic exhortations. Regimes who murder in the name of progress, whether the victims are the *kulaks* or the Jews, are peculiarly immune from moral suasion. If they were moral, in our sense of the word, they would not conceive of such policies in the first place. How determined they were is clearly illustrated by the fate of Hungarian and Slovakian Jewry. Here murder was committed when Berlin knew the war was lost and within full view of an alerted world.

The secular outlook that, as I have noted, played such havoc with American Jewry's ability to perceive and respond to the crisis, was no less a factor among officials in Berlin, Washington, or London who implemented policy. It was as difficult to enlist them in the cause of rescue in the Allied camp as it had been easy earlier to enlist them in the cause of genocide in Nazi-occupied Europe. Subject to a *raison d'état* that viewed Jews as inimical, American officialdom matched that of Germany in being coolly inured to loss of life. It would seem that the role of a self-initiating bureaucracy that is central to totalitarian regimes is also present in latent form in the governments of democratic nations.[27] They, too, produce a bureaucratic objectification that blocks the human agony from entering their consciousness. By their nature, bureaucracies are interested in programs, not people.[28] Phillips, Robert Borden Reams, J. Pierrepont Moffat, Long in America; Richard Law, Emerson, Winterton in Britain, the officials who managed the crisis, were, in their pervasive anti-Semitism and their sense of urgency to get the job done, the match for an Adolf Eichmann or a Reinhard Heydrich. Against such odds and such power, what little influence American Jewry had, came almost to nought.

Examined here are two of the internal reasons for American Jewry's ineffectiveness during the Holocaust years. Stated briefly, it comes to this: The historical development of American Jewry, especially the more recent process of secularization and acculturation in a free and open society, significantly altered its internal governing threshold so that the requisite coherence and will to play its advocacy role was diminished. By the 1940s, American Jewry had virtually lost its corporate communal character, and the new coherence based on voluntarism and managed by professionals had not yet taken its place. Yet, historians will hardly need to mention that change because it made little difference in the larger picture. Even a more powerful American Jewry would not appreciably have changed the picture. The same process of modernization inured non-Jewish bureaucrats from sympathizing with the Jewish plight. In Washington and London, the Jewish death toll was seen as numbers as much as it was in Berlin. Bureaucratic objectification is, after all, universal.

Finally, those who argue that American Jewry was indifferent to the plight of their European brethren need to read American Jewish history. A concern for Jewries abroad virtually defines the American Jewish persona. They may have been ineffective, but that is a far cry from being indifferent. Those who draw up the indictment against American Jewry, and the number grows yearly, are really unhappy with what American Jewry had become through an inexorable historical development. They would have liked it to be something else. It is like arguing with the direction of the wind. The real historical question is whether American Jewry did what it could within the parameters of what it had become and what was possible. I suspect that the answer to such a question will yield a more balanced, less polemical, history.

13

Who Shall Bear Guilt
for the Holocaust?

A SIMPLE SEARING TRUTH emerges from the vast body of research
and writing on the Holocaust. It is that European Jewry was ground
to dust between the twin millstones of a murderous Nazi intent and
a callous Allied indifference. It is a truth with which the living seem
unable to come to terms. Historians expect that, as time moves us
away from a cataclysmic event, our passions will subside and our
historical judgment of it will mellow. But that tempered judgment is
hardly in evidence in the historical examination of the Holocaust.
Instead, time has merely produced a longer list of what might have
been done and an indictment that grows more damning. There are,
after all, six million pieces of evidence to demonstrate that the world
did not do enough. Can anything more be said?

Given that emotionally charged context, it seems at the least
foolhardy and at the most blasphemous to question whether the
characterization of the Holocaust's witnesses as callously indifferent
does full justice to the historical reality of their posture during those
bitter years. There is a strange disjuncture in the emerging history of
the witnesses. Researchers pile fact upon fact to show that the witnesses did almost nothing to save Jewish lives. And yet if the key
decision makers could speak today, they would be puzzled by the
indictment because they rarely thought about Jews at all. Roosevelt
might admit to some weakness at Yalta, and Churchill might admit

This essay appeared originally in *American Jewish History* 48, no. 3 (Mar. 1979):
261–82, under the title "Who Shall Bear Guilt for the Holocaust: The Human Dilemma."

that the Italian campaign was a mistake. But if they recalled Auschwitz at all, it would probably be vague in their memories.

Historical research in the area of the Holocaust is beset with problems of no ordinary kind. It seems as if the memory of that human-made catastrophe were as deadly to the spirit of scholarship as was the actual experience to those who underwent its agony. The answers we are receiving are muddled. The perpetrators have been found to be at once incredibly demonic but also banal. The suspicion that the victims were less than courageous, that they supposedly went "like sheep to the slaughter," has produced a minor myth about heroic resistance in the Warsaw ghetto and the forests of Eastern Europe to prove that it was not so. Like the resistance apologetic, the indictment against the witnesses is as predictable as it is irresistible.

That is true because, in theory at least, witnessing nations and agencies had choices, and there is ample evidence that the choices made were not dictated by human concern as we think they should have been. In the case of America, the charge of indifference is heard most clearly in the work of Arthur Morse, who found the rescue activities of the Roosevelt administration insufficient and filled with duplicity, and Saul Friedman, who allowed his anger to pour over into an indictment of American Jewry and its leadership.[1] One ought not to dismiss such works out of hand. And yet it is necessary to recognize that they are as much cries of pain as they are serious history.

The list of grievances is well known. The Roosevelt administration could have offered a haven between the years 1938 and 1941. Had that been done, had there been more largess, there is some reason to believe that the decision for systematic slaughter taken in Berlin might not have been made or at least might have been delayed. There could have been threats of retribution and other forms of psychological warfare that would have signaled to those in Berlin and in the Nazi satellites that the Final Solution entailed punishment. Recently, the question of bombing the concentration camps and the rail lines leading to them has received special attention. The assumption is that physical intercession from the air might have slowed the killing process. American Jewry has been subject to particularly serious charges of not having done enough, of not using its considerable political leverage during the New Deal to help its brethren. Other witnesses have also been judged wanting. Britain imposed a White Paper limiting migration to Palestine in the worst moment of the refugee crisis, the pope failed to use his great moral power against the Nazis, the International Red Cross showed little daring in interpreting its role vis-à-vis the persecution of the Jews. The list documenting the witnesses' failure of spirit and mind could be extended; but that would take us away from the core problem faced by the historian dealing with the subject.

The historian must determine what the possibilities of rescue actually were. Failure cannot be determined until we have some agreement on what was realistically possible. There is little agreement among historians on what these possibilities were, given Nazi fanaticism on the Jewish question. Lucy Dawidowicz, for example, argues compellingly that once the ideological and physical war were merged in the Nazi invasion of Russia in June 1941, the possibilities for rescue were minimal. That, incidentally, was the position also taken by Earl Winterton, who for a time represented Britain on the Intergovernmental Committee on political Refugees, and Breckinridge Long, the assistant secretary of state responsible for the potpourri of programs that made up the American rescue effort during the crisis. Other historians, including myself, have pointed out that the Nazi *Gleichshaltung* on the Jewish question was nowhere near as efficient as generally assumed. The war mobilization of their economy, for example, was not achieved until 1944. Opportunities for rescue were present especially during the refugee phase, when the Final Solution had not yet been decided upon and possibilities of bribery and ransom existed. It was the momentum of this initial failure during the refugee phase that carried over into the killing phase.

The point is that, in the absence of agreement on possibilities, historians are merely repeating the debate between power holders and rescue advocates that took place during the crisis. The latter group insisted that not enough was being done, and the former insisted that the best way to save the Jews was to win the war as quickly as possible. Nothing could be done to interfere with that objective, including, ironically, the rescue of the Jews. When Stephen Wise pointed out that, by the time victory came, there would be no Jews left in Europe, he exposed what the argument between rescue advocates and their opponents was about. It concerned priorities, and beyond that, the war aims that ordered those priorities. What rescue advocates were asking then, and what the historians of the role of witness are asking today, is: Why was not the Jewish question central to the concern of the witnesses as it was to the Nazis who spoke about it incessantly? But we cannot solve that question of priorities until we have an answer to the question of what World War II was all about and what role the so-called Jewish question played in it.

Clearly, Allied war leaders were wary of accepting the Nazi priority on the Jewish question. The war was not one to save the Jews, and they would not allow war strategy and propaganda to be aimed in that direction. None of the conferences that worked out war aims and strategy—the Argentia meeting which produced the Atlantic Charter (August 1941); the several visits of Churchill to Washington; the Casablanca conference (January 1943); the Quebec conference (August 1943); the Moscow conference (October 1943); the Tehran conference (November-December 1943); and, finally, the Yalta and Potsdam conferences (February and July-August 1945)—had anything to say about the fate of the Jews. The silence was not solely a consequence of the fact that Allied leaders did not remotely fathom the special significance of what was happening to Jews in Nazi concentration camps. Even had they understood, it is doubtful that they would have acknowledged the centrality of the Final Solution. To have done so would have played into Nazi hands and perhaps interfered with a full mobilization for war. Hence, Roosevelt's insistence on using a euphemistic vocabulary to handle what Berlin called the Jewish problem. There was distress in the Oval Office when George Rublee, who had unexpectedly negotiated a Statement of Agreement with Hjalmar Schacht and Helmut Wohlthat in the spring of 1939, spoke of Jews rather than the "political refugees," the preferred euphemism. The two agencies concerned with Jews, the Intergovernmental Committee for Political Refugees, which grew out of the Evian conference, and the War Refugee Board carefully avoided the use of the word *Jew* in their titles. When the American restrictive immigration law was finally circumvented in the spring of 1944 and a handful of refugees were to be interned in Oswego outside the quota system, just as had been done for thousands of suspected Axis agents active in Latin America, Robert Murphy was cautioned to be certain to select a "good mix" from the refugees who had found a precarious haven in North Africa. Undoubtedly, what Roosevelt meant was not too many Jews. The crucible of the Jews under the Nazi yoke was effectively concealed behind the camouflage terminology conceived by the Nazi bureaucracy and the Allies. Even today in Eastern Europe, unwillingness persists to recognize the special furor the Nazis reserved for the Jews and the relationship of the Jews to the Holocaust. The former Soviet government did not acknowledge that it was Jews who were slaughtered at Babi Yar; and in Poland, the Jewish victims became in death what they were never allowed to be in life, honored citizens of that nation. In the East, it became the Great Patriotic War, and in the West it was ultimately dubbed the Great Crusade—never a war to save the Jews. Those who examine the history textbooks continually note with despair that the Holocaust is barely mentioned at all.

The low level of concern about the fate of the Jews had a direct effect in strengthening the hands of those in Berlin responsible for implementing the Final Solution. They became convinced that the democracies secretly agreed with their plan to rid the world of the Jewish scourge. "At bottom," Goebbels wrote in his diary on December 13, 1942, "I believe both the English and the Americans are happy that we are exterminating the Jewish riff-raff." It was not difficult even for those less imaginative than Goebbels to entertain such a fantasy. Each Jew sent to the East meant, in effect, one less refugee in need of a haven and succor. Inadvertently, the Final Solution was solving a problem for the Allies as well. Nazi propaganda frequently took note in the early years of the war of the reluctance of the receiving nations to welcome Jews. They watched London's policy of curtailing immigration to Palestine, American refusal to receive the number of refugees that might have been legally admitted under the quota system, the pope's silence. Goebbels's impression was after all not so far from the truth. Smull Zygelbojm, the Bundist representative to the Polish Government-in-Exile, came to much the same conclusion shortly before his suicide.

Yet Zygelbojm, who was very close to the crisis, was bedeviled by the dilemma of what to do. He was dismayed by the assumption underlying a request for action that he received from Warsaw in the spring of 1943. The message demanded that Jewish leaders "go to all important English and American agencies. Tell them not to leave until they have obtained guarantees that a way has been decided upon to save the Jews. Let them accept no food or drink, let them die a slow death while the world looks on. This may shake the conscience of the world." As Zygelbojm wrote to a friend, "It is utterly impossible, they would never let me die a slow lingering death. They would simply bring in two policemen and have me dragged away to an institution." The bitter irony was that although Zygelbojm had come to have grave doubts about the existence of a "conscience of the world," his former colleagues in Warsaw, who were aware of the fate that awaited Jews at Treblinka, could still speak of it as if it were a reality.

Once such priorities were in place, it proved relatively easy for

State Department officers like Breckinridge Long to build what one historian has called a "paper wall," a series of all but insurmountable administrative regulations to keep Jewish refugees out of America. He informed Adolf A. Berle and James C. Dunn on June 26, 1940, "We can delay and effectively stop for a temporary period of indefinite length the number of immigrants into the U.S. We could do this by simply advising our consuls to put every obstacle in the way and resort to various administrative advices [sic] which would postpone and postpone." That is precisely what was done; only in the year 1939 were the relevant quotas filled. During the initial rescue phase the mere existence of strong restrictionist sentiment reinforced by the depression proved sufficient. After the war started, the notion that the Nazis had infiltrated spies into the refugee stream was used. The creation of a veritable security psychosis concerning refugees triggered the creation of a screening procedure so rigid that, after June 1940, it was more difficult for a refugee to gain entrance to the neutral United States than to wartime Britain. During the war, a similar low priority for the rescue of Jews might be noted in the neutral nations of Latin America and Europe and by the Vatican and the International Red Cross. There was no agency of international standing that could press the Jewish case specifically. But that is a well-known story that need not be retold here.

The question is, why did not the witnessing nations and agencies sense that the systematic killing in the death camps by means of production processes developed in the West was at the ideological heart of World War II, and therefore required a response? Why were they unable to fathom that Auschwitz meant more than the mass destruction of European Jewry? It perverted the values at the heart of their own civilization; if allowed to proceed unhampered, it meant that their world would never be the same again. Roosevelt, Churchill, and Pius XII understood that they were locked in mortal combat with an incredibly demonic foe. But as the leaders of World War I sent millions to their death with little idea of the long-range consequences, these leaders never had the moral insight to understand that the destruction of the Jews would also destroy something central to their way of life. Even today, few thinkers have made the link between the demoralization and loss of confidence in the West and the chimneys of the death camps. The Holocaust has a relatively low priority in the history texts used in our schools. It is merely another in a long litany of atrocities. Today as yesterday, few understand that a new order of events occurred in Auschwitz and that our lives can never be the same again.

Yet, how could it have been different? If the key decision makers at the time were told what Auschwitz really meant, would it have made a difference? They would have dismissed the notion that they could make decisions on the basis of abstract philosophy even if the long-range continuance of their own nations was at stake. They were concerned with concrete reality, with survival for another day. Until the early months of 1943, it looked to them as if their enterprise would surely fail. And if that happened, what matter abstract notions about the sanctity of life? The sense that *all* life, not merely Jewish life, was in jeopardy may have been less urgently felt in America, which even after Pearl Harbor was geographically removed from the physical destruction wrought by war. In America, it was business as usual. What was being done to Jews was a European affair. Roosevelt viewed the admission of refugees in the domestic political context, the only one he really knew and could control to some extent. He understood that the American people would never understand the admission of thousands, perhaps millions, of refugees while "one third of the nation was ill housed, ill fed and ill clad." In case he dared forget, Senator Robert Reynolds, a Democrat from North Carolina in the forefront of the struggle to keep refugees out, was there to remind him, and did so by using the president's own ringing phrases.

That brings us to one of the most bitter ironies of all concerning the role of America. The Roosevelt administration's inability to move on the refugee front was a classic case of democracy at work, the democracy that American Jewry revered so highly. The American people, including its Jewish component before 1938, did not welcome refugees. So strong was this sentiment that it would have taken an act of extraordinary political courage to thwart the popular will. Had Roosevelt done so, there was a good chance, as Congressman Samuel Dickstein, the Jewish chairman of the House Committee on Immigration and Naturalization pointed out, that there would have occurred a congressional reaction of even more restrictive laws in the face of the crisis. Roosevelt was occasionally capable of such political courage, especially on a major issue. Witness his action on the destroyer-bases deal that he implemented by Executive Order in September 1940. But in the case of refugees, even Jewish refugee children, he chose to be more the fox than the lion. He settled first for a politics of gestures. That is perhaps the key to the mystery of his invitation to thirty-two nations to meet at Evian in March 1938 to consider the refugee problem. The invitation was carefully hedged. It stated that the United States would not alter its immigration regulations and did not expect other states to do so. That, of course, consigned the Evian conference to failure.

Soon, the "politics of gestures" became more elaborate. Among other things, it featured an enthusiasm for mass resettlement schemes. That usually amounted to tucking away a highly urbanized Jewish minority in some tropical equatorial rain forest or desert to "pioneer." The Jews predictably could not muster much passion for it. Resettlement imposed on Jews, whether conceived in Berlin or in Washington, they understood as a concealed form of group dissolution, and they would have little to do with it. Thus, it was doomed to failure.

By the time Henry Morgenthau Jr., Roosevelt's secretary of the treasury and perhaps his closest Jewish friend, was enlisted in the rescue effort, it was already late in the game. Morgenthau did succeed in convincing the president to establish the War Refugee Board in January 1944. He prepared a highly secret brief that demonstrated that the State Department had deliberately and consistently sabotaged efforts to rescue Jews. It was a devastating document, and the WRB that it brought into existence did play an important role in saving those Hungarian Jews in and around Budapest who survived the war. But it was created too late to save the millions.

Similar practical concerns dictated the response of other witnessing nations and agencies. Pressed unwillingly into a life-and-death struggle for survival, British leaders predictably viewed German anti-Jewish depredations within the context of their own national survival. It was a foregone conclusion that in balancing the needs of the Jews against their own need for Arab loyalty and oil should there be a war, the latter would win out. Within that context, they were, according to one researcher, more generous to Jewish refugees than the United States. Apparently, moral considerations did bother some British leaders after the betrayal of the White Paper. It was partly that concern that led to the hedged offer of British Guiana for a small resettlement scheme. That colony had been the scene of two prior resettlement failures and posed many other problems, so that except for some territorialists like Joseph Rosen, Jews did not welcome it with enthusiasm and Zionists certainly did not see it as a substitute for Palestine. The indifferent response of Jewish leaders exasperated Sir Herbert Emerson, chairman of the Intergovernmental Refugee Committee. The subtle anti-Semitism in his reaction was not uncommon among middle-echelon bureaucrats in London and Washington. He complained in Washington in October 1939, "The trouble with the refugee affair was the trouble with the Jews and most eastern people, there was always some other scheme in the background for which they were prepared to sacrifice schemes already in hand."

The problem with assessing the role of the Vatican as witness is made complex by the fact that such power as it had was in the spiritual rather than the temporal realm; and yet the pope faced a problem of survival that was physical, involving as it did the institution of the church. Just as we expected the leader who introduced the welfare state in America to demonstrate a special sensitivity to the plight of the Jews, so to the pope, who ostensibly embodied in his person the moral conscience of a good part of the Christian world, was expected to speak out, to use his power. He did not, and it does not require a special study of church politics to realize that its priorities were ordered by crucial requirements in the temporal rather than the spiritual sphere. During World War II, church officials also sensed that it faced a struggle for mere survival. The Vatican probably possessed more precise information on the actual workings of the Final Solution than any other state. And although the pope had none of the divisions Stalin later sought, he had an extensive, brilliantly organized infrastructure that might have been brought into play for rescue work and a voice that had a profound influence with millions in occupied Europe. Yet, the pope remained silent, even as the Jews of Rome were deported "from under his window." That posture contrasted sharply with the activities of certain Dutch and French bishops and some lesser officials like Cardinal Roncalli, later Pope John, who were active in the rescue effort. But they did not bear the responsibility for the survival of the institution of the church itself.

One need not search out the reason for the pope's silence in his Germanophilia or in his oversensitivity to the threat the church faced from the Left. The latter had been demonstrated under the Calles and Cardenas regimes in Mexico and during the civil war in Spain. But observing that the church genuinely felt the threat of "Godless Communism" is a long way from concluding that therefore Pius XII accepted the Nazis' line that they were the staunchest opponents of a Communist conspiracy that was somehow Jewish in nature. The immediate threat to the church during the years of the Holocaust emanated from Berlin, and we know today that Hitler did indeed intend to settle matters with the church after hostilities were over.

The Nazi ideology posed not only a physical threat but also divided the Catholic flock. Over 42% of the SS were Catholic, and many top-ranking Nazi leaders, including Hitler, Himmler, Heydrich, and Eichmann, were at least nominally so. The war itself had placed the Vatican in a delicate position because Catholics fought on both sides. The pope's primary problem was how to walk that delicate tightrope. The determination not to speak out on Jews, which was at the very center of Nazi cosmology, should be viewed in that light. His choice was not basically different from that of the British in the Middle East or of Roosevelt on refugee policy.

The International Red Cross also thought in terms of its viability as an agency whose effectiveness was based on its ability to maintain a strict neutrality. It faced a legal dilemma; for although the Nazis spoke endlessly about the threat of "international Jewry," the Jews of Germany were legally an "internal" problem during the refugee phase. After the deportation and internment in camps began, their status became even more difficult to define. When Denmark requested the Red Cross to investigate the fate of Danish Jews deported to Theresienstadt, it could do so because the request indicated that Denmark continued to recognize them as Danish citizens. But such requests were not forthcoming from other occupied countries. And the Danish request set the stage for one of the cruelest hoaxes of the war. The Red Cross delegation that visited Theresienstadt to carry out that charge apparently was totally taken in by the Potemkin village techniques and gave the "model" camp a clean bill of health even while inmates were starving to death and being deported to Auschwitz behind the façade. Overly sensitive to the fact that it was a voluntary agency whose operation depended on the goodwill of all parties, it did not press the case concerning Jews with determination. Food parcels were not delivered to camps until 1944, nor did it press for a change of classification of certain Jewish inmates to prisoners of war. That tactic, suggested by the World Jewish Congress, might have saved many lives. It was for that reason that A. Leon Kubowitzki, the leading rescue proponent of the World Jewish Congress, found that "the persistent silence of the Red Cross in the face of various stages of the extermination policy, of which it was well informed, will remain one of the troubling and distressing riddles of the Second World War." Yet here, too, one can observe how the integrity and well being of the agency took precedence over the rescue of the Jews. It may well be that the priorities of nations and international agencies are directed first and foremost to their own well-being and cannot be readily transferred, for altruistic reasons, to a vulnerable minority facing the threat of mass murder.

We come next to a question that embodies at once all the frustrations we feel at the failure of the witnesses and is, for that reason, posed with increasing frequency in Holocaust symposia and in publications on the catastrophe. The question of bombing Auschwitz and the rail lines leading to the camp raises the twin problems of assessing the failure of the witnesses and of determining the range of possibilities and their relationship to strategic priorities. The assumption is that interdiction from the air was, in the absence of physical control of the death camps, the best practical way to interrupt the killing process.

An article in *Commentary* by Professor David Wyman and another by Roger M. Williams in *Commonweal* demonstrate beyond doubt that, by the spring of 1944, the bombing of Auschwitz was feasible.[2] Thousands of Hungarian and Slovakian Jews might have been saved had the American Fifteenth Air Force, stationed in Italy and already bombing the synthetic oil and rubber works not five miles from the gas chambers, been allowed to do so. Moreover, by the fall of 1944, Auschwitz was well within the range of Russian dive bombers. Given that context, the note by Assistant Secretary of War John J. McCloy that bombing was of "doubtful efficacy" and the Soviet rejection of the idea are the most horrendously inhuman acts by witnesses during the years of the Holocaust. All that was required was a relatively minor change in the priority assigned to the rescue of Jews.

Yet, a perceptive historian cannot long remain unaware of the seductive element in the bombing alternative. All one had to do, it seems, was to destroy the death chambers or the railroad lines leading to them, and the "production" of death would cease or at least be delayed. Things were not that simple. Jewish rescue advocates were late in picking up the signals emanating from Hungary for bombing, and even then there was little unanimity on its effectiveness. It was the World Jewish Congress that transmitted the request for bombing to the Roosevelt administration; but its own agent, A. Leon Kubowitzki, held strong reservations about bombing because he did not want the Jewish inmates of the camps to be the first victims of Allied intercession from the air. There was then and continues to be today genuine doubts that, given German fanaticism on the Jewish question and the technical difficulties involved in precision bombing, bombing the camps could have stopped the killing. The *Einzatsgruppen*, the special killing squads that followed behind German lines after the invasion of Russia, killed greater numbers in shorter order than the camps. The Germans were able to repair rail lines and bridges with remarkable speed. And, of course, Auschwitz was only one of the several camps where organized killing took place.

Most important, the bombing-of-Auschwitz alternative, so highly touted today, does not come to grips with the question of the fear that the Germans would escalate the terror and involve the Allies in a contest in which the Germans held all the cards. In a recent interview, McCloy cited this reason rather than the unwillingness to assign war resources to missions that were not directly involved in winning the war as the reason uppermost in Roosevelt's mind when the bombing alternative was rejected. An almost unnoticed subtheme in McCloy's August 14 note spoke of the fear that bombing might "provoke even more vindictive action by the Germans." Survivors and rescue advocates might well wonder what "more vindictive action" than Auschwitz was possible. But that views the bombing alternative from the vantage of the Jewish victims—which, as we have seen, is precisely what non-Jewish decision makers could not do, given their different order of priorities and sense of what was possible. The people who conceived of the Final Solution could in fact have escalated terror. They could have staged mass executions of prisoners of war or of hostages in occupied countries or the summary execution of shot-down bomber crews for "war crimes." Their imagination rarely failed when it came to conceiving new forms of terror, nor did they seem to possess normal moral restraints as one might find in the Allied camp. That was one of the reasons why the Final Solution could be implemented by them.

Nevertheless, one can hardly escape the conclusion that bombing deserved to be tried and might conceivably have saved lives. The failure to do so, however, is best viewed in the larger framework of the bombing question. It began with a collective *démarche* delivered by the governments-in-exile to the Allied high command in December 1942. That request did not ask for the bombing of the camps, but for something called "retaliatory bombing." That notion too was rejected because of the fear of an escalation of terror, and rescue advocates did not pick up the idea until it was all but too late. There is good reason to believe that retaliatory bombing offered even greater hope for rescue than the bombing of the camps themselves.

In 1943, when the death mills of Auschwitz and other death camps ground on relentlessly, bombing was in fact not feasible, but retaliatory bombing was. That was the year when the heavy saturation bombing of German cities was in full swing. In one sense, the bombing of Hamburg in July 1943 and the savaging of other German cities, including the bombing of Dresden, which many Germans consider a separate war atrocity, make sense today only when considered in the context of the death camps. Albert Speer and our own postwar evaluation of saturation bombing inform us that it had almost no effect on curtailing German war production. Not until one industry, fuel or ball bearings, was target-centered did the Nazi war machine feel the pinch. Yet, it might have furnished rescue advocates with an instrument to break through the "wall of silence" that surrounded what was happening to Jews. Even bombing interpreted as retaliatory could have had remarkable effects, especially in the satellites. When Miklós Horthy, the Hungarian regent, called a halt to the deportations on July 7, 1944, he did so in part out of fear that Budapest would be subject to more heavy raids as it had been on June 2. It was the bombing of Budapest, not Auschwitz, that had the desired effect. We know that Joseph Goebbels, in his perverse way, fully expected such a quid pro quo and had even taken the precaution of planning a massive counteratrocity campaign should the Allies make a connection between bombing and the death camps. Himmler also had already made the link. We find him addressing his officers on June 21, 1944, on the great difficulties encountered in implementing the Final Solution. He told the gathered group that, if their hearts were ever softened by pity, let them remember that the savage bombing of German cities "was after all organized in the last analysis by the Jews."

Yet, the natural link between bombing and the Final Solution made by Nazi leaders was not shared by Allied leaders or by Jewish rescue advocates. Had they done so, it is not inconceivable that the fear of disaffection and the terrible price the Reich was paying might have led more rational-minded leaders in the Nazi hierarchy to a reevaluation of the Final Solution, which was, after all, a purely ideological goal. Not all Nazis were convinced that the murder of the Jews was worth the ruin of a single German city. We do not know if such a rearrangement of Nazi priorities was possible. The theme of retaliatory bombing was not fully picked up by rescue advocates; and by the time the notion of bombing the camps came to the fore in March 1944, millions of Jews were already in ashes. That is why the twelve-point rescue program that came out of the giant

Madison Square Garden protest rally in March 1943 is as startling in its own way as McCloy's later response to the plea to bomb Auschwitz. It was silent on the question of bombing. It seems clear that those researching the role of the witnesses in the future will have to place failure of mind next to failure of spirit to account for their inaction during the Holocaust.

I have saved the discussion of the role of American Jewry for the end because it is the most problematic of all. For those who remain convinced that American Jewry failed, how the problem is posed does not really matter because the answer is always the same. Still, how did it happen that American Jewry, possessing what was perhaps the richest organizational infrastructure of any hyphenate group in America, experienced in projecting pressure on government on behalf of its coreligionists since the Damascus blood libel of 1840, emerging from the depression faster than any other ethnic group, boasting a disproportionate number of influential members in Roosevelt's inner circle, and chairing the three major committees in Congress concerned with rescue,[3] despite all this was appreciably unable to move the Roosevelt administration on the rescue question?

Stated in this way, the question provides not the slightest suggestion of the real problem that must be addressed if an adequate history of the role of American Jewry during the Holocaust is ever to emerge. For even if all of these assets in the possession of American Jewry were present, one still cannot avoid the conclusion that American Jewry's political power did not match the responsibilities assigned to it by yesterday's rescue advocates and today's historians. We need to know much more about the character and structure of American Jewry during the thirties, the political context of the host culture in which it was compelled to act, and the ability of hyphenate or ethnic groups to influence public policy.

The political and organizational weaknesses of American Jewry during the thirties have been amply documented. It seems clear that the precipitous shift of the mantle of leadership of world Jewry found American Jewry unprepared. A communal base for unified action simply did not exist. Instead, there was fragmentation, lack of coherence in the message projected to policy makers, profound disagreement on what might be done in the face of the crisis, and strife among the leaders of the myriad political and religious factions that constituted the community. It may well be that the assumption of contemporary historians that there existed a single Jewish community held together by a common sense of its history and a desire for joint enterprise is the product of a messianic imagination.

One is hard-pressed to find such a community on the American scene during the thirties. Even those delicate strands that sometimes did allow the "uptown" and "downtown" divisions to act together vanished during the crisis. The issues that caused the disruption stemmed from the crisis and seem appallingly irrelevant today. There was disagreement on the actual nature of the Nazi threat, the efficacy of the anti-Nazi boycott, the creation of a Jewish army, the commonwealth resolution of the Biltmore conference, the activities of the Peter Bergson group, and the way rescue activities were actually carried out around the periphery of occupied Europe. There was something tragic in the way each separate Jewish constituency was compelled in the absence of a unified front to go to Washington to plead separately for its particular refugee clientele. In 1944, Rabbi Jacob Rosenheim, director of the Vaad Ha-Hatzala, the rescue committee of the Orthodox wing, explained why he found it better to act alone. He observed that the rescue scene "was a dog eat dog world [in which] the interest of religious Jews [is] always menaced by the preponderance of the wealthy and privileged Jewish organizations especially the Agency and the Joint." Clearly for Rosenheim, the Nazis were not the only enemy. It did not take long for the unfriendly officials in the State Department to learn about the strife within the community. In 1944, we find Breckinridge Long writing in his diary: "The Jewish organizations are all divided amidst controversies. . . . there is no cohesion nor any sympathetic collaboration [but] . . . rather rivalry, jealousy and antagonism." It was a fairly accurate observation.

But, one can have doubts whether the administration's rescue policy would have been appreciably changed had the Jews had a pope, as Roosevelt once wished in a moment of exasperation. In the American historical experience, the ability of pressure groups to reorder policy priorities has been fairly circumscribed. The Irish Americans, perhaps the most politically astute of all hyphenate groups, tried to use American power to "twist the lion's tail" in the nineteenth and twentieth centuries. Yet with all their political talent, they were unable to prevent the Anglo-American reapprochement that developed gradually after 1895. During the years before World War I, the German Americans were a larger and more cohesive group than American Jewry during the thirties. Even so, they failed to prevent the entrance of America into war against their former fatherland. And adamant opposition of Polish Americans did not prevent the "Crime of Crimea," the surrender of part of Poland to the Soviet Union at Yalta.

There are more examples that could be cited to establish the fact that hyphenate pressure has not been distinctly successful in pulling foreign policy out of its channels once it has been firmly established that a given policy serves the national interest. Despite the rantings of some individuals and groups, Jews have done no better than other groups in this regard. That it is thought to be otherwise is part of the anti-Semitic imagination, which has always assigned Jews far more power and importance behind the scenes than they possessed. It is one of the great ironies of our time that many Jews share the belief that they possess such secret power. It is a comforting thought for a weak and vulnerable people. It should be apparent to any Jew living in the time-space between Kishinev and Auschwitz that such can hardly be the case. A powerful people does not lose one-third of its adherents while the rest of the world looks on.

The charge that American Jewry was indifferent to the survival of its brethren during the Holocaust is not only untrue but would have been highly uncharacteristic from a historical perspective. Much of American Jewry's organizational resources in the nineteenth and twentieth centuries—the Board of Delegates of American Israelites, the American Jewish Committee, the Joint Distribution Committee, and the various philanthropic organizations that preceded them, the American Jewish Congress, the various Zionist organizations and appeals—were structured in relation to Jewish communities and problems abroad. From its colonial beginnings, when American Jewry welcomed "messengers" from Palestine, it has consistently demonstrated a strong attachment to Jewish communities overseas. The Holocaust years did not mark a sudden change in that pattern. A close perusal would indicate that virtually every means of public pressure, from delegations to the White House to giant public demonstrations—techniques later adopted by the civil rights movement—were initially used by American Jewry during the war years to bring their message to American political leaders. They were not terribly effective because leaders were not fully attuned to Jewish objectives and because the war itself tended to mute the cry of pain of a group trying vainly to convince America that its suffering was inordinate and required special attention.

Given the circumstances, American Jewry seemed bound to

fail. Sometime, one is tempted to believe that such was the case with everything related to the Holocaust, including the writing of its history. Those who despair of the role of American Jewry forget that, throughout the war years, the actual physical control of the scene of the slaughter remained in Nazi hands. Wresting that physical control from them, the most certain means of rescue, required a basic redirecting of war strategy to save the Jews. Even under the best of circumstances, military strategists never would have accepted such restrictions. British historian Bernard Wasserstein, searching through recently declassified British documents, discovered that at one point, as the war drew to a close, Churchill and Eden actually favored a direct military effort to save the Jews. But they did not succeed in breaking through the middle echelons of the bureaucracy and the military command to effect it. That is the reason why the American failure during the refugee phase (1938–1941) and the failure to support the notion of retaliatory bombing and the bombing of the camps and rail lines leading to them looms so large today. Such steps were possible without a massive redirecting of strategy and without great sacrifice of lives and material. Aside from the possibility of ransoming proposals, which came at the beginning and end of the Holocaust, there seemed to be no other way to rescue appreciable numbers.

Besides the lack of precedent for responding to such a situation, American Jewry was plagued by its inability to get the fact of systematized mass murder believed. Few could fathom that a modern nation with a culture that had produced Goethe, Heine, Bach, and Beethoven, and the German *Kulturgebiet*, which Jews especially linked to progress and enlightenment, had embarked on such a program. It beggared the imagination. The immense problem of gaining credibility was never solved during the crisis and contributed notably to the failure to activate decision makers to mount a more strenuous rescue effort. The role of the State Department in deliberately attempting to suppress the story of the Final Solution, a now well-known and separate tragedy, made breaking through the credibility barrier even more difficult.

It is in that context that the role of Rabbi Stephen Wise in asking Sumner Welles to confirm the Riegner cable, which contained the first details of the operation of the Final Solution, is best viewed. American Jewish leadership might be accused of ignorance, ineffectiveness, or just sheer lack of stature, as Nahum Goldmann has observed, but the charge of betrayal is unwarranted and unfair. The contents of the Riegner cable, which spoke of the use of prussic acid and the production of soap from the fat of the cadavers, was so horrendous that to have publicized it without confirmation would have resulted in widening the credibility gap. Middle echelon State Department officials were not remiss in accusing Jewish leaders of atrocity mongering. In the context of the history of the thirties, that charge was far from innocent. The notion that Americans had been skillfully manipulated by British propaganda into entering World War I was common fare in the revisionist history which made its debut in the thirties. A warning that British and Jewish interests were plotting to bring America into World War II had been a major theme in a speech delivered in September 1941 in Des Moines by Charles Lindbergh, a greatly esteemed national folk hero. It was but a small jump for the isolationist-minded American public to believe that it was happening all over again. The neutrality laws passed by Congress in the thirties were based on the same supposition.

Although the delay in several months in publicizing the Riegner report was probably costly, it was necessary to gain credibility. A duplicate cable had also been forwarded to the British branch of the World Jewish Congress, so that there was little danger that the story could have been permanently suppressed by the State Department. Eventually, even the department's attempt to cut off the flow of information at the source was discovered and used to remove its hand from the rescue levers.

The inability to believe the unbelievable was not confined to Washington policy makers. It plagued Jewish leaders who were right on top of the operation and had every reason to believe it. The strategies developed by the Jewish Councils in Eastern Europe, "rescue through work" and "rescue through bribery," and finally the surrender of the aged and the infirm in the hope that the Nazis did not intend to liquidate useful Jews, were based on the assumption that the Nazis did not intend to kill *all* the Jews.

Even after the press made public news of the Final Solution, most Americans, including many Jews, simply did not absorb the fact of what was happening. A poll of Americans in January 1943, when an estimated 1,000,000 Jews had already been killed, indicated that less than half the population believed that mass murder was occurring. Most thought it was just a rumor. By December 1944, when much more detail was available, the picture had not drastically altered. Seventy-five percent then believed that the Germans had murdered many people in concentration camps. But when asked to estimate how many, most answered 100,000 or fewer. By

May 1945, when Americans had already seen pictures of the camps, the median estimate rose to 1,000,000, and 85 percent were then able to acknowledge that systematic mass murder had taken place. But the public was oblivious to the fact that the victims were largely Jewish. The inability to understand the immensity of the crime extended to the Jewish observers around the periphery of occupied Europe. They underestimated the number who had lost their lives by 1,500,000. The figure of 6,000,000 was not fully established until the early months of 1946.

The credibility problem was at the very core of the reaction of the witnesses: they could not react to something they did not know or believe. The problem of credibility takes us out of the realm of history. We need to know much more about how such facts enter the public conscience. How does one get people to believe the unbelievable? Rescue advocates did not succeed in solving that problem during those bitter years; and that, in some measure, is at the root of their failure to move governments and rescue agencies. In democracies, it requires an aroused public opinion to move governments to action. Without that impetus, there is little hope that governments who are naturally reluctant to act would do so.

Thus far, no historians have probed the role of Jewish political culture, those assumptions and qualities of style and habit that shape relationships to power and power holders, in accounting for the Jewish response. To be sure, there are some untested observations in Raul Hilberg's *Destruction of European Jewry* and Lucy Dawidowicz's *War Against the Jews*. But no systematic study of its workings during the Holocaust years has been published. It is such an elusive subject that one can seriously wonder if it can be examined by modern scholarship. Yet, it is precisely in that area that one of the keys to our conundrum regarding the Jewish response may lie.

Underlying the response of Jewish victims and witnesses at the time is an assumption about the world order so pervasive that we tend to forget that it is there at all. Jews believed then that there existed somewhere in the world, whether in the Oval Office or the Vatican or Downing Street, a spirit of civilization whose moral concern could be mobilized to save the Jews. The failure to arouse and mobilize that concern is the cause of the current despair regarding the role of Jewish witnesses and leads to the search for betrayers. It is an assumption that continues to hold sway in Jewish political culture, despite the fact that there is little in recent Jewish experience that might confirm the existence of such a force in human affairs.

To some extent, that despair is present in most literary works dealing with the Holocaust, especially in the speeches and works of one of the leading spokesmen for the victims, Elie Wiesel. It is a contemporary echo of what the Jewish victims felt before they were forced to enter the gas chambers. Emmanuel Ringleblum and others recorded it in their diaries. They wondered why no one came to their rescue and often assumed that the civilized world would not allow such a thing to happen. It can be heard most clearly in the message sent to Smull Zygelbojm which asked Jewish leaders to starve themselves to death if necessary in order to "shake the conscience of the world." The assumption was and continues to be that there is a "conscience of the world."

American Jewry, no less than others, shared that belief. Most Jews were convinced that Roosevelt's welfare state, which reflected their own humanitarian proclivities, was a manifestation of that spirit of concern. That is why they loved him so; after 1936, even as other hyphenates began to decline in their political support, American Jewry raised the proportion of its pro-FDR vote to over 90 percent. Yet had they searched for deeds that actually helped their coreligionists, they would have found only rhetoric. That and their support of FDR's domestic program proved sufficient to hold them even after he had passed from the scene.

It may be that Jewish voters had not resolved in their own minds the problem of possibilities of rescue or even the need for it. They assumed privately that the "authorities" were doing all that could be done. American Jewish leaders, who were aware of the previous dismal record of government intercession in the Jewish interest, nevertheless were hard-pressed for an alternative. They might have recalled how hard Jews had fought for an equal rights clause in the Romanian Constitution at the Congress of Berlin in 1878, only to see it almost immediately thwarted by the Romanian government. They surely were aware that dozens of diplomatic intercessions on behalf of Russian Jews at the turn of the century had come to nothing. Surely, they knew that the most successful single effort to bring better treatment for their coreligonists, the abrogation of the treaty of 1832 with czarist Russia in 1911 had come to nothing. They might have recalled that when Louis Marshall turned to the Vatican in 1915 with a request that it use its influence to halt the anti-Jewish depredations in Poland, the response had been indifferent. The League of Nations, which many Jews imagined would house the spirit of humanity and even amplify it, had become a

dismal failure by the thirties. They must have noted Roosevelt's nig-
gardly response to the refugee crisis and Britain's reneging on the
promise contained in the Balfour Declaration. They must have seen
how drastically the situation had deteriorated even since World War
I. At that time, one could at least hint that Berlin would do for Jews
what London would not and gain concessions. In short, they could
not have failed to understand that, for Jews living in the thirties, the
world had become less secure and benevolent than ever. But living
with the knowledge of total vulnerability in an increasingly barbaric
world is a reality almost too painful to face. One had to choose
sides, and clearly Roosevelt, with all his shortcomings, was still better than the alternatives. There were in fact no alternatives, not on
the domestic political scene and not in the international arena. The
truth was that, during the years of the Holocaust, Jewish communities were caught in the classic condition of powerlessness that, by
definition, means lack of options. That was true of American Jewry
as well.

In that context, the central assumption of pre-Holocaust Jewish
political culture becomes understandable. It was based as much on
powerlessness as on residual messianic fervor or the universalism of
democratic socialism that large numbers in the community adhered
to. As a general rule, it is precisely the weak and vulnerable who call
for justice and righteousness in the world. The powerful are more
inclined to speak of order and harmony. It is in the interest of the
weak to have a caring spirit of civilization intercede for them. That
may explain why Jews especially called on a threatened world to be
better than it wanted to be.

For American Jewry, the notion of benevolence and concern in
the world was not totally out of touch with reality. Bereft of specific
power, Jews did in fact make astounding economic and political ad-
vances in the eighteenth, nineteenth, and twentieth centuries. Despite occasional setbacks, the idea that progress was possible, even
inevitable, was deeply ingrained in American Jewry's historical experience. More than other Jewries who lived in the West, American
Jews had, to some degree, been disarmed by their history; and so
they never fully understood the signs that all was not well in the
secular nation-state system. The most important of these signs was
the relative ease with which the nations ordered and accepted the
incredible carnage of World War I. That experience contained many
of the portents of the Holocaust, including the use of gas and the
cheapening of human life. The rise of totalitarian systems in the in-

terwar period, which extended further the demeaning of individual human dignity, was not part of their experience; therefore, they did not understand what the massive bloodletting in the Soviet Union and the transferring of populations like so many herds of cattle signified. They did not understand that the nation-state was dangerously out of control, that all moral and ethical restraints had vanished, and only countervailing power held it in check.

Many Jews still looked to the nations for succor; they sought restraints. As Alexander Donat writes, "We fell victims to our faith in mankind, our belief that humanity had set limits to the degradation and persecution of one's fellow man." The countering facts were of too recent a vintage to seep into their historical consciousness and alter their visions and assumptions about the world in which they lived. Jewish leaders and rank and file blithely disregarded the mounting evidence that states and other forms of human organization, even those like the Holy See, which professed to a humanizing mission through Christian love, were less than ever able to fulfill such a role. The behavioral cues of states came from within and were determined by the need of the organization to survive at all costs. With a few notable exceptions, the rescue of Jews during the years of the Holocaust did not fit in with such objectives, and they were allowed to perish like so much excess human cargo on a lifeboat.

The indictment of the witnesses is based on the old assumption that there exists such a spirit of civilization, a sense of humanitarian concern in the world that could have been mobilized to save Jewish lives during the Holocaust. It indicts the Roosevelt administration, the Vatican, the British government, and all other witnessing nations and agencies for not acting, for not caring. And it reserves a special indignation for American Jewry's failure to mobilize a spirit that did not in fact exist. It is an indictment that cannot produce authentic history. Perhaps that cannot really be written until the pain subsides.

Notes

Selected Bibliography

Index

Notes

Introduction

1. *Accounting for Genocide* (New York, 1979).

2. (New Brunswick, N.J., 1970).

3. Arthur Morse, *While Six Million Died* (New York, 1968) and David Wyman, *Paper Walls* (Amherst, 1968).

4. *Why Did The Heavens Not Darken* (New York, 1988).

5. *Judenrat: The Jewish Councils in Eastern Europe Under Nazi Occupation* (New York, 1972); *Eichmann In Jerusalem: A Report on the Banality of Evil* (New York, 1963).

6. Ben Halpern, "What Is Antisemitism?," *Modern Judaism*, 1, no. 3 (Dec. 1981): 251–62.

7. James H. Kitchens III, "The Bombing of Auschwitz Re-examined," *The Journal of Military History* 58, no. 2 (Apr. 1944): 233–66.

8. Emanuel Celler, *You Never Leave Brooklyn* (New York, 1957), 89.

1. The Uniqueness of the Holocaust

1. Arthur A. Cohen, "Thinking the Tremendum: Some Theological Implications of the Death Camps." New York: Leo Baeck Memorial lecture 18, 1974, 3; Jacob Katz, "Was the Holocaust Predictable?" uses the term *novum*.

2. New York Board of Education, *The Holocaust, A Study of Genocide*, Curriculum Bulletin 1978–1979 no. 13 (New York, 1979), xvi ff.

3. Helen Fein, *Accounting for Genocide* (New York, 1979), 9–10.

4. Alexander I. Solzhenitsyn, *The Gulag Archipelago*, I–II, (New York, 1973); Roy A. Medvedev, *Let History Judge* (New York, 1973). The comparative approach placed under a generalized category of totalitarian terror is best illustrated in Irving L. Horowitz, *Genocide: State Power and Mass Murder* (New Brunswick, N.J., 1976).

5. The practice began in earnest when the noted novelist James Baldwin characterized Angela Davis, a recently arrested Black Marxist activist, as "the Jewish housewife on the way to Dachau." See an "Open Letter to My Sister, Miss Angela Davis," in *The New York Review of Books*, Jan. 7, 1971.

6. That was the thrust of a paper delivered by John Murray Cuddihy "The

Latent Issue in the Uniqueness Debate," Meeting for the Sociological Study of Jewry, Boston, Aug. 26, 1979.

7. See Arthur R. Butz, *The Hoax of the Twentieth Century*, London, n.d. (ca. 1976).

8. Cuddihy, "Uniqueness Debate," 16–17. Sociologists generally experience difficulty in handling the concept of uniqueness. Cuddihy, for example, needs to fit all such Jewish claims whether it be for the general behavior (or lack of it) in society or their Holocaust experience under a category he calls "metaphorical chosenness."

9. Emil L. Fackenheim, *The Human Condition After Auschwitz: A Jewish Testimony A Generation After*, The B. G. Rudolph Lectures in Judaic Studies, 1971, Syracuse Univ., 9.

10. Such a projection was made by Teilhaber, a German Jewish demographer, in 1911.

11. Speech to Wehkreis (n.d. ca. Aug. 1943): "However hideous it may be, it has been necessary for us to do it. . . . If we lose our nerve now, we shall have to march once again; we shall simply be repeating in the next century the political idiocies of the last thousand years." Helmut Krausnick, et al. *Anatomy of the SS State* (New York, 1965), 388–89

12. *Nazi Conspiracy and Aggression* (Washington, D.C., 1946), 6:787–90, Affidavit of Rudolf Hess.

13. The term *modernizing elite* is used in preference classifications like *revolutionary elites* or *conscious pariah*, as employed by Hannah Arendt or *creative wanderers*, as used by George Steiner, or the rubric *change agents*, as employed in contemporary managerial science. The term *modernizing elite* is at once more neutral and more encompassing. *Revolutionary elite* presents a particular problem because only a small minority of the Jewish group favored violent revolutionary change. Russia between 1880 and 1890, when a disproportionate number of the arrested members of terrorist groups like Narodnaya Volna were Jewish, was an exceptional case. Generally, what the Jews in the modernizing elite had in common was a sense that change was necessary and a generally optimistic vision of what the world might become.

14. George Steiner, "A Kind of Survivor," *Commentary*, Feb. 1965, 32–38; "The Unique and the Universal," *Commentary*, May 1970, 4–10.

15. J. L. Talmon, *Israel Among the Nations*, 11–12.

16. Ibid. 72.

17. George Steiner's reply to Robert Alter, *Commentary*, May 1970, 8.

18. Hannah Arendt to Gershom Sholem, June 24, 1963, in Ron H. Feldman, ed. "Hannah Arendt," *The Jew as Pariah* (New York, 1978), 246.

19. Y. L. Peretz "Advice to the Estranged" in *The Faith of Secular Jews*, ed. Saul L. Goodman (New York, 1976), 140.

20. Simon Dubnow, "The Secret of Survival and the Law of Survival," ibid., 187.

21. Quoted in Nahum Glatzer, ed., *On Judaism* (New York, 1973), 28.

22. Feldman, "Arendt," 67–90.

23. Robert S. Wistrich, "Eduard Bernstein on the Jewish Problem," *Midstream*, Dec. 1979, 12.

24. J. L. Talmon, *The Unique and the Universal*, London, n.d., 83.

25. Peter Gay, *The Berlin Jewish Spirit: A Dogma in Search of Some Doubts* (New York, 1972), 3–4.

26. Feldman, "Arendt," 67.

2. Like Sheep to the Slaughter: The *Judenrat*

1. Jacob Robinson, *And the Crooked Shall Be Made Straight: The Eichmann Trial, the Jewish Catastrophe and Hannah Arendt's Narrative* (New York, 1965); Gideon Hausner, the chief Israeli prosecutor, whose conduct of the trial Arendt also found wanting, has written his own account, *Justice in Jerusalem* (New York, 1966).

2. Isaiah Trunk, *Judenrat* (New York, 1972).

3. "If pagans should tell them 'Give us one of yours and we shall kill him, otherwise we shall kill all of you' they should all be killed and not a single Jew should be delivered." *Mishne Torah Hilkhot Yesoday Hatorah*, chap. 5, para. 5.

4. Stanley Hoffman, *In Search of France* (Cambridge, Mass., 1963).

3. The Resistance Question

1. Uri Suhl, *They Fought Back* (New York, 1967); Lucien Steinberg, *Not as a Lamb* (London, 1970).

2. Lester Eckman and Chaim Lazar, *The Jewish Partisans in Lithuania and White Russia 1940–1945* (New York, 1977).

4. Allied Foreign Policy and the Holocaust

1. The most recent work on the witness role of the Roosevelt administration almost completely discounts the part of anti-Semitism as an element in its indifference to rescue. See Richard Breitman and Alan M. Kraut, *American Refugee Policy and European Jewry, 1933–1945* Bloomington, Ind., 1987. Anti-Bolshevism takes precedence over "Judeophobia," to which it is linked, in Arno J. Mayer, *Why Did the Heavens Not Darken? The "Final Solution" in History* (New York, 1989).

2. See Sarah Gordon, *Hilter, Germans, and the "Jewish Question"* Princeton, 1984; Lucy S. Dawidowicz, "Towards A History of the Holocaust," *Commentary* 47 (Apr. 1969): 51–56; for an explanation of the new biological anti-Semitism see J. L. Talmon, "European History—Seedbed of the Holocaust," *Midstream* 19 (May 1973): 7.

3. Morris D. Waldman, *Nor by Power* (New York, 1953), 79.

4. Karl Schleunes, *The Twisted Road to Auschwitz: Nazi Policies Towards the Jews, 1933–1939* (Urbana, Ill., 1970).

5. Charles Reznikoff, ed., *Louis Marshall, Champion of Liberty, Selected Papers and Addresses* (Philadelphia, 1957); L. Marshall to Charles E. Hughes, Apr. 27, 1921, 1:174–75.

6. US House Committee on Immigration and Naturalization, *Hearings Before the House Committee on Immigration and Naturalization*, "Restriction of Immigration," 68th Cong., 1st sess., Jan. 3, 1924.

7. See, for example, *The War Diary of Breckinridge Long*, ed. Fred L. Israel (Lincoln, Neb., 1966). Entry Jan. 23–24, 1940, 55–56.

8. Richard D. Breitman and Alan M. Kraut, "Anti-Semitism in the State Department, 1933–44: Four Case Studies," in *Anti-Semitism in American History*, ed. David A. Gerber (Urbana, Ill., 1986),167–97.

9. David Engel, *In The Shadow of Auschwitz: The Polish Government-in-Exile and the Jews, 1939–1942* (Chapel Hill, N.C., 1987); Marjtin Gilbert, *Auschwitz and the Allies* (New York, 1981), 106.

10. Michael J. Cohen, *Churchill and the Jews* (London, 1984).

11. Gilbert *Auschwitz*, 76–77.

12. Ibid., 107.

13. Raul Hilberg, *The Destruction of the European Jews* (New York, 1973), 207–8.

14. Dov Levin, "The Attitude of the Soviet Union Toward Rescue Attempts During the Holocaust," *Proceedings of the Second Yad Vashem International Historical Conference*, Apr. 9–17, 1974, 230–35.

15. Owen Chadwick, *Britain and the Vatican During the Second World War* (Cambridge: Cambridge University Press, 1986); Michael R. Marrus, *The Holocaust In History* (Hanover, NH: University Press of New England, 1987), 179–183; John Morley, *Vatican Diplomacy and the Jews During the Holocaust, 1939–1943* (New York: Ktav, 1980).

5. Roosevelt's New Deal Humanitarianism

1. *Proceedings of the Intergovernmental Committee*, Evian, July 6–15, 1938.

6. Could Mass Resettlement Have Saved European Jewry?

1. The Black Book Committee, *The Black Book: The Nazi Crime Against the Jewish People* (New York, 1946), 91.

2. *Christian Science Monitor*, Aug. 3, 1938, 1.

3. James McDonald to Frederick P. Keppel, Nov. 21, 1938, McDonald MSS.

4. George Warren to Cordell Hull, Nov. 25, 1938, McDonald MSS.

5. Lawrence Duggan to Joseph Chamberlain, Dec. 9, 1938, McDonald MSS.

6. Franklin Roosevelt (hereafter FDR) to Cordell Hull, July 3, 1940, F. D. Roosevelt Library/Official File (hereafter FDRL/OF) 3186.

7. *New York Times* (hereafter *NYT*), Nov. 16, 1938, 22.

8. NA/SDDF, 840.48, Refugees 9851/2, Nov. 26, 1938; FDRL/OF, 76-c, Nov. 26, 1938.

9. Robert G. H. Tallman, "The Alaskan Resettlement Corporation for Refugees," Oct. 20, 1938 (mimeographed), McDonald MSS.

10. Lewis Strauss, *Men and Decisions* (New York, 1963), 124–25.

11. George Warren to Myron Taylor and George Rublee. (Statement by Commings, former US Health Surgeon and at the time head of the Pan-American Sanitary Bureau), Dec. 15, 1938, McDonald MSS.

12. Rexford Tugwell, *The Democratic Roosevelt: A Biography of Franklin D. Roosevelt* (Baltimore, 1969), 345.

13. That such proclivities persisted in Washington is attested to by George Ball, who blames the Vietnam adventure partly on the fantasy of nation building. George W. Ball, "The Lesson of Viet Nam, Have We Learned or Only Failed?", *NYT Magazine*, Apr. 1, 1973, 13.

14. Warren, Circular letter to members of PACPR, n.d. (probably Oct. 1939), McDonald MSS.

15. Official Minutes of the Officers of the Intergovernmental Committee on Political Refugees, Oct. 17, 1939; Minutes of the twenty-ninth meeting of the President's Advisory Committee on Political Refugees, Oct. 23, 1939, FDRL/OF, 3186; Warren Circular Letter to "Members of President's Advisory Committee," Nov. 6, 1939, McDonald MSS.

16. Van Zeeland to Hull, Dec. 1, 1939, *FRUS*, 2:154–55.

17. FDR memorandum to Sumner Welles, Dec. 4, 1939, FDRL/PSF, box 24.

18. David S. Wyman, *Paper Walls: America and the Refugee Crisis, 1938–1941* (Amherst, Mass., 1968), 59.

19. Alex Hŕdlička to FDR, May 27, 1942, Long MSS.

20. Max Gottschalk to McDonald, May 15, 1941, McDonald MSS.

21. McDonald to Albert Einstein, May 30, 1935, McDonald MSS (Leo Baeck Institute).

22. McDonald to Felix Warburg, Sept. 9, 1935, McDonald MSS (Leo Baeck Institute).

23. Memorandum of meeting called to consult with Jaretzki and Warren on colonization projects, Dec. 1938, McDonald MSS.

24. Kurt Battsek to Lord Victor Rothschild, Mar. 27, 1938; Battsek to McDonald, May 30, 1938, McDonald MSS.

25. Minutes of the Third Meeting of the PACPR, June 2, 1938, Wise MSS.

26. Charles S. Dewey to Myron Taylor, Feb. 9, 1939, McDonald MSS.

27. Hotchkiss to McDonald, Apr. 13, 22, and Dec. 21, 1938, McDonald MSS.

28. Leopoldville to State Department, Feb. 8, 1939, NA/SDDF, 855.55 J/1.

29. McDonald to Paulo Carneiro (secretary of agriculture, Pernambuco), Apr. 12, 1935, McDonald MSS (Leo Baeck Institute).

30. *NYT*, Dec. 1, 1938, 12.

31. Ibid., July 18, 1938, 4.

32. FDR to Gonzalez, June 3, 1938, FDRL/PSF, State Department File.

33. Evian Proceedings, July 21, 1938.

34. B. W. Hebsch to McDonald, Feb. 28, 1941, McDonald MSS.

35. Memorandum by Col. Waley Cohen, Dec. 14, 1938, McDonald MSS.

36. Warren to Stephen Morris (State Department), July 31, 1939, McDonald MSS.

37. Ibid.

38. Warren to Taylor and Rublee, Dec. 15, 1938, McDonald MSS.

39. Stephen Wise to McDonald, Dec. 21, 1938 and McDonald to Stephen Wise, Dec. 28, 1938, McDonald MSS; Memorandum, Division of American Republics, Mar. 3, 1939, NA/SDDF, 840.48, Refugees 1531; Isaiah Bowman's group later made a positive study of resettlement possibilities in Lower California, Bowman to McDonald, Apr. 17, 1941, McDonald MSS.

40. Ibid. (McDonald to Stephen Wise).

41. Warren to Taylor, June 16, 1939, McDonald MSS.

42. Ibid.

43. Welles to FDR, Jan. 5, 1939, FDLR/OF 3186.

44. Anthony de Rothschild to Warren, Jan. 25, 1939, McDonald MSS.

45. Warren to Taylor, Feb. 9, 1939, McDonald MSS.

46. Nathan Goldberg, "Immigration Attitudes of Mexicans: An Insight," *Rescue*, July/Aug. 1945, quoting from the *Inter-American Monthly*, Dec. 1942.

47. Leo Sach to FDR, Dec. 5, 1939, NA/SDDF, 840.48, Refugees/1115.

48. Warren to Evans Clark, Jan. 29, 1940, McDonald MSS (20th Century Fund).

49. *FRUS* 1:787 (Sept. 13, 1938); Rublee to Hull, *FRUS* 1:772 (Aug. 25, 1938).

50. McDonald to Warburg, Apr. 30, 1935 and McDonald to Walter Rotschnig, Apr. 4, 1935, McDonald MSS.

51. *NYT*, Dec. 1, 1938, 12.

52. Isaiah Bowman, *Limits of Land Settlement: A Report on Present-day Possibilities* (New York, 1937), 319–37.

53. *NYT*, June 25, 1939, 22.

54. Confidential memorandum, Mar. 25, 1941, and McDonald to Welles, Apr. 1, 1941, McDonald MSS.

55. Welles to McDonald, Apr. 21. 1941, McDonald MSS; Jefferson Caffrey to Hull, Apr. 19, 1941, NA/SDDF, 840.48, Refugees/2543.

56. Strauss, *Men and Decisions*, 124.

57. Ibid., 125.

58. Ibid.

59. Warren to Taylor, June 7, 1939, McDonald MSS.

60. Rosenman memorandum to FDR, Dec. 5, 1938, FDRL/PPF, 64.

61. Strauss, *Men and Decisions*, 126.

62. Elliot Roosevelt, ed., *FDR: His Personal Letters, 1928–45*, vol. 2 (New York, 1950), 951.

63. Bowman to FDR, July 5, 1942, Long MSS.

64. Bowman to McDonald, Apr. 17, 1941, McDonald MSS.

65. Bowman to FDR, Nov. 4, 25, 1938, FDRL/PPF 5575. See also J. H. Wellington, "Possibilities of Settlement in Africa," in Bowman, 279–82.

66. Ibid., 281.

67. In the case of the former German colony of Tanganyika, e.g., both Berlin and certain Zionist spokesmen were opposed to Jewish colonization, *German Documents*, Series D, 4:333–41 (Nov. 18, 1938); *British Documents*, 3d Series, 3:295–96 (Nov. 24, 1938); Wise to Taylor, Nov. 23, 1938, Wise MSS.

68. Welles memorandum to FDR, Jan. 12, 1939, FDRL/OF 3186.

69. FDR to Taylor for transmission to Chamberlain, Jan. 14, 1939, *FRUS* 2: 67–69.

71. Ibid.

72. Ibid.

73. Taylor to FDR, June 25, 1939, *FRUS* 2:127.

73. Hull to Taylor, Feb. 15, 1939, *FRUS* 2:70.

74. Achilles to Bowman, May 26, 1939, NA/SDDF, 840.48, Refugees/1640.

75. Pell memorandum of conversation with Van Zeeland, Nov. 8, 1939, *FRUS* 2:154.

76. Jacob Rosenheim (Agudas Israel) to McDonald, May 26, 1943, McDonald MSS.

77. Ibid.; see also Charles Liebman to Taylor, June 10, 1943, NA/SDDF 840.48, Refugees/4022.

78. Phillips to State Department, June 12, 1939, *FRUS* 2:64.

79. Phillips to FDR, Dec. 10, 1938, NA/SDDF 840.48, Refugees/1319 ½; see also *Ciano Diaries, 1939–1943* (London, 1947); and *German Documents*, Series D, 4:548.

80. *NYT*, Oct. 17, 1939, 25.

81. Letter to State Department announcing organization of group, Dec. 12, 1943, NA/SDDF 840.48, Refugees/4967.

82. Kraft to McDonald, Mar. 28, 1939, McDonald MSS.

83. Joseph L. Blau and Salo W. Baron, eds., *The Jews of the United States, 1790–1840: A Documentary History* (New York, 1963), vol. 3, document 314, 895.

84. "Memoir Addressed to Persons of the Jewish Religion in Europe, On the subject of Immigration to, and Settlement in, One of the Most Eligible Parts of the United States of North America," Oct. 20, 1819, Morris U. Schappes, ed., *A Documentary History of the Jews in the United States, 1654–1875* (New York, 1950), document 68, 141.

85. Joseph Brandes, *Immigration to Freedom: Jewish Communities in Rural New Jersey Since 1882* (Philadelphia, 1971), 323–25.

86. Refugee Economic Organization, Annual Reports, 1939–1943.

87. As early as June 1938, Paul Baerwald, director of the JDC, had suggested mass resettlement in the interior of the country, where the Rotary and YMCA would retrain the refugees. Minutes of the Third Meeting of the PACPR, June 2, 1938, Wise MSS.

88. "What Is Free Ports?", *New York Post,* Apr. 5, 1944.

89. Robert J. Caldwell, "The American Far North," *Foreign Affairs,* 1939, 516.

90. Minutes of the Fifth Meeting of the PACPR, June 10, 1938, Wise MSS.

91. McDonald to Alsberg, Aug. 8, 1938, McDonald MSS.

92. The Alaska Resettlement Corporation, Oct. 20, 1938, McDonald MSS.

93. Charles Buckley to FDR, Nov. 18, 1938; and State Department to Buckley, Dec. 7, 1938, FDLR/OF 3186.

94. Meeting of individuals called to consult with Jaretzki and Warren on colonization projects, Dec. 2, 1938, McDonald MSS.

95. Warren to Taylor, Jan. 27, 1939, McDonald MSS.

96. Harry Slattery, "The Problem of Alaskan Development," McDonald MSS, 38–41.

97. Klaus to McDonald, Aug. 15, 1940, McDonald MSS.

98. Ickes to FDR, Oct. 18, 1939, FDRL/OF 3186.

99. FDR to Welles, Oct. 19, 1939, FDRL/OF 3186.

100. Harold L. Ickes. *The Secret Diary of Harold Ickes*, vol. 3, "The Lowering Clouds" (New York, 1954), 56–57; Wyman, *Paper Walls* 102–3.

101. *NYT*, Aug. 27, 1939, section 4, 7.

102. Minutes of the Thirteenth Meeting of the PACPR, Dec. 8, 1938, McDonald MSS.

103. Herbert Frieder to Charles Liebman, Dec. 8, 1938, McDonald MSS.

104. Memorandum of conversation, McNutt and Welles, Dec. 16, 1938, Na/SDDF 840.48, Refugees 116 ½.

105. Warren to Rublee, Dec. 9, 1938, McDonald MSS.

106. Warren to Taylor and Rublee, Jan. 3, 1939, McDonald MSS.

107. *NYT*, Apr. 23, 1939, 33.

108. Karl J. Pelzer to Warren, Memorandum on Settlement Possibilities on the Island of Mindanao, Jan. 21, 1939, McDonald MSS.

109. Morris (State Department) to Department of Interior, July 14, 1939, McDonald MSS.

110. Survey Commission Report on Settlement Possibilities on Mindanao, Oct. 17, 1939 (mimeographed), Wise MSS.

111. Pell to McDonald, Nov. 21, 1939, McDonald MSS.

112. Liebman to McDonald, Nov. 21, 1939, McDonald MSS.

113. Warren to Taylor and Rublee, Dec. 15, 1938, McDonald MSS.

114. Memorandum on British Immigration to British Guiana (excerpts from 1927 report), Dec. 12, 1938, McDonald MSS.

115. Letter to the Editor, *Times*, Dec. 16, 1938.

116. Warren to Taylor and Rublee, Jan. 3, 1939, McDonald MSS.

117. Preliminary draft of Report on Settlement Possibilities in British Guiana and Surinam (Bowman), Jan. 1939, McDonald MSS; Hull to FDR, Nov. 21, 1939, FDRL/PSF, Hull folder.

118. Warren to Taylor and Rublee, Jan. 3, 1939, McDonald MSS.

119. Bowman to Wise, Feb. 6, 1939, Wise MSS.

120. Wise to McDonald, May 19, 1939, McDonald MSS.

121. Rothschild to Warren, May 26, 1939, Wise MSS.

122. Joseph A. Rosen, "Problem of Large Scale Settlement of Refugees from Middle European Countries in British Guiana," Apr. 14, 1939.

123. Ibid.

124. Ibid.

125. *Report of the British Guiana Refugee Commission to the President's Advisory Committee on Political Refugees of the United States of America*, May 1939.

126. Moffat diary, June 1, 1939.

127. Minutes of the Twenty-fifth Meeting of the PACPR, Apr. 20, 1939.

128. Memorandum on the Report of the British Guiana Commission—Remarks Submitted by Isaiah Bowman, May 19, 1939, McDonald MSS.

129. Pell to State Department, transmitted to Warren, May 12, 1939, McDonald MSS.

130. WCF to Taylor, June 5, 1939, McDonald MSS; *FRUS* 2:139–40, (July 7, 1939); Minutes of the Twelfth Meeting of the PACPR, Nov. 21, 1938.

131. WCF to Taylor, June 5, 1939, McDonald MSS.

132. Ibid.

133. "The German Refugee Transfer Plan, Memorandum Submitted by Dr. Joseph Tenenbaum," July 1939, McDonald MSS.

134. Ibid.

135. Ibid.

136. Pell to State Department, June 15, 1939, McDonald MSS.

137. Pell to Hull, July 13, 1939, *FRUS* 2:34.

138. Pell to State Department, June 22, 1939, McDonald MSS.

139. Held to JDC, July 12, 1939, McDonald MSS.

140. Warren to Pell, July 13, 1939, and Warren to Taylor, July 14, 1939, McDonald MSS.

141. Cable from Rosenberg, Jaretzki, and Hyman to Lewis Strauss, July 13, 1939, McDonald MSS.

142. Pell to Moffat, Apr. 17, 1939, Moffat MSS.

143. Memorandum of Lewis Strauss, Aug. 21, 1939, McDonald MSS.

144. Ibid.

145. Alfred Houston to Charles Liebman, Jan. 2, 1939, McDonald MSS.

146. Hull to Rublee, Jan. 18, 1939, *FRUS* 2:70–71.

147. Official Minutes of the Meeting of the Officers of the Intergovernmental Committee on Political Refugees, Oct. 17, 1939.

148. Warren to Pell, Nov. 8, 1939, McDonald MSS.

149. Pell to McDonald, Nov. 15, 1939, McDonald MSS.

150. McDonald to Welles, Jan. 24, 1941, McDonald MSS.

151. Welles to McDonald, Jan. 28, 1941, McDonald MSS.

152. Unsigned confidential memorandum, Dec. 1, 1942, NA/SDDF 840.48, Refugees/4839.

153. McDonald to Epstein, Apr. 10, 1942, McDonald MSS.

154. *Congress Weekly*, Jan. 15, 1943, 8–9.

155. "Large Scale Settlement in the Eastern Mediterranean," *Bulletin of the Economic Research Institute of the Jewish Agency* 2, no. 9–10 (Sept./Oct. 1938), 159.

156. David H. Popper, "A Homeland for Refugees," *Annals*, 203 (May 1939), 178.

157. Memorandum by Colonel Waley Cohen, Dec. 14, 1938, McDonald MSS.

158. Chaim Weizmann, "Palestine's Rôle in the Solution of the Jewish Problem," *Foreign Affairs* 20, no. 2 (Jan. 1942), 324–38.

159. A. G. Price, "Refugee Settlement in the Tropics," *Foreign Affairs* 18 (July 1940), 659–70.

160. Memorandum on the Report of the British Guiana Commission—Remarks submitted by Isaiah Bowman, May 19, 1939, McDonald MSS.

161. Joseph Rosen, "Problem of Large Scale Settlement of Refugees from Middle European Countries in British Guiana," Apr. 14, 1939.

162. Rudolph Stahl, "Vocational Retraining of Jews in Nazi Germany," *Jewish Social Studies* 1, no. 2 (Apr. 1939), 171; Bruno Blau, "The Jewish Population of Germany, 1939–1945," *Jewish Social Studies* 12, no. 2 (Apr. 1950), 161–72.

163. Ernest Hamburger, "One Hundred Years of Emancipation," *Leo Baeck Institute Year Book* 15 (New York, 1969), 59.

164. Taylor to Welles, June 25, 1939, *FRUS* 2:127.

165. Moffat diary, Feb. 15, 1939.

166. Welles to McDonald, Apr. 21, 1941, McDonald MSS.

167. Bowman, *Limits of Land Settlement*, 2.

168. As early as April 1935, McDonald spoke of "accumulating evidence of the contagious character of Nazi propaganda of Anti-Semitism, often disguised as ardent nationalism. Already there are indications that Jewish young men are being excluded from certain of the professions. . . . For example medicine and the Police. The Argentinians are very prone to copy and unfortunately just now they are inclined to copy the Germans." He also observed that anti-Semitism had made great inroads among Latin American officialdom. McDonald to Felix Warburg, Apr. 30, 1935, McDonald MSS.

169. Evian Proceedings, July 9, 1938, 31.

170. Memorandum, conversation of Berle, Wise, and Goldmann, Dec. 10, 1940, NA/SDDF 840.48, Refugees/2350.

171. Nathan Goldberg, "Immigration Attitudes of Mexicans: An Insight," *Rescue*, July/August 1945, 3.

172. NA/SDDF 840.48, Refugees/5846, May 25, 1944.

173. Rosen, "Problems of Large Scale Settlement", Apr. 14, 1939, 5.

174. Vickers to Harold Lucas, June 6, 1939, McDonald MSS.

175. Bowman, *Limits of Land Settlement*, 1.

176. Interview with George Backer, Oral History Division, Institute of Contemporary Jewry, Hebrew University of Jerusalem, Oct. 20, 1966 (not verbatim).

177. Yehuda Bauer, *From Diplomacy to Resistance: A History of Jewish Palestine, 1939–1945* (Philadelphia, 1970), 61–67, 116–18.

178. Wise to Taylor, Nov. 23, 1938, Wise MSS.

179. Wise to Pesach Rosenblatt, July 19, 1937, Wise MSS.

180. Wise to Rosenblatt, May 9, 1938, Wise MSS.

181. Stephen S. Wise, *As I See It* (New York, 1944), 130.

182. Memorandum submitted to the Bermuda Refugee Conference by the World Jewish Congress, Apr. 14, 1943, Wise MSS.

183. *Jewish Forum*, May 1942 (editorial).

184. Laurie and Maurice Cowan, *The Wit of the Jews* (Nashville, 1970), 71.

7. The American Effort to Save the Jews of Hungary

1. *New York Times*, Mar. 25, 1944, 1.

2. After Switzerland turned down Washington's request to house the conference of thirty-two nations, a French offer of the spa at Evian was accepted. Held July 6–15, 1938, the conference brought forth yet another committee to grapple with the refugee problem. Myron Taylor, head of the American delegation, despite the gambits conceived by the State Department, was never able to convince the delegates of the sincerity of Roosevelt's intentions.

3. Breckinridge Long, former ambassador to Rome, led a coterie of State Department personnel in successfully blocking all efforts at a more energetic rescue effort until 1944.

4. See Louis P. Lochner, ed. and trans., *The Goebbels Diaries, 1942–1943* (New York, 1948), 241, entry for Dec. 13, 1942.

5. Franklin D. Roosevelt MSS, Franklin D. Roosevelt Library, Hyde Park (FDRL), President Secretary's file (PSF), box 24, Dec. 4, 1939. President's memorandum to Welles for oral transmission to Van Zeeland.

6. For his pessimism regarding resettlement, see Isaiah Bowman, *Limits of Land Settlement: A Report on President-Day Possibilities* (New York, 1937).

7. The first reports of the State Department's attempt to suppress the news of the Final Solution were published by Henry Morgenthau Jr., "The Morgenthau Diaries VI—The Refugee Run Around," *Collier's*, Nov. 1, 1947, 22.

8. Cited in Gideon Hausner, *Justice in Jerusalem* (New York, 1966), 134.

9. A. Leon Kubowitzki, *Unity in Dispersion: A History of the World Jewish Congress* (New York, 1948), 184.

10. Papers of the War Refugee Board, FDRL/WRB) Feb. 11, 1944, Pehle to Stettinius. Pehle thought that "a program of this character offers the best potentialities for saving hundreds of thousands of lives. The number we can save by changing attitudes far exceeds the number by evacuation."

11. FDRL/WRB, Pehle to Harrison, Mar. 7, 1944. A second message was sent on Mar. 24, 1944, to Stockholm, Lisbon, Madrid, Ankara, and Cairo for transmission to Budapest. Included in it were instructions for intensive circulation of the president's speech.

12. FDRL/WRB, Morgenthau memorandum to FDR, Mar. 22, 1944. He urged Roosevelt to make a unilateral declaration promptly because time was short. What may have convinced the president was Anne O'Hare McCormick's observation that criticism of the rescue program "has become so vocal that policy makers cannot ignore it." *New York Times*, Mar. 25, 1944, 4.

13. *New York Times*, Mar. 25, 1944, 1.

14. Ibid.

15. FDRL/WRB, McClellan to Pehle, Apr. 13, 1944. A full description of the IRC activities is presented in a typed report, "Summary Report of the Activities of the WRB with Respect to Jews in Hungary," Oct. 9, 1944.

16. FDRL/WRB, Pehle to Harrison and McClellan, May 25, 1944. In Sept. 1944, the IRC became involved in delivering food packages to certain camps; but not until October did it risk approaching the German Foreign Office with a request that all foreigners in the camps be recognized as civilian prisoners of war.

17. FDRL/Official File (OF), Hull folder, FDR confidential memorandum to Hull, Oct. 2, 1939.

18. For an account of the position of the church on the Holocaust, see Guenter Lewy, *The Catholic Church and Nazi Germany* (New York, 1964). A different version is given by Pinchas Lapide, *Three Popes and the Jews* (New York, 1967).

19. FDRL/WRB, Pehle to Cicognani, Mar. 24, 1944.

20. Quoted by Raul Hilberg, *The Destruction of the European Jews* (Chicago, 1961), 539.

21. FDRL/WRB, Olsen to Pehle, Aug. 10, 1944.

22. Hausner, *Justice in Jerusalem*, 141.

23. *Interpreter Releases*, 21, June 1944, 213.

24. *Jewish Forum*, May 1944.

25. FDRL/WRB, McClellan to Pehle, June 24, 1944.

26. FDRL/WRB, Johnson to Pehle, enclosure, "Informal Statement of Bulgarian Minister Balabanoff," June 28, 1944.

27. FDRL/WRB, Pehle to McCloy, June 29, 1944.

28. FDRL/WRB, McCloy to Pehle, July 4, 1944; see also Memo of Conversation, Friedmann, Kubowitzki, Goldmann, Mereminski with Pehle, Aug. 10, 1944.

29. FDRL/WRB, Pehle to Harrison, May 25, 1944. Similar cables were sent to Ankara, Lisbon, Madrid, and Stockholm.

30. FDRL/WRB, Pehle to Harrison, June 6, 1944.

31. FDRL/WRB, McClellan to Pehle, Record of Expenditures from Board Discretionary Fund, May 1–Oct. 31, 1944. Especially interesting are the funds received by Nathan Schwartz, representative of the Jewish Agency, to finance the flight of 2,000 Jews to Romania, 250 to Slovakia, and 500 to Yugoslavia.

32. FDRL/WRB, Olsen to Pehle, July 7, 1944. (Contains account of instructions given to Wallenberg.)

33. FDRL/WRB, Johnson to Pehle, Enclosure of Swedish newspaper article on Wallenberg's activities in Budapest based on interviews with survivors, Mar. 7, 1945.

34. FDRL/WRB, Wallenberg to Olsen, Oct. 12, 1944.

35. This approximation reached the WRB via underground reports emanating from Bratislava and relayed through Bern. They were tabulated by railroad workers counting trains and cattle cars. The figure is confirmed by Veesenmayer, Berlin's minister and plenipotentiary on the scene, who estimated that a total of 437,000 had been deported while Hoess, commandant of Auschwitz, estimated that 400,000 had been gassed in a forty-six day period.

36. International Military Tribunal (IMT), *The Trial of Major War Criminals Before the IMT* (Nuremberg, 1949), 15, 424–25, Jodl testimony.

37. Hausner, *Justice in Jerusalem*, 142.

38. Ibid. 143. Quoted from Veesenmayer's dispatch to the Foreign Office.

39. A first attempt to sneak out a transport after the cancellation of deportations on July 14 had been foiled by Hungarian gendarmes; but a few days later, using a clever ruse, Eichmann successfully snatched his pound of flesh.

40. FDRL/WRB, McClellan to Pehle, June 24, 1944. This dispatch contains an enclosure that appears to be identical to the one described by Sztójay. It also contains a list of seventy Hungarian and German officials involved in the deportations. A supplementary message with the same request was also received on Aug. 24, 1944.

41. FDRL/WRB, Zollinger to State Department, July 25, 1944. The offer was simultaneously submitted to the British Foreign Office.

42. FDRL/WRB, State Department to Rio de Janeiro, Havana, Bogota, et al., Apr. 4 and 12, 1944. Reopening Latin America to refugees brought forth renewed

concern regarding spies among the refugees and apprehension about commercial competition. Both fears were prevalent in Latin American capitals during the earlier infiltration. See, e.g., Spruile Braden to Stettinius, Apr. 24, 1944.

43. *Rescue* 1, May 1944, 9. Reprint of Grafton's article, "What Is Free Ports?"

44. FDRL/OF 3186, Memorandum of the Executive Committee of the War Refugee Board to the President, May 8, 1944.

45. Ibid.

46. FDRL/OF 3186, FDR to Murphy, May 29, 1944.

47. *New York Times*, May 31, 1944, 4.

48. Ibid., May 4, 1944, 18.

49. *Washington Post*, May 29, 1944, 9.

50. *New York Times*, June 3, 1944, 15. He suggested that the Sicilian resort of Taormina might be used as a haven.

51. *New York Times*, June 10, 1944, 1.

52. *New York Times*, June 13, 1944, 1. The arguments used by the president as well as the strategy of bypassing Congress are found in a special memorandum prepared for the president by Pehle. FDRL/OF 3186, June 8, 1944, Pehle to Early. The expected restrictionist response came in a letter from Senator Reynolds to the solicitor general, Francis Biddle, FDRL/WRB, June 14, 1944. Biddle reminded Reynolds that Long, by admitting unfriendly aliens from Latin America, had established the precedent. FDRL/WRB, June 23, 1944.

53. FDRL/WRB, Stettinius to Winant, Aug. 4, 1944

54. Josiah E. Dubois Jr., *The Devil's Chemists* (Boston, 1952), 198.

55. FDRL/WRB, Pehle to Harrison for transmission to Budapest, Aug. 11, 1944.

56. FDRL/WRB, Pehle to McClellan, Aug. 23, 1944.

57. FDRL/WRB, McClellan to Pehle, Sept. 22, 1944. McClellan was reporting on a conversation held with Swiss Foreign Minister Feldscher, who had received this news from the German Foreign Office on Sept. 8, 1944.

58. FDRL/WRB, McClellan to Pehle, Aug. 11, 1944.

59. Some indication of this can be gleaned from the trials of Schacht and Eichmann. Both maintained that the Allies shared responsibility in the Final Solution because they failed to take advantage of Berlin's offer to sell lives. See *International Military Tribunal* 22, 389, Schacht testimony; and Hausner, 408, Servatius summation.

60. Winston Churchill, *The Second World War*. Vol. VI: *Triumph and Tragedy*. (Boston, 1953), 693.

61. FDRL/WRB, Hirschmann to Pehle, June 24, 1944. Such assurances were necessary because the British, in order to discredit the Brand mission, had begun to circulate the story that he was a Gestapo agent.

62. US State Department Archives, 840.48 Refugees/6344, Shertok to Goldmann, June 19, 1944. At the time, Moshe Shertok was head of the political division of the Jewish Agency; and Nahum Goldmann had recently been appointed, over considerable State Department opposition, the official agent of the agency in Washington. Both men tried desperately to convinced the administration to prolong the talks and to send Brand back to Budapest.

63. Hausner, *Justice in Jerusalem*, 249, quoting from the minutes of a meeting between Stettinius and Goldmann held on June 7, 1944.

64. FDRL/WRB, Pehle memorandum to Leahy for FDR, July 8, 1944.

65. FDRL/WRB, Jerusalem to State Department with enclosure, July 11, 1944.

66. FDRL/WRB, Steinhardt to Pehle, June 22, 1944. The request came from

Chaim Barlasz, Jewish Agency representative in Ankara, who had received word that the SS meant the Brand mission only as a feeler. Lisbon was considered more suitable because it was a distance from the pernicious influence of London. Pehle quickly rejected the proposal because of the growing suspicion that Berlin was trying to split the Allies.

67. A memorandum by Reuben Resnick, representative of the Joint Distribution Committee, clearly pointed to this possibility. FDRL/WRB, June 1944. But the World Jewish Congress and the Jewish Agency did not entirely agree. Brand later confirmed this theory when he testified at the trial of Krumey and Hunsche. "It is now clear to me," he observed, "that Himmler sought to sow suspicion among the Allies." *Herald Tribune,* May 21, 1964, 18.

68. FDRL/WRB, Hull to Harriman, June 9, 1944.

69. FDRL/WRB, Vishinsky to Hull, June 19, 1944.

70. FDRL/WRB, Hull to Harriman, July 7, 1944.

71. Even as late as Feb. 1945, the new ambassador in Moscow, George Kennan, fearing a further undermining of confidence, recommended not informing the Kremlin of such offers, "in view of the extreme suspicion with which the Soviet Government views all financial transactions with Germany conducted through Swiss channels." FDRL/WRB, Kennan to State Department, Feb. 17, 1945.

72. *Die Lage,* Aug. 23, 1944. Quoted in *Nazi Conspiracy and Aggression,* Supplement A, document D908, 1062–63.

73. FDRL/WRB, Johnson to State Department, Aug. 22, 1944, cites a Swedish report of a particularly cruel deportation in Budakalász, in which Hungarian gendarmes participated.

74. FDRL/WRB, Pehle to McClellan for transmission to Budapest, Oct. 6, 1944; and McClellan to Pehle, Dec. 7, 1944, Budapest's response.

75. FDRL/WRB, WRB to Harrison for transmission through IRC to Budapest.

76. Marches replaced cattle cars after the rail lines to Auschwitz were partially destroyed and the camp itself was being dismantled. FDRL/WRB, Kubowitzki to Pehle, Oct. 8, 1944. Wallenberg's observations were contained in a special dispatch, Johnson to WRB, Dec. 2, 1944.

77. This was done by giving the Germans Swiss F300,000,000, collected from local sources and holding out the hope that additional money could be made available from blocked accounts in Switzerland.

78. *Nazi Conspiracy and Aggression,* Supplement B, 5: 315–25. Kasztner's testimony at Nuremberg.

79. FDRL/WRB, McClellan to WRB for Ackerman, Sept. 15, 1944.

80. FDRL/WRB, McClellan to Pehle, Sept. 16, 1944.

81. FDRL/WRB, McClellan to Pehle, Nov. 18, 1944.

82. FDRL/WRB, Pehle to McClellan, Jan. 6, 1945. Pehle approved of the deposit of Swiss F20,000,000 in a blocked account with the proviso that none of the money could ever be expended without prior approval of the WRB.

83. Falling into this category is the Kleist offer made to Olsen via Felix Kersten, the negotiations with Himmler through Jean Marie Musy, and the Himmler talks with Norbert Masur.

84. This is an early estimate found in the American Jewish Committee's *American Jewish Yearbook, 1947–8,* 49: 740. It includes Jews from the newly annexed areas. Higher estimates based on the statistics of theAnglo-American Committee cite 220,000 as the number surviving. This includes 60,000 Jews who returned to Hungary from Germany. For German estimates of the number of Hungarian Jews killed, see n. 35.

85. Hausner, *Justice in Jerusalem*, 155. Quoted directly from the Sassen tape.

86. After some pressure and a great deal of waiting, the administration finally issued license W-2115 to the World Jewish Congress on Dec. 18, 1943. It allowed for payment of persons in Romania and France "for goods and services." John Pehle, at the time chief of the Foreign Funds Control Division of the Treasury Department, was instrumental in making this breakthrough. But at the time of the Mayer-Becher-Kasztner negotiations, the policy on trading with the enemy had again been reversed and did not shift until Dec. 1944.

87. The contention in Ben Hecht's controversial *Perfidy* (New York, 1961), is that there was a conscious betrayal by leaders like Kasztner, who ostensibly guaranteed order in the delicate concentration and deportation procedure by keeping the truth, which they knew to be gassing at Auschwitz, hidden from Jews in the provinces. In turn for this service, they were, according to this position, allowed to rescue certain small, hand-picked, Zionist groups.

88. FDRL/WRB, Olsen to Pehle, enclosure Wallenberg description, Aug. 14, 1944.

89. Ibid., Aug. 10, 1944.

8. Governmental Response to Human Crisis

1. See, e.g., Rolf Hochhuth, *The Deputy* (New York, 1964); Arthur D. Morse, *While Six Million Died: A Chronicle of American Apathy* (New York, 1967); Saul S. Friedman, *No Haven For the Oppressed: United States Policy Toward Jewish Reguees, 1938–1945* (Detroit, 1973).

2. Besides the works cited above, see also Henry L. Feingold, *The Politics of Rescue: The Roosevelt Administration and the Holocaust* (New Brunswick, N.J., 1970); David Wyman, *Paper Walls: America and the Reguee Crisis, 1938–1941* (Boston, 1968). A second volume will appear shortly. On the role of Great Britain, see A. J. Sherman, *Island Refuge: Britain and Refugees From the Third Reich 1933–1939* (Berkeley, Calif., 1973) and Bernard Wasserstein, *Britain and the Jews of Europe 1939–1945* (New York, 1979). The works focusing on the White Paper and policy toward the *Yishuv* are too numerous to list here. The most objective work on the Vatican continues to be Günter Lewy, *The Catholic Church and Nazi Germany* (New York, 1964). Others include Carlo Falconi, *The Silence of Pius XII* (Boston, 1965); Anthony Rhodes, *The Vatican in the Age of the Dictators, 1922–1945* (New York, 1973); Saul Friedländer, *Pius XII and the Third Reich* (New York, 1966). The best work detailing the activities of the Red Cross and other agencies remains *Unity in Dispersion, A History of the World Jewish Congress* (New York, 1948). The most complete anthology of relevant articles is *Rescue Attempts During the Holocaust: Proceedings of the Second Yad Vashem International Historical Conference* (Jerusalem, Apr. 8–11, 1974; Jerusalem, 1977).

3. See Henry L. Feingold, "The Roosevelt Administration and the Effort to Save the Jews of Hungary," in Randolph Braham, ed., *Hungarian Jewish Studies* (New York, 1969).

4. For an elaboration of this point, see Karl A. Schleunes, *The Twisted Road to Auschwitz 1933–1939* (Urbana, Ill., 1970); also, Feingold, *Politics of Rescue*.

5. A biographical sketch of Breckinridge Long is included in Fred L. Israel, ed., *The War Diary of Breckinridge Long: Selections from the Years 1939–1944* (Lincoln, Neb., 1966), xi–xxv (hereafter: *Long Diary*).

6. See Jerold A. Auerbach, "From Rags to Robes: The Legal Profession, Social

Mobility and the American Jewish Experience," *American Jewish Historical Quarterly* 66 (Dec. 1976), 265 ff.

7. *Long Diary*, Jan. 23, 1940.

8. Ibid., Apr. 22, 1942.

9. Sherman, *Island Refuge*, 264–65.

10. This phrase was first used by A. L. Kubowitzki, *Unity in Dispersion*, 160.

11. Long MSS, Manuscript Division, Library of Congress, Intradepartmental Memorandum, May 14, 1943.

12. See, for instance, the revisionist work by H. C. Peterson, *Propaganda for War: The Campaign Against American Neutrality, 1914–1917* (Norman, Okla., 1939).

13. Ernest R. May, *The World War and American Isolation 1914–1917* (Chicago, 1966), 180 ff.

14. Charles Stember, ed., *Jews in the Mind of America* (New York, 1966), 141.

15. Long Diary, Jan. 20, 1942 (unpublished section, Manuscript Division, Library of Congress).

16. The helpful role of Eleanor Roosevelt is examined by Jason Burger in chap. 3 of an unpublished doctoral dissertation now being completed at the Graduate Center of the University of the City of New York.

17. Haim Genizi, "American Catholic Attitude Toward Catholic Refugees from Nazis, 1933–1945," Bar Ilan Univ., Aug. 1977 (unpublished). Genizi's research finds that the record of the Catholic Church in relation to its refugees was characterized by less interest and less effectiveness than that of the American Jewish community toward Jewish refugees.

18. John M. Blum, *Roosevelt and Morgenthau: A Revision and Condensation of From the Morgenthau Diaries* (Boston, 1970). Probably the best single source for Morgenthau's relationship to the Holocaust.

19. Henry L. Feingold, Review of John M. Blum, *Roosevelt and Morgenthau*, *American Jewish Historical Quarterly* 60 (Dec. 1970), 207.

20. Morgenthau Diaries, 693, 212–29, and 694, 194–202, Franklin D. Roosevelt Library.

21. See, e.g., Cordell Hull, *The Memoirs of Cordell Hull* (New York, 1948), 2: 471. Morgenthau denied the ethnic source of his bitterness toward Germany. He claimed it stemmed from World War I, when he observed the behavior of German officers in Turkey while acting as his father's assistant.

22. Blum, *Roosevelt and Morgenthau*, 582–83.

23. Long MSS, memorandum from Long to Adolf Berle and James C. Dunn, June 26, 1940. Manuscript Division, Library of Congress.

24. *Long Diary*, Sept. 18, 1940.

25. That is the underlying theme of Wyman, *Paper Walls*, and is also prominent in Feingold, *Politics of Rescue*.

26. Frances Perkins, *The Roosevelt I Knew* (New York, 1946), 95.

27. Leo Szilard, "A Personal History of the Bomb," in *The University of Chicago Roundtable* (Chicago, 1949), 3–7.

28. Henry L. Feingold, "Roosevelt and the Resettlement Question," *Rescue Attempts During the Holocaust* (Jerusalem, 1977), 123–80.

29. See Geoffrey Smith, *To Save a Nation: American Countersubversives, The New Deal and the Coming of World War II* (New York, 1973).

30. *New York Times*, Sept. 12, 1941. Lindbergh's threat was reminiscent of those emanating from Berlin: "Instead of agitating for war the Jewish groups in this country

should be opposing it in every possible way, for they will be among the first to feel its consequences."

31. Stember, *Jews in the Mind of America,* 128, 129,133–34. See also, Nov. 1938 and Opinion Research Corporation, May 1938 through Nov. 1939, on various aspects of fear, dislike, or distaste of the Jews.

32. See, for instance, Lucy S. Dawidowicz, *The War Against the Jews, 1933–1945* (New York, 1975), chap. 5; also, Eberhard Jäckel, *Hitler's Weltanschauung: A Blueprint for Power* (Middletown, Conn., 1972).

33. Frank Freidel, *FDR, Launching the New Deal* (Boston, 1973), 274.

34. Sherman, *Island Refuge,* 100, 113.

35. Paul C. Conkin, *The New Deal* (New York, 1967), 5.

36. Feingold, *Politics of Rescue,* 105.

37. Sherman, *Island Refuge,* 103.

38. Meir Dworcezki, "The International Red Cross and Its Policy Vis-à-Vis the Jews in the Ghettos and Concentration Camps in Nazi-Occupied Europe," *Rescue Attempts During the Holocaust* (Jerusalem, 1977), 71–110. See also the unpublished paper by Monty N. Penkower, "The World Jewish Congress Confronts the International Red Cross During the Holocaust Years," Touro College, New York, 1978.

39. Feingold, *Politics of Rescue,* 168.

9. PBS's Roosevelt: Deceit and Indifference or Politics and Powerlessness?

1. Arthur Schlesinger Jr., "Did F.D.R. Betray the Jews?" *Newsweek,* Apr. 18, 1994.

2. See, e.g., Lucy Dawidowicz, "Could the United States Have Rescued the Jews From Hitler," *This World,* no. 12 (Fall 1985), 15–30; and "American Jews and the Holocaust," *New York Times Magazine* Apr. 18, 1982 by Holocaust Library.

3. See my review in *Jewish Social Studies* 48, no. 1 (Winter, 1986), 83–86.

4. Henry L. Feingold, *The Politics of Rescue: The Roosevelt Administration and the Holocaust, 1938–1945* (New Brunswick, NJ., 1970, 1980).

5. *American Refugee Policy and European Jewry, 1933–1945* (Bloomington, Ind., 1987).

6. Quoted in Henry L. Feingold, *A Time for Searching: Entering the Mainstream* (Baltimore, 1992), 214.

7. *The Juggler: Franklin Roosevelt as Wartime Statesman* (Princeton, 1994).

8. *The Crooked Road to Auschwitz: Nazi Policy Toward German Jews, 1933–1939* Urbana, Ill., 1970); Christopher R. Browning, "The Decision Concerning the Final Solution," in *Unanswered Questions: Nazi Germany and the Genocide of the Jews* (New York, 1989), 96–118.

9. Sharon Lowenstein, *Token Refuge: The Story of the Jewish Refugee Shelter at Oswego* (Bloomington, Ind., 1986).

10. Long MSS, Long memorandum to Adolf A. Berle Jr. and James C. Dunn, June 26, 1940, Manuscript Division, Library of Congress.

11. Feingold, *Politics,* 121.

12. Aaron Berman, *Nazism, the Jews and American Zionism, 1933–1948* (Detroit, 1990), 142–44; Feingold, *Politics,* 300–301.

13. Leonard Dinnerstein, *Antisemitism in America* (New York, 1994), xix.

14. See Fred Israel, *The War Diary of Breckinridge Long* (Lincoln, Neb., 1963), 216.

15. Editors of *Fortune*, *Jews In America* (New York, 1936), 1–5.

16. See, e.g., Arno J. Mayer, *Why Did the Heavens Not Darken? The "Final Solution" in History* (New York, 1988).

10. Was There Communal Failure Among American Jews?

1. The latest example is Rafael Medoff, *The Deafening Silence: American Jewish Leaders and the Holocaust* (New York, 1987). There are others as well. Haskell Lookstein, *Were We Our Brothers' Keepers? The Public Response of American Jews to the Holocaust, 1933–1945* (New York, 1986); Seymour M. Finger, ed., *America Jewry During the Holocaust* (New York, 1984); Saul S. Friedman, *No Haven for the Oppressed: United States Policy Toward Jewish Refugees, 1933–1945* (Detroit, 1973).

2. See, e.g., Henry L. Feingold, " 'Courage First and Intelligence Second': The American Jewish Secular Elite; Roosevelt and the Failure to Rescue," *American Jewish History* (June 1983), 459 pp.; and "Rescue and the Secular Perception: American Jewry and the Holocaust," in *Organizing Rescue: Jewish National Solidarity in the Modern Period*, ed. Selwyn I. Troen and Benjamin Pinkus (London, 1992), 154 66.

3. Emanuel Celler, *You Never Leave Brooklyn: The Autobiography of Emanuel Celler* (New York, 1953), 81; House Committee on Immigration and Naturalization, *Restriction of Immigration*, H.R. 5, 105, 561, 68th Cong, 1st sess., Jan. 3, 1924, 388–89.

4. *American Hebrew*, Sept. 26, 1924, 30.

5. *American Hebrew*, Oct. 13, 1922, 593; see also Paul E. Anderson, "Are Jewish Children Brighter?" *American Hebrew*, May 17, 1926, 886.

6. Nathan Reich, "The Role of the Jews in the American Economy," *Yivo Annual of Jewish Social Science* 5 (1950), 198–202; Jacob Letchinsky, "The Position of Jews in the Economic Life of America," in *Jews in a Gentile World*, ed. I. Graeber and S. H. Britt (New York, 1942), 406–15.

7. Isaac Metzker, *A Bintel Brief: Sixty Years of Letters from the Lower East Side to the Jewish Daily Forward* (New York, 1971), 160–61.

8. Quoted in "The War of Nerves: Hitler's Helper," *Fortune* 22 (Nov. 1940), 85–86, 108–10.

9. Editors of *Fortune*, *Jews in America* (New York, 1936), pp. 3–5.

10. *Jewish Telegraphic Agency Community News Report* 32, no. 2, as reported in issue of Jan. 10, 1992, 2.

11. Henry L. Feingold, *The Politics of Rescue: The Roosevelt Administration and the Holocaust, 1938–1945* (New York, 1980), 41–42; Deborah Lipstadt, *Beyond Belief: The American Press and the Coming of the Holocaust, 1933–1945* (New York, 1986), 98–104.

12. Konrad Bercovici, "The Greatest Jewish City in the World," *Nation* Sept. 12, 1923, 261.

13. Metzger, *Bintel Brief*, 150–51.

14. Charles Reznikoff, *Louis Marshall, Champion of Liberty: Selected Papers and Addresses* (Philadelphia, 1957), 2: 786–89.

15. Moshe R. Gottlieb, *American Anti-Nazi Resistance, 1933–1945* (New York, 1982), 45–75. A highly partisan examination of the transfer agreements is presented by Edwin Black, *The Transfer Agreement: The Untold Story of the Secret Pact Between the Third Reich and Jewish Palestine* (New York, 1984).

16. David Shapiro, "From Philanthropy to Activism: The Political Transformation of American Zionism in the Holocaust Years" (Ph.D. diss., Hebrew University of

Jerusalem, n.d.), 147; Dan Kurtzman, *Ben Gurion, Prophet of Fire* (New York, 1983), 235–37.

17. Arthur A. Goren, *Dissenter in Zion* (Cambridge, Mass., 1982), 46–47.

11. Jewish Leadership During the Roosevelt Years

1. The statistics on the Jewish population in America were tabulated by the government census of religious bodies conducted in 1936–1937. See H. S. Linfield, "Jewish Communities in the United States," *American Jewish Yearbook* 42 (1940): 216, 220.

2. Albert J. Menendez, *Religion at the Polls* (Philadelphia, 1977), 24–35, tables 16–19. Lawrence H. Fuchs, *The Political Behavior of American Jews* (Glencoe, Ill., 1956), 177–87.

3. Deborah D. Moore, *At Home in America: Second Generation New York Jews* (New York, 1981), 210–11.

4. Samuel Lubell, *The Future of American Politics* (New York, 1956), 36–37; Fuchs, *Political Behavior*, 66.

5. James M. Burns, *Roosevelt, The Lion and the Fox* (New York, 1956), 104; Mark R. Levy and Michael S. Kramer, *The Ethnic Factor: How American Minorities Decide Elections* (New York, 1973), 103.

6. Cyrus Adler and Aaron Margalith, *With Firmness in the Right, American Diplomatic Action Affecting Jews 1840–1945* (New York, 1977); Louis L. Gerson, *The Hyphenate in Recent American Politics and Diplomacy* (Lawrence, Kans., 1964); Gary D. Best, *American Jewish Leaders and the Jewish Problem in Eastern Europe, 1890–1914* (New York, 1982); Naomi Cohen, *Not Free to Desist* (Philadelphia, 1972).

7. An exploration of the process is found in Henry L. Feingold, *The Politics of Rescue: The Roosevelt Administration and the Holocaust, 1938–1945* (New York, 1980), 5–44.

8. Fuchs, *Political Behavior*, 99–107, 177–87.

9. Burns, *Lion and Fox*, 453–55.

10. Alfred O. Hero Jr, *American Religious Groups View American Foreign Policy* (Durham, 1973), American Institute of Public Opinion (AIPO) listing, 145–46, 279–84. Polls also reflect the intensity of Jewish support of the welfare-state measures, 144, 466.

11. Fuchs, *Political Behavior*, 171–77.

12. Hero, *American Religious Groups*, 279–84.

13. See David Brody, "American Jewry, the Refugees and Immigration Restriction, 1932–1942," *Publication of the American Jewish Historical Society* 45 (June 1956), 219–47; Hero, *American Religious Groups*, 202.

14. Jerold S. Auerbach, *Unequal Justice, Lawyers and Social Change in Modern America* (New York, 1976), 184–89; see also "From Rags to Riches: The Legal Profession, Social Mobility and the American Jewish Experience," *American Jewish Historical Quarterly* 46 (Dec. 1976), 249–84; Lubell, *Future*, 83–84.

15. Quoted in Auerbach, *Unequal Justice*, 187.

16. Ibid., 188.

17. Daniel J. Kevles, *The Physicisist: The History of A Scientific Community in Modern America* (New York, 1979), 212–21, 278–79, 288; Laura Fermi, *Illustrious Immigrants: The Intellectual Migration From Europe, 1930–1941* (Chicago, 1969); *The Intellectual Migration: Europe and America 1930–1960*, ed. Donald Fleming and Bernard Baylin (Cam-

bridge, 1968); and Leo Szilard, "A Personal History of the Bomb," in *The University of Chicago Roundtable* (Chicago, 1949), 3–7.

18. Irwin Howe, *Decline of the New Intellectuals* (New York, 1978); Stephen J. Whitfield, "The Imagination of Disaster: The Response of the American Jewish Intellectuals to Totalitarianism," *Jewish Social Studies*, 42 (Winter, 1980), 1–20; Charles Kadushin, *The American Intellectual Elite* (Boston, 1968).

19. Jacob Fisher, *The Response of Social Work to the Depression* (Boston, 1980); Roy Lubove, *The Professional Altruist* (New York, 1969).

20. Feingold, *Politics*, 149–53; David Wyman, *Paper Walls*, 96–97.

21. Feingold, *Politics*, 126–66.

22. See Samuel Rosenman, *Working with Roosevelt* (New York, 1952); Samuel B. Hand, *Counsel and Advise: A Political Biography of Samuel I. Rosenman* (New York, 1981); and Jordan A. Schwarz, *The Speculator, Bernard M. Baruch In Washington, 1917–1965* (Chapel Hill, 1981).

23. Joseph Proskauer, *A Segment of My Time* (New York, 1950); Louis M. Hacker and Mark D. Hirsch, *Joseph M. Proskauer: His Life Time* (Mobile, 1978); *Challenging Years: The Autobiography of Stephen Wise* (New York, 1949); Melvin I. Urofsky, *A Voice that Spoke for Justice: The Life and Times of Stephen Wise* (Albany, 1982); and Morris D. Waldman, *Nor by Power* (New York, 1953).

24. Michael E. Parrish, *Felix Frankfurter and His Times, The Reform Years* (New York, 1982); Bruce A. Murphy, *The Brandeis Frankfurter Connection, The Secret Political Activities of the Two Supreme Court Justices* (New York, 1932); and H. N. Hirsch, *The Enigma of Felix Frankfurter* (New York, 1981).

25. *Roosevelt and Frankfurter: Their Correspondence, 1928–1945*, ed. Max Freedman (Boston, 1967), 474–75; also Frankfurter to Astor, June 2, 1938.

26. Parrish, *Frankfurter*, 132.

27. Frankfurter to Roosevelt, June 6, 1942; Tully to Frankfurter, July 17, 1942; Freedman, *Frankfurter/Roosevelt Correspondence*, 451, 611, 667.

28. Parrish, *Frankfurter*, 206.

29. *Dissenters in Zion: Fron the Writings of Judah L. Magnes*, ed. Arthur A. Goren (Cambridge, 1982), 22, 154–55 (document no. 24); see also Parrish, *Frankfurter*, 131–32, 242.

30. Jan Karski, "Reaction of Frankfurter, Wise and Goldmann to First Reports of Warsaw Ghetto Uprising and Belzec Death Camp," in *The Impact of the Holocaust on Judaism in America* (Colloquim, American Univ., Washington, D.C., Mar. 23, 1980), 34.

31. John M. Blum, *Roosevelt and Morgenthau: A Revision and Condensation of From the Morgenthau Diaries* (Boston, 1970), xvi.

32. Parrish, *Frankfurter*, 142, 224, 248.

33. Transcription of telephone conversation, Morgenthau and Rosenman, Jan. 13, 1944, 11:35 A.M., Morgenthau Diaries, book 693, 205–10, Roosevelt Library, Hyde Park, New York.

34. Feingold, *Politics*, 182–183; 239–44.

35. Blum, *Morgenthau*, 582–83.

36. Monty N. Penkower, "In Dramatic Dissent: The Bergson Boys," *American Jewish History* (Mar. 1981), 296; Sarah E. Peck, "The Campaign for an American Response to the Nazi Holocaust, 1943–1945," *Journal of Contemporary History* 15 (Apr. 1980), 386–87.

37. See *Challenging Years: The Autobiography of Stephen Wise*; and Melvin I. Urofsky, *A Voice That Spoke For Justice: The Life and Times of Stephen S. Wise* (Albany, 1982).

38. Urofsky, *Wise*, 258.

39. Moshe Gottlieb, "In the Shadow of War: The American Anti Nazi Boycott Movement in 1939–1941," *American Jewish Historical Quarterly* 42 (Dec. 1972), 146–61.

40. Henry L. Feingold, "Stephen Wise and the Holocaust," *Midstream* (Jan. 1983), 45–48.

41. Urofsky, *Wise*, 327.

42. Stephen Wise, *As I See It* (New York, 1944),123–24.

43. For a similar analysis of Wise's posture, see Louis Lipsky, *Memoirs in Profile* (Philadelphia, 1975), 192–200.

44. Feingold, *Politics*, 302.

45. Janes A. Farley, "F.D. R. the Man." in *F.D.R.'s America*, ed., David E. Kejrig (New York, 1976), 23.

46. Quoted Richard T. Goldberg, *The Making of Franklin D. Roosevelt, Triumph over Disability* (Cambridge, Mass., 1982), 1, 36.

47. Paul K. Conkin, *The New Deal* (New York, 1977), 5.

48. Such a development is considered by David Wyman, "American Jews and the Holocaust," *New York Times Magazine* (May 8, 1982), 94.

49. Eliyho Matzozky, "An Episode: Roosevelt and the Mass Killing," *Midstream* (Aug./Sept. 1980), 17–19.

50. *Jews In The Mind of America*, ed., Charles H. Stember et al. (New York, 1966), 128, 158.

12. Rescue and the Secular Perception

1. Jacob R. Marcus, *Early American Jewry* (Philadelphia, 1953), 2: 1,041–44.

2. Cyrus Adler and Aaron Margalith, *With Firmness in the Right: American Diplomatic Action Affecting Jews, 1840–1945* (New York, 1977), 261–98.

3. Naomi Cohen, *Not Free to Desist: The American Jewish Committee, 1906–1966* (Philadelphia, 1972?), 3–18.

4. Ibid., 54–80.

5. John Snetsinger, *Truman, the Jewish Vote and the Creation of Israel* (Stanford, Calif., 1974). For another opinion see Zvi Ganin, *Truman, American Jewry and Israel, 1945–1948* (New York, 1979), 170–89.

6. Estimates vary considerably on the number of Jews in the International Brigade because volunteers were listed under their nationalities. Thus Cecil Ely, *Between the Bullet and the Lie, Volunteers in the Spanish Civil War* (New York, 1969), does not make an estimate. C. V. Lipschitz, *Franco's Spain, the Jews and the Holocaust* (New York, 1984), 15, observes only that the percentage of Jews was "disproportionately high." On the other hand Haim Avni, *Spain, the Jews and Franco* (Philadelphia, 1982), 50, estimates that 10 percent, or 3,000 to 5,000 of the International Brigade, which consisted of approximately 40,000 volunteers, were Jewish. The most confidently stated figures come from Albert Prago, "Fifty Long Years Later, Commemorating the Spanish Civil War," *Jewish Currents* (Mar. 1987): 4–7. He estimates that 18 percent of the total Brigade, approximately 7,000 volunteers, were Jewish, and about 30 percent of the Lincoln Brigade were Jewish. But the highest percentage belonged to Palestine, which sent 300 volunteers, a few of whom were Arabs. High percentages were also to be observed in the Italian and Polish detachments. The latter sent 5,000 volunteers, fully 40 percent of whom were Jewish. It contained a segregated Jewish company (Dombrowski) composed almost entirely of Jews.

7. See Monty Penkower, "In Dramatic Dissent: The Bergson Boys," *American Jewish History* 70, no. 3 (Mar. 1981): 281–309. An emotional account of the attempt to create the army is contained in Yitshaq Ben Ami, *Years of Wrath, Days of Glory: Memoirs from the Irgun* (New York, 1982), 248–52.

8. Melvin Urofsky, *A Voice That Spoke for Justice: The Life and Times of Stephen S. Wise* (Albany, N.Y., 1982).

9. Carl Voss, *Rabbi and Minister: The Friendship of Stephen S. Wise and John Haynes Holmes* (Cleveland, Ohio, 1964), 39.

10. Arthur Morse, *While Six Million Died* (New York, 1967); David Wyman, *Paper Walls*; Henry L. Feingold, *Politics*; Saul Friedman, *No Haven for The Oppressed* (Detroit, 1973); David Wyman, *The Abandonment of the Jews* (New York, 1985). In addition, there are two new books in the pipeline and innumerable articles have published in the journals.

11. See, e.g., Frederick A. Lazin, "The Response of the American Jewish Committee to the Crisis of German Jewry, 1933–1939," *American Jewish History* 58, no. 3 (Mar. 1979): 283–304.

12. David Brody, "American Jewry, the Refugees and Immigration Restriction, 1932–1942," *Publications of the American Jewish Historical Society* 45 (June 1956): 219–84.

13. Henry Feingold, *Politics*, 237–39, 300–301. See also Aaron Berman "American Zionism and the Rescue of European Jewry: An Ideological Perspective," *American Jewish History* 70, no. 3 (Mar. 1983), 320–30.

14. Marc Raphael, *A History of the United Jewish Appeal, 1939–1982* (Providence, R.I., 1982), 5–11.

15. Larence Fuchs, *The Political Behavior of American Jews* (Glencoe, Ill., 1965), 97–107, 177–87.

16. Deborah Moore, *At Home In America: Second Generation New York Jews* (New York, 1981), 23.

17. Alfred Hero, *American Religious Groups View Foreign Policy; Trends in Rank and File Opinion, 1937–1969* (Durham, N.C., 1973), 279–84.

18. Deborah Lipstadt, *Beyond Belief: The American Press and the Coming of the Holocaust, 1939–1945* (New York, 1986), 240–78.

19. Naomi Cohen, *Not Free*, 69–70. See also Irving Howe, *World of Our Fathers* (New York, 1976), 377–78.

20. Henry Feingold, *A Midrash On American Jewish History* (Albany, 1982), 46–48. Also Gary Best, *American Jewish Leaders and the Jewish Problem in Eastern Europe, 1890–1914* (New York, 1982).

21. Selig Adler, "Franklin Roosevelt and Zionism, The Wartime Record," *Judaism* 21 (Summer 1972): 256–76.

22. This observation and those which follow are fully developed in Henry Feingold, "'Courage First and Intelligence Second:' The American Jewish Secular Elite, Roosevelt and the failure to Rescue," *American Jewish History* 72, no. 4 (June 1983): 424–60. See also Peter Lowenburg, "Walter Rathenau and Henry Kissinger: The Jew as a Modern Statesman in Two Political Cultures," *Leo Baeck Memorial Lecture*, no. 14 (New York, 1980).

23. Morgenthau, Lehman, and Brandeis are interesting exceptions. They were Jews of Central European descent. Brandeis was a third-generation descendant of a Prague family; Lehman and Morgenthau were second-generation German Jews. All were fully Americanized.

24. Bernard Wasserstein, *Britain and the Jews of Europe, 1937–1945* (Oxford, 1979), 353–54.

25. Henry Feingold, "Courage First," 443–48.

26. "American Jews and the Holocaust," *New York Times Magazine*, 8 May 1982, 94.

27. On the role of bureaucracy generally during the Holocaust, see Raul Hilberg, *The Destruction of the European Jews* (New York, 1985), 3: 993–1,029. For the self-initiating process of the bureaucracy in Vichy France, see Michael R. Marrus, "The Theory and Practice of Anti-Semitism," *Commentary* (Aug. 1982), 39ff.

28. Henry Feingold, "The Bureaucrat as Mass Killer: Arendt on Eichmann," *Response*, no. 39 (Summer 1980): 45–51. Also Feingold, "The Government Response," in *The Holocaust: Ideology, Bureaucracy and Genocide*, ed. Henry Friedlander and Sybil Milton (New York, 1980), 245–59.

13. Who Shall Bear Guilt for the Holocaust?

1. Arthur D. Morse, *While Six Million Died* (New York, 1965); Saul S. Friedman, *No Haven for the Oppressed* (Detroit, 1973).

2. *Commentary* 65 5 (May, 1978): 37–46; *Commenweal*, Nov. 24, 1978, 746–51.

3. Congressman Sol Bloom, House Foreign Affairs Committee; Congressman Samuel Dickstein, House Committee on Immigration and Naturalization; Congressman Emanuel Celler, House Judiciary Committee.

Selected Bibliography

Part One: Holocaust: The Historical Problem

Arendt, Hanna. *Eichmann in Jerusalem: A Report on the Banality of Evil.* New York, 1963.

Arno, Mayer, *Why Did the Heavens Not Darken? The Final Solution in History.* New York, 1988.

Bauer, Yehuda, and Nathan Rotenstreich, eds. *The Holocaust as Historical Experience.* New York, 1981.

Berenbaum, Michael, ed. *A Mosaic of Victims; Non-Jews Persecuted and Murdered by the Nazis.* New York, 1990.

Dawidowicz, Lucy. *The Holocaust and the Historian.* Cambridge, Mass., 1981.

Fein, Helen. *Accounting for Genocide: National Responses and Jewish Victimization During the Holocaust.* New York, 1979.

Gilbert, Martin. *Auschwitz and the Allies.* New York, 1981.

Gordon, Sarah. *Hitler, Germans and the "Jewish Question."* Princeton, 1984.

Guttman, Israel. *Resistance: The Warsaw Ghetto Uprising.* New York, 1944.

Hilberg, Raul. *The Destruction of the European Jews.* 3 vols., rev. ed. New York, 1985.

Katz, Jacob. *From Prejudice to Destruction: Anti-Semitism, 1700–1933.* Cambridge, Mass., 1980.

Kren, George M., and Leon Rappoport. *The Holocaust and the Crisis of Human Behavior.* New York, 1980.

Marrus, Michael M. *The Holocaust in History.* Hanover, 1987.

Schleunes, Karl. *The Twisted Road to Auschwitz: Nazi Policies Towards the Jews, 1933–1939.* Urbana, Ill., 1970.

Tec, Nechama. *Defiance: The Bielski Partisans.* New York, 1984.

Trunk, Isaiah. *Judenrat.* New York, 1972.

Part Two: America and the Holocaust

Abella, Irving, and Harold Troper. *None Is Too Many: Canada and the Jews of Europe, 1933–1948.* Toronto, 1982.

Breitman, Richard, and Alan Kraut. *American Refugee Policy and European Jewry, 1933–1945.* Bloomington, Ind., 1987.

Dinnerstein, Leonard. *America and the Survivors of the Holocaust.* New York, 1982.

Feingold, Henry. *The Politics of Rescue: The Roosevelt Administration and the Holocaust, 1938–1945.* New Brunswick, N.J., 1970.

Friedman, Saul S. *No Haven for the Oppressed: United States Policy Towards Refugees.* Detroit, 1973.

Laqueur, Walter. *The Terrible Secret: An Investigation into the Suppression of Information about Hitler's "Final Solution."* London, 1980.

Lipstadt, Deborah. *Beyond Belief: The American Press and the Coming of the Holocaust, 1933–1945.* New York, 1986.

Morse, Arthur. *While Six Million Died: A Chronicle of American Apathy.* New York, 1967.

Penkower, Monty. *The Jews Were Expendable: Free World Diplomacy and the Holocaust.* Urbana, Ill., 1983.

Wyman, David. *The Abandonment of the Jews: America and the Holocaust, 1941–1945.* New York, 1984.

———. *Paper Walls: America and the Refugee Crisis, 1933–1941.* Amherst, Mass., 1967.

Part Three: American Jewry and the Holocaust

Belth, Nathan. *A Promise to Keep: A Narrative of the American Encounter with Anti-Semitism.* New York, 1979.

Berman, Aaron. *Nazism, the Jews and American Zionism, 1933–1945.* Detroit, 1990.

Dinnerstein, Leonard. *Antisemitism in America.* New York, 1994.

Feingold, Henry L. *A Time for Searching: Entering the Main Stream, 1920–1945.* Baltimore, 1992.

Gerson, Louis. *The Hyphenate in Recent American Politics and Diplomacy.* Lawrence, Kan., 1964.

Halperin, Samuel. *The Political World of American Zionism.* Detroit, 1967.

Hero, Alfred Jr. *American Religious Groups View Foreign Policy: Trends in Rank and File Opinion, 1937–1969.* Durham, N.C., 1973.

Howe, Irving. *World of our Fathers: The Journey of the East European Jews to America and the Life They Found and Made.* New York, 1976.

Kaufman, Isidore. *American Jews in World War II: The Story of 550,000 Fighters for Freedom.* 2 vols. New York, 1947.

Lowenstein, Sharon R. *Token Refuge: The Story of the Jewish Refugee Shelter at Oswego.* Bloomington, Ind., 1986.

Moore, Deborah. *At Home in America: Second Generation New York Jews*. New York, 1981.

Morgenthau III, Henry. *Mostly Morgenthaus: A Family History*. New York, 1991.

Urofsky, Melvin. *American Zionism: From Herzl to the Holocaust*. New York, 1976.

Index

Achad Ha'Am, 28–29
Achilles, Theodore, 121
Adler, Cyrus, 208
Adorno, Theodor, 20
Advisory Commission on Political Refugees. *See* United States President's Advisory Commission on Political Refugees
Africa, 120, 135, 139. *See also* North Africa; "United States of Africa" (proposed); West Africa
African Americans, 20, 37, 185, 199
Agro-Joint, 120, 126, 138
Agudath, 111, 245
Aguinaldo, Emilio, 119
Alaska, 80, 100, 102, 113–17; Ickes and, 115, 116–17, 144, 174; F. Roosevelt and, 116, 178; State Department and, 115, 177; Wise and, 139
Alaskan Development Bill, 115–17
Alaskan Development Committee, 115
Alaskan Resettlement Corporation for Refugees, 114
Aliyah Bet, 138
Alliance Israélite Universelle, 34
Allied Powers: American Jewry and, 223; anti-Semitism of, 6–7, 67–68, 253; attempted split of, 162, 164, 291nn. 66, 67; bombing proposed to, 64–65, 88, 182, 265–66, 267; Hitler on, 154; Hungarian Jewry and, 151, 155, 160–62, 164, 165–66,

167; indifference of, 51, 67, 87, 252–53, 255; Lakatos and, 163; Nazi defendants on, 290n. 59; priorities of, 15, 16, 59–69, 180, 258; refugee problem of, 81; resettlement issue and, 8, 94–95, 139; successes of, 10, 14; variables uncontrolled by, 90; will of, 168, 187
"America and the Holocaust" (TV program), 10–11, 183–201
"America First" committee, 185, 211
American Federation of Zionists, 235
American Friends Service Committee, 104
American Jewish Committee: anti-Nazi boycott and, 237; commonwealth resolution and, 220; establishment of, 34, 243–44; on Hungarian Jewry, 291n. 84; Jewish elite and, 250; "Marshall law" and, 12; Rosenman and, 233; Russian Jewry and, 249
American Jewish Conference, 220, 247–48
American Jewish Congress, 112, 124, 195, 237, 249
American Jewish Joint Agricultural Corporation, 120, 126, 138
American Jewish Joint Distribution Committee: British Guiana and, 124, 125–26; Crimea and, 216; funds raised by, 218; ghetto sur-

305